Write to the Limit

Write to the Limit

Christopher J. Thaiss

GEORGE MASON UNIVERSITY

Holt, Rinehart and Winston, Inc.

Fort Worth • Chicago • San Francisco • Philadelphia
Montreal • Toronto • London • Sydney • Tokyo

Publisher	Ted Buchholz
Acquisitions Editor	Michael Rosenberg
Developmental Editor	Stacy Schoolfield
Editorial/Production Services	Editorial Services of New England, Inc.

Library of Congress Cataloging-in-Publication Data

Thaiss, Christopher J., 1948–
    Write to the limit / Christopher J. Thaiss.
      p.   cm.
    Includes index.
    ISBN 0-03-014089-7
    1. English language—Rhetoric.   2. English language-
-Grammar—1950–   3. Interdisciplinary approach in education.
I. Title.
PE1408.T39   1991
808'.042—dc20   90-49356
                                             CIP

ISBN: 0-03-014089-7

Address for editorial correspondence: Holt, Rinehart and Winston, Inc., 301 Commerce Street, Suite 3700, Fort Worth, TX 76102.

Address for orders: Holt, Rinehart and Winston, Inc., 6277 Sea Harbor Drive, Orlando, Florida 32887. 1-800-782-4479, or 1-800-433-0001 (in Florida).

PRINTED IN THE UNITED STATES OF AMERICA

0 1 2 3 090 9 8 7 6 5 4 3 2 1

Holt, Rinehart and Winston, Inc.
The Dryden Press
Saunders College Publishing

Preface

I love to write. I dream that everyone will enjoy writing as much as I do.

Most people I meet don't enjoy writing, though they manage to do it when pressed. Most people I meet don't like to talk about writing. It makes them squirm. It makes them think of failure.

I wrote this book because I enjoy writing. I enjoy it so much that it is one of the few things that I want to make time for. I didn't always enjoy writing. For many years, particularly all my years as a student in school, then college, then graduate school, I did the writing I was assigned because I had a strong sense of responsibility—and I wanted good grades from my teachers. But I struggled to write. I took no joy in it.

I did all the things that this book shows people how to avoid. Like putting off writing until the deadline loomed. Like sitting for hours before a blank page, rejecting every idea that came into my head. Like starting over ten times after I'd written no more than a sentence. Like hiding my writing from anyone until I was forced to hand it in to my teacher—then being too afraid to pick up the graded paper, much less look my teacher in the eye—even if I'd received a high grade.

Even after I began to teach writing, I carried my fear, my lack of ease and confidence. I tried to hide this from my students, but I no doubt communicated my disability in the way I taught. (For one thing, my own fear of writing failure was translated into my grading too easily and expecting too little.)

But it was as a teacher of writing that I came to know the ideas that inspired this book. The methods of other teachers that I cite throughout the book, and that I've modified through my own teaching and writing, came to me because those teachers had the confidence and good will to write their ideas. Without their joy in writing I could not have acquired my own joy and I could not pass it on to you.

How should you use this book?

If you are reading this because you have been assigned to by a teacher, most likely that person has a purposeful order for your reading and for your use of the exercises and projects placed throughout. But I wish, as I imagine most authors do, that you would establish your own relationship with the book. I mean for the book to be read from beginning to end. I realize that many teachers will not assign it this way, but rather in chunks, so that you will dip in and out. Hence, I've included a lot of cross-referencing. If, for example, you dip in at the start of Chapter 5 (Four Common Tasks for College Writers), you'll see references to the earlier chapters and the stern warning that you would be well served to read those chapters first.

This book will fulfill my intent if you thoroughly digest the earlier ideas before moving on. Your specific anxiety about "the research paper" or "literary analysis" or "correct grammar" may lead you to jump into the chapters on those topics first, but you will not get much out of them unless you have successfully dealt with more basic skills—particularly writing without anxiety—first. "Thoroughly digesting" the earlier ideas includes using the exercises to let you feel, not only acknowledge, the ideas in the text. Reading and writing go together in this book; you will understand the reading if you do the exercises as you go. So it's not meant to be a "quick read," even though I hope it's not the style that slows you down.

The title, *Write to the Limit,* with its connotations of speed, pressure, and deadlines, speaks to the situations most of us find ourselves in as writers, whether in school, on the job, or in those few quiet moments, so limited by our responsibilities, that allow us to reflect on our lives. It speaks to the intensity of the writing act, as we use writing to probe the far reaches of our understanding, or to harness our ideas so that others may understand them. It speaks honestly to the limits of our endurance, for writing is intensely physical, and all writers must learn when to stop and rest, as well as how to get going again.

USING THIS BOOK FOR REFERENCE

Once you've savored the book chapter by chapter, you can refer to specific sections, as needed, to remind yourself of particular strategies. I've included specific features for reference purposes:

- **Checklists:** At the end of each chapter is a brief checklist of the procedures to follow to reach certain goals; at the end of the last chapter is a Checklist of Checklists to remind you of key procedures in each chapter.

- **Cross-referencing:** I frequently refer to pertinent sections of previous or later chapters in order to facilitate your search for specific information.

- **The Grammar Handbook Section of Chapter 8:** These pages list the most frequently broken rules of Standard Written English and cite examples of incorrect and correct construction.

IF YOU ARE TEACHING THIS BOOK

Teachers of writing classes can assign this book chapter by chapter in accordance with a one- or two-semester schedule. There are too many exercises and projects to assign all of them, so I'd recommend a judicious selection. For those of you who customarily assign several substantial projects or "papers" throughout a course, I've included Projects for Writers at the end of each chapter. These reinforce the emphasis of each chapter, so they do not require more sophisticated knowledge than one would get through careful reading and through practice of the exercises. (Please see the Instructor's Manual for many other teaching ideas.)

I think the book works best if assigned from first chapter to last. I'm assuming that the principal reader of this book is not already a confident and virtuoso writer. The early chapters most directly address what I see as the "basics" for writers: the discipline to write regularly, the confidence to try new things, and the many uses of writing to enhance thought and learning. If your students are adept in these ways, by all means start with later chapters. And, of course, I encourage you to write to me, in care of the publisher, if you strike on an order that works better for you than the one I've set forth here.

IF YOU TEACH IN A WRITING-ACROSS-THE-CURRICULUM PROGRAM

This book doesn't depend on a teacher superintending each part of it in order to be effective. The book is meant to be readable by writers; its exercises are built-in teaching tools. Nevertheless, you may want to highlight certain sections that seem most applicable to your course and subject area. However, let me repeat the caution I noted above. The specific sections on such "types" of writing as the research paper, literary analysis, and essay exams—to name a few types I discuss here—will be much more useful to writers who have already achieved the basic skills that are the heart of Chapters 1 through 3. This book will be a more effective teaching aid if you advise students to digest these chapters first.

ACKNOWLEDGMENTS

In Chapter 7, I suggest to readers that they not skip over the Acknowledgments pages of the books they read, because no part of a book more clearly shows how collaborative all writing is. Authors get the credit for the time and love of everyone who comments on a manuscript, says a comforting word, writes a work that the author reads, or carves out the clean hours for the author's authoring.

I cannot thank all who deserve thanks. I'll mention a few.

Thanks to Donald Murray, who convinced me a few years ago that writing textbooks contributes substantially to the growth of knowledge in our profession, and whose own textbooks best justify that conviction.

Thanks to Donald Gallehr, Karen Hickman, and the three hundred Teacher/Consultants of the Northern Virginia Writing Project, who prove every day, year in and year out, that writing is joy.

Thanks to the reading/writing group of Cathy Garea, Kate Hodges, Marian Mohr, and Courtney Rogers, who, back in 1978, showed me how the "helping reader" can give the writer that vital boost in confidence. Thanks to the 1987 group of Neal Hutt, Sharon Jeffrey, Zada Pierce, and Melissa Rice, who provided valuable perspectives on the first draft of Chapter 2. Thanks also to Marie Nelson and Barbara Esstman for their comments on portions of the manuscript.

Thanks to the students of English Composition and Advanced Composition at George Mason University who have used portions of this text in draft and whose comments I have used in revision. Thanks also to the students of the Plan for Alternative General Education whose writing across the curriculum provided me with so many of the examples I cite. In particular, I thank former and current students Omar Altalib, Ali Ghobadi, and Christine Sorge for the time they gave to the interviews in Chapter 9.

To colleagues in the composition and writing-across-the curriculum programs at George Mason University, all of whom sustain my joy in writing and teaching, and nurture that joy in thousands of students, let me express my gratitude for your ideas spoken at "brown bag" meetings on teaching, your sharing of apt articles from the journals, and those impromptu problem-solving sessions that occur every day in the corridors and offices. Special thanks to Robert Clark of the Department of Public Affairs and Ray Chapman of the George Mason Institute for the time they gave to the interviews in Chapters 9 and 3, respectively.

Special thanks, too, are owed to members of the writing community outside George Mason who gave their time for interviews: Douglas Ayers, Stephen Gladis, Mary Redenius, and Taejung Welsh.

Thanks also to the scholars/teachers/program directors around the country who reviewed various drafts of the manuscript and whose comments pushed me to make this a richer text: Victoria Aarons, Trinity University; Chris Anson, University of Minnesota; Walter H. Beale, University of North Carolina, Greensboro; Mary Bly, University of California, Davis; Christopher Burnham, New Mexico State University; Patricia Connors, Memphis State University; Mary H. Dickson, Trinity College; Alexander Friedlander,

Drexel University, Larry G. Mapp, Middle Tennessee University; Alma E. Nugent, Villa Julie College; John O'Connor, George Mason University; and Mark E. Rollins, Ohio University.

At Holt, Rinehart and Winston, Michael Rosenberg rekindled my commitment and smoothed the way toward completion, and Stacy Schoolfield made me feel that authors do count in the publication process. My thanks to both of them.

To Flannery, Christopher, James, Jeffries, and Ann Louise Thaiss a few special words: Flann, here's to your fame as a new poet; Crink, here's to the "Lotza Mysteries" series; Jim, here's to Logenburg, "Robbie and Me," and John Cranial; Jeff, here's to Newsbag, the plays, and the songs; Ann Louise, here's to your future with glorious words. May each of you always write with joy.

My deepest thanks are owed to Ann Jeffries Thaiss, for her comments on Chapter 1, for the interview in Chapter 4, for her spontaneous feedback on sections throughout the book, for her tough but gentle judgment as writer and editor, and most of all for her courage and vision. May I always support her writing as she supports mine.

Contents

Write to the Limit

1 Getting Started and Sticking with It

*I go to encounter for the millionth time the reality
of experience and to forge in the smithy of my soul
the uncreated conscience of my race.*
> —James Joyce
> *from* A Portrait of the Artist
> as a Young Man

COMMON PROBLEMS WRITERS FACE

The Blank Page

Right now I'm staring at a blank page. At least I was until I started writing on it. What it says may not make a lot of sense yet. But at least I've got a place to keep going from, and I can keep on writing—spinning out ideas—until I get tired or until I stumble onto an even better idea. Then I can go back to the start and change the beginning. In writing, anything can be changed. That's the fun of it. I can try out any words I want, let them sit for a while so I can look at them from different angles, then change them or add to them or take some away, whatever I wish. If I like what I see, I may want to show them to someone else. The important thing is that I've got something to show; and in writing, something is always better than nothing.

Every writer faces a blank page. The more you write, the more blank pages you face. But many people feel threatened by the blank page. They stare at it in hopes that the right words will magically appear before them. (Before I started writing this sentence, I was staring at the page, wondering what I would write next.) There has never been a writer who hasn't stared at a blank page or screen, and there never will be. Every writer always wonders, "What will I write next?" And that's exactly why people who love to write love to write, for the adventure!

Then why do people consider the blank page a problem? That's a good question to write about. As a matter of fact, I'd like you to write about that right now.

EXERCISE: Why is the blank page a problem for people? Put another way, why is writing hard for people? Why do they sometimes fear it, and often try to avoid it? Is it a problem for you? When? Why? Take a few minutes to jot down some thoughts about these questions. ∎

Now that you have done some real thinking (that is, writing) about the blank page, I'll share with you some of my ideas about why people find writing difficult and sometimes frightening. Use your writing from the previous exercise to see what I've left out.

Lack of Motivation

Let's face it. Sometimes I just don't have a reason to write. Particularly if I find writing difficult (every writer finds some kinds of writing more difficult than others), I'll look for every excuse I can to avoid it. If I want to get a message to someone, I might telephone rather than write a letter. If the message is complex or unpleasant, I might give up altogether. Maybe I feel tired and I just want to relax, to do something that doesn't tax my brain. Maybe I have a million other things to do, such as raking the leaves that I'm staring at right now or trying to find the leak in my radiator hose. Even if I find writing exciting and enjoyable, there are times when I'd rather do something else.

And even when writing is fun, it is still exercise. It takes energy—lots of it—because it involves thought and imagination (and often pencil-chewing and pacing around the room). So the writer has to *want* to do it.

Why do I want to do it? First, I like the adventure. Whenever I sit down to write (or stand or lie down, depending on where I am and how I feel), I can't really predict what will emerge on the page. Writing is a unique kind of thinking: as teacher and writer Janet Emig has said, writing is the kind of thinking that uses the hand, the eye, and the brain, all working together. Every time I put a word on that blank page, it gains life and power. As I look at that word, it sets off a chain reaction in my brain; that word suggests pictures, recalls memories of old conversations, reminds me of books I've read; and one idea leads to another. (Try this: Put one word, any word, on a blank sheet. Even as you write it, your mind will leap ahead to offer you pictures and other words somehow related to that word.)

Second, I'm motivated to write because I feel the need to make sense of things, which is another way of saying that, like all other humans, I want to have some control over my world. When I put words on a page, I deliberately give a shape, *my* shape, to something in my world. That shape may turn out to be totally ridiculous (like many weather forecasts or sportswriters' predictions, for example), but if I don't write down something, my thoughts are like weeds blown about in a hurricane. My imagination keeps pumping images and words and my senses keep picking up on the world around me, but I never grab on to any of this, capture it, so that I can look at it and think about it before it flies by.

Third, I write because I have to, because I can't get along in the world unless I communicate with other people. And as tough as the work often is, much of that communicating has to go on through written words because only written words can be kept, looked at, and thought about. Most of what has meaning in human culture is written, from laws to contracts to music to blueprints to history to stories to money to love letters to our signatures. Whatever work people choose, they will discover that words, written words, are essential for understanding what they think and see, and for working with others. The fact that my work—indeed everything I love and enjoy and feel—has meaning for others when I write about it is a powerful motivation to write.

Keeping these three motives in mind helps me to keep hammering away at my writing when I'm tired (writing a comment on the sixty-fifth term paper in a group of eighty), when I'm confused (writing to understand my feelings about a complex issue, such as writing), or when I'm distracted (writing a report of a committee meeting while everyone else in the family is going out to play football). The three motives—adventure, control, and communication—don't always work to keep me writing, but they are always strong enough to keep me itching to write again.

Lack of Perseverance

I have a friend who's always starting pieces of writing, but never finishes one. At least this is what he thinks. In fact, he has finished enough writings to get almost all the way through a double major in English and business marketing, while working full time as a mid-level manager for a large corporation. Yet he sees himself as a person who loses interest in a project after the first excitement has faded and who doesn't have what it takes to keep plugging away. Indeed, it's true; there are many projects that this imaginative man has begun but not completed. But what he has accomplished defines him better.

If you sometimes feel about yourself as a writer the way my friend does, then you and he are in good company: every writer's career is full of false starts, dead ends, and failed experiments. But these so-called failures do not add up to failure. They merely show the creative mind at work. I have a paperweight somewhere in my clutter of belongings that says, "Geniuses are rarely tidy." This doesn't mean that every slob is a genius, but it does mean that you can't tie up loose ends without having loose ends to tie up. Put another way, before you can find writing to finish, you have to generate a lot of possibilities. That's another reason why rule number one for all writers is *Write!* Part of the adventure of writing is discovering that rich vein of ore that will keep you adding one word after another until you've got something you feel is complete. But you've got to keep spilling out the words, like the prospector sifting endless pans of gravel, until the strike comes.

Moreover, that surge of energy that some people call inspiration rarely comes unless you work hard to make it happen. Something else has to take over in order to keep you going from day to day.

What is that something else? Writers call it discipline (so do athletes, scientists, health workers, artists, philosophers, parents, and everyone else who knows the difficulty of accomplishing anything worthwhile). There are no quick and easy ways to become a good writer, no instant formulas to follow. It doesn't matter what kind of writing you do, whether a school assignment, a love letter, a job application, or a poem; to become a better writer and to write more easily, you have to write regularly. If this book convinces you of nothing else, it will have succeeded if it convinces you of that.

Here are some tips for regular writing:

- *You choose the writing or let the writing choose you.* For developing your writing muscles, it doesn't matter what you write about. If you have a school or job assignment, work on that. If not, or if you want to vary the exercise, write about anything else that strikes you: describe the world outside (or inside), spout off about someone or something that makes you mad, create rhymes for a song or birthday poem, record a conversation or funny story you don't want to forget, anything. The crucial thing is to keep that hand-eye-brain coordination smooth and well oiled.

- *Don't worry about writing the perfect draft.* Unless you have a deadline (I'll talk more about deadlines later), don't let the worry of finishing get in the way of your writing. Many people don't begin writing because they fear that it won't be perfect and complete the first time. So what? You can't make something better until you see what you've got. Moreover, who knows what's perfect? If you knew what perfection was, you wouldn't be human. If you can forget the ideal of perfection for a while each day and just begin the adventure of discovering—through writing—what goes on in your head, you might make something pleasing to yourself, even if it isn't perfect.

- *Set easy, concrete goals.* Prize-winning journalist Donald Murray describes an easy writing goal: never a day without a line. Here's another easy goal: write for five minutes every day. Don't worry about how good the writing is: check the time and *begin*. You'll be surprised to discover that you don't need to think hard about your writing before doing it, as long as you've turned off that little voice that keeps telling you that you have to be perfect. There's plenty going on in your brain that's just begging for a chance to come out on the page. Let it. (This technique is called *freewriting*. More on it later in the chapter.)

Fear of the Reader

This is the big one. We go through life always afraid of "messing up" in front of someone whose opinion matters to us: our parents, friends, teachers, in-laws, bosses, coworkers, the list goes on and on. When it comes to writing, we can mess up in two ways: first, we can write something that offends someone; second, we can write it wrong. Indeed, fear of the reader is so great a barrier for most writers that I'll devote a large part of this book to tactics for making your reader your ally, rather than your enemy, in the writing process.

Many of us are taught to think about writing as something that we only do for other people, on command. You may be reading this book because you are taking a required writing course. If we only write because we have to show the writing to someone else for their approval, we'll be as unprepared as the athlete who only plays on game days. Writers who write well do most of their writing for themselves, just like the child playing with toys, the computer whiz at the keyboard, or the dancer, chef, mechanic, farmer, or singer. Here's the great irony: the performer who gets the most applause is the one who worries least about getting the applause and who is most in the performance, the art, itself.

What does this mean? It means that as a writer you have to set up a "space" around yourself, a place in your mind for only yourself and your writing. It takes much practice and discipline to achieve this state of mind, but all successful writers, who face deadlines and tough critics, achieve it. This space doesn't demand physical separation; it certainly doesn't mean isolation from readers, which is another source of fear. The naturalist Henry David Thoreau called this space "solitude" and said that one could have it anywhere, even in a crowd. You can achieve this solitude in many ways, some of which we'll explore in this chapter.

Lack of Information

Sometimes we don't write because we don't know enough about a particular topic to write about it. More often, however, we use lack of information as an excuse. Experienced journalists, even when assigned stories about which they know little or nothing, have to do some writing before they begin to collect information. Why? Because they must plan whom they will try to contact, what questions they will ask, and what other sources they may try to locate. Experienced writers also use this planning strategy before they begin their research: they write as much as they think they know and use this writing to discover what they have questions or doubts about. And, of course, they rely on readers they trust to give them advice. See Chapters 2 and 7 for more details on this and other methods for collecting information.

Most of us already know something about the topics we choose or are given. In fact, we probably know much more than we think we do. But if we are inexperienced, we rarely just sit down and write out everything we know or think about a topic. Every experienced writer knows that just doing this exercise improves our ability to recall. The writing acts the same as a conversation with an old friend: once we start talking we keep remembering more and more to talk about.

Often, though, there is another problem. We let our fear of the reader convince us that what we know isn't worth taking seriously. We fear that the reader will contradict what we say, "You don't know what you're talking about!" or the reader will find it childish or trivial, "So what? Everyone knows that." This is a serious block for many writers . . . but it is not a problem of information. It's vital for us, as writers, to separate our sense of what we know from our sense of what others may say about our writing. Even if you doubt that others will find you well informed and convincing, you can still write for yourself regularly as long as you trust your own experience. And, again, doing the writing is the first and most important step.

Fear of Error

Sometimes it's not our fear of ignorance that stops us, but our fear of the language. We have good reason to be afraid. Even though we recognize the cruelty and unfairness of it, we continually judge

people by how they talk—their accents, their grammar, their vocabulary—and how they write—their neatness, their spelling, their
punctuation, their sentence structure, their vocabulary. When we
talk, we fear that we'll stutter, stammer, choose the wrong words, or
keep silent at the wrong times. When we write, we fear that we'll
misuse words, write too much or too little, or make some terrible
grammatical error that will brand us illiterate. It takes real courage
for people to express themselves when they lack confidence in their
knowledge of the "right" words. Most of us overcome this fear
when the need is great enough: when we must survive in a foreign
country, for example. I, for one, would have no hesitancy to speak
my few words of ungrammatical Spanish if I needed food or a place
to stay in a Central American country. But my fear of error in that
language keeps me from using it in most other circumstances.

On the other hand, I'll never learn Spanish well unless I use it
over and over, making many errors. The same thing is true for one's
native language. Even the most skillful speakers or writers are
always in the process of learning their language. Why? First, the
language is constantly growing, new words are added and the
meaning of others change. Second, every language is spoken in
different, interesting ways by different groups of people. If we want
to reach people, we must, as we say in conducting business, "speak
their language," meaning that we must continually learn new vocabularies and new ways of speaking if we want to communicate.
Unfortunately, nobody learns without making errors. Fortunately,
our errors show us where we most need improvement.

As painful as it is, making errors shows that we're trying.
Always remember that anything we write we can change. Every
experienced writer knows that writing really means rewriting.

Just as with the fear of ignorance, don't confuse fear of language with fear of the reader. For example, just because a teacher
may have harshly criticized your spelling or found ten usage errors
in your one-page theme, don't think that your English is so bad that
you can't write about what you know and feel, or that you can't
write that job or school application. There are many ways to edit,
correct errors in, the pieces you write. (Chapter 8 is specifically
devoted to this.) The prospect of making errors should never keep
anyone from filling a blank page.

Isolation from Other Writers

Here's the best-kept secret about writing well: if you want to be a good writer, and a confident one, look for other writers with whom to share your work. Other writers are not hard to find. If you're in a writing class, or in any other class where writing is required, writers are all around you. All you lack is an introduction. Fortunately, more and more writing classes are being set up to provide this introduction. The teacher sets them up workshop-style, allotting class time for small groups of students to read their writing to one another, to talk about their problems with their writing, and to help one another. (See Chapter 4 for tips on how to get the most out of your writing group.) Indeed, once you get beyond the required writing course, you'll find that almost all advanced writing classes are taught workshop-style, with the students reading to and helping one another.

Did I say "helping one another"? Indeed I did. I wouldn't be surprised if your immediate response to that statement is "But that's cheating!" Somewhere in the past, when people began to use written tests as a way of separating "winners" from "losers," writing began to be associated with competition. If you think about it, this is a strange mixture. If writing is a way of reaching other people, why should it become a way of separating them? The answer isn't a mystery. If people helped one another on written tests, there would be no easy way of assigning grades to individuals. Eventually, most people associated writing with testing. And if you think of all writing as a test, the following things can happen:

• you worry
• you avoid it like the plague
• you fear making errors, because errors mean failure
• you don't think of rewriting, because who rewrites tests?
• you don't ask for help: you don't ask another writer's help, because supposedly that's cheating, and you don't ask your teacher's help, because the teacher is the one grading the test

So people think of writing as something you do by yourself and never show to anyone until it's perfect. Ridiculous! Every serious writer knows the secret: share your work with other writers early and often. Ask their advice. Offer yours to them.

Why other writers? Why not just anyone? Because other writers know what you're going through. They also try to make sense out of the jumble of ideas; they also fear some readers; they also stare at blank pages.

✍ **EXERCISE:** Quickly review the six reasons why people find writing difficult. On a sheet of paper, list each one, with space between them. After each reason write briefly about a time when you experienced that reason.

Now look over your writing. Which of the six reasons strikes you most powerfully? On a separate sheet, write about that reason. Use your writing to help you recall people and situations that might have caused you to experience it.

Now think about my advice regarding that reason. Would any of my suggestions have lessened your difficulty in those situations? Can you think of another strategy that might have helped you? ∎

VICTORY OVER THE BLANK PAGE

On the shelf next to me, I have a picture of William Shakespeare. In this miniature painting Shakespeare sits at a writing desk. I asked my son, who loves to write stories, what Shakespeare is doing. He said, of course, "writing." Yes. All of us writers know that Shakespeare isn't looking *at* anything, nor is he glued to the paper. He is doing what writers do most of the time: thinking. This is what I imagine he is thinking: with his mind's eye he is looking at some characters he is creating, maybe Hamlet and Queen Gertrude, and he imagines them saying some lines he has just written. As he watches them, they keep talking to each other, in words that he has not yet written. But the scene doesn't just keep rolling on. It keeps replaying, again and again, and every time, the words they speak are different, their movements are different, their expressions are different. Eventually, Shakespeare writes down some of these words. But even as he writes them, the scene plays and different ideas arise. Sometimes he changes a line; sometimes he tosses a page aside and begins again. Sometimes, in the midst of writing, he gets a completely new idea for a play and makes a note to himself in the margin of this one.

Since literary detectives have yet to find an actual manuscript of a Shakespeare play, one can only imagine what his pages looked like. His fellow playwright Ben Jonson wrote that Shakespeare "never blotted a line," but Jonson meant this as criticism, not praise, so we can take it with a grain of salt. More likely, if Shakespeare was anything like every other writer, he blotted thousands.

More important, Shakespeare wrote and wrote and wrote. He kept filling page after blank page. Most important of all, he was always *ready* to write, pen at hand, paper in reach, and his mind's eye clear and focused.

When we talk about victory over the blank page, we're talking mainly about readiness. Author Flannery O'Connor was at her writing desk every morning, not because she always had the words ready to spill out, but, as she said, "in case the words came." She didn't just wait, of course. Every writer has tricks for opening the floodgates and other tricks for keeping the flood between the banks. In this part of the book, I'll share with you some of the tricks for getting started that I've adapted for my writing and teaching.

Nonstop Writing or Freewriting

Associated with writers/teachers Ken Macrorie and Peter Elbow, nonstop writing, or freewriting, is designed to keep your hand moving on the page (or your hands moving over the keyboard). It's meant to keep you so busy writing that you don't have time to think about how hard it is to find the right words. It doesn't usually produce excellent writing; sometimes it produces a mess. But it always produces a string of ideas—it gives the writer something to work from. And sometimes the results are surprisingly good.

Here's how to do it:

1. Forget all the "have to's" of writing: you "have to" be neat, you "have to" spell correctly, you "have to" think before you write, you "have to" sound good and make sense.

2. Instead, record as fast as you can whatever goes through your mind. Yes, *whatever* goes through your mind. Don't censor or edit anything. Remember, you're writing this for yourself. You don't "have to" show it to anyone.

3. With some sort of timer (human or mechanical), set a time limit, say five or ten minutes. As with any other physical exercise, it's good to start slowly. True nonstop writing can tire you out, until your muscles get used to the exercise.

4. Start the timer. Write. If you find that you have nothing to say, keep writing "I have nothing to say," until you have something to say. Remember, the goal here isn't to produce prize-winning prose, but to strengthen that hand-eye-brain coordination.

    Here's a five-minute nonstop sample I wrote. Note that I didn't stop to correct punctuation:

> How I love that song the Water Is Wide! I told Ann that it was a perfect song—I wish I could write one like it. She said that I had written songs like it. but I think she was just being kind. I'm glad she was being kind. I love her for that. She didn't have to say that I could write good songs, but she made me feel really good when she did. I don't know what to write. I'm a bit nervous right now. I know I'm doing a freewriting to show nonstop writing—unfocused—and this sure does lack focus. I'm feeling some fear of my reader at this point—I'm also worried that my handwriting is so bad that I won't be able to read it when I go to type it into the computer. Damn this pen . . . it's running out of ink. It can't keep up with my thoughts. Is 5 minutes up yet? Not yet. One minute to go. See. I said this was going to be a mess—and it is. But it'll give me ideas to keep going from if I want. I'd like to write more about the song—it really is beautiful. Is it because of the words—"Give me a boat that's just for two"—that line knocks me out.

5. When the exercise stops, read over what you have. Find a sentence or passage that interests you. If you wish, use this sentence or passage as the beginning of a new nonstop writing.

6. Whether you use the writing or not, save it (save all your writing), because it might prove a source of inspiration at another time.

Focused Nonstop Writing

After your hand-eye-brain coordination has been improved through nonstop writing, you're ready for a more advanced, focused form. In the focused form, you write nonstop as quickly as you can while trying to stay focused on a topic. This is difficult compared with regular nonstop writing, so don't practice it until you're comfortable with the easier exercise.

While plain freewriting is a fine way to find something to write about, focused freewriting is an ideal starter once you've been given a topic or at least have a vague idea of what you'd like to write about. Because focused freewriting is more complex, it involves a preliminary exercise. Here are the steps:

1. Again, forget all the *have to's*. Even though this form of freewriting requires that you stay with a train of thought, you still don't have to worry about making sense. That is, you should still feel free to write anything at all about your topic. And if a better topic strikes you while you're writing, you can always pursue it.

2. Before you write, try to relax for a minute or two. Sit comfortably, relax your muscles. Then, let your imagination give your mind's eye a picture of an object or a scene closely related to your topic. This is called *visualization.* For example, if you're writing about a personal experience, you might imagine yourself going through that experience. If you're writing about a story, you might picture an episode or a character. Concentrate on that picture for a minute or so. See it in detail. Note its parts, its colors; try to feel its atmosphere, hear its sounds. In short, try to bring your topic as alive as you can in your mind.

3. Set the timer and begin. Write without stopping; try to capture as much of the scene as you can, its sights, sounds, sensations. When an idea strikes you about the topic, write it down. Again, don't censor or edit anything you want to say.

    Here's a sample based on my nonstop writing:

> It's an old song. I love old folk songs that have been set to major seventh chords. I love the effect of the major seventh chord. Not a tonic. Something slightly different. Bluesy. An

edge. I get the feeling of a person who's alone, looking at the sea. imagining her lover across it. She can't reach him. The longing, the loneliness is terrible. At the same time, she has a nostalgic feeling, a feeling that he still loves her, and that someday they'll be together again. That image of the boat built for two. I see them together on the waves. In a storm even. Both rowing—"And we'll row, my love and I." That feeling that together they can survive, as long as both pull together. Each is in the other's hands. The idea of the ship deeply loaded—what a metaphor—"but not as deep as the love I'm in"—I wonder what the circumstances of the song were. Who wrote it? When? When was it first sung? Was it really written by a person standing by the sea and thinking about her love? The writer can imagine such scenes and be inspired just by the thought, the image.

4. When the exercise ends, read over your work. You should find that you've produced much more than you thought you knew about the topic. You should at least find that you've written several sentences that can be the basis of another freewriting.

5. If you wish, repeat the exercise. Each time you repeat it, you should find that your ideas about the topic are becoming clearer. On the other hand, you may find that you are moving further away from your original topic. If so, you have at least two options: (a) you could allow your writing to follow the new direction; (b) you could ask yourself the question "How can I bring my writing back to my original topic?" Use this as the first line of a new focused freewriting, and see where it leads.

6. Save all writings. You may find later, in going over these freewritings, that words and ideas you had ignored may be just what you need in a later draft.

Brainstorming

Brainstorming is like freewriting because you accept anything you write and pay no attention to the *have-to's*. But it isn't a nonstop exercise. Another name for brainstorming is *listing*, because that's what you do: make a list of ideas, facts, sights, sounds, people, and so forth, that can help you either get started on a project or move a project along.

You can brainstorm individually or in a group. Group brainstorming brings out many ideas that can help each member of the group. I'll describe both methods.

Individual Brainstorming. Individual brainstorming is usually used after you have an idea of your topic. If you don't, I'd recommend freewriting at least once until you have a clear idea in mind. Then brainstorm a list of items you might include in your writing about the topic.

Let's look at an example. A common brainstorming exercise is making grocery lists. People are usually aware of several factors that limit what goes on the list: what they already have at home, how much they can carry, how much they can spend, what's nutritious, what tastes good, and how long it will be until they can shop again. (Note: I just brainstormed that list of factors. What would you add to the list?) These factors are part of the topic for the list. Most adults have written so many grocery lists that it would be silly to write down the topic before making the list, but for the purpose of this exercise I'll note the topic. For example:

Things We Need for the Next Three Days, Including Breakfast, Lunch, Dinner, Snacks—These Things Should Be Nutritionally Balanced, Inexpensive, and Tasty (Since I'll have the car I can carry as much as I need to.)

milk (2 gallons?)	soup	apples
margarine	crackers	oranges
eggs	lettuce	ground beef
cereal (hot? cold?)	celery	chicken
bread	peppers	juice
paper towels	onions	cookies
pasta	potatoes	
tomato sauce	cheese	

Now let's look at the list. Actually there are two lists. The first is the list of factors, my topic, that I use to determine the kinds of things I want to buy. The second is the list of items. This is really how brainstorming works. First, you generate one list; then you generate another list based on the first. You could take any item on the food list and generate another list based on that. Take pasta, for example. When I get to the store, I'll have to choose the type of pasta to buy: spaghetti, linguini, macaroni, shells, tortellini, etc. For your writing, the important thing to note is that whenever you take one item from one list and use it to create another list, you are making your writing more clear and more vivid for your reader. Brainstorming is not yet sentences and paragraphs—that's a different step— but, like freewriting, it gives you the "stuff" to work with.

Notice something else about the list: the order. When you brainstorm, just as when you freewrite, your brain tends to give out information in patterns. The next thing you write always relates in some way to what you wrote before it. Notice that the items on the list sometimes seem to be in groups: *lettuce, celery, peppers, onions, potatoes* form a group of vegetables. I brainstormed these items together because I saw in my mind's eye that part of my local grocery store where these things are displayed. I saw myself walking through the vegetable section picking up the items I needed.

On the other hand, the things you write are often related in other ways. For example, *soup, crackers* are together because I saw myself eating soup and then eating a cracker with the soup. Likewise, *cheese* follows *potatoes* because I saw myself grating Colby cheese on a baked potato, a dish my family and I like. Someone else reading my list might think it strange that *cheese* follows *potatoes,* but there is always a reason, a logical pattern, to brainstorming.

Those patterns always have something to do with what we see with our mind's eye. That's why the most important step in brainstorming is to concentrate on the pictures, scenes, sounds, smells, and other sensations in your mind. Thus, the steps in brainstorming are similar to those needed for focused freewriting:

1. Relax
2. Visualize
3. Write
4. *Don't* censor or edit anything
5. Review what you've written
6. Go on to the next step (another list, another freewriting)
7. Save your writing

Group Brainstorming. In school, this technique is often used to generate many ideas about a topic (for example, reasons why people either vote or don't vote in elections). It's also used to generate a list of topics from which students can choose. In business and government, group brainstorming is one of the most common tools used in solving problems (for example, How can we advertise our new product? What items should we ask for in next year's budget?). It is a powerful tool for thinking because it uses the combined power of many minds.

However, it has to be done right. The most important step in group brainstorming is that the group members allow anything to be suggested, no matter how strange. If someone in the group criticizes another member (saying perhaps, "Are you kidding? That would never work!"), the members will be afraid to say anything else. At the start of the brainstorming session, it's good to remind others not to criticize or laugh at anything that is suggested. Remember, this is a time for imaginative thinking, and the imagination doesn't work when we're afraid of what others might say.

How does a group, a college class, go about brainstorming? Let's say, for example, that a history class has been studying China. A library research paper is a class requirement and the students choose their own topics for this paper. The professor decides to use group brainstorming to help each person choose a topic of interest. Here's one useful way in which the session might proceed:

1. In class, each student does a focused freewrite on "What am I interested in studying more about in relation to China?" *Or* each student brainstorms individually on the same question.

2. The session leader (the professor or a designated student) then asks for suggestions and writes them on the blackboard or a flip chart so that all can see the growing list. The goal is to use the visible list to stimulate your imagination further. For example, if one student suggests "Trade Between China and the United States," you might be reminded of the newspaper article you read on the desire of Chinese youth for designer clothes from the United States. You might suggest this as a subtopic on trade. One of the good effects of group brainstorming is that an idea from one person can lead to a more focused suggestion from another.

As you'll see in Chapter 7, a more focused idea is easier to research and usually leads to a clearer, more interesting paper.

3. The class reviews the list. Do the suggested topics tend to fall into categories: "trade," "warfare," "culture," "education," "government"? Have any significant parts of life been left out: "religion," "games," "transport"? If so, brainstorm some topics in these categories. Remember, the brainstormed list is always used for generating further ideas.

4. The group session could be followed by a second freewriting by each person. For example, each person could write with this focus: "Now that I've looked over the list, what looks interesting? How could I make this topic more focused so that I have a clear direction for my research?"

Imaginary Dialogues: The Reader and You

Writers do this so much that they are probably not even aware of it as a technique for getting started or sticking with it. Indeed, we use it in different ways in different situations. For example, we use this when we have a general idea of what we want to write about and also know who our reader will be. In this situation, we use imaginary dialoguing as a way of attacking our fear of the reader, not by avoiding or ignoring the fear but by trying to understand it. In the imaginary dialogue the writer imagines that he or she is talking with the reader about the topic. The writer visualizes the reader in as much detail as possible. Like Shakespeare watching his characters move through a scene in his mind, the writer observes the reader hearing what the writer is saying about the topic. The writer tries to put himself or herself into the mind of the reader and to imagine what questions the reader will ask in response to each statement the writer makes.

Remember, the goal of this technique is to get as much useful writing on the page as possible. We visualize the reader asking questions because the questions can move our thinking and writing along. (For example, when I wrote the first sentence of this paragraph, I imagined a reader asking me, "How does this technique help me get useful writing on the page?" My next sentence answers that question.) It's very important that we visualize the reader conversing with us because that gives us words to write. If we have a mental picture of the reader frowning at us or shaking his or her head, that increases our fear. Unfortunately, fearful writers always have a picture like that in their minds. If we can get beyond that image to an image of the reader asking us questions about our words, then we can at least break through our fear and get words on the page. (Note: Ideally, this exercise can also help us discover questions that we should ask our reader. In Chapters 3 through 7, I suggest many other specific ways of making your audience your ally and not your enemy.)

Imaginary Dialogues: Both Sides of the Coin

Because it's natural to talk with others, it's natural to think of our writing as a kind of talk between ourselves and someone else. In fact, one of the oldest forms of writing is the dialogue, which we can read today in the writings of the Greek philosopher Plato. Plato's strategy was simple: he imagined his teacher, Socrates, conversing with his pupils about important ideas such as justice, good government, love. In a typical dialogue, one of the pupils would ask Socrates a question and Socrates would suggest an answer and ask the student another question. Besides being a dramatic, interesting way to write, dialogue kept Plato's imagination working.

You can make dialoguing work for you, too. Here is one dialoguing strategy:

1. Begin with a freewrite (a focused freewrite if you already have a rough idea of your topic).
2. From your freewrite, pick out a statement that interests you, for example, "I have a hard time getting up on Monday mornings."
3. Write this statement; then write a question, for example, "So what? Doesn't everybody else?" or just "Why?"
4. Then answer your question.
5. Keep asking questions and answering them. Try becoming argumentative. When you write an answer (for example, "I don't like Monday mornings because I've gotten used to sleeping late on weekends"), think up a snappy reply: "Well, dummy, why not go to bed earlier on Sunday night?" or "Come on, admit it. Isn't it just as hard for you to get up on Tuesday and Wednesday?"

The beauties of this strategy are that you keep your writing alive by testing everything you say against an imaginary opponent and that the writing makes sense because every statement is connected to the one before and the one after.

Here's another dialoguing strategy:

1. If you have a rough idea of your topic, begin by brainstorming two characters who'll have a conversation about it. The characters can be anyone you find interesting: friends, relatives, famous people, or total inventions. Like Shakespeare, you can visualize them talking in a scene.
2. Follow the steps as in the first strategy. Be sure that the characters are different from one another so that each one challenges what the other says.
3. You may find that someone else, you, will want to get into the conversation after a while. Feel free to add another character, as long as that character adds another perspective on the issue.

You can use the imaginary dialogue as a strategy for getting started with any kind of writing. You may find, in fact, that the dialogue so appeals to you that you'll want to revise it into a piece of writing to show others. While Plato is the best known practitioner of this form, you need only do a little looking to see how often dialogue is used today in many types of writing. It's particularly effective for trying to explain a difficult idea or trying to prove a point to someone who's hard to convince. For example, many instruction guides (computer manuals or car maintenance guides) use a question-and-answer format, a kind of dialogue. Also, a high percentage of commercial and political ads are in dialogue forms: think how often a commercial presents one person talking with another person who holds a different point of view. We pay attention to this writing because of the constant give-and-take between people who disagree.

Moreover, you'll find practice with dialoguing particularly helpful when you are given any kind of school assignment that involves proving a point, or thesis. For any persuasive or argumentative piece of writing, it's vital to show the give-and-take between different points of view. (See Chapters 3 and 5 for more on persuasive writing, plus descriptions of other popular, useful forms.)

Graphic Display

Up to this point, I've been stressing the importance of visualizing in sparking your imagination to write. Now, I'd like to show two techniques that use the blank page itself to map your thinking process. The first, called *mindmapping* or *clustering*, involves writing your topic in the center of the page and showing your following thoughts radiating from it, like rays of the sun. The second, which we'll call the *double-entry* method, involves writing on the left and right sides of the page to show thoughts of different kinds.

Both methods are offshoots of brainstorming, but they look different on the page. Try them out a few times to get the hang of the techniques, and see how they work for you.

Mindmapping. Because we're used to writing from left to right and down the page, mindmapping takes some getting used to. But many writers like it because it shows how each idea connects with others. These connections help them turn their brainstormings into written drafts.

1. In the center of an unruled page, write your topic and draw a circle around it.

2. Relax and visualize, as described for focused freewriting (p. 13).

3. When you are fully visualizing your topic, list the images and ideas that come to you. Mindmapping is a shorthand designed to get as many images and ideas as possible on the page, so write only single words or short phrases. Write them in a circle around the center topic. As you write each one, you will probably think of other images and ideas that relate to it. Write these related images and ideas near the word that sparked them, but farther out from the center. Each time you add a word, draw a line from it to the word to which it is related.

4. Your map should look something like wheel spokes radiating from the central topic, with other words branching off in a widening circle.

5. Review your map. As you read the words, you may become aware of other connections that you did not see before. Draw a

dotted line between each pair of words that you now wish to connect.

6. The map can be used to create the outline of a draft, since the connections among ideas have already been made. The map can also be used as the basis for another mindmap if you wish to take one of your ideas and make it a new center.

   Below is my mindmap for the topic Double-Entry Mindmapping. Note how I use the map to describe double-entry mindmapping in the next section.

Double-Entry Mindmapping. Double-entry mindmapping uses a ruled page, divided into left and right halves. On the left side, write the images and ideas about your topic that come to you after you relax and visualize. The method is like brainstorming since you write these down the page; however, in double-entry mindmapping, you leave several empty lines between each image or idea. You leave these spaces because on the right half of the page opposite them, you will write other ideas related to those you've written on the left.

   The method is called "double-entry" because your first entry, on the left, introduces an image or idea in a word or a short phrase; and your second entry, on the right, expands on the left-hand entry either with other brief phrases or by a longer statement of explanation, whatever you wish.

As with mindmapping, you can enter your ideas in any order. For example, you may choose to jot down in the left column a long list of words and phrases and then go back and expand on each idea in the right column. However, as your imagination gives you ideas, you may want to jot your brief image on the left and then immediately expand on that idea to the right. When writing your map, don't worry about keeping the main ideas on the left and the related ideas on the right. This isn't a formal outline. It's a way of giving you space and freedom to let your imagination work.

Of course, as with mindmapping, the blank space on the page also gives you the freedom to go back later and fill in more information as it comes to you. You need not hurry to get it all down at once. Indeed, one of the benefits of both mindmapping methods is that the more you look at the words and phrases, the more ideas spark in your mind.

On page 24, in double-entry form, is a version of the mindmap I drew earlier. The words and phrases in the left column are the spokes of the wheel in the mindmap. In the right column are the ideas that branched off from the spokes. Note how I've used the double-entry format to add ideas in short sentences.

As you can see, any method of mindmapping, or freewriting, dialoguing, or brainstorming, gives you more raw material than you may need in a later draft. For example, I've not up to this point mentioned that I first heard about double-entry mindmapping from writing teacher Dixie Goswami, who described it as a way of taking notes and keeping a journal about the ideas one studies (see more on this technique in Chapter 2.)

EXERCISE: Review the techniques for getting started. Try each one in turn. In fact, try each one a couple of times so you get the feel of it. If you are like most of us, you are not used to using your imagination in these ways, so you may feel awkward at first. Be sure to follow the steps in order; for example, make sure to take the time to relax and visualize before brainstorming. (Reminder: These techniques tap

Double-Entry Mindmapping

relax	visualize images, scenes, sounds
left, right	let ideas on one side spark ideas on other side
short phrases	right side lets you write sentences — more space
main ideas	write related ideas or longer explanations on right. Fill in questions as they occur in rereading
images lined page	not really essential, but it provides order
not an outline	freedom to think of new ideas, fill in as you reread, should be freeing, not restricting
Goswami	suggested this as a journal-keeping method

your imagination, so don't let someone else tell you what to free-write or brainstorm or dialogue about, at least the first few times you practice. After that, you'll find the techniques just as useful for getting you started with topics you've been given as they are for helping you discover your own topics.) ■

✍ **EXERCISE:** Do a focused freewrite about your best experience as a writer. What did you do? Why was it successful? You may discover that your best experience contained a technique for getting started that I've not mentioned here. If so, write about it. ■

A BRIEF LOOK INSIDE THE BRAIN (*OR* WHY ARE WE DOING THESE THINGS?)

Freewrites? Brainstorms? Dialogues? Mindmaps? Why can't we just *write*? The simple answer is because our brains won't let us. The better answer is the more practice we get, the more regular writing we do, the more relaxed we become and the easier any writing task becomes. Learning to write with confidence does not happen overnight. It happens with time, with patience, and with practice.

This statement makes sense when we consider what researchers have learned about how the brain works. Scientists often picture the brain as an incredibly complex network of interconnected cells, called *neurons* (Fig. 1). Each neuron holds information. When we think—whether consciously (aware) or unconsciously (unaware) or asleep—we send information in electrical impulses from one neuron to many others. In other words, we are connecting each bit of information with many others. (The mindmap is a rough picture of this process.)

Not only do we send impulses along existing lines to existing neurons, but we also are constantly creating new neurons and new

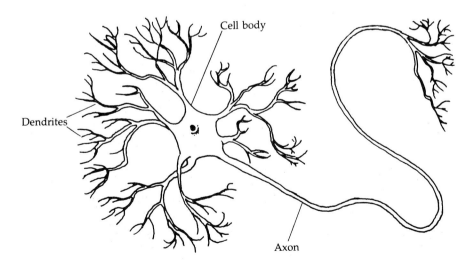

Figure 1. Neuron

connecting lines (called *dendrites* and *axons*) as we think (Fig. 2). Just as important, every time we practice the same exercise or use the same words or concentrate on the same idea we physically strengthen all the cells and lines that pertain to that practice, those words, or that idea. Thus, the more we practice something, the easier it becomes for our brains to control. This is certainly true of writing.

But, you may ask, why is writing still difficult, even for people who've been doing it regularly for a long time? The answer has two parts. First, for the experienced writer, much writing *is* easy. A professional journalist can write a clear, vivid report of last night's event in time for a midnight deadline. An experienced office manager can dash off a brief, clear memo to an employee. A doctoral student isn't daunted by an assignment for a five-page paper in her specialty. If you've done a certain kind of writing enough times, your brain has made and strengthened all the necessary neurons and pathways so that the task isn't hard.

But life always offers new challenges, new adventures to every writer. And writing to meet these challenges means that we can't do things in the old, easy ways, so the work is sometimes very difficult indeed. Besides, people who love to write are always looking for the challenges, so they're always going to be facing difficult tests.

Second, no matter how many times you've written that newspaper report or that office memo or that five-page paper, there's an

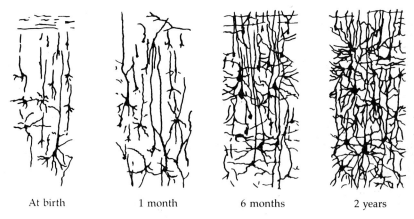

At birth   1 month   6 months   2 years

Figure 2. Growth of the Neuron Network (Relative Complexity)

element of difficulty about even the easiest writing task. That difficulty is caused by the way that your brain handles information. When you write, you have to turn many pictures and feelings into words. Think back to your visualization exercises. When you relax and visualize, your mind offers pictures, sounds, smells, feelings—only occasionally does it offer words. Even less often does it offer whole sentences. For example, the newspaper reporter may have vivid pictures of a house fire. In her mind, she may still hear the sirens and the weeping of the cold, homeless victims. She may still smell the acrid smoke and see the fire fighters rushing into the collapsing building. But what words should she use to describe these things so that they make sense to her and to someone else? As she writes, she builds new connections in her brain between the neurons that hold the sights, the sounds, and the smells, and the other neurons that exist in the language centers of the brain. Some new pathways must be created. For example, perhaps a person has been killed in the fire, and the writer has never reported such an event before. She has to consider carefully how to report this without being either too matter-of-fact or too emotional. In addition, most of the connecting lines lead through other neurons that hold data that may confuse the writer; for example, in her mind the writer needs to separate this fire from others she has reported or experienced, even though her process of thought keeps taking her back to those earlier experiences. Thus, the brain must find the right word. It is a physical process that requires time and energy.

Furthermore, scientists such as Nobel prizewinner Roger Sperry have discovered evidence that the centers of language and the centers of feeling and visualizing are in separate halves of the brain, though this evidence is still very controversial. These halves, called *hemispheres* (Fig. 3), are connected by a dense body of cells called the *corpus callosum*. If the theory is correct, the impulses that go back and forth from what we see in our mind's eye to the words we want to use must travel long distances. Though reaction time is measured in milliseconds, the back-and-forth search for that right word can cost any writer, as we well know, many milliseconds indeed!

This is why techniques such as freewriting, brainstorming, dialoguing, and mindmapping are suggested. In a physical sense, these are exercises that strengthen the connections between what

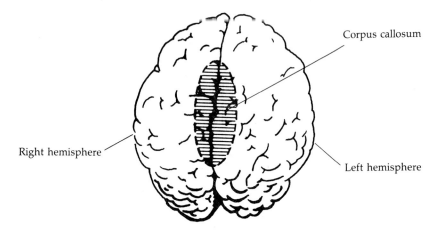

Figure 3. Hemispheres of the Brain and Corpus Callosum

we see, hear, smell, taste, and feel and the language we have for expressing this information. If we borrow Sperry's theory, we can say that writing is a complex act that depends on smooth coordination between both halves of the brain. Only writing itself, including such tested exercises as I've described above, can make this coordination relaxed and smooth.

EXERCISE: Try an experiment: Relax. Close your eyes, and concentrate on what you see in your mind's eye. For a few moments just observe what you see and don't try to put it into words. Then try to *write* a description of what you saw. What happens as you write? How does your mind help you do this writing? How does your mind make the writing difficult? Make a note of how the mind helps and hinders you. ■

STICKING WITH IT

Now that we've solved for the moment the problem of getting started, I'd like to turn back to the problem of perseverance, sticking with it. Earlier (p. 5), I suggested that getting into the habit of regular writing (remember Donald Murray's "Never a day without a line"?) was the best way to stay disciplined and motivated. The theory is simple: the more you do it, the more you'll appreciate it, the better you'll do it, and the more you'll want to do it. Simple.

That's part of the story, but only the first, most basic part. You'll find, as you grow in writing experience and in the complexity of studies and career, that your writing tasks will grow more complex and occur more frequently. You already may have had those days when anything seems more pleasant than the writing you have to do. Moreover, you may have put it off and put it off until the final deadline is breathing down your neck or until it's gobbled you up.

Discipline and Motivation

Why should it be so difficult to stick with a writing task, once you have learned the first secret, regular writing, and the second secret, how to get started?

Well, one reason is complexity; sometimes a project seems so complicated that we fear we'll never get it done. Another reason is tedium; it's hard to work on the same thing, day in, day out. A third reason is that the more we write, the more we get weighed down by what we've written. When we've invested a lot of time in a piece of writing and then realize that we have to make basic changes, sometimes we'd rather give up the whole thing than make the necessary revisions. Let's look at these three factors and consider some techniques for dealing with them.

"It's Too Complicated." This book will deal with some fairly complicated writing tasks, including the library research paper (see Chapter 7) and the proposal, which is one of the most common and important forms of writing in business and government (see Chapter 3). People who do such projects as a regular part of their work break up the complex task into manageable parts. Otherwise, they would feel overwhelmed by the amount of work. You'll see how this works for the library research paper and the proposal when you get to the appropriate chapters.

As a first exercise, a writer looks at the entire project and at the amount of time before the deadline (if there is no deadline, the writer may make up one to help plan out the steps of the project). Then the writer lists (brainstorming helps here) the different things that need to be done, such as going to the library, taking notes on books and articles, interviewing, writing a draft of each section of the paper, and making changes. Then the writer sets up mini-deadlines; for example, "by the twentieth, I'll have finished taking notes; by the twenty-second, I'll have written my working outline; by the twenty-fourth, I'll have written a draft of the first section."

The key is to make sure that the pieces are small enough so that you can meet the goal of each day. If you know that you won't have much time to give to the project each day, do your planning right away and get started, so you won't find yourself with two days left and half the project to do. Completing a little bit of a project each day keeps you feeling that you're making progress. In addition, you'll be using less physical energy each time, so you'll be fresher and sharper each time you return to your writing.

"It Gets Boring." All of us, including people who love to write, get bored with anything if we have to keep at the same thing hour after hour. Professional writers know this, so they use tricks to keep their interest high.

- The novelist William Faulkner said, "I always quit when I still have more I want to say. That way, I'll keep wanting to get back to it." That is, quit for the day while you're still excited, not when you can't stand one more minute.

- Try stopping for the day in the middle of a sentence. For instance, the last time I worked on this chapter, I stopped with the words, "The novelist William Faulkner said . . . ." By doing this, I could get started again with something easy, something I already knew how to say. And once you get started, it's easier to keep going.

- The advice for working on complicated writing tasks applies for boredom, too. If you set reachable goals for each day, you don't have to keep going until you drop from exhaustion. You will be happier all the time you are working.

- Take a break. Get some exercise. If you get tired of drafting your library research paper, run an errand, make that phone call you've been putting off, take a brisk walk, or take a look through a book about a different subject. Then come back to the paper. Even better, if you schedule your breaks, then you've got something to look forward to and you'll take your break when you're not tired of your project.

- Shift your focus. If you get stuck trying to draft something that seems particularly difficult to you, turn your attention to another part of the project: reread a part you've already drafted and make any changes you think it needs; or do a focused freewrite on the idea you're having trouble with; or look over your notes and see if you spot any new ideas that you could work into your writing.

Besides saving your energy and keeping up your interest, these tricks have an added benefit: stopping when you're still fresh, taking a break, or shifting your focus lets your unconscious mind keep working on your writing. Students of the mind have been telling us for centuries that our brains continue to work on problems even when we're not consciously thinking about them. Some have said that our ideas incubate in the unconscious part of our brains; that is, they grow and mature like fertilized eggs kept in a warm place.

Think of a time when you suddenly got a good idea or remembered a name you'd forgotten or thought of a solution to a problem that had stumped you. Chances are that you had some of these good ideas—scientists call them *insights*—when you were thinking about something totally different. The idea just popped into your head. This, scientists say, is how incubation works.

Artists and scientists, people whose business is thinking, learn to use this process and depend on it. Scientific history is full of stories about discoveries that were made when the thinker was taking a break, shifting focus, or even asleep! Remember the story of Isaac Newton under the apple tree: when the apple bounced off his head, he suddenly understood gravity. Remember the story of Archimedes: while he relaxed in his bathtub, he suddenly understood why objects float. Albert Einstein remarked that he got some of his best ideas while shaving. These were men who had devoted long, conscious hours to their study of scientific problems, but they also knew that their minds didn't stop working when they shifted their attention to something else. The same process can work for you.

EXERCISE: Stop reading the chapter now. For a minute or two do a freewrite, on anything. Go back to the chapter then. Some time later, an hour or a day, reread your freewrite, then do a second freewrite focused on the same topic. Compare the two. Consider the unconscious thought that has occurred during incubation. ■

"I Have So Much Revising to Do, It's Just Not Worth It." The best part of writing is that you can change anything you don't like. The toughest reality of writing is that you rarely get it just the way you want it the first time or the second time, or maybe even the twentieth time. The imaging part of your brain keeps telling the writing part that it's made the wrong choice: "Nope, that's not it. Try again." Then, too, you will find that your readers, your teacher, your fellow students, your boss, will want you to make revisions, to do it their way. The more you write, the more you'll come to accept that making changes, sometimes major changes, is a major part of writing.

How can you keep the need to revise from turning you off to the entire project? Here are some hints:

First, just realizing that writing is rewriting should be some motivation to keep going.

Second, if you know that you'll have to revise, build revision time into your schedule. All experienced writers do this. For example, book publishing companies always build into their production schedules long periods of time, sometimes several months, during which drafts of parts of the book are sent out for reviewers to read and make comments on. Then the author revises, deciding which comments are most important and how to respond to them. After revisions are made, the new drafts are often sent out again, sometimes to different readers. Writers expect this and plan for it. (In Chapters 3–7, you'll see different ways in which you can use readers' comments to improve any kind of writing.)

Third, remember that every time you go back to a project you are, in a way, getting started again. All the techniques you practiced earlier are useful at any stage. For example, if you have collected a lot of information from books and articles for a library research paper, you may be confused about how to organize your data into a coherent report. This would be a fine occasion for a freewrite or a mindmap on the question "What's my most important idea in this paper and what's my best information?" Using these techniques and others can suggest a path to follow.

Fourth, reread periodically. Rereading what you've already written creates momentum. Instead of coming back to your manuscript where you left off, reread either the whole piece or a large chunk of it. This will help you get into the flow of your draft and make it easier to continue writing. When the right words are coming particularly hard, rereading gives you a confidence boost. As you read, say to yourself, "I've accomplished this." Congratulate yourself on your intelligence and hard work; after all, the evidence is right in front of you.

EXERCISE: Recall a project, not necessarily writing, that you thought was complicated, but that you successfully completed. What made the project complicated? Were you at any time bored by the project? How did you overcome boredom? What techniques or attitudes helped you finish the project? If any of the techniques that worked for you are different from those described above, note them for future reference. They may work again! ■

CRAFTSPERSON? ARTIST? ATHLETE?

If you haven't guessed it by now, the most essential part of writing is psychological. Of course, pen, ink, and paper (or computer hardware and software), muscles, blood, nerves, and sweat all go into the work; but, to get you started, keep you going, and keep you happy as a writer, you have to stay "psyched." In other words, you play mind games.

Aside from all the techniques and tricks I've described, one of the most enjoyable and useful mental games is *role-playing*. *Role-playing* by a writer means seeing the connection between writing and other vocations that you either admire or find very intriguing. For example, in this chapter, I've talked at length about the discipline of writing, and have compared writing to the work of athletes, scientists, philosophers, explorers, and artists. These comparisons are not pretense; the adventure, the difficulty, the beauty, and the discipline of writing make it very much like the work of these other people. Moreover, all these other adventurous people spend some part of their lives as writers, so the connection is real to that degree.

Since it is very easy for a writer, experienced or beginning, to sometimes feel small, frustrated, clumsy, and alone, it helps to see himself or herself as part of a grander community in which all are doing important and valuable, though often painful, things.

Sometimes, the writer makes the comparison vivid in his or her writing. The nineteenth-century British poet Percy Bysshe Shelley called poets the "legislators of the human race"; the American poet Walt Whitman, in his *Song of Myself*, said of himself as "singer":

> Of every hue and caste am I, of every rank and religion,
> A farmer, mechanic, artist, gentleman, sailor, quaker,
> Prisoner, fancy-man, rowdy, lawyer, physician, priest.

In this century, a powerful metaphor for the writer was built around the life of American novelist and newspaperman Ernest Hemingway. Hemingway was pictured by himself and others as a rugged outdoorsman—soldier of fortune, big-game hunter—whose writing was always honest, cutting right to the heart of an event. Balancing this macho image was that of British novelist and essayist Virginia Woolf, who saw her writing and her womanhood as inseparable: "A woman's writing is always feminine; it cannot help being feminine; at its best it is most feminine; the only difficulty lies in defining what we mean by feminine." In the last fifteen years, another popular metaphor for the writer has emerged, that of detective. Journalists Carl Bernstein and Bob Woodward gave rise to this comparison through their discoveries about the Watergate break-in, which toppled the Nixon administration.

Finding the Model for You

It may help to keep you going as a writer to imagine yourself following in the footsteps of these writers or to see yourself as these different writers saw themselves. But I'd like to offer a few other metaphors.

The Craftsperson. The writer makes real things that work and that serve real purposes. As a writer, you can give important information to people that need it; you can use your writing to preserve the present so that future generations can relive it. You can use your writing to meet personal goals: getting a job, making your business grow, convincing a special person of your love. You can use your writing to help others: that job recommendation for a friend, that letter to the town council to keep bus service available to the poor and the elderly, that proposal to business and government for safe disposal of hazardous waste. The writer at his or her desk, brainstorming, revising, risking the criticism of readers, makes something just as tangible and useful as the dedicated farmer, carpenter, mechanic, or engineer.

The Artist. All writing can be beautiful. We think poems or great speeches or profound plays are beautiful. But we can feel proud of the beauty in a letter that consoles a person in pain or that expresses thanks; in a letter to the editor that expresses our point of view without disregarding the views of others; in a report that shows our careful study of an event or an idea; in a proposal that convinces our reader. The artistry of the writer whose ideas fit together and whose words fit the ideas compares with the artistry of the dancer performing the perfect pirouette, the poet who perfectly blends the sound and the image, and the painter whose colors and textures capture the feelings of the subject.

The Athlete. Runners take joy in the smooth working of their bodies, in the growing resistance of their minds to fatigue and pain. Basketball players take joy in their deception of gravity, their improving ability to shoot with grace and accuracy while on the move. Skiers and gymnasts take joy in achieving calm balance in the face of breathtaking risks. Writers do all these things. Though the muscles, moves, and risks may be different, writing is as physical, as unpredictable, and as scary as any sport. It is also just as satisfying for the person who, like the dedicated athlete, practices regularly to reach gradually greater goals. Sure, there are bad days as well as good; sure, one has to fight the mental fatigue of practicing the same things over and over. But the rewards can be great. Indeed, the rewards for the writer can exceed those for other athletes. No one has put this difference better than physical educator and writer James Metcalf:

Peak motor expression demands the vigor of youth, it is therefore difficult to incorporate much life experience into the expression. . . . Contrarily, the written mode offers ample opportunity for artists to incorporate life experience into their work. Indeed, the tools of expressive craft here are sharpened as the artist's perceptions are refined by age and experience. Even if the writer's skills erode later, [the] writing has already transformed ideas and insights into permanent artifact, the quality of which is now independent of the writer's competence. . . . So, no wonder that I, a physical educator, am fascinated by the writing process. Written expression, like motor expression, is a statement and affirmation of self. Yet, while the tools and products of motor expression are ephemeral, writing makes the art eternal. The former athlete must ultimately accept that "it is better to be a used-to-be than a never-was . . . but I really can't prove that I am a used-to-be." The writer simply says, "I am I . . . and I always will be."

EXERCISE: Reread the quotation from Walt Whitman (p. 34). Using the double-entry format, list each of the jobs or vocations to which he as a "singer" compares himself. Then, in the space next to each term, write at least one way in which that job or vocation is similar to writing. If you don't know the definition of some of the terms (some of Whitman's nineteenth-century language has disappeared from common use), either ask someone who knows or go to the library and find an annotated edition (one that has notes for the modern reader) of *Song of Myself*. ▪

EXERCISE: Again use Whitman's list of jobs and vocations and the double-entry format. This time, however, next to each term write at least one way in which it is clearly different from writing. Compare your lists of similarities and differences and reflect on what you've written. Then write a definition of the writer that uses the similarities and differences that seem the most accurate and interesting to you. ▪

EXERCISE: Relax. Visualize yourself writing something difficult. What model or metaphor of the writer helps you to keep going and feeling good about your work? Is it different from any of the models that have been mentioned in this chapter? Use this visualization as the subject of a focused freewrite. Revise the freewrite so that it says what you want it to say about you. ▪

✍ PROJECTS FOR WRITERS

Write Your Own. Use Getting Started and Sticking with It as the title of a guide you will write about a skill, craft, sport or other activity that you greatly enjoy. Imagine that you're writing it for someone who has heard of this activity and who may even have tried it but who just hasn't found in it the joy you have. Try to put yourself in the mind of that person (visualizing and dialoguing might help here). What fears or mistaken ideas might have kept that person from getting started? How might the person overcome these blocks? What tricks of the trade have you picked up that can help the person?

Now, how do you stick with it when the going gets rough? Do you ever feel tempted to give it up? How do you cope with this temptation? What have you learned from other enthusiasts that can help you in these situations?

In writing this guide, use any and all suggestions made in Chapter 1. When you have written down as much as you want to say, take the plunge and show it to another writer. If you have any anxiety about this part of the writing process, read ahead in Chapter 4 the section entitled Getting Help from Friends, Relatives, and Fellow Students. Use the techniques described there for asking good questions about your writing.

Connecting with Fellow Writers. Brainstorm a list of people you know who write, perhaps in school, perhaps on the job, perhaps through letters to friends. Teachers, bosses, co-workers, and fellow students will do.

Shorten the list to four or five who seem to you to be comfortable with the writing they do and who seem to enjoy it. Interview them about their writing. (To learn more about how to interview, see How to Do Personal Interviews in Chapter 7.) Find out how they get started in writing and stick with it. How do they overcome the blank page? How do they cope with the fears of the writer? What tricks do they have to share?

As for sticking with it, how have they acquired the discipline to write? How do they plan their writing? How do they set schedules? Do they have favorite metaphors for the writer that help them get through the difficult times?

Write up these interviews into an informal report. Do you observe similarities among these writers? Differences?

As with Write Your Own, show your draft to a fellow writer and use Chapter 4 to ask this reader a few good questions that can get you the "feedback" you need to help you revise the report.

Free Experiment. Use any theme or technique in this chapter. Give your imagination room to work. Use any form of writing or any medium with which you're comfortable to explore the idea you choose. Some examples are:

• a story (or a video play) about a person terrified to write
• a parody guidebook, for example, *Procrastination: Getting Started and Sticking with It*
• a newly discovered letter from Shakespeare about how he really wrote his plays.

Chapter Checklist

Write regularly

Try these tricks for getting started:
Nonstop Writing or Freewriting
Focused Freewriting
Individual Brainstorming
Group Brainstorming
Imaginary Dialogues: The Reader and You
Imaginary Dialogues: Both Sides of the Coin
Mindmapping
Double-Entry Mindmapping

For each of these tricks to be successful, always remember to:
Take time to relax
Take time to visualize
Ignore the *have to's*
Review your work
Repeat the technique (as needed)

Try these tricks for sticking with it:
To simplify a complex project:
    Plan your project schedule now

Set small, reachable goals for each day
Set mini-deadlines, and keep them
To keep from getting bored:
Stop each day while you still have more you want to say
Stop each day in the middle of a paragraph or sentence
Reread periodically to build momentum
Schedule breaks, and take them
Shift your focus
Let incubation work for you
To make the necessary revisions:
Remember that writing is rewriting
Include revision time in your schedule
Reread to congratulate yourself on what you've accomplished

To keep going and stay happy: find the model of the writer that works for you.

Words to Write By

Write regularly.

Anything you write you can change.

Something is always better than nothing.

I've learned to write anywhere—in a motel, in a plane, on a bus. . . . I give myself no excuses for not writing.
—Carlos Fuentes
novelist and statesman

2 The Basics of Writing: Discovery, Experiment, Knowledge

Words . . . are the wildest, freest, most irresponsible, most unteachable of all things. Of course, you can catch them and place them in alphabetical order in dictionaries. But words do not live in dictionaries; they live in the mind . . . all we can say about them, as we peer at them over the edge of that deep, dark, and only fitfully illuminated cavern in which they live—the mind—all we can say about them is that they seem to like people to think and to feel before they use them, but to think and to feel not about them, but about something different.
—Virginia Woolf

People who write honestly and self-critically, trying to say what they mean, will often find that what passed for a truth when floating vaguely in the mind looks a lot like an error when moored to the page. Better still, they will discover truths they didn't know they had.
—Donald McCloskey, economist
"Economical Writing"

THE WRITER-EXPLORER, THE WRITER-SCIENTIST

You may have noticed, when you freewrote and did other exercises in Chapter 1, that a lot of what you wrote surprised you. That is, before you started writing, you wouldn't have guessed that you'd come up with what you did. That's what happens when you start tapping your brain through writing: you stumble onto some really interesting stuff that you don't know you have. Sometimes these discoveries take you so by surprise that you feel the writing must have come from somewhere, or someone, else. Plato called such a moment "divine fury"; other writers have called it "genius" or "inspiration." Brain scientists would say that these writers, through experience, knew how to use their writing to make greater use of their minds.

With this idea of discovery in mind, let me add two more models to the list we generated in the previous chapter: the writer-explorer and the writer-scientist. Each time we write, no matter what we intend to write or how much planning we have done, we are setting out, like explorers, into strange lands. We are taking pencil and paper to chart what we come across, and we know that we'll have to keep revising our maps as we move and discover different angles. Why do we keep these charts, our writings? We keep them so that we'll know how we have come, so that we'll know each place we have been, and so we'll be able to predict, or at least guess, what lies farther on. We keep them so that the next time we come this way the going will be easier. We also keep them so that we can take them back to the world we left, show the charts to others, and say, "I was here and here and here—and this is how I got there."

Each time I write, every word I write is a way of saying, "I know this." Maybe it's not that emphatic; maybe it's more like saying, "For this moment, I think I know this." Each word I write, like each mark added to an explorer's map, is a way to test what I think I know. And so the writer is also a scientist, who constantly experiments with words rather than seeds, acids, or atomic particles. Once I put a word on a page, I can look at it, study it, and test to see if it continues to feel like truth. Sometimes, putting that word on the page makes me realize that I'm not sure of what I think I know. The explorer might have thought that the stream he crossed was flowing east, but when he marks it on the map, he sees the scene again in his mind, and he recalls the sun being in his eyes. "Maybe I'd better go back and look again," he thinks. So he does, and finds not only that he had been wrong about the stream, but also that there are many other sights, such as wildflowers, animal tracks, shining metal in a rock, that he had missed.

> I have learned that what I have not drawn I have never really seen, and that when I start drawing an ordinary thing I realize how extraordinary it is, sheer miracle: the branching of a tree, the structure of a dandelion's seed puff. "A mouse is miracle enough to stagger sextillions of infidels," says Walt Whitman. I discover that among the Ten Thousand Things there is no ordinary thing. All that is, is worthy of being seen, of being drawn.
>
> —Frederick Franck
> *The Zen of Seeing*

There is nothing more basic to writing than the urge to discover, to explore what you think you know. You may have been told that the basics of writing are spelling and grammar, but people who like to write never learn these things before they start writing. Give a child a pencil and paper and watch that youngster cover the page with a picture, an idea, of something in his or her thoughts. Ask about that drawing, and the child will give you the name of every part of it and maybe even tell you a story about it. Keep listening to the child and you'll see that the pictures change, grow more detailed—now the eyes have lashes and brows, the houses have windows and chimneys. Keep talking with the child and you'll hear the stories change, grow more full of events and characters. The child is writing and revising, even though letters have not yet been added to the pictures and the talk.

Sadly, many of us lose our childhood excitement with pictures and words as we get caught up in other people's expectations about correct writing. We have to relearn how to use writing to discover, to test our discoveries, and to know. That's what this chapter is about. It's also about ways to improve our writing as a tool for knowing.

RESCUING THE EXCITEMENT

Whatever you want to know, or need to know, or are told that you have to know, writing can help you know. But before your writing can help you discover, test your discoveries, and know, you have to go through the basic steps outlined in Chapter 1. That is, you must

• Relax
• Visualize
• Forget about the *have to's*

When you write to discover, you have to forget that you are writing and concentrate on what you see in your mind's eye or what you hear from a lecturer or observe in the lab. You might not even think of the writing you are doing as writing; instead, you will more likely consider it recording data, working out the problem, taking notes, sketching the plan, making a list, drawing a conclusion, telling the story, or explaining how you feel. Whenever you can forget about the writing itself and get involved with what you're trying to accomplish, then you can make discoveries with your writing. Furthermore, that's when you can get back to the same excitement and the same efficiency of effort that the child knows with a pencil, a pad of paper, and that mental picture he or she is aching to draw.

EXERCISE: Think about ways in which you like to express yourself. Focus on a time when you just had to express an idea through words, music, pictures, movement, or whatever other form you chose. Why did you have to express it? What did that self-expression enable you to do? What did you learn from putting these thoughts and feelings into a form?

Try a focused freewrite or other exercise to express your thoughts about these questions. ∎

WRITING TO DISCOVER, TEST, AND KNOW: AN EVERYDAY EXAMPLE

Let me give an everyday example of how writing to discover can work: the grocery list. In Chapter 1 I used the grocery list as an example of individual brainstorming. There, I emphasized the power of this tool to generate useful data from scratch. Recall that to create my list I relied on visualization: I imagined myself walking through my local store and observing the various displays I passed. I also paid attention to at least one other visual process: the scene of my sitting at the table and eating a meal, which helped me realize other items I wanted to buy.

For the purpose of this chapter, the key is to use brainstorming as a discovery tool: I have no idea what I want to buy before I start the process, but I am confident that brainstorming will give me the information.

However, once I make my initial discovery, I still don't know for certain what I will buy. Here's where the next step, the test, comes in. Recall from Chapter 1 that after I brainstormed the first list I could then look at the list to help me make more careful, definite choices. For example, with "pasta" on the list, I could decide whether I wanted spaghetti, macaroni, shells, or another pasta. I could also do other kinds of tests; for example, I could look over the entire list and test to see if I could put together meals for three days from the items I had brainstormed. I might set up a simple grid into which to put the items:

	Day 1	Day 2	Day 3
Breakfast			
Lunch			
Dinner			

Doing this test, I might find that I needed more variety for dinner or that I needed more nutritional balance for breakfast, so I'd add some items to my list. This test would also help me to determine the quantities of some items I needed, such as two gallons of milk or two dozen eggs, so that I could make my list more specific.

Testing the list could also include weighing it against my budget. I could do a rough price estimate of the items and see if I want to spend that much. If not, I could revise the list to cut costs. If I discover that my list comes in under budget, I could think about adding something special. And so on.

Perhaps the most important idea to draw from this example is that even as commonplace an activity as grocery shopping is so complex that most of us need to use simple tools, such as lists and charts, to help us discover and test our information. Perhaps just as important an idea is that these tools are simple, so simple that few of us would think of them as pieces of writing. Nevertheless, they are forms of writing, potentially powerful forms. When we don't use these tools, we find ourselves, like the scientist without a notebook, unable to keep track of the data and thus unable to know when something significant has happened. Moreover, like many grocery shoppers I know (including myself on some occasions), if I wait until I get to the store to discover and test, I find that three unpleasant things happen: one, I spend more time walking and wondering than I would have spent brainstorming and revising; two, I spend more money than I would have needed to spend; and three, as I walk out of the store with my groceries, I remember, that is, discover, three or four things that I forgot to buy.

The everyday grocery list exemplifies writing to discover, test, and know: the person who makes good lists and charts is writing to the purpose. The shopper is rarely aware of writing, but the writing makes the difference. The rest of this chapter will describe other purposes and techniques that can make a difference as you seek to learn and to know.

EXERCISE: With the grocery list example in mind, think of another type of writing you do that you might not consider writing, but that helps you discover ideas, test ideas, or organize information. (If you have trouble thinking of something, remember to relax and visualize. You might freewrite or brainstorm.)

Write answers to the following questions about this type of writing:

What purpose do you use the writing for?
How did you learn to use it?
Are there times when you don't use the technique? Why?
    What happens? ■

STRATEGIES FOR DISCOVERY, EXPERIMENT, AND KNOWING

Writing to the Limit

In his book *Searching Writing,* teacher-writer Ken Macrorie advises students to begin any process of research (he calls it *I-Search* because I do the work to learn what I really want to know) with some writing about the topic. He says that we must do this for two reasons. First, we cannot know where to begin our research until we have a sense of what we already know about our subject, and the best way to get that sense is through writing. Second, since we always have more knowledge, or at least more ideas about a topic than we think we do, writing is an excellent way to uncover this knowledge. As we write, each piece of information calls up other memories and sparks connections with related information.

Such writing can be called writing to the limit, the limit of what we know about a subject. When we write to the limit of what we know, or think we know, we discover where we feel firm ground and where the ground feels shaky. (For example, in writing, above, about Ken Macrorie, I felt confident writing about the principle of writing to the limit, but I discovered that I was not sure if Macrorie himself had used that term in the book. So I made a note to double-check the text.) Whenever our footing feels loose, we've discovered something that our research needs to pay attention to. The best research questions come from the doubts that we run into as we try to explain what we know.

Taking you through the process of writing to the limit is probably the best way to explain it. Remember, of course, that I'll be describing only one way of proceeding and that you may discover other methods that work just as well or better.

Step One: The Topic. Freewrite, brainstorm, or mindmap some topics that you want to learn more about. School assignments or controversial public issues are good examples. If a topic doesn't come to you right away, let freewriting or other methods help you discover what you'd like to write about.

Step Two: Writing to the Limit about Your Topic. Say that you choose that research assignment from your government or sociology course: "Choose one public issue that has been mentioned in the course thus far. With help from several books or articles pertinent to the topic, write a two-thousand-word paper in which you state your view of the issue, summarize other points of view, and cite evidence that supports your position. If you have personal experience relevant to the issue, use it as one type of evidence."

Following the guidelines in Chapter 1, you use one of the getting-started techniques to find the public issue about which you want to write: homelessness. This topic intrigues you because on your walks in American cities you have seen shabbily dressed, weather-beaten people lying on park benches or on the sidewalk on heating grates, and you have occasionally been asked for spare change. Because you have heard many opinions about these people, you have a confusing mixture of thoughts and feelings about them. You'd like to know the facts. Your biggest initial problem in doing the assignment, however, is that homelessness has been mentioned only briefly in class and your textbook doesn't mention it at all. Where do you start?

Your first impulse might be to head for the library to look at books and articles on the homeless. But before you search for more information and other opinions, try to grasp what you already know and think. Write to the limit. Remember, you chose this topic because you'd already had some first-hand experience with the homeless and you'd heard some opinions about the homeless issue. If you are like most writers, you know more bits and pieces than you think you do, but you haven't taken the time to write them down. In fact, you might already have the beginnings of a fascinating paper, a solid launch pad for your research. Here's how to tap that reserve of facts and ideas.

Start by heading your paper "What I Already Know about the Homeless." After getting relaxed and visualizing, start writing down anything that comes to mind. You can do this in a list, as in brainstorming, or in phrases and sentences, as in focused freewriting. Your list or your freewrite will probably contain some odd bits and pieces that don't seem closely connected, such as

the man who asked me for money and offered to show me the scars on his neck

the shelter on Central Avenue has barbed wire around it.
Why?
Karen and I hid from the woman who was talking to herself.

Don't worry about lack of connections. The goal is to write down as
many details as you can remember. Each detail can trigger other
memories that you may find useful later; moreover, the details you
write now may give your final draft life and power.

In this part of writing to the limit, you should try to stick to
facts. As writers and thinkers, we all have a strong tendency to
ignore the facts and jump ahead to an opinion about them. For
example, in building your lists of facts, you may be tempted to write
an opinion only, such as "Most homeless people are alcoholics,"
rather than the facts that you are using to support your opinion. For
example, you may have been led to this opinion by these details:

> I heard my uncle say that all homeless people are alcoholics
> and my father agreed with him.
> Last winter, I saw these two guys on the street who were
> walking like they were drunk.

Sticking to the facts means writing your memories of what you have
seen, heard, felt, smelled, and tasted. This is not to say that we can
always trust what our senses tell us (I frequently hear something
that hasn't been said, for example), but a big part of learning to write
is training your mind to pay close attention to your senses.

Step Three: Do the Personal Experience Test. Review your list or
freewrite to see if you've stuck to the facts. All the items on your list
should be things you have directly experienced. If you find any
items that don't follow this rule, next to the item write where you
heard it said or saw it in print. For example, revise the item "900
men sleep every night in the D.C. shelter" to show the source: "TV
news and the *Washington Post* said that 900 men sleep every night in
the D.C. shelter."

Let's say, however, that you've written a detail, such as
"Homeless people can't vote because they don't have a fixed ad-
dress," but you can't remember who said it or where you read it.
Don't cross the detail off your list; instead, mark it in some way so

that you won't forget about it. The detail isn't a mistake; it's just a gap that needs filling in. Indeed, these are the gaps you want to find in your list or freewrite, because they give you starting points for your research. Research is always easier when you have something definite to look for.

Step Four: More Lists and Freewrites. Writing to the limit doesn't restrict you from using as many tools as you need to get the facts and ideas down on paper. For example, writing to the limit for your assignment may mean generating several different lists or freewrites. On homelessness, you've already written and reviewed one list, "What I Already Know about the Homeless." But the assignment asks you to state your view of homelessness as a public issue *and* to summarize other viewpoints. A good second list on this topic might be headed "What Opinions Do I Hold about Homelessness?" A good third list would be "What Opinions Have I Heard about Homelessness?" An alternate list, or maybe a fourth list, might be "What Are the Issues to Be Decided? What Are Some Possible Outcomes?"

Let's say that you choose to compose the second list. You can start by taking from the first list all those facts that really turned out to be opinions, once you did the personal experience test. Thus, you might head your list of opinions with "Most homeless people are alcoholics." Then write other things that you think are true about the topic, even though you are not sure. Remember, this is not the place to hesitate to express your views. Try to write everything down. If you wish, put a question mark next to each statement that you're not sure of.

Here's one student's lists about homelessness:

WHAT OPINIONS HAVE I HEARD ABOUT HOMELESSNESS?

"Let them eat cake." (Marie Antoinette)
Get them off the streets because they're an eyesore.
If you give money to a homeless person, they'll just use it to
    buy liquor.
The poor will always be with us.

The government should build shelters for the homeless.

People are homeless because they're too lazy to work for a
   living.

Homeless people can't hold jobs because most of them are
   mental patients who should be in hospitals.

Homeless people don't look for work because they are
   afraid.

If a homeless person asks for money, give it to him because
   you would want to be treated the same way if you were
   in his shoes.

Don't give them money, because a handout just encourages
   them to be lazy.

Homeless people are uneducated and don't contribute anything to society.

WHAT OPINIONS DO I HOLD ABOUT HOMELESSNESS?

Middle-aged men are the largest group of homeless. (Why?)

Most homeless people are alcoholics. ?

Homeless people don't get jobs because employers are
   afraid of them.

A homeless person is potentially as capable as anyone else,
   but the homeless haven't been encouraged by others.

How do people get to be homeless? (I don't know.)

Most homeless people would like to work, but they don't get
   opportunities.

Every person, or family, should have a place to live, but it's
   impossible for the government to provide this.

I think there must be many homeless families, but I haven't
   seen any. (Where do they go?)

Now review the student's lists. If you find that you, like the
student, have written question marks after any items, you've found
a focus (or more than one) for your reasearch. Change your statement into a question, and you may have the central idea of your
paper. For example, if, like the student above, you're not sure that
"Most homeless people are alcoholics," then your paper could
attempt to answer the question "Are most homeless people alcoholics?" Once you have this focal question, you have a clear purpose
when you go to the library or look for experts to interview.

But what if you have no question marks and you're sure about everything you've written? Then you have to review your list in a different way. You have to keep poking at your statements until you find something that you do have a question about. Poke at each statement in turn. Let's take one of the statements in the student's list:

> Every person, or family, should have a place to live, but it's impossible for the government to provide this.

Start your poking by doing the same thing you did with the facts list, by writing next to the item who said it, where you read it, or what direct, personal experience you are using as evidence. If you can't remember, then you've found a focus for your research. Turn the statement into a question: "Could it be possible for the government to provide an affordable place to live for every person or family?" If you can remember where you heard the statement, the second test is: how did that source know? If you can't answer that question, then you have a definite reason for tracking down that source and getting the facts. Likewise, if you can think of some direct personal experience that backs up your opinion, test it this way: compare your opinion with your evidence. Ask yourself, "If I were trying to convince someone who doesn't share my opinion, what other evidence would I need besides my personal experience?" Even if you think that your personal experience is pretty good evidence, this question gives you a clear direction for starting your research. Writing to the limit has worked for you.

EXERCISE: Write to the limit on a topic of your choice. Follow steps one through four and see what you discover. (Besides finding that you know both more and less than you thought you did, you'll also find that the exercise helped you read the chapter better. See the next section for more on the reading-writing connection.) ■

Planning to Read, Listen, and See

Let's say that you are about to leave for a weekend in a place you've never visited. (Take a moment here to visualize the situation.) What do you do? Do you just get the thought in your head, hop into the car, and go? Of course not. You plan. Why? Because if you don't plan, your trip will be ruined because of what you forgot to do beforehand: reserve a place to stay, withdraw money, pack a suitcase, put gas in the car, and so on. In fact, most of us would agree that planning, anticipation, is at least half the fun, because we visualize all the exciting things we might do.

As sensible as it is to plan for new experiences, few of us in school or on the job think to plan for new experiences that are a normal part of our studying and working lives. What are those everyday new experiences? Statistically speaking, students and professionals spend most of their time reading, talking with people, and writing. Students know that they'll be expected to read a lot and to remember what they read. They know that they'll be expected to listen a lot and remember what they hear. They also expect to write and, in some classes, to be called on to talk. Most students have learned that they have to spend some time planning their writing and talking (much of this book has to do with making your planning of the writing as efficient and rewarding as possible). But how many students or professionals put any planning time into what they are about to read or listen to?

Planning to Read. Let's take an example. You're in an economics class and you've been assigned to read the first chapter of the textbook. You've been told by the professor that you'll be responsible for the chapter on a test. What do you do? Most likely, you'll plunge in and hope for the best. You'll look at each word in succession until all the words of the chapter have passed before your eyes. At which point you'll believe that you've finished the assignment.

But have you really *read* the chapter? People who study the reading process agree that we can't get anything out of our reading unless we bring something to it, either some prior knowledge of the subject or some definite questions that we want the reading to answer. Otherwise, the words will just go by us; we won't know what's important to remember and we won't know how to fit the reading into our minds. As a result, students will conclude that the assignment is boring or too complicated to understand. With planning, however, readers can turn a frustrating experience into a rewarding one.

How do you plan for reading? Let's go back to the economics

assignment. What did you bring with you to the chapter? If you only brought the warning that you will be responsible for the reading, you are at a clear disadvantage. Since you don't know what you'll be responsible for, you don't know where to focus your attention: will you have to memorize dates, places, and names? Will you have to define vocabulary words? Will you have to apply the ideas to solving problems? The simplest strategy is the most direct: ask "How should I focus my reading?" or "What are the most important things for me to pay attention to?" Chances are that the instructor can give you some guidance, even though he or she does not yet know precisely what will appear on the test. But even if the teacher says only, "I'd like you to read for the main ideas," you have a direction for your reading.

Here's where the writing comes in. Now that you have a direction, a question, for your reading, you can further plan by doing a bit of writing to the limit. Just as newspaper reporters write what they think they know about a topic before they go out to observe or interview, you can write to discover your thoughts and feelings before you read. Suppose that the chapter is titled "A Brief History of Economics" or perhaps "What Is Economics?" Before you read the chapter, write the title at the top of a piece of paper and write as much as you think you know of economic history or try to answer the "What Is Economics?" question. Here's one student's answer to "What Is Economics?"

> Economics is the study of how the monetary system of a society affects every facet of the society.

Here's what a second student wrote:

> Economics has to do with business and paying bills and politics and government and taxes and stocks and a lot of other things. But I can't really say what it *is*.

Though the first student's answer is very general and the second student's answer admits his confusion, the writing serves two real purposes: (1) the writing has started the writer thinking about the topic and (2) it has given the student some ideas to test when beginning to read. Once into the text, the student can go back to the writing and revise it with new information from the book. The reader who approaches a text in this way will not just read over the words, but will actually read them.

Many textbooks include study questions at the end of each chapter. Instead of reading the study questions after you've read the chapter, use the questions as a stimulus for writing before you do the reading. Even if you can't answer the questions at this point, trying to answer them will focus your attention on important ideas in the text. Imagine that one of the study questions for the first chapter of an economics text is

> What is the difference between *macroeconomics* and *microeconomics*? Explain with examples.

You probably won't know the answer before you start to read, but if you write down what you think the difference might be, you'll already have done some essential work before you get into the chapter.

Planning to Listen. While relatively few students use writing to plan their reading, even fewer use writing, or any other means, to plan their listening, even though most classes are taught through lecture. Some lecturers know the importance of planning so that their audience can listen well. These lecturers plan for their listeners by starting their lectures with challenging questions: "What would have happened if the British had won the American Revolution?" "How many earthquakes occurred in the United States last year?" "Have you ever been inside a prison? What is it like?" Sometimes a lecturer will ask the students to attempt to answer the questions. As with planning for reading, such an exercise provides a goal. It also lets the listener discover what he or she thinks and test those thoughts against what the lecturer says.

Usually, however, the planning is up to you. What can you do? If the lecture has a title, you can do the same exercise that you did for the title of the assigned reading. If you only have a brief topic notation on a class syllabus, "Feb. 24   Smooth Muscles," "June 13   Introduction to Yeats," it is enough to give you some food for thought. After all, everyone knows something about muscles—if only how much they hurt after the first day of practice—but it's surely enough to get you started on a freewrite or mindmap that will give you plenty of ideas to test against what the lecturer says.

On some occasions the only thing you'll be able to write is "I've never heard of this person." (Everyone knows muscles, but not everyone knows Yeats.) In such cases, you may want to write, "OK, I'll just wait until the lecture to find out." But remember, once the lecture begins, you're like the unprepared reader just moving your eyes over the page, like a car skidding over an ice-glazed road. You'll need something to grab onto, something to focus on and direct your attention to. A better strategy would be to use your ignorance as an incentive to look through the dictionary or the encyclopedia for preliminary data on Yeats. Even if you find only what you get from the *American Heritage Dictionary:*

Yeats, William Butler. 1865–1939. Irish poet and playwright,

that will still be plenty for a useful freewrite or mindmap.

Planning to See. As visual technology becomes more common-place, more and more of the learning that is expected of us in school, on the job, and in our communities comes to us in pictures, most of which move and change quickly. Because a video picture changes so quickly, it seems that it is doing the work for us and we may be fooled into thinking that we are learning more from this medium than we could learn from a quiet book or a lecturer. But precisely because the images change so fast, which means that we have less time to pay attention to them, it is even more important to plan before we watch than it is to plan before we read or listen. It is rare for a film or video presentation to prepare us at all for what is to come. The burden is on the viewer to get more than just some blurry impressions. How can we use writing to help us plan?

Suppose that you have been assigned to view a film about plate tectonics for geology class, or a film about a new technical procedure for your job, or a production by the Royal Shakespeare Company for your drama class. Suppose also that you'll be watching the film with a group and won't be able to stop and replay portions that you don't understand. You've been advised to take notes on the film, but you realize that every time you pause to reflect and write, you'll miss more of the film. You also realize that without some idea of what to watch for, your notes are likely to be random and confusing.

It's useful to do a little detective work before you see the film, to plan your viewing and note-taking. Read an encyclopedia article or the textbook section about plate tectonics; read the article or the manual on the technical procedure; read the Shakespeare play. These will give you ideas about what to expect from the film. They may also give you questions that you hope the film will answer such as, "What happens at the edge of plates? What do photographs show?" "How does one reach the A-valve without disturbing the B and C circuits?" "How would an actor playing King Lear say, 'Never, never, never, never, never'?" Writing down these questions gives you a focus for viewing the film and a plan for your note-taking (see more on taking notes in the next section). You will also better appreciate the power of film and video to show you what words can only approximate. (Note: Watching a film or video is never a substitute for reading the article, the manual, or the play. It's faster, but more complicated. Just as with reading, we can only get a lot out of viewing a film or video if we put in a lot of thought and planning.)

Here's one more writing trick to help you plan for viewing: remember that a film or video is made up of both sight and sound. Sometimes sight and sound are closely tied, as in a film of a person making a speech. Facial expressions, dress, gesture, and background all affect how we understand and react to the speech. Sometimes sight and sound give us different messages, as in a film that shows starving children while we hear other children talking about the expensive toys they are expecting for Christmas. In short, the meaning of the speech comes from a mixture of what we see and hear. So, before we view a film or video we can mindmap, brainstorm, or freewrite on the different kinds of things we'll need to be aware of in the event. For example, here's a management student's list of things to watch and listen for in a film about "business practices in Japan":

- interaction of managers and workers
- incentives
- atmosphere of the workplace—do they have tea? paint, pictures on the walls? windows?
- how are people treated?—respect—how do workers talk with each other? how do supervisors talk to workers?

- on a production line, do people smile? do they talk while working? do they move around? are they closed off from each other?
- how does the workplace look? government-like? military? home-like? what kind of music is playing? is there music?
- eating areas? work while eating? places to congregate? pace of work attitudes on productivity—what mental crutches can people use to get through long days?
- outside activities—teams, parties—do people on the job socialize after hours?
- dress code? uniforms?
- how do managers show appreciation? how do workers show appreciation? parties for individuals?
- skills levels—a mixture—are people of one level kept together? do people of different levels work together?
- are any of these characteristics general throughout the country?
- does the film show differences from one company to another? does the film show a range of types of practice or does it want to make a point about one "management style"?

Note that the student uses the exercise to generate questions. Although many of the things she wants to know about may not be in the film, many of them may, and the freewrite has given her a clear sense of purpose and direction for viewing the film.

Note also that she is making herself aware of many different kinds of sights and sounds. Among other things, she prepares herself for

- people talking
- expressions
- gestures
- clothes
- setting—walls, windows, decoration, architecture, etc.
- music
- variety of examples
- the filmmaker's point of view

You can use these kinds of sights and sounds for your own planning. Use them as ideas for the left side of a double-entry brainstorm and fill in the right side with the specific questions you have about the film or video you are about to see.

The Questing Note Taker

It's easy to see that the student who wrote the questions for the Japanese business film will be prepared to watch and hear the film; she'll also be ready to take notes that mean something to her and that won't take her attention away from the film. Why? Because by using her writing to think and to plan, she has prepared her brain to receive the film. This means that she'll remember the film without having to scribble everything down. Because her brain has already made a network of neurons and dendrites for the memory, she can devote her note-taking to more creative and interesting work.

Many people take notes to remember a lecture. Have you ever heard someone say, "I don't have to take notes today in class, because I'm going to record the lecture on tape"? Sure, if you can tape the class, why knock yourself out trying to write down everything the speaker says? It's both impossible and tiring unless you've had the education and the practice of a court stenographer.

The experienced note-taker knows that taking notes is a tool for thinking, not recording. Taking notes meets two purposes: answering questions and asking them. The good note-taker is always on a kind of quest: if he or she has planned for the reading, the lecture, or the film, then the first goal is to answer those questions that the brainstorm has discovered: "What *is* economics?" "What did Yeats say about Ireland?" "Do Japanese factories look more like homes or warehouses?" The second goal takes the note-taker beyond the planning stage. He or she uses the reading, lecture, or film to generate more questions: "Economists think that everything is part of economics—what *isn't* economics?" "Did Yeats think that everyone in Ireland knew as much about Irish legends as he did? Did they?" "Can Americans understand Japanese business ideas without living in Japan?" The creative note-taker uses notes to catch ideas that come to mind as the reading, lecture, or media event continues. When you take notes this way, you can use your notes to think about the event later or to give you questions that you can ask people later or find the answers to from other sources. Great paper topics can come from a question that pops into your head as you read, listen, or view.

The Five General Questions. If you've made the sort of list that the student made before watching the film on Japanese business practices, you've already got a framework for your notes. But even if you don't have such an elaborate guide, there are a few questions that can guide your note-taking in any situation:

1. Is there a main idea (or two or three) that the lecture (or film, chapter, etc.) emphasizes? (This may be stated at the outset or it may be repeated several times.)
2. What key terms need to be understood in order to follow the lecture, film, chapter, etc.? Do you understand them? If the definitions are fuzzy to you, or if the meanings seem to change, write this down. This is something to ask questions about.
3. What seems hard to follow or difficult for you to accept? For example, in your notes about the economics chapter, you might write, "If economics is a science, why do economists disagree so widely in their views?"
4. "What's the connection with _____?" or "How does this apply to _____?" For example, as you watch the film on Japanese business practices, you might ask the question, "How are the attitudes of Japanese workers related to Japanese religions and traditional culture?"
5. Any other question that comes into your mind.

With questions such as these, though they are not as good as the questions you'll come up with through planning, you'll be an active thinker about the chapter, lecture, or film, rather than a passive recorder. The notes you take in this active role will look different from the bits and pieces of data that the passive recorder jots down. You probably won't write as much during the lecture or film because you'll listen and observe more than the hurried recorder does. But the notes and questions you do write will help you better organize and understand, as well as remember, the presentation.

During the presentation, the questing note-taker behaves differently than the passive recorder. Where the recorder starts writing with the first word, the note-taker listens for the key word and the important idea. Like an investigative reporter, the note-taker is in a kind of conversation with the lecturer, writer, or narrator. During a political speech, a reporter listens in order to formulate the best questions to ask the speaker. That is, the reporter acts like a participant in the speech, not just a member of the audience. To do a

good job of note taking, the note-taker has to have the same attitude, even though he or she can't ask questions directly of a textbook or a videotape!

✍ **EXERCISE:** Play the role of the questing note-taker as you hear a
lecture, watch a film or videotape, or read a text chapter (you might
try it on this chapter). Try it two different ways:

1. Use one of the planning strategies described on pages 51–57 to
   help you focus your attention and generate questions; then take
   notes that help you answer those questions.
2. Use the five general questions described on pages 58–59 to
   guide your note-taking.

Use each method several times until you become comfortable with
it. (If you are doing this as a class exercise, compare your notes with
those of another student: what are his or her main ideas and key
terms? What questions has he or she asked? What other note-taking
tricks has he or she used that you might be able to apply?) ∎

Writing to Summarize

The writer-scientist always seeks to make sense of his or her experiences. The daily writings of Charles Darwin or Henry Thoreau
never try to account for all that happens during sixteen or more
waking hours. Their diaries focus on key details and main ideas—
the thoughts that they don't want to forget, the words that capture
the meaning of the events. These close observers of nature write to
summarize their experiences.

Summarize means, literally, "add it all up." A summary isn't a
list: "At 6 A.M. I woke up. At 6:20 I got up to turn off the clock radio.
At 7:00 I decided to get up to go to work. . . . " A good summary
covers the main points, tells the choicest news, lets someone else
know what it all means. Writing a summary can be one of the most
powerful tools of thinking because it forces us to make order out of
details, to think about how the bits and pieces fit together.

The questing note-taker summarizes as he or she takes part in
the chapter, lecture, or film, trying to find main ideas and key terms.
But even the best notes are lists of a sort because you write items as
they occur to you. A summary follows from well-written notes
when you add up the notes to see what they mean.

In fact, proficient note-takers see summarizing as a key part of note-taking itself. In the summary stage, the writer reviews the notes, looking for patterns of thoughts, connections between ideas, and confusing statements that should spark the reader's questions. In this stage, the note-taker might draw arrows between notes, write in question marks, or jot down comments or questions.

The summary itself may be a freewrite, a mindmap, or some other form that helps you to make sense of the experience and to remember key points. What does it mean to *make sense* of an experience? You make sense of an experience when you understand how it compares to what you already know. That means that your summary should:

1. Use your own words to explain new terms or to describe the most vital scenes. (Your own words are words you feel comfortable using; if you copy someone else's definition or language, you'll neither understand nor remember what the person is talking about.)

2. Tell how the lecture, film, music, game, etc., is like, and is different from, something else. (For example, you might say, "The actress reminded me of Meryl Streep in the way she tossed her hair to show she was upset except she did it more nervously, with less cool.")

3. Pay particular attention to things that don't seem to make sense. If an idea contradicts the main idea of the lecture or the film or the chapter so that you can't seem to include it in your summary, don't pretend it isn't there. Be honest about your quandary. Sometimes, writing about your confusion can help you understand. Indeed, some teachers ask their students to write about confusing ideas because they know that writing often leads to a solution. The same is true for summaries: if an idea doesn't seem to fit, writing about the difficulty can often help you see how the idea might fit. Remember, writing stimulates the brain to make connections, to strengthen the pathways among neurons. As you write about your failure to connect two ideas, your brain may discover the link.

4. Describe the main idea and show how the rest of the experience relates to it. One way to start your summary might be: "The most

important idea in the lecture was. . . . " or "What the movie really said to me was. . . . " or "The author's main point is. . . . " If you show how the experience relates to the main idea, you've made sense of the experience and your summary works. On the other hand, your summary might be something like this: "First, she said that there are millions of illegal immigrants in the United States; then she went on to describe the sanctuary movement. Then she told us about the Geneva conventions regarding political refugees. . . . " This isn't a summary; it's just a list. It can't make sense unless a connection is made between the main idea and the rest of the experience.

When should you summarize? As a learning-thinking tool, summarizing is most effective if done as soon as possible after an event, while the images and words are fresh. For example, summarizing for five to fifteen minutes right after a lecture is more useful than spending two hours weeks later trying to recall the lecture for a test. Making sense while an experience is still fresh is so important that many people who run workshops for professionals require participants to write about the workshop after every session. Until you write about a new experience, it's hard to know where and how it fits into your life. Until you write, it's just as hard to know what to doubt or question about what you've seen or heard. For example, an extended sales pitch may sound great when you hear it, but writing a summary of it right away might save you from the agonizing discovery later that you should have asked questions.

Writing Summaries for Other People. Summaries are essential in college and in professional careers; they are a key part of almost all school and career documents. But those summaries are different from the summaries I'm describing here because they are written to meet other people's needs. The summarizing here meets your own purpose of adding it all up. Nevertheless, the skills you practice here, looking for main ideas, looking for key terms, looking for connections, looking for what doesn't fit, and asking questions, will help you write summaries for others. Indeed, if you get into the habit of summarizing for yourself while an experience is fresh, you'll find it easier to report the experience to others. In the next chapter, I'll take up the task of turning the writing we do for ourselves into writing for other people.

✍ **EXERCISE:** Use the method I've described to summarize this section on summarizing. Note how the method pushes you to question both what you have read and how well you remember it. Be sure to use your own words, not mine, to express the ideas in the section. The method will work for you if you reread the text to understand it better. ∎

Writing to Reflect and Speculate

Albert Einstein once imagined that he was riding on a beam of light. He wrote about this in his notebook so that he might better understand what would happen to space and time as one approached the speed of light. The person who writes to imagine, to speculate, goes beyond writing to the limit and writing to summarize. He or she asks what might be, what could be, what would happen if. . . .

In a way, the questing note-taker writes to reflect and speculate. Every time we write down a question (note the link between *question* and *quest*), we look into the future and wonder *what if?* But the reflective-speculative writer does this deliberately. As explorer and scientist, this writer sets out to be original, to discover something new, or to find a new way to say things.

> My ability to fantasize has been of more use to me than any knowledge I've ever acquired.
>
> —Albert Einstein

Anyone whose work involves planning, design, or problem solving can profit from training and practice in speculative thought. Writing promotes speculative thought, just as it promotes the ability to analyze for key ideas or to make connections between new experience and what is already known. Writing to reflect and speculate is a kind of creative writing anyone can do because everyone imagines and fantasizes. However, few people have been taught to see the connection between imagination and so-called *practical* work. Instead, they call imagination *daydreaming*, wasting time on wishful thinking while the real work piles up.

Yet every successful writer, artist, scientist, or businessperson knows that nothing gets written, painted, discovered, or negotiated without imagination. Creative techniques such as brainstorming and role-playing (see Chapter 1) are standard in every successful concern, although the processes don't always go by those names.

Chapter 1 showed how writing focuses the power of brainstorming and role-playing. In this chapter, I'll describe two other speculative techniques and the purposes they serve.

"What if?" Writing. In "What if?" writing, we imagine a situation and write to see what happens next: "What if I didn't go to class today?" "What if we buy three PC's for the office? What else would we have to buy? What would it save us?" "What would have happened if the French hadn't helped the United States against the British?" "What will happen if a cure for AIDS isn't found?"

We ask ourselves "What if?" questions all the time. Our choices come from this question. But writing in response to "What if?" forces us to concentrate on the situation. When we concentrate, we imagine more possibilities, more images, and more scenes of what might occur. Writing also lets us keep track of what we imagine: it slows down the flow of information so that we can manage it, so that we won't be overwhelmed—"Wow, there are too many options, too many risks. I don't want to think about it."

As an exercise, try a "What if?" writing about some choice that you have to make: "What would (or could) happen if I choose _____?" Chances are that a number of alternatives will come to mind, as they did for the writer who asked, "What if I ask Sandy to marry me?"

If I decide to ask Sandy to marry me, it might scare her so much that she'll break up with me. But if I don't ask her to marry me, she'll probably get tired of waiting. Why am I so worried about this? What am I afraid of? Maybe I could think more clearly if Mom and Dad weren't pushing me to settle down, whatever that means. Maybe I could think more clearly if Danny and Caroline hadn't broken up. But I never thought that they had much going for each other. They liked to show off their relationship at parties, but Danny never seemed to want to spend much time with her, and she didn't seem to care. It was pretty stupid for them to get married, when you think about it. Now me and Sandy. Most of the time it feels like we're already married—and it feels pretty damn good! What am I afraid of? I guess the best thing is to ask Sandy about it.

The writer uses his speculation to identify a source of his fear, the broken marriage of his friends, and to see that their situation is not analogous to his own. His writing also pushes him to consider the advantages and the disadvantages of his choice.

Another type of "What if?" writing, called *Pros and Cons*, makes this decision making graphic. It is one of the most common tools of formal decision making. At the top of a page in your notebook, write a choice, for example, "What if I drop out of school?" "What if I buy the van rather than the sedan?" "What if I accept the offer from Apex Research?" "What if the Congress cuts military spending?" Draw a line down the middle of the page; at the top of the left column write *Pros* (advantages) and at the top of the right *Cons* (disadvantages). List items in each column. If the choice is one you tend to favor, then it should be easier to list pros; if the choice is one you dread, cons will come more quickly. However, writing the lists will push you to think about both kinds of effects. Most people who use this tactic find that every pro gets them thinking about a corresponding con; in other words, when you write down an advantage, the method pushes you to think about its disadvantage. Many writers go back and forth as each item sparks an opposing thought: "The van will give me more room than the sedan, but the van will use more gas. But if I'm hauling stuff I'll need to make fewer trips, though how often will I be hauling stuff?" Because your brain spins out pros and cons quickly in any decision-making situation, this writing tactic lets you sort through your feelings and judge what is most important.

The Big Wish. While "What if?" and *Pros and Cons* help us discover choices and their consequences, the *Big Wish* helps us discover what we want or how we'd like the world to be. Though this writing lets our fancy run free to conjure up exotic, exciting visions, it is also practical writing. If, like me, you spend some of your day vaguely or even sharply uneasy about the way things are, you may wish for things that will make you happy for the moment: "Oh, I just wish you'd shut up!" or "I wish today were Saturday" or "I wish that she would call!" To a great extent we spend our days trying to gratify these momentary wishes. How often do we look back on a day and realize that it disappeared as we chased after every little wish—a cup of coffee, a bit of gossip, that song on the radio?

The Big Wish invites us to write about and thus think deeply about what we really want, what our ideal world might be, and then how to make the ideal happen. We focus on the important wishes so that we can avoid the distraction of all the little wishes. People do Big Wish writing when they want to plan their futures or to think about their values; groups of people do Big Wish writing when they establish governments or begin long-range enterprises. Goals statements, five-year plans, and constitutions are all Big Wishes.

Try some Big Wish writing. Since most people rarely do this, don't be surprised if you discover ideas and visions that you never knew you had. You can get your Big Wish started in a couple of ways. You can put *My Big Wish* or *What I Really Want Out of Life* or *How I See Myself in Ten Years* at the top of a page and write freely. You can begin with *What I Hope I Never Become* or *My Greatest Fear for the Future* or *A World I Don't Want to Live In*. Some of the most powerful writings of the century, such as *1984* and *Brave New World*, have been nightmare visions. Even more powerful writings, such as Plato's *Republic*, the *Declaration of Independence*, and Martin Luther King, Jr.'s, speech "I Have a Dream," show how big wishes make history.

As you write your Big Wish, or big nightmare, remember to use the twin tools of relaxation and visualization. Be aware of your senses and the images in your mind. As you write, you may move back and forth, as in Pros and Cons, from something you wish to something you don't wish, and vice versa. If the writing takes you toward the nightmare side, go with it. Sometimes it's easier to visualize horrors. For most writers, however, exploring what we don't want sharpens our notion of what we do want, and so we'll reverse directions once again.

You may also find as you gaze into the future that you'll imagine ways to get where you want to go and ways to avoid going where you don't want to go. Besides giving more insight into self, Big Wish writing is meant to do just that. People such as systems engineers, financial counselors, and career counselors, who make careers out of helping other people plan, know that you can't design the ways to get there until you've thought carefully about what you want. More than one city has the weed-choked highway that ends abruptly because the plans were drawn and the concrete poured before anyone explored the city's big wishes. And think about all the time and money you waste to gratify the little wish when a real need comes along.

Here's an excerpt from one student's Big Wish, drawn from his English class journal. Notice how the writer moves back and forth from wish to nightmare and how he starts making plans:

I'm not sure about this big wish idea. It might be a waste of time because I'm always changing my mind. But I've never really thought about wishing for the future, beyond college, that is. I guess I've always wanted things to be as set as they could be, so there wasn't a lot of wishing involved. Accounting degree, job with a good accounting firm, and all that. But I guess that's wishing isn't it? It looks more like wishing all the time, if I don't pass Business Calculus. Well, I can take it again in the summer. I hope Mike is right about the summer session being easier. And even if it isn't, I won't be taking any other courses.

Big Wish: I don't want to get stuck in a boring job that takes all my time, so that I can't enjoy the fine starting salary I'll probably be making (I hope!). Dad spends all his time working. I couldn't hack that. If I had to make a choice between having a new car or a bigger house and having leisure time for my music and my friends, I'd take the time, no question. (I hope I can stick to that!) Dad always looks like he'd rather be working in the garden, but I guess he's got to pay for things. Like me going to college!

Do I want kids? The sociology teacher asked us that the other day. Hell, do I want to get married? Does anybody want to marry me? Let's take 'em one at a time, OK? No, really, if I ever do have kids, I'll love them. I will have time for them and I won't get hung up on buying things I don't need. Whoever I marry is going to have to understand that.

You may find that you'll want to write your Big Wishes fairly frequently. As the student says, "I'm always changing my mind." Writing Big Wishes can be a way of keeping in touch with ourselves as events and people affect us. You might even start a Big Wishes collection, a record of yourself as you grow. Moreover, as with "What if?" and Pros and Cons, Big Wish can be a tool for making difficult life decisions that often confront us.

A WORLD OF JOURNALS

> The thing that he was about to do was open a diary. This was not illegal (nothing was illegal, since there were no longer any laws), but if detected it was reasonably certain that it would be punishable by death . . .
>
> —George Orwell
> *1984*

Have you ever kept a diary? Have you ever kept a notebook of little sayings and clippings that you don't want to forget? Have you ever kept a log of research data, of progress toward a goal, or of sights and experiences on a trip? Have you ever felt the urge to keep a running commentary of your opinions of the world and people in the news? Have you ever for a course in school kept a record of your reactions to what you've read and talked about? In short, have you ever kept a journal?

Journals go by many names, some of which are *diary, notebook, log, running commentary,* or *record.* A journal can be about almost anything. It can be for almost any purpose or it can be for many purposes. A ship's log is a journal, a photo album with your comments is a journal, a scientist's research notebook is a journal, a poet's collection of lines and observations is a journal, an artist's sketchbook is a journal, a mother's record of her child's accomplishments is a journal, a collection of frequent letters to a friend is a journal. *Journal* comes from the French word for day, *jour.* What all journals have in common, and what makes them powerful, is that they are kept regularly. They may not be kept every day but they are kept often and consistently.

If you have kept a journal, you know that you have to make room in your day for it and you know what you miss when you let everything else crowd it out of your life. If you have kept a journal, you are aware of its power. If you have not, then you may not yet know what you are missing.

What is the power of a journal? Every strategy for thinking and knowing uncovered in this chapter, from writing to the limit to the Big Wish, can help you the first time and each time you use it. But the first time you try it, it will feel uncomfortable, like a new baseball glove, stiff and unoiled. The more you use it, the better it fits, until it almost becomes part of you. That's when you can really use it, and that's part of the power of a journal. If you wrote to the limit on a different topic every day or wrote to summarize or wrote to reflect each day, you'd be a master of the form and you'd have a terrific journal. But if you varied the exercise each day, and if you used your summary from Wednesday as a boost for your "What if?" on Thursday, that's keeping a journal, too, and the other part of the power. Journals give us practice so that we become experts. Journals also give us history so that we can grow and watch ourselves growing.

Some Common Purposes for Journals

To Record Events and How You Feel about Them. Diarists (people who keep diaries) keep personal histories to record the flow of events and to reflect on them. The diary is a statement of the importance of one's life and of the present. The diary lets a person step back from events and emotions to focus on those that seem particularly worth remembering, to sort out feelings about those key moments, and often to discover a fuller understanding of what has happened.

The diarist in a quiet way makes history for everyone. How fortunate are those families who have had a diarist, a person who treasures the present and keeps it alive for the future. Think what it would mean to discover that someone in your past, a grandparent, for example, had kept a diary and could give you entry into your family history.

Some diarists write with future readers in mind. Some parents keep diaries about their young children and give them to the children when they've grown. Public figures, such as state leaders, keep diaries to turn them into books or memoirs when they leave office. But even if the diarist writes only for himself or herself to summarize and to reflect, the diary can give future generations insights into the past, insights that no public records or official historians can tell. The diary kept by Samuel Pepys, an English businessman, gives us one of our best ideas of the thoughts of people in seventeenth-century England. The diary of Anne Frank, the child of an obscure Dutch family swept up in the terrors of war, provides a memory of thought and spirit that stirs the heart.

To Keep an Ongoing Public Record. Adventurers, captains, explorers, legislators, project managers, reporters. Anyone who wants or is required to keep an account of official business can do so in a journal. Often such an account is called a *log*, after the ship's or captain's log that is an essential part of sea voyages. Many logs record daily details that the writer needs to remember. The ship's log, for example, records latitude and longitude, the direction of the ship, and any noteworthy events, such as foul weather or illness among the crew. Such a log usually does not include the captain's reflections or speculations about the day's events. Similarly, business managers often keep logs on the progress of a project.

Most large organizations keep staff meeting minutes that serve two vital functions. First, the minutes provide the history of decision making in the organization; second, they are the raw material for the reports that keep the members of the organization informed. Keeping the minutes may not seem an important role in the decision-making process, since the minute keeper may not say much during a meeting, but it's the minute keeper who decides what's important to record and what isn't. If you have kept minutes, you know that writing up the notes of a meeting means summarizing, choosing what to keep and what to omit. For the members of the organization not present at the meeting, it's the minute keeper's viewpoint that comes across. Moreover, when the decision makers have forgotten the back-and-forth talk, they turn to the minutes.

Because the keeper of the public record is not merely a recording device, but a feeling and thinking human being, logs can sometimes contain dramatic and moving expression. The log of Robert Falcon Scott, leader of an ill-fated expedition to the South Pole in 1912, was found by the rescue party that arrived too late:

> I do not think that human beings ever came through such a month as we have come through. . . . Had we lived, I should have had a tale to tell of the hardihood, endurance, and courage of my companions that would have stirred the heart of every Englishman. These rough notes and our dead bodies must tell the tale, but surely, surely a great rich country like ours will see that those who are dependent on us are properly provided for.
> [March 19, 1912]

> Since the 21st we have had a continuous gale. . . . We had fuel enough to make two cups of tea apiece and bare food for two days on the 20th. Every day we have been ready to start for our depot *eleven miles* away, but outside the door of the tent, it remains a scene of whirling drift. I do not think we can hope for any better things now.

We shall stick it out to the end, but we are getting weaker, of course,
and the end cannot be far.
  It seems a pity, but I do not think I can write more.

—R. Scott

For God's sake look after our people.
[March 29, 1912; final entry]

To Make Close Observations for Scientific Purposes. A friend of
mine, a chemistry professor, was telling me about her scientific
journal. I asked her if her students knew about the importance of
the journal, or *notebook* as it is commonly called, to scientists. She
looked surprised. She assumed that students already knew. "I
thought everyone kept one," she said.

A scientist's notebooks hold the details of experiments and the
scientist's efforts to understand his or her observations. The scientist can read over entries to see patterns in the data and thus begin to
draw conclusions, or hypotheses, about them.

While sometimes the scientist uses the journal exclusively to
record statistical measurements, important in itself, the journal also
lets the writer do the vital work of putting into words new experiences that flash before the senses. Sometimes such a journal appears to be in shorthand. Remember, unless it's a public record, the
journal is meant to make sense to the writer, not necessarily to
another reader! Here's an example from the "Red Notebook" kept
by the great naturalist Charles Darwin on his travels in South
America in 1831–36:

> The Tertiary formation South of the Maypo at one period of elevation
> must in its configuration have resembled Chiloe
>   In De La Beche, article "Erratic blocks" not sufficient distinction is
> given to angular & rounded.—
>   Fox Philosoph. Transactions on metallic veins. 1830 P. 399.—
> Carne. Geolog. Trans: Cornwall

Darwin records an observation, expresses an opinion, and thinks of
other writers who may have commented on a similar phenomenon.
Such a notebook provides a sound, accurate basis for later revising
into a public document. Darwin's *The Voyage of the Beagle*, one of the
most important books of the nineteenth century, was based in part
on the "Red Notebook."

A good example of scientific journal keeping that is also public record comes from Meriwether Lewis and William Clark, who amazed America in 1803–6 with their scientific exploration of the newly acquired Louisiana Territory. The journal helps them describe and understand complex, dazzling events:

> *Monday, November 5* . . . Late at night we were awaked by the sergeant on guard to see the beautiful phenomenon called the northern light: along the northern sky was a large space occupied by a light of a pale but brilliant white color which, rising from the horizon, extended itself to nearly twenty degrees above it. After glittering for some time its colors would be overcast and almost obscured, but again it would burst out with renewed beauty; the uniform color was pale light but its shapes were various and fantastic: at times the sky was lined with light-colored streaks rising perpendicularly from the horizon and gradually expanding into a body of light in which we could trace the floating columns sometimes advancing, sometimes retreating, and shaping into infinite forms the space in which they moved . . .

> *Monday, October 29* . . . In the evening the prairie took fire, either by accident or design, and burned with great fury, the whole plain being enveloped in flames. So rapid was its progress that a man and woman were burnt to death before they could reach a place of safety; another man with his wife and child were much burnt, and several other persons narrowly escaped destruction. Among the rest a boy of the half-white breed escaped unhurt in the midst of the flames. His safety was ascribed to the great medicine spirit, who had preserved him on account of his being white. But a much more natural cause was the presence of mind of his mother, who seeing no hopes of carrying off her son, threw him on the ground, and, covering him with the fresh hide of a buffaloe [sic], escaped herself from the flames; as soon as the fire had passed, she returned and found him untouched, the skin having prevented the flame from reaching the grass on which he lay. . . .

Of course, what makes such a journal scientific is not that the writer is a scientist, but that the writer uses the journal to sharpen the senses, to do the tough job of turning sensations into words. Any writer can practice this skill. When President Thomas Jefferson hired Lewis and Clark to undertake this journey into lands previously unknown to Europeans, he knew they were men who could observe closely and patiently. Although they did not call themselves scientists, they were capable of important scientific work.

To Explore Your Emotions, Memories, and Images. A college student wrote about the journal she has kept since she was twelve:

> One thing I do in my journal—I write about a problem until I've looked at it from every angle I can. I try to wrestle it down so that I can understand how and why I was thinking as I was. I'd learned earlier that the writing let me admit things that I would have had a hard time saying: this process doesn't always solve my problems, but if I keep at the writing it usually helps.

This student's journal also meets other needs: in it she records events, practices writing styles, reflects on the books she reads or the films she sees, and so on. At any time she feels free to delve more deeply into the why of her reactions and opinions. In a sense, she uses the journals to get some distance between herself and her feelings. This is one of the great freedoms that journal writers enjoy, no matter what other purposes their journals serve.

As you become more adept at journal keeping, you'll find ways to look at yourself and change your usual ways of reacting to the joy, pain, and mystery of life. Emily Chamlee, the student quoted earlier, found while in high school that she could step back by experimenting with her point of view, by pretending that she was looking at herself:

> When I was in Europe, I wanted to record as vividly as possible: I wanted to avoid my usual tendency to reflect. So I pretended that I was one of my favorite writers, Joseph Wambaugh, writing about the place, with me as one of the characters in it. Instead of writing, for example, "Today Jean and I walked along the Left Bank," I'd say, "There's Emily from America, with the red pack on her back, just meeting Jean."

Psychologists use journal writing as a way to learn more about who we are, who we've been, and who we wish to become. Carl Jung, one of the founders of the modern science of psychology, recorded his dreams and fantasies in what grew to be a six-volume journal. British psychologist Marion Milner (under the pen name Joanna Field) wrote in 1934 *A Life of One's Own*, in which she described the process and benefits of her eight years of journal keeping. Anaïs Nin, the novelist whose published diaries are masterpieces, developed a theory of journal keeping out of her work with psychologist Otto Rank.

Another psychologist, Ira Progoff, has studied the exploratory journal more fully than anyone else. In his two books about the intensive journal, Progoff describes more than twenty different techniques for journal keeping. Among the tricks he teaches are several types of dialogues. The dialoguing you practiced in Chapter 1 can give you a head start on this kind of exploring. Other Progoff exercises begin with listing. In *Steppingstones*, you begin with relaxation and visualization and brainstorm eight to twelve key moments in your life. As you read over the list of steppingstones, you see, in Progoff's words, "the wholeness of life as it has been lived over the years." You use the list as a springboard to deeper writing about one, then more, of the steppingstones. As you write, your memories increase; the person you are now meets the person you used to be.

Steppingstones can be an introduction to journal keeping for writers at any age and level of writing experience. Here, for example, is a list created by my eleven-year-old son Jimmy:

1. Born	7. Little League
2. Crink's birth	8. New house
3. Nursery school	9. Kids on Stage
4. My stitches	10. Big Shots screen test
5. Homeschool	11. Quitting Small World
6. Flann's birth	12. Nutcracker

You'll note that some of the entries are easier for you to comprehend than others. Remember that, as in all exploratory journal keeping, you write so that you, and not necessarily anyone else, will understand. If you and I can understand the journal keeper's entries, so much the better; but the writer gets the most out of a journal when it's written to and for himself or herself, not for another reader.

Writing for yourself makes the exploratory journal different from the more public journals of Robert Scott or Meriwether Lewis. Writing for yourself gives the journal its power. The exercises of Chapters 1 and 2 should make it easier for you to write for yourself. When the journal writer achieves this ability, the results ring with freedom and personal insight. Look at these three excerpts from journals by three very different writers. Don't worry if you can't easily follow what they write or if you don't agree with their points of view. They wrote to understand their lives and emotions, not to convince you or me. Watch as they play freely with ideas and images.

First, from Emily Chamlee's journal:

> I'd love to have a dime for every minute women (or men) spent thinking "How do I look? How do I appear?" I feel that I'm especially aware of this problem having grown up in dance studios—mirrored dance studios. In those clothes, if you ate an extra portion of alfalfa sprouts, everyone knows it . . . You are constantly judged by the image you project. Higher leg. More turns. More eyes. Every aspect of your body must work for that projection, so of course your brain is preoccupied with appearance. Unfortunately, that preoccupation does not stay in the studio. A performer's life, if gone unchecked, is quick to become one big production—everything done for the proper reaction. . . . reality and your projection of reality become hard to differentiate. Carried to the extreme, you have the "washed up" performer who is too old, the "fat" dancer (who weighs 102 lb.), the "has been" chorus girl who can't get that leg extension any more, who are alcoholics, drug addicts, and anorexics. THAT'S SHOW BIZ!!

Second, from *The Journals of Anaïs Nin*, April 1936:

> The suffering of the world seemed to me to be without remedy, except by what we could give individually. I did not trust any movement or system. But now the drama is going on, and Spain is bleeding tragically, and I feel tempted to engage my allegiance. But I must find a leader I trust and would die for, seeing only betrayal and ugliness so far, and no ideals, no heroism, no giving of the self. If I met a revolutionary who was a great man, a man, a human being, I could serve, fight, die. But meanwhile I help in a small radius, and I wait.

Third, from *Markings*, the journal of Dag Hammarskjöld, former secretary general of the United Nations:

> Soaked, dark, woollen garments. Deprecating glances. Tired mouths. It is late.
> The business proceeds with indifference and dispatch. At the polished black marble tombstone of the counter, many are still waiting.

A sexless light from white ramps is reflected in glass and enamel. Outside stands the darkness. The street door bangs and a wave of raw dampness breaks in upon the dry air, saturated with chemicals.

. . . then he looks up from behind the scales on one of the high desks—wise, good-natured, withdrawn in concentration. Deep wrinkles in a gray skin bear witness to a gentle irony, born of experience and a long life within four walls.

Here and now—only this is real:
The good face of an old man,
Caught naked in an unguarded moment,
Without past, without future.

To Think and to Learn in Any Subject. If the basics of writing are discovering, exploring, and knowing, then how can these be done better than through regularly keeping a journal? You can keep a journal on any subject to help you remember, make connections, solve problems, and reach new heights of knowing. The scientist does this in the notebook; the student of every other field can do this, too.

In math, for example, you can use the journal to wrestle with tough concepts, to try to put them into your own words, or even just to figure out why you can't understand something. Watch what happens in this entry from a sophomore's math journal:

In going back and reviewing my notes on the . . . lecture, I do recall being quite confused toward the end of the lecture. I understood and was able to pick up the initial steps in creating a model which are similar to problem solving techniques in understanding a problem. The speaker seemed to emphasize that in making a model, errors are expected. But without making these attempts, through trial and error, a solution most probably cannot be reached. Models can also be distorted by making assumptions, as indicated well with the problems at the end of the lecture. Boy, I think I just cleared up my confusion at the end of the lecture . . . Thoughts are just coming to me!

This student wrote to express her confusion about the theory of mathematical modeling; but as she wrote—*because* she wrote—she worked through the confusion and figured out the concept. This often occurs in these learning journals, which my colleague Anne Wotring calls *think books* because of their power as an understanding and problem-solving tool.

The learning journal can also be a laboratory in which the writer reaches insights beyond the textbook or lecture. Look at this entry from a world politics journal in which the student makes connections between several details from a lecture and reaches his own bold conclusion:

> The majority of African states had to fight their way to independence, seeing how the European colonizers were unwilling to give them up. The European countries did not recognize the political rights of the black inhabitants, even when the locals tried to obtain representation through the European model. Kenya's population, for example, tried to copy Western forms of trade unions and political parties to "legitimately" practice the right to self-rule. The British colonialist government proved itself hypocritical, as it always had, by continuously changing the rules to frustrate the black man's efforts. Thus the white man could legitimize his rule through democracy and "civilization" and modernity, while the black man was not even allowed to practice the Western forms of democratic governance. It comes as no surprise to me, then, that current African regimes are not democratic. The colonial governments left Africa without passing on the experience of government to their population . . . It was nothing short of a colonial conspiracy to justify the white man's return to Africa and continue its exploitation.

A freshman writer in a fine arts class uses her journal to ask questions about a film she has seen and to experiment creatively:

> Sometimes I can't decipher between the sounds in the background and the music itself. The instruments quite often imitate the subject of the dialogue. Bertrande is worried about the wolves coming down from the mountain. Is that a wolf I hear in the background? No, it's a French horn. She is frightened by the spirits. Is that what is making the noise? No, it's a violin . . . I'm not sure which came first in this film, the musical

score or the cinematography but it's amazing how well the two passages complement the film. The "colors" of the music would be the soft blues and greens of the French country-side . . .

The "think book" lets us compare what we read and hear with what we've done and felt outside school. In this geology journal, a student's beach vacation takes on scientific relevance:

> (Off the North Carolina coast,) I have done my fair share of surfing and enjoy the sport very much. I have also noticed that the weather is greatly affected by the currents of the ocean. For example, when surfing one day me and my friends were confronted with an approaching storm from inland. The storm let loose on the beach and soon passed over into the vast region of the ocean. We knew it was the time for the best surfing as the storm backlashes on the beach and the waves are the highest. However, I became very aware of the power of the currents, as the inward current of the ocean proceeded to bring the storm back onto the beach and chase us off the waves. That was quite an experience—to see something as powerful as a rainstorm be shifted and controlled by the inward flow of the water and wind currents.

To Respond to Books, Magazines, and Newspapers. In most careers, much of what we learn comes to us through what we read. Earlier in the chapter I described a way to increase learning by using writing to plan for reading. But how can writing help you remember and use what you've read?

You can use a reading response log in any class or with the reading you do on the job or for pleasure. In this type of journal you play the role of the fellow writer, commenting on another person's work or responding to it in some other creative way. Try out these roles as you comment on your reading:

The Critic: Commenting can be saying what you like and dislike about a book, as a critic would in writing a review. The critic gives convincing reasons for likes and dislikes, and you can practice this in your journal. You might pretend that you are a critic writing a review: the public will either buy or avoid the book based on your comments. You might pretend that you are two critics, one who likes the book and one who doesn't, having a dialogue. Both try to defend their opinions and show why the rival critic is wrong.

The Historian: The historian asks, "What does this book tell me about the time when it was written? How does this book fit into its time and place?" The historian writing about *1984*, for example, would note that the book was written in 1948 in England and might write about events in Europe at that time that could have influenced the book.

The Technical Expert: The technical expert asks, "What does this book or article teach me about how things work or how something is done? How does it relate to what I know and do?" In *1984*, the technical expert might consider Orwell's details about the workings of the telescreens or the torture techniques, for example.

The Avid Reader: The avid reader asks, "What other reading does this remind me of? What is similar? What is new? What does this writer do better or worse than other writers who write about the same things?" The avid reader might compare *1984* with other science fiction or fantasy novels or might compare Winston Smith with other heroes or O'Brien with other villains.

Other creative responses to reading include these techniques:

- *Imitate style.* Write about an incident in your life using the style of an author you are reading or practice writing the same idea or description using the styles of two or three different writers. There is no better way to learn how a person writes than by trying to write like he or she does!

- *Do a "what if?" piece.* Imagine a new ending to a story you've read, a character from one story meeting a character from another, your economics teacher summarizing the plot of the novel you've read, or a novelist rewriting your economics textbook.

- *Write your own story, poem, or article about the same topic or situation as that chosen by an author.*

• *Switch forms.* Write a poem about a newspaper editorial, a newspaper editorial about a poem, a short story about a play, a play about a short story, and so on.

No matter what forms and roles you experiment with in your reading response log, they will help you remember and use your reading. Why? Because, first, you focus your attention on the words, rather than skim. Second, you focus on what the writer means. Third, you make the reading belong to you by responding to it in your own words.

Many people who say that they hate to read enjoy the reading response log because it lets them relate to whatever they read in an imaginative, personal, way, different from the analytical papers they are often assigned. Another pleasant surprise for these reader-writers is that the reading response log can give them good ideas for assigned papers. Some journal entries, they may discover, can even work well as papers themselves. Why not? It's always been true that what we most enjoy writing about for ourselves usually turns out to be what others most enjoy reading.

A JOURNAL FOR YOU: BEGINNING "THE HISTORY OF A WRITER"

From the title of this section, you may think that I'm about to assign a different species of journal, titled "The History of a Writer." In fact, if you have been doing the exercises from Chapter 1 and if you've tried some of the writing-to-think techniques in Chapter 2, you have already begun this journal. Indeed, you may already have a considerable folder or notebook of entries. Remember, there are only three requirements for a journal:

• write regularly
• keep your writings together
• occasionally look back over earlier entries

Take the time now to scan the writing you've done since the beginning of this book. Spend a few minutes reading over your first entries. Do you remember writing about the ways in which writing is difficult for you? As you reread those first pieces, jot down on a separate sheet a few words or phrases that stand out, words or phrases that seem particularly true to you, that now seem wrong to you, that surprise you ("Did I really write that?"), or that you can no longer understand ("What did I mean by that?").

Now write a new entry. Freewrite, if you wish, about any of the words or phrases you jotted down. One of the best ways journals work for us is by showing us where we have been so that we can go back later and question, revise, or be proud of our thinking.

For a different focus, write about something you've learned since beginning the book, something that has changed your outlook as a writer. What is new in your perspective? What questions do you have? What problems do you still perceive? Answering these questions will give you another milestone to look back on from future plateaus.

Now that you have officially begun the history of yourself as a writer, be sure to keep in your growing collection all the writings you do, either in relation to this book, classwork, or on the job. From time to time, I'll ask you to refer to this history and to add other milestones to it.

REVISION IS ALWAYS DISCOVERY, EXPERIMENT, AND KNOWLEDGE

In the chapters that follow, our focus will shift from the basics of writing—discovery, experiment, and knowledge—to the types of writing that build on the basics. Most importantly, we will focus on the process of writing for other people, to meet their demands and to communicate what we know and believe. Keep in mind that if your basics are strong, if you can use your writing to think, to understand, and to imagine for yourself, the writing that you do for others will be strong as well.

To help you plan for the coming chapters, I'll tell you that the main idea is revision. When we move from the basics, writing for ourselves, to writing for others, we are talking about *re-vision*, literally, "seeing again." And when this happens, we always make more discoveries as writers because imagining others reading our words always teaches us something about who we are and what we think and say. Experienced writers look forward to this because they know that they will learn from other people and that their writing and knowledge will grow as a result.

PROJECTS FOR WRITERS

Write Your Own. This chapter has described many ways that writing can help us to learn. But writing is only one of many learning tools that humans have. What are other tools that have helped you to discover, test, and know?

Focus on a skill, craft, art, sport, or other activity that you love. (If you wish, continue with the one you identified in the Write Your Own project in Chapter 1.) Visualize yourself doing this activity and concentrate on how you learn to do it better. How do you discover new refinements? How do you test these discoveries to see if they are true and not just mistaken perceptions? What do you mean when you say, "I know how to do this," and "I know that this is a better way than that"? What tells you that you may be wrong? Remember, think of all the ways by which you learn this skill or craft.

Keep a log of your thinking on this issue; better yet, use the log to help you think. When you're ready, write up your reflections in an informal guide for the readership described in the Write Your Own project at the end of Chapter 1.

Connecting with Fellow Writers. As an individual or group project, find out how experts in different fields use writing, as it is broadly defined in this chapter, to increase their knowledge. Caution: if you ask this question directly, you may get a blank look because many people don't think of their writing-to-learn tactics as writing. Instead, ask what kinds of notes they make for themselves or if they keep logs of any kind. If you can visit them at their workplace, keep an eye out for the kinds of writing they deal with, and ask questions about anything interesting you see.

Ask them how they read. Do they write in the margins of books and articles? Do they summarize their reading? What other writing tricks do they use to read well?

Include your data in a report and share it with other members of your group. In discussing what you've found, identify common writing practices among experts and practices that you might want to adapt to your own learning process.

Free Experiment. Try something new. Begin learning words in a foreign language, play a few notes on a new instrument, try a new software package, practice a new sport, whatever you'd like. Keep a learning log as you progress. Use the log in any way that helps you get the most out of your new venture. Refer to the techniques in this chapter. For example, to monitor your progress in learning to play the piano, write to the limit every other week or so; see how much you've learned, how far you've come since the last entry. If you're learning a new language, the log would be a perfect place for exercises and self-composed drills. The goal is to put into practice the skills this chapter teaches so that learning another skill can be easier and more rewarding.

Chapter Checklist

Use your writing to help you think and learn. Remember:
Relax
Visualize
Forget the *have to's*
Concentrate on *what* you are writing, not *how* you are writing

Use strategies to discover, experiment, and know
Write to the limit
    Use lists, freewrites, and so on
    Stick to the facts
    Question your opinions
    Repeat (as needed)
Plan before you read
    Develop focus questions
    Write to the limit
    Test your writing against the reading
    Use study questions, if available
Plan before you listen
    Develop questions about the topic

Write to the limit
Do detective work in reference sources
Test your writing against the lecture
Plan before seeing a film or video
    Use reading if available
    Develop focus questions
    Pay attention to both sight and sound
    Brainstorm things to watch and listen for
    Use double-entry brainstorm
Take questing notes
    Write to think, not to record
    Ask questions
    Try to answer them
    If needed, use the five general questions
Write to summarize
    Use your own words
    Compare and contrast
    Find what doesn't make sense
    Describe the main idea
    Write while the experience is fresh
Write to reflect and speculate
    Try "What if?"
    Try Pros and Cons
    Try the Big Wish
Keep a journal, log, or notebook for one or more of these purposes:
    Record events and how you feel about them
    Keep an ongoing public record
    Make scientific observations
    Explore emotions, memories, and images
        Experiment with point of view
        Use steppingstones and other tricks
        Write for yourself first, others later
    Think and learn in any subject
    Respond to your reading
        Role play
        Imitate styles
        Try "What if?"

Write your own story, poem, article
Switch forms
Keep a history of yourself as a writer

Words to Write By

How can I know what I think till I see what I say?
—Graham Wallas
The Art of Thought

We write in order to think, not to record what we have thought.

To learn from my writing, I must write honestly to myself.

Writing is always a test of what we know.

3 How to Write to Others

*I think the writer ought to help the reader as much as he
can without damaging what he wants to say.*

—James Joyce

TAKING THE FEAR OUT OF WRITING FOR A READER

I wanted to title this chapter "Getting to Know Your Audience"
because that's part of my formula for learning how to write well to
other people. But I decided that most readers wouldn't understand
that title without an explanation, so I chose a title that I hoped
would be more direct. That's the difference between writing for
myself and writing for someone else. When I write for myself, I'm
happy if I write what I understand and what I feel is true. When I try
to revise what I've written so that someone else can understand it,
my brain has to switch into a different gear.

I'm thankful, of course, that I've learned how to write for
myself first. Using the techniques from Chapters 1 and 2, I produce
raw material that I can then reshape for another reader. Imagine
how difficult it would be to try to generate raw material and reshape
it at the same time. I'd feel like a fantasy machine that takes in clay,
wood, and nails at one end and produces finished, custom-made
houses out the other. Fortunately, as a writer I don't need to do that.

However, many inexperienced writers have the idea that writing is like being one of those machines. When they are given an
assignment ("Write a thank-you note to Aunt Lucy" or "Write a

memo to the accounting office explaining why we're short three hundred dollars"), they sit down in front of that blank page expecting to produce in one draft a perfect note that Aunt Lucy will love or a perfect memo that will satisfy the accounting office. With that expectation, no wonder writing is so hard for most people! The person who writes well to other people knows how to revise. Period.

Yet people resist revision. Why? Because it takes strenuous thinking, usually some legwork, and a good deal of time. Many people feel that this pain and time shouldn't be necessary. When they read published work, they can't see on the clean page the sweat, doubt, and anguish that went into the writing. As the great sportswriter Red Smith once wrote, "Writing is easy. I just sit there until drops of blood appear on my forehead." The people who enjoyed his columns found the writing funny and relaxed, as if Smith were talking with them over a beer and snacks after a game. They couldn't see him staring at his draft, scratching out his words, making phone call after phone call to track down and verify information. If you think about your own writing, I'm sure you'll see that you, too, are striving for that appearance of smoothness and easiness. What makes it hard to achieve? For one thing, remember how our brains work in the writing process. What we put on paper never fully satisfies the vague image in our heads. As one of my students recently wrote, "When I write it down, it never looks right." For another thing, consider how little we know about our readers. How can I write something that appears smooth and easy when I don't know what my readers think is good writing?

Chapters 1 and 2 discuss solutions to the first problem. This chapter deals with the second problem.

Let's do a problem-solving exercise. Here again is the problem, slightly restated:

> How can I write what *appears* good to someone else if I don't know what that person *thinks* is good?

Stop here a moment and jot down a possible solution.

Now, whatever you wrote, chances are that it involved some strategy for finding out what the reader thinks is good. That makes sense. You probably did not write anything like, "The writer should just stare at the writing and worry that the reader isn't going to like it," even though inexperienced writers often approach the problem that way.

More likely, you wrote something that fits into one or more of these three categories: ask for advice; find an example of good writing to guide you; get a reader's reaction, feedback, to what you've written. I'll say a few words about each of these and then describe a method that uses all of them, in sequence, to help a writer with any writing task for any audience.

Ask Advice

The most direct way to find out what people think about something is to ask them. Of course, it's not always possible to ask your reader what he or she likes. Red Smith couldn't ask his millions of readers their likes and dislikes, and it would probably be inappropriate to ask your Aunt Lucy what she'd like to see in your thank-you note. But it's always possible to get some kind of advice on what readers want, even if you can't reach every reader. For example, newspaperman Red Smith had an editor who read the copy, perhaps shortened it to fit within the allotted space, and gave advice. If Smith had trouble with a story, he could call his editor, or another person whose judgment he trusted, and ask advice. Similarly, if a child writes that thank-you note to Aunt Lucy, it's a good idea to ask Mom or Dad what Aunt Lucy might like to hear, especially if Mom or Dad is picky about what goes into thank-you notes.

While it's easy to say that a writer should ask advice, it's not always easy to know whom to ask or what to ask. I will discuss those questions later in the chapter.

Find Good Examples

Sometimes adapting good writing examples for your own use is easy, sometimes it's hard, and sometimes it's impossible. Here's an example of an easy way to adapt good writing:

> The club president has to write the invitation to the annual picnic for members, spouses, and friends. The president looks through the files and pulls out last year's invitation; by changing only the date and time, the same invitation can go out again. The president remembers receiving compliments on the clarity and grace of last year's invitation and is confident about sending it again with little revision.

Fortunately, the president has a good filing system. (Note: The more writing you do and the more efficient you have to be in completing writing tasks, the more important you'll find your filing system.)

Here's an example of a hard way to adapt a good example:

> The club president has to write the invitation to the annual picnic. New directions are needed because this year's picnic is at a new location. The program committee has changed some of the activities and has asked the president to make them sound exciting in the invitation. The task is more difficult; however, to save time, the president can use the beginning and ending of last year's invitation and can keep the information in the same order. The task is really not very different from the previous year. The president must show the invitation to the program committee to make sure the new activities sound exciting enough.

Most writing tasks are like the second example: sources can serve as partial models, even though we have to produce a good deal of new material. Note that the president relies on feedback from the committee before sending out the invitations.

Here it's impossible to use a previous example as a model:

> The club president has to write the invitation to the annual picnic. Last year's picnic was a fiasco: the beer ran out early, the band didn't show up, and the softball game resulted in two broken windshields and two lawsuits. This year everything's been well planned and the president has to assure the members that the picnic will go smoothly. Last year's invitation is no help.

What can the president do? While many writers would be stymied, the president won't be daunted if he or she knows useful getting-started and writing-to-discover techniques. After doing some beginning writing, the president can then use the writer's best tool: feedback from readers.

Get Feedback on What You've Written

To take the fear out of writing for a reader, get feedback on your work before you write the final draft that you hand in. Professional writers take comfort in the fact that at least one editor will review the article or story before it goes into print. Professionals always look for people of good judgment who can give honest, detailed feedback. In writing this book, for example, I relied not only on my editor, but

also on other writers, teachers of writing, and my students to give
me suggestions for improvement. Knowing that these people were
there gave me the freedom to experiment and took away the fear
that I would embarrass myself in front of my readers.

If you have never shown a draft of your writing to another
person, you will need courage to do so. But remember, what you
show to another person is not a finished piece, but a work in
progress that you intend to make better. Besides, most people are
flattered to be asked for advice.

This is not to say that you should ask just anyone for advice,
nor that you should just walk up to someone and say, "Here, read
this, and tell me what you think of it." Later in this chapter I discuss
talking to the right people and asking the right questions. In Chapters 4, 5, and 6, I deal with these issues regarding college assignments.

✍ **EXERCISE:** Write about a time when you asked someone for advice
about something you were making (not necessarily a piece of writing). Whom did you ask? Why did you ask that person? What did
you ask? Why did you ask those questions?

How did the advice affect what you did? If you could do it over
again, would you change anything you did? ■

A WAY TO HANDLE ANY WRITING TASK
FOR ANY READER

I say here *a* way; this doesn't mean the only way. As you read you'll
see that I mention many ways to approach writing, most of which
are optional. Besides, as I've done throughout the book, I encourage you to think of your own ways that will work better.

One thing is not optional: no matter how you go about your
writing, you must remember that writing to other people means
working with other people. My way brings other people as much as
possible into your act of writing.

Rather than explain my way abstractly, as if it were the same for
everyone in all situations, I'll explain it through two case studies:
The Finance Company Memos and What I Really Did on My Summer Vacation.

Case Study: The Finance Company Memos

"What's this!?" roared Mr. Pemblechook as he entered the cubicle of finance officer George Jenkins at the Security Reliable Savings and Loan. As Jenkins looked up from the letter he was composing, Pemblechook waved in his face some pieces of company stationery. "Jenkins, don't you know how to write a simple memo?" asked Pemblechook, though it didn't really sound like a question.

Startled by the interruption, Jenkins stammered, "Yes, sir. Yes, I know how to write memos. I wrote memos every day at my old company, and everyone said I wrote good ones."

Pemblechook shook his head, "Then how do you explain this?" He showed Jenkins the paper he was holding.

Jenkins recognized the paper immediately. It was a three-page memo he had sent to the vice-president to inform him of all the new accounts in the past month. It was just like the memos he had sent to the vice-president at his old company, the company he had left to take this higher-paying job at Security Reliable. In fact, Jenkins thought the memo was perfect. He had included the investors' names and addresses, the amounts of their initial investments, plus the interest rates at the time of deposit. It was what he had always done at his old company. What could be wrong? "I'm sorry, Mr. Pemblechook, but I can't see what's wrong with the memo." He looked at his boss with honest bewilderment.

Pemblechook stared at him, "Why, everything's wrong with it! First, you sent it directly to the vice president. Don't you know that all memos to the VP are supposed to go through me first? Second, you used the blue stationery. Didn't anyone tell you that blue is for proposals only, and that yellow is for monthly reports? Third, why are all these figures here? And why these addresses? Don't you know that the VP keeps track of those things in the computer? Fourth, where are the projections?"

Jenkins was really puzzled, "What projections?"

"The projections! Every monthly report of new accounts includes a brief projection for each account—what you think the investor is likely to do in the next quarter."

Jenkins was hurt, and more confused than ever, "But nobody told me how to write these reports. We never did them this way at my old company."

"Nobody told you?" shouted Pemblechook. "It's your job to find out what you need to know."

"But how was I to know that things were different here than in my old company?"

"Because things are always different until you find out otherwise. You say that you're a good writer. Well, every good writer knows that every company has its own rules and it's the writer's job to find out what they are. They're not written down any place. You just have to find out what they are."

"But how?" wondered Jenkins.

EXERCISE: How indeed? Pretend that you are Jenkins. Brainstorm or freewrite a plan of attack so that you can avoid further embarrassment in front of your boss. If possible, share your ideas with other writers in your group. ∎

Here's what I imagine Jenkins did. Compare your plan of attack with this one. After Jenkins got over his surprise and embarrassment, he realized that he'd learned a valuable lesson: good writing at one company is not necessarily good writing at another. Moreover, he realized that his boss had already told him a few of the rules for writing at Security Reliable. Next time, his monthly report would not include the figures and addresses, it would include the brief projections, and he'd use the yellow stationery (which sounded like a little thing, but obviously was important to Pemblechook). He also realized that he was lucky: because his reports to the vice-president were supposed to be reviewed by Pemblechook, he could ask Pemblechook to look at a draft of his next report before it went to the vice-president.

But this wasn't all that he did. Jenkins did two things that he should have done earlier:

1. He went carefully through the recent files of company memos, letters, and other documents to discover the unwritten rules of writing at Security Reliable. He looked for patterns: he noticed, for example, that memos tended to be addressed to "Ms. This" and "Mr. That," rather than to "Mary This, Director of Accounting" or "John That, Director of Investments"; he noticed that the monthly reports to the vice-president were never more than five

pages long and never less than three; he saw that the brief projections sometimes were two lines long and sometimes as long as a page—he'd need a lot of practice and feedback on those! He also saw that some things didn't make sense: why were some memos handwritten and some typed? Why did some reports begin with a summary while others did not? He jotted down these observations so that he could ask questions.

2. Jenkins began to ask questions of employees who had been with Security Reliable longer and who had written the different kinds of documents. When, for example, Pemblechook asked him to prepare the quarterly report on investment accounts, he looked at recent reports and talked them over with the two other finance officers and with Pemblechook. By referring to the documents and by asking questions about what to include and what to leave out, he was able to build a picture of the quarterly report he had to write.

With this information, and with his knowledge of writing to discover and experiment, he could then draft the summary and the speculative writing, "Projections for the Next Quarter," that were important to the report. Then he could write a draft of the report to show to Pemblechook.

Jenkins had, nevertheless, not completed his education in the rules for writing at Security Reliable. He had, in fact, only begun. He knew that with each new task—proposals to the president, letters to new clients—would come different rules. However, he had built a strategy for getting advice, finding models, and getting feedback that would help him handle each writing task.

Format: What It Is and What to Ask. Before going on to the second case study, What I Really Did on My Summer Vacation, I want to point out a distinction between *form* and *format* that should help you ask questions during the advice and feedback stages of the writing process. When Jenkins learned to use blue stationery for proposals and yellow for reports, he learned about *format*. When he learned that memos used "Mr." and "Ms." rather than first names and titles, he learned format information. Format has to do with the way material is presented rather than the content of the material. It

tends to be relatively simple information that people can give you
clear advice about. For example, an income tax return has a clear
format: fill in the lines with the figures requested. Formats are
important to learn, because they can make communication easier
and faster between writers and readers. For example, if you understand the income tax return (I didn't say that all formats were easy to
learn!), the only writing you do is filling in the figures; what they
mean will be immediately clear to the person reading them. Imagine how difficult it would be for the Internal Revenue Service to read
tax returns if taxpayers made up their own formats and used their
own words and figures in whatever order they chose.

Learning the Proper Format. The most important thing about
formats is that they vary from situation to situation. No matter what
someone asks you to write or what you want to write to someone,
find out as much as you can about the format. There is no such thing
as *the* proper format for a business letter, a college application, a job
résumé, or anything else, even though some books try to suggest
models to follow. Jenkins wrongly assumed that his old company's
format: names, addresses, figures, and interest rates, would work
at Security Reliable. He learned the hard way that he should have
checked the files and talked with people before writing his report.

Luckily, organizations that recognize the importance of format
do their best to inform their writers. For example, colleges send
application *forms* (short for "formats") that give detailed instructions for each writing task. People in business who compete for
contracts or grants from the government fill out long, detailed forms
so that the people who judge the applications can make fair comparisons. Publishers send detailed guidelines to writers because most
publications have strict ideas about length, acceptable topics, and
writing style.

No matter what your task, learn to ask format questions, and
look for writing samples, if they are available. If your reader does
supply a format, be sure to ask that reader or some other reliable
person format questions. Here are some format elements to keep
in mind:

• minimum or maximum length (number of words or pages)
• acceptable size, color, weight of paper

- acceptable print form: typing? handwriting? word processing?
- width of margins
- name and address of person to whom writing is sent
- types of information to include and the preferred order for this information (for example, a potential employer might ask for your educational background, your qualifications for a job, and your reasons for seeking a job, in that order; remember, don't guess, ask!)

Form = Time + Practice. While your readers and other knowledgeable people can give you clear advice about the format for a particular task, they cannot give you clear advice about its *form*. When Jenkins searched the files, he quickly discovered some of the rules of format. The rules of form in any organization and for any writing task are harder to pin down. The only way to learn them is through the formula *time + practice*: you have to do much writing, get feedback from many readers, and be patient to become adept at form. For example, although Jenkins knew that the *format* of the monthly reports called for projections, he had to practice to learn the *form*, how to write them and what to say.

We use many vague words to define the form of a piece of writing. We say, for example, that an author has a certain *style* or *voice*. We say that a letter or a memo has a certain *tone*. We use other vague words to describe these styles and tones. We say that someone has a *lively style*, an *intimate voice*, or a *somber tone*. We try to put into words a feeling that comes through that person's writing. All those words attempt to describe *form*.

If a writer asks a reader for advice about style or tone, the writer is likely to get an unclear answer, something like "Oh, I don't know. You should make it serious, but not too serious. We want to see that you're sincere, but don't sound like you're begging." This can't be much help. Readers would like to be more helpful, but can't put their feelings precisely into words, especially when they haven't seen any of your writing yet.

The simple truth is that the more you write, read, and talk with people, the more you learn about form and all its varieties. For example, if you keep a reading response journal (see Chapter 2) in which you imitate the style of another author, say Virginia Woolf or

Ernest Hemingway, you'll find that with practice you'll become good at imitation. The more you imitate it, the more you'll discover about that author's style. The more practice Jenkins gets in writing those monthly reports, the better he'll be at writing those projections.

However, even though you and Jenkins will become adept in your chosen form of the writing, neither of you will be able to tell others clearly how to do it. They will have to go through the same process that you did. You can show them the books you used (or the company files) and you can offer feedback on their writing, but they'll just have to read and practice and keep asking questions.

I know that it's not comforting to hear that there are no quick guidelines for learning form, but it would be unfair to pretend that there are. Think of it this way: writing to people and reading their writing is part of building relationships with them. The writing we do for others is part of our roles as friends, co-workers, lovers, neighbors, customers, and so on. To pretend that we can learn to write well to others without practice and patience would be like pretending that we can learn to understand and get along well with people without practice and patience. Through time, including some difficult moments, we learn how to read another person's gestures, expressions, actions, and words. Through time we learn how to act and speak toward that person so that we can be understood. The same is true with writing.

The Rewards of Time + Practice. Happily, as we practice writing to ourselves and as we read different kinds of writing in different situations, it gets easier to write in *new* situations. In his old job, Jenkins wrote letters to many investment clients and became adept at writing to people about their investments. Even though he is writing to different people in his new job, he can use what he has learned. This doesn't mean that he won't make mistakes, as he did with the report to the vice-president, but he sees mistakes as part of learning and he can correct the errors. He knows that he can write effectively to a range of clients and he has confidence in his ability to write to new people.

Sometimes, it takes surprisingly little experience to learn the form of writing in a new situation, as long as we use what we already know and follow the three-step process of asking advice, using examples, and getting feedback. To illustrate, I present a second case study.

Case Study: What I Really Did on My Summer Vacation

It was the first day of English 101 and Margaret Ellis couldn't believe what she was hearing. "All right, folks, your first assignment will be to write an essay titled, 'What I Did on My Summer Vacation.' Please turn it in in class on Wednesday. Any questions?"

"Not that old thing," thought Margaret. "I did that in sixth grade. You'd think she could come up with something herself." She lazily jotted down the assignment and vowed to wait until her free hour before Wednesday's class to write the—what did the professor call it?—oh yes, the "essay."

This somewhat puzzled her. She looked at the word in her notebook. How could one write an essay about summer vacation? She thought of an essay as something that took a stand, made a point, argued an idea. She remembered her sixth grade summer vacation piece as a dull list of activities that were fun to do, but were boring to report: "I went to the beach for a week in July with my family. In August, we took a trip to visit my grandparents. Mostly I played with my friend Jennifer." Later, in high school, when another unimaginative teacher had given the same assignment, she had been clever enough to put in other activities, some of which she made up, that the teacher would probably want to hear: "When we went to the beach, I spent part of my time reading, because reading is one of my favorite things. I also went to the library a lot."

"Oh well," she thought, "she probably doesn't really mean an essay. Teachers call everything essays." She decided to write a slightly more sophisticated version of her high school paper and just take her chances.

Her musings were interrupted by her professor's voice. "A question? Yes?"

"Professor Lang," a woman across the room began, "when you say 'What I Did on My Summer Vacation,' I think of those reports that I used to write on the first day of elementary school. 'I went to the beach, I visited my grandparents'—that sort of thing. Is that what you want? Sort of a list?'' The woman's tone was vaguely sarcastic, as if she, too, expected more of a college class.

Professor Lang smiled. "I'm glad you asked. Yes, that's why I gave you that title. But no, that's not what I'd like you to write. Remember, I said that I wanted an essay—I want you to make a statement, a point, about something you did, or discovered, or that happened to you during the last few months. You might say that the title, 'What I Did on My Summer Vacation,' is ironic, because that title usually means some dull, harmless writing that doesn't mean anything to you or the reader. I want the opposite of that. I give you this topic because your memories of the summer are still fresh and because maybe you haven't had a chance yet to take stock of the important things that happened in your life or that you thought deeply about during those months. What happened during the summer that really made a difference for you? That's what I want to hear about."

Margaret was getting nervous. She was thankful that the other woman had had the courage to say what she herself had been thinking. But now she knew that other questions needed asking. Like "Aren't you asking us to write something pretty personal?" Margaret could think of a couple of things that had happened in the summer that she could write about; her sister's accident, her father being laid off, and the family having to sell their house. Those events had indeed made a difference in her life; but she didn't feel like writing about them, especially to a total stranger. Still, she was afraid to let the teacher know that the assignment made her nervous.

Again, someone in the class read her mind. "Do you mean that you want us to write about something personal?"

"Yes," said Professor Lang, "but I don't want you to feel that you have to embarrass yourself. Let me mention something, though. One of my goals in this course is to make it easier for you to write about things that really matter to you. This means that you'll have to take a few risks in your writing. No matter what kinds of writing you do in your life, you have to learn the courage to express yourself.

"Let me assure you that I won't be making moral judgments

about your life or your feelings. Because this is a first assignment and because I want you to concentrate on writing honestly, I won't even be paying attention to whatever errors you make in spelling or grammar. I'll only make marks on your paper when I can't understand something you have written. Then I'll ask a question about it in the margin to help you when you revise the essay."

There was stirring in the class. Now Margaret could read their minds: "Revise?" she thought. "What would we revise for?" She found herself raising her hand. "Professor Lang," she asked, "when you say something you 'can't understand,' what kinds of things are you talking about? I know that it's hard to answer that without seeing our writing, but, in general, are there some things we should look out for when we're writing?"

Margaret had surprised herself; she rarely spoke out in class. She could see other students just as interested in the professor's response as she was. "You're right," said Professor Lang. "I can't talk specifically until I see your writing. However, let me suggest a couple of factors to keep in mind about the form of writing I'm looking for. Since this is an essay of a personal nature—in fact, the general form is called the personal essay—you'll be telling a story about your summer in order to build up to a statement, a point, that you want to make sure the reader, in this case, me, understands clearly. If you wish, you may begin your essay with the statement and then tell the story that illustrates the point. Either way is all right with me. But, whatever way you organize your material, two things have to happen: first, the point you make really does have to be relevant to the story (and vice versa); second, the story has to show the reader, through action and the scenes you paint, that your point makes sense. You want to make the reader feel that your point is true, not just think it." She paused. "Does that make it any clearer for you?"

"Yes," said Margaret, "it does." She said this without conviction. While she could follow the teacher's explanation, she wondered how she could be sure that anything she would write would meet the criteria for the form.

Professor Lang seemed to sense her uncertainty, for she spoke again. "I know that what I'm saying can't be very clear. But I hope it's enough to get you started. I'm going to ask you to trust the writing process. Write a draft of the essay, I'll give you some feedback on it, and then you can revise."

Margaret felt somewhat reassured by this. She appreciated the teacher's offer of help toward revision; still, she could not put out of her mind the uncertainty of writing in a new form about a personal topic to someone she did not really know.

Margaret became aware of the sounds of people closing their notebooks and rising from their desks. As students began to move toward the door, Professor Lang spoke above the end-of-class noise. "By the way, if you have trouble understanding the personal essay form, you can come by my office during office hours tomorrow. I have some collections of personal essays written by students in previous classes. They're not about summer vacations, but there are some good examples of the form. You're welcome to browse through them if you wish and ask me questions."

Margaret jumped at the suggestion, and wondered why Professor Lang had not mentioned the sample essays earlier; but as she walked across the September campus, she reasoned that she should probably attempt her own draft of the essay before she looked at someone else's on a different topic. She had become curious to see what she might write and didn't want other students' ways of writing coming between her and the task too soon. "After all," she reasoned, "if I want to use something from someone else, I can always revise."

✍ **EXERCISE:** Stop here a moment and reflect on the change in Margaret Ellis's view of the assignment. What had Ellis assumed about the form of the writing? Why has her view changed? Do a reflective writing in your journal on this topic. ∎

✍ **EXERCISE:** You are a student in the same class as Margaret Ellis. With the advice you have heard from Professor Lang, try your own draft of "What I Did on My Summer Vacation." Use focused free-writing or any other of the Chapter 1 techniques to help you get started. As you write, record other questions that emerge that you would like to ask Professor Lang. ∎

Here is Margaret Ellis's discovery draft:

I was going to write something on this assignment very trite and dull, like what I wrote in sixth grade. I'm still not very confident writing about what really happened this summer, but you're right, it does make more sense to write something meaningful. But it's still painful to do it.

Anyway, I thought summer was going to be really great. I'd been accepted to college, I had a track scholarship (I run the 400 and 800 meters), and I'd gotten invitations to three important track meets. Then the night before I was supposed to leave for Chicago (the first meet), while my parents and I were eating dinner and I was talking on and on about my great plans, we got a phone call from my Uncle David in Philadelphia. He's my mom's favorite brother (she doesn't say so, but he is) and she always jokes a lot with him on the phone. But she could tell something was wrong as soon as he said hello, because the first thing she said was, "What's wrong, Dave?" I had this feeling that something had happened to Marilyn, my sister—she moved to Philadelphia last year to work and to help my uncle and my Aunt Sarah take care of my grandmother, who's eighty-five. I don't know. We're always worried that Uncle Dave is going to call us about Grandma, but I just felt that there was something wrong with Marilyn. Mother got real quiet on the phone, and my father got up from the table and stood next to her and held her hand. It was like he could hear what my mother was hearing just by touching her.

I was so scared. Finally, I asked my mother, "Is it Marilyn?" She nodded. "Is she all right?" She held up her hand to say "Wait a second," and then she said into the phone, "Dave, Margaret's here and I'd better talk to her for a minute." She put down the phone and put her arms around me. "It's going to be okay, honey. Your sister had an accident. She got hit by a car, but Uncle Dave said it wasn't going too fast, so she wasn't too badly hurt." I asked if she was in the hospital and my mother said she was in Intensive Care, but she wasn't unconscious. I wanted to ask my mother a lot more questions, but I couldn't help it, I started to cry, and she just held me. My dad got on the phone and talked to my uncle, trying to sound real calm. He got the number of the hospital and then he asked about Aunt Sarah and my grandmother.

We found out that Marilyn had been paralyzed from the waist down when they brought her to the hospital, but that she was beginning to regain feeling in her legs. The doctor said she had multiple fractures, but was incredibly lucky (those were his words) that no permanent injury had been done to her back.

It wasn't until the next morning that we could talk to her on the phone. She sounded very tired, but she said I shouldn't worry and that the best thing I could do to help her heal would be to win my meet. I found out later that she'd been hit while crossing the street to a pay phone, where she was going to call me to wish me good luck.

So what makes this an essay? I'll never forget standing on the track before my first race two days later. I thought about Marilyn in her hospital bed, her legs in casts, totally helpless. I felt the blood coursing through my own legs, the muscles tighten and relax, and my feet press against the warm cushion of the surface. I couldn't imagine any feeling more wonderful or beautiful and I felt incredibly guilty about all the self-pity I'd had through the years over the pulled muscles, cramps, and bruises that are part of the lucky runner's life.

Margaret decided to take the draft with her to Professor Lang's office the next afternoon. She figured that the professor might not mind looking over her essay, since she had offered to answer questions about the assignment and sample essays.

Professor Lang read Margaret's draft while Margaret leafed through a two-year-old anthology of student essays. Though a few research papers and book interpretations were in the stapled collection, most of the pieces were stories from the students' lives. Some of these were quite personal, on the death of a grandparent or a childhood memory of an embarrassing or frightening experience. A few candidly related some act of meanness or jealousy by the writer. Margaret suddenly felt no longer alone in having written about her family and about her own sense of guilt.

In comparing her own draft with these revised pieces, Margaret was pleased most by her effort to describe the phone call from Philadelphia and her feelings on the track. She had wanted, almost like a filmmaker or a painter, to show her reader that picture she had in her mind of her mother and father when the phone call came, and she wanted to have her reader feel, physically, what she had felt standing on the track in Chicago. As she read parts of the essays in the book, she found herself most attracted to those sharp scenes where the feeling came through:

> . . . when we'd go to Poppy's house for Sunday dinner and Grandma would always be in her armchair, neat and silent in her padded robe, her eyes never moving, even when we kissed her goodbye.

> . . . so we went out to the playground, where my friends were already gathered to gossip. Now it was me they were whispering about behind their notebooks. I wanted to run away from Hermie; instead I walked closer to him and just tried to stare down those creeps.

The essays showed her quickly a couple of ways to revise her draft. To help her get started with the draft, Margaret had addressed her own writing to the teacher and included some comments about the assignment. She was more comfortable writing to someone directly than she was writing according to a form, an essay. But she could see that these revised pieces were not at all about the assignment and did not seem addressed to any particular person. They were about the characters and the plot (even if the main character was usually the writer); the reader could have been anyone. Her fingers itched for a pen so that she could revise these qualities into her essay.

To give Margaret a few more minutes to read through the essays, Professor Lang waited after reading Margaret's draft. Now, as the student looked up from her reading, the professor asked if she were ready to talk about the assignment.

"I think I already know some ways I want to revise it," said Margaret.

"Really? Did you get some ideas from the stories?"

"Yes. Actually, I'm pretty happy with what I've written, especially the way I tell the story, but I'd like to cut out the stuff at the beginning, up to where I start telling about the summer. And I need to change the beginning of the last paragraph: I don't like the first sentence, but I don't know if I need another sentence in the same place."

Professor Lang was slightly startled by Margaret's initiative.

Students usually acted as if they wanted the professor to tell them
what to change. She was pleased at Margaret's taking charge of her
own writing. "Fine. Let's look at the paragraph and see how it reads
without the first sentence."

Teacher and student looked together at the draft. Margaret
crossed out "So what makes this an essay?" and reread the last
paragraph. Really, it seemed to her that nothing else was needed
there. But she couldn't be sure what a reader would think. "How
does it read to you?" she asked.

"I like the way you've revised it. The sentence about crossing
the street to the pay phone shows me why you might have felt guilty
about the accident, so you're not really changing the mood when
you start telling about how you felt on the track. As a matter of fact, I
find it very powerful writing. I can feel what you were going
through."

Margaret didn't know if she could handle the praise because
she was not used to being praised for her writing. She decided not
to let it go to her head. "Thank you. Can I ask you what you think
about the beginning of the essay?"

"Sure. What would you like to know?"

"Well, if I cut out the first paragraph, does it sound all right to
start with the second?"

Professor Lang read the beginning, imagining the deletion of
the first paragraph. "I think you could do that. The first paragraph
isn't about the accident per se, and I don't think another reader
would understand why it's there, though of course I do. As I reread,
however, I have a question about the first sentence of the second
paragraph: 'I thought summer was going to be really great.' I
wonder if 'great' is the best word there. From reading the essay, it
doesn't seem to me that your sister's accident made the summer not
great for you. Because of what you say in your final paragraph, it
seems that your sister's accident made you see something even
greater about yourself than the scholarship and the invitations to
the meets. So it wasn't that the summer was less great; it was just
that things didn't turn out the way you'd expected."

Margaret thought about this. Yes, that was what she was trying
to say, though it came through in different words. Maybe what she
needed to show at the start was that she'd been so wrapped up in

her honors and her plans that she'd forgotten about what was most basic and beautiful in her life. Clearly the professor had some insight into this. It amazed her that so much meaning could depend on the choice of one word. No wonder a person couldn't get a blueprint for writing a personal essay. You had to start writing and then figure out what you wanted to say and how to say it.

"Maybe what I need to say there is that I thought I had it all together, that things were all in place, and that the summer would be all smooth sailing, except for my worries about myself—the races and getting ready for college and all that. What do you think?"

"That sounds plausible to me. Why don't you try playing around with those ideas? I don't think it will take you a lot of extra work. You've really got some good writing there. I'll look forward to reading your next draft."

✍ **EXERCISE:** Consider the scene in Professor Lang's office. What does Ellis learn about form from reading the other essays? What does she learn about form from her conversation with Professor Lang? On what factors does the form of Ellis's essay depend? ▪

✍ **EXERCISE:** Reread your own personal essay. As you reread, think about how you might like to revise it. Consider (1) examples of writing by others and (2) a reader that could help you revise the essay. What would you look for in those examples? What questions would you ask the reader? ▪

MORE ON FINDING GOOD EXAMPLES

When George Jenkins went through the files at Security Reliable, he found clues to help him with format. When Margaret Ellis read through the personal essays in the class anthology, she found out about form. Jenkins had an easier task than Ellis: he merely had to note the color of the paper, the usual length of the documents, the way to address the recipients of memos, and so on. He could precisely follow what other writers had done. Ellis, on the other hand, could copy nothing. When reading others' stories she had to pay attention to her own reactions as a reader. She had to think about what she liked and didn't like; what seemed clear and what seemed vague; and what seemed logical, consistent, genuine, and honest, all those ideas that are hard to express.

She learned something from the examples that helped her to revise, but what she learned was relatively minor: not to address her teacher and not to refer to the assignment. Indeed, these instructions could have been written into the assignment and she would not have needed to look at the anthology. The anthology helped her feel good about what she had already written. This was important help, but she didn't need it to get started. What did she need?

Diving In and Swimming Around

In Chapter 1, I said that the best way to start writing is just to start. The first technique presented was unfocused freewriting, in any form and about anything, wherever your mind takes you. But the secret behind freewriting and all the other techniques is that your mind can only take you to places it's already been in some sense. A person who's never used words, who's never spoken, heard, written, or read, can't freewrite. It would be like telling you to freewrite in Chinese when you know none of the symbols of the language. You discover new ways to put words and ideas together when you write, but you can't start from nowhere and expect to get somewhere.

In fact, Margaret Ellis was able to write a pleasing first draft because (1) she had taken part in that useful class discussion of the personal essay and (2) she had experience using language to deal with her feelings and the events of her life. When she first heard the teacher's instructions, she thought she was unprepared. In truth, she already had most of what she needed to do the assignment well. If you reread her first draft, you'll notice that she has no trouble describing the phone call or her sensations before the race. Yet, without practice, it is very difficult to write so effectively. How can we account for Margaret's success?

Margaret Ellis, like most of us, brings to her assignment a history of writing, reading, speaking, and listening that helps her write in this new form. For example, if she has ever kept a diary (see Chapter 2), she has already written in a form similar to that of the personal essay. If she likes to read novels, stories, or magazine articles about places and events, she has seen how writers create scenes and pictures through words. If she enjoys storytelling—intricate, descriptive conversations with friends or family ghost story sessions on winter evenings—she has had experience in using words. By diving in and swimming around in descriptive writing—her own and others'—she has absorbed a great deal.

There are several lessons in this case study that we can use in our own search for good examples.

First, all writing and reading that you have done is relevant to any new writing task. Ellis had never before written a personal essay per se, but her other writing and reading helped her. Likewise, experienced writers of poetry do not panic if they have to write a grant proposal to a government agency; the lawyer, who writes many legal briefs, is not unprepared to write a short skit for the P.T.A. entertainment night at his or her child's school. The student who can write thorough lab reports in chemistry class can keep a good reading response log in literature class. Whenever we approach a new form of writing, we have much to learn about style, vocabulary, and format, but we have the basics as long as we have good histories as readers and writers. (See Chapter 2 for discussion of the basics.)

Second, most of what we learn about form—style, tone, voice—we must learn slowly and patiently through practice. Despite their minor problems with form and format, both Ellis and Jenkins adapted quickly to new writing tasks because they'd had years of practice as writers, readers, and speakers. Ideas such as style, tone, and voice are hard to define because you learn them by feel, by experience. Swimming around in a new form is crucial. The person who would write mystery novels has to read mystery novels as well as other kinds of novels and stories, to learn how one person's style differs from another's. Without knowing the differences, you can't know style at all. Swimming around also shows the range of tricks and techniques that you might be able to use. To learn how to write the monthly projections, Jenkins read through many reports. He learned when to be brief and when to expand, what things to include and what things to avoid, when to use his imagination and when to estimate conservatively. The writer is like the athlete who observes other athletes for possible ways to stand, move, and fool the opposition. No matter what form of writing you work in, dive into examples and swim around in them until the water feels warm.

✍ **EXERCISE:** Look again at your first draft of the personal essay. Do a freewrite or brainstorm on books, stories, or articles you have read that might have had some influence on your ability to write this essay. What other parts of your own history as a language user might have been useful to you in this task? ■

✍ **EXERCISE:** Think of a very specific type of writing (such as a job application, spy novel, or advertising brochure) that you need to do or would like to do. How could you dive in and swim around in this type of writing to learn its form? If there is a precise situation for which you will write (such as applying for a summer job with the National Park Service or writing a spy story for a national magazine), plan how you will learn the appropriate format. As you plan, let these questions guide you: (1) What have you already read or written in this form? (You might refer to those works.); (2) Where might you find precise information on format? (For example, the U.S. government provides formats for applications; national magazines publish guidelines for their articles); and (3) What people could you ask for suggestions of works to read in the form? ■

ADVICE AND FEEDBACK FROM THE RIGHT PEOPLE

The best person to give you advice and feedback is your reader. Rather than stare at a blank page in anxiety over the approval or disapproval of your work, make your reader your ally, your associate, in the writing process. Chapter 4 talks in detail about writing for the college teacher and how to bring the teacher, as well as fellow students, into your writing and revision. Here, I'll mention briefly some ideas to remember as you write for other audiences and situations.

The Natural Way to Get Advice and Feedback

In most situations, we write to people as part of our work and community lives. We talk on the phone, we write memos or letters, we reply to those letters and memos, we talk some more, and so on.

If we think about it, the reason we write to other people is to create more opportunities for conversation. Jenkins writes to inform and impress his boss, so that he can talk about his clients and gain more prestigious assignments. You send a postcard while you are on vacation to keep your relationships strong, so that you and your family will have more to talk about when you get home.

Every time that you talk or correspond with a person, you are in effect getting advice from your reader, even if you never actually ask that person about your writing. Every interaction teaches us what to say and what to avoid, and which words that person will be comfortable with and which will seem strange or offensive. Humans are marvelously adept at picking up cues from one another. We quickly learn how to adjust our manners and language for different people.

I call this the natural or environmental way to get advice and feedback on our writing. Although it's the best and surest method, it takes much patience because we undoubtedly make mistakes, as Ellis and Jenkins did. But if you keep the lines of oral and written communication open, your writing will definitely improve.

Your Reader Doesn't Know What He or She Wants— Until You Ask

Remember Professor Lang's conversation with her students? Remember Pemblechook's stormy discussion with Jenkins? Neither Professor Lang nor Pemblechook told the writers how to do the assignment until the writers asked questions. Like anyone else who gives an assignment, they didn't know what the writers needed to know until the writers asked. As Pemblechook said, it's the writer's job to find out the unwritten rules. As I said earlier, some organizations publish formats, but in most situations you'll have to ask format questions. And, of course, no one can give you clear advice about form until you ask a specific question, as Margaret Ellis did about the first paragraph of her personal essay.

This is why it is important to do some discovery writing on an assignment before you ask your reader for advice. Discovery writing forces you to make choices about your ideas, the order of your ideas, and your words. Your choices help you frame specific questions for your reader, which are easier to answer than vague ones. (I explore the question-asking process in detail in Chapter 4.)

Because the reader lacks awareness of what you need to know, the best advice for your writing comes from feedback on a draft you've written. When he saw Jenkins's report, Pemblechook immediately saw what Jenkins needed to do. Professor Lang immediately saw the problem with Ellis's first sentence when she read the draft. Neither reader could have given such good advice without seeing the text. Remember, it's never valid for a writer to say, "I couldn't do it because I wasn't told how to."

Always Avoid the Shot in the Dark

You might ask, "What if my reader won't give me feedback?" or "How can I get feedback if my reader is far away and I don't know him or her?"

Readers who deliberately refuse to give feedback seriously hurt their organizations. I once interviewed a mid-level manager in a government agency who said to me, "I won't talk with my employees about their writing. They're supposed to know how to do it." No wonder this man complained about how bad his employees' reports were. Fortunately, attitudes like his are not common. The fact is that many readers don't give feedback because they don't know how effective it is and because no one asks them. Don't assume that your reader doesn't want to give feedback. Ask for it.

Don't assume that your reader is too remote or is unidentifiable. Say that you want to respond to an ad for a job with a company in another state. The ad says, "Send letter and résumé by June first" and includes a brief job description along with the company's name, address, and phone number. Try two things: (1) write a discovery draft of your letter and résumé to discover questions about what to say and how to say it and (2) call the company and speak to the person who placed the ad. Tell this person that you're composing your letter and résumé and need some information. Then ask your questions (remember to ask about both form and format). You may discover that this person, like other readers, does not know what he or she wants until you ask the questions. Don't be surprised if the person gets curious and asks you what you have put into your draft or gives you clues about the company and the job.

Anyone's the Right Person—Except the Wrong Person

It's pretty hard to find anyone who's not a good source of advice and feedback. Even if someone is not your intended reader, that person can still help you in some way. For example, you can ask a good speller to check your job application before you mail it, even if he or she can't tell you if it will impress the personnel director. You can ask someone's opinion of your work, "What seems to you to be the most important idea in my essay?" as long as you don't let that one opinion outweigh the opinion of your intended reader.

Your reader can be the wrong reader if you have unreasonable expectations. If you write a book review, don't expect someone who hasn't read the book to tell you if your review is accurate. Your reader may be able to tell you what your main idea is and if you stay on it and may also be able to show you whether or not the review holds his or her attention. But don't expect more than the reader can deliver. (In Chapter 4, I talk in detail about how to train readers to give you the feedback you need for school assignments.)

To avoid having unreasonable expectations, think about why you want a certain person to read your work. What does this person have in common with the person you are writing to? How is he or she different? What special talents or knowledge does this person have that can make him or her a good reader? Is this person likely to give you an honest response, or will he or she be too kind, or too bored, to answer honestly? By asking yourself these questions you will get the most help from your readers.

Finding a Mentor

In the two case studies that conclude this chapter, The Engineer and The Speechwriter, you'll read about *mentors.* Writing mentors are people who have had experience writing in situations similar to yours. They can give you good feedback on an assignment and can be relied on in diverse situations. These people have learned through time and practice what to say and what not to say.

How do you find a mentor? Sometimes the choice seems obvious. For George Jenkins, Pemblechook is the best candidate. Not only does he know company rules and employees, but, as boss, he bears some responsibility for the quality of Jenkins's work. Most important, he has already shown a willingness to help and give feedback, even if he didn't deliver it gently. Likewise, Professor Lang, who is clearly willing to answer questions and offer whatever help she can, can be a mentor to Margaret Ellis and other students.

Remember, though, that Jenkins and Ellis must take the initiative and avail themselves of the help. If Jenkins is put off by Pemblechook's gruffness, the opportunity is lost. If Ellis is overawed or too embarrassed to show her teacher the draft, she, too, misses the chance.

Often, the choice of mentor is not as obvious. All people who write well can name one or more people on whose judgment they rely. They may not think of these people as mentors, but as friends or co-workers with whom they can easily discuss their work. Mentors might be fellow students "who like to listen to what I'm writing and always say something helpful," or fellow employees "who always seem to know where to send the memos and what to say." The help may be mutual, with the mentors coming to the student for advice or feedback.

Relationships with mentors don't happen suddenly; as with anything else worthwhile, they take time to mature. One doesn't really go out to find a mentor, but takes the initiative to get responses to his or her writing. If you do this conscientiously and consistently, sooner or later you'll realize that there are one or a few people with whom you are always comfortable to share your writing and who always give good advice. These are your mentors. Having such friends may be the greatest reward of writing.

THE THREE-STEP PROCESS IN ACTION: TWO WRITERS' STORIES

The following interview reports illustrate the three-step process by which any writer can write for any reader: asking advice, finding examples, and getting feedback.

The Engineer

Ray Chapman learned industrial engineering in college, then pursued a career in engineering management for more than twenty years with private industry, the U.S. Department of Defense, and the U.S. Department of Energy. As associate director of the George Mason Institute of Science and Technology, he organizes university projects in cooperation with corporations and government agencies. Among his latest projects is the establishment of the Japanese Technical Information Research Service, the first on-line access in the United States to Japanese-language databases of technical research.

Every job he does requires him to write, though he does not call himself a writer per se. As a creative man who wants his ideas to become reality, he has to make his ideas interesting to his financiers. For twenty-five years he has written proposals to convince his financiers that spending their money or time will be worthwhile. He has to know what the reader wants to hear and how to convince the reader that he can do what he promises. Because writing proposals is competitive and others vie for the same funds, he has to make his ideas more exciting and useful than the competition. Proposal writing is so important to government and industry that Ray Chapman says confidently, "I can guarantee that there are jobs for anyone who can write in an organized, interesting way."

Through years of proposal writing, Ray Chapman has learned that every situation is different, in format and form. He must ask countless questions of many people, read all pertinent documents, and get feedback throughout the process.

He always goes straight to the funding source to learn as much as he can about what will be funded and what sorts of information should be included. Because he writes many of his proposals to government agencies or to Congress, he reads detailed documents called Requests for Proposals, or RFP's, in which funding sources tell proposal writers what they want to spend money for and give the writers an outline and a format for the proposal. RFP's may be short or long, depending on the complexity of the information requested from proposal writers. When RFP's are available, Chapman relies heavily on their advice. When they are not available, he creates his own from answers to his questions about format and form.

But getting an RFP is only the beginning of the process. Since Chapman proposes projects that need the work of several, maybe many, people, he has to talk with each person about how much

money is needed, why it is needed, and what work will be contributed. As he drafts the proposal, he must get feedback from each one
to be sure that he has pictured their situation accurately and fully.
"All proposal writing," he says, "is a mesh between the people who
have the money and the people who'll do the work." Both groups,
in effect, are readers. The proposal writer must stay in touch with
both as the proposal grows.

Equally important to the writing process are other people who
can give useful feedback. Chapman says, "I am always looking for
experts in the field to use as sounding boards for my ideas. Experts
help me discover aspects of my ideas that I hadn't considered, or
different uses for what I'll do. They also alert me to possible problems. I need to know what other groups are doing or have done that
is similar to what I am proposing, so that I can show how my work
will contribute."

Finding the best people to consult is always an adventure. "I'm
on the phone a lot. I start with someone who I think can help, and I
ask him or her to give me names of others to call. Then they put me
on to others, and so on. To do this well, you also have to get out of
the office and rub elbows. Some of my best contacts have come from
casual conversations at meetings, at lunch, or at social gatherings."

Besides learning through discussion, most proposal writers
also read whatever might be of use. Computerized databases keep
writers up to date on related research and lead them to pertinent
books and articles. These in turn suggest other sources. And certainly, every proposal writer must dive in and swim around in the
files of successful past proposals. Funding sources are usually glad
to give a person access to past proposals, since it's easier to show a
writer someone else's successful work than to explain how to write
it. By reading proposals and asking questions about them, the
proposal writer gets a feel for the writing itself.

Discovery Writing: Scoping and Storyboarding. Besides asking
advice, proposal writing requires much discovery writing to plan
the project and experiment with ideas. Among experienced proposal writers such as Ray Chapman, two techniques are essential
early in the process: *scoping* and *storyboarding*. Writers scope out an
idea by projecting the work involved into the future: "How long

until the project is completed? Three years? Five? How much time does that give us for the first phase? The second?" Scoping forces writers to visualize the project. As they watch, they understand the intricacy of the plan—the time needed, the problems that may arise, the materials required. These data will enable them to write a full and accurate proposal. Scoping also helps better estimate the all-important budget for the project.

Through storyboarding the writers brainstorm what they want to include in the proposal. Often a group exercise (see Group Brainstorming in Chapter 1 for a variation), storyboarding frequently uses a chalkboard, or large sheets of paper taped to a wall, on which the writers experimentally list facts, figures, and ideas for the final proposal. Items are continually added, deleted, or moved around as the writers review what they've written. Storyboarding gives a preliminary outline for a draft proposal and also is a kind of writing to the limit in which writers see what they feel confident about and what requires more research, reading, phone calls, or interviews.

The Final Audience. Because many of the proposals Ray Chapman writes and reviews ask for large sums of taxpayer money, they undergo intense screening by readers at several levels before they reach the final approval authority. Most are rejected at lower levels.

The purpose of the proposal is to convince the buyer, whether in government or industry. In government, proposers want to present the proposal to the source selection board. If the project is of national importance, the proposal might be presented to select committees of Congress. Once the proposal is among the finalists a new round of planning—reading, writing, and asking questions—begins. Since the writers know who is in the decision-making group, they can tailor their work to the needs of that audience. Government experience has taught Ray Chapman the importance of the first part of the proposal, the Executive Summary. "Since members of Congress and other selection authorities have little time and there are many competing proposals, the summary has to be exciting to the reader. That means that each agency head or member of Congress has to see immediately how the proposal ties into his or her mission. We have to know what's important to each member of the committee and try to show how our proposal will help the member accomplish that." (See the section on summary writing in Chapter 2.)

Presentation goes beyond merely presenting proposal documents to the committee. The skilled proposal writer must also know how to package the proposal so that the live presentation is effective. At this stage, presenters often use slides, flip charts, scale models, or videotapes.

However, Chapman points out that the most important part of the presentation may occur when the presenting is over. "Always finish your presentation at least ten minutes before your allotted time. Then ask for questions. Involving your audience in dialogue lets you find out what they really want and where they have problems with the proposal. Talking with them really lets you get things done." Perhaps nothing better captures the idea that writing is a process of working with people than the notion that this large enterprise of proposal writing culminates in ten minutes of intense talk.

The Mentor. Because throughout the process of proposal writing the number and variety of readers is so great, a proposal cannot be custom-made for one reader. Therefore, it is important to talk with people, be available to answer questions, get feedback from different readers, and study other proposals. Also important is experience.

Ray Chapman says to the newcomer to proposal writing, "Find those rare people who really know the environment, who can tell you whom to ask and can judge what you've written. You have to have a mentor in order to learn the ropes." He matter-of-factly includes himself in that group, "I really enjoy trying to answer the questions. That's one of the reasons I'm on the phone all the time!" But from observing Ray Chapman, I know that he's also on the phone because he practices what he preaches. Even the mentor never knows it all, but he does know that he must keep on asking.

EXERCISE: Think about a proposal you would like to make to a funding source (family, employer, government, and so on) for something you would like to buy or do. What are the details of the request: how does your plan benefit the funding source? Why are you asking that source? What will you spend the money for? Why do you need so much?

What do you know about the funding source (your reader) that will help you know what to say and what not to say? Whom can you call on for good feedback on a draft of the proposal?

Try using scoping and storyboarding to help you discover what to say. ■

The Speechwriter

Special Agent Steve Gladis of the FBI writes speeches for the director. As chief of the speech unit, Gladis supervises three other writers and works closely with the director, William S. Sessions, and high-ranking Bureau officials. An agent for fifteen years, several spent supervising an antiterrorist squad, Gladis taught writing and public speaking at the FBI Academy in Quantico, Virginia, before assuming his current post. He has written three successful books on the craft of writing and for the past few years has kept a regular journal, which he says contains some of the most interesting writing he does.

I interviewed Gladis about how he and his staff write speeches. "It's not a matter of sitting there, wringing your hands, and wondering if the director will like what you say . . . It's staying in touch with the director throughout the process, making suggestions and getting his feedback . . . It's researching the audience for the speech, so that we know as much as we can about the group and why they want the speech . . . It's getting facts and figures from every division of the bureau and documenting what we say . . . And it's asking for ideas and feedback from the other members of the team." Even though the speeches that come from the unit are given by the director, Gladis says that the director calls the speeches "ours," not his. Gladis points out that this group responsibility has two consequences. "On the one hand, it means that we all have some ownership in the project. On the other, it means that we have to be able to listen to everyone else. We have to be willing to take suggestions and make changes."

Speechwriting at the FBI follows a system that Gladis designed. First, the team, including the director, must decide if they'll accept a request. The Director assigns us to research the group and why they've requested the speech. So we make calls and we read. If we feel that the occasion will allow the director to make an important statement to a significant audience, then we'll suggest acceptance. Of course, he can and does at times turn down our recommendation."

Though the director, by necessity, accepts some invitations on short notice, most acceptances give the team two months or more to prepare. "Understand that these are important speeches, both because of the group hearing it and because they usually articulate Bureau policy on controversial issues, such as terrorism and drugs. We need time to work with the divisions to acquire statistics, to verify the facts and figures, to get feedback from the divisions on how we have worded their information." Of course, the unit is working on several speeches over this time frame—another reason why the process has to be systematic.

After the director accepts an invitation, the unit gets to work on what Gladis calls the "thesis note": a half-page sketch of the speech written to the director. The note contains the central thesis of the speech and the main ideas that support that thesis. The note also describes the audience, its size, location, and so on. A lot of work goes into writing this half page. This detailed note also lets the director give detailed feedback to the writers. Once the writer understands what the director wants to convey, the writer talks with the divisions to find out what the agency can say on the topic based on the current state of affairs. Throughout this part of the process, the team meets regularly in conferences to work out the details, much as Ray Chapman's proposal-writing team scopes and storyboards.

The director's comments and input from the divisions help the writer compose the next document, a formal outline. "We use a formal outline structure—roman numerals, capital letters, and all that. But this is only a 'working' document, a piece of think-writing. We use the outline to help us put our thoughts into a logical plan— it's essential that a speech be logical—but we'll typically revise the outline several times before sending it on to the director." This, too, occurs in conference. "I won't let my writers write in a cave," says Gladis.

About three weeks before the speech is to be given, the director reviews the outline, again suggesting changes and asking questions. "Sometimes he may question the language or the use of a particular statistic. Clarity and accuracy are essential. We all appreciate this. If we don't understand a comment or question from him, we ask."

The next step is to write a rough draft. When Gladis himself drafts the speech, he follows guidelines of style and form that he has learned over many years of writing, reading, and hearing speeches, and teaching others public speaking. "When I draft, I come to my writing through talking. I role-play the speaker before that particular audience; I talk a discovery draft of the speech into the tape recorder. I call it 'free-speaking,' because it's like free-writing."

How does he know how to role-play? "That takes research and practice. Of course, we've already checked out the audience, so we know some things about them to use in writing the speech. Besides, many of the groups are similar—they are usually large professional groups, such as the American Banking Association or the U.S. Chamber of Commerce, for whom we've prepared other speeches. That makes the task easier. But we also have to know a lot about the speaker. When we met Director Sessions for the first time, we wanted to find out such things as the books he enjoys and his attitudes toward new ideas. We also looked at some of his previous speeches, to begin to get a sense of his style. Of course, learning someone's style takes time—the best way is to work with the person on speech after speech."

Through experience, Gladis has learned other stylistic devices that give him a partial format for every speech. He uses transitional words such as *however* and *nevertheless*. The listener is not likely to be confused if the speaker gives a signal that a transition will occur: "Even though crime is up 10 percent over last year, it is down 10 percent over the last five." Gladis says that he learned this from years of listening to speeches and paying attention to his reactions. "Hearing speeches makes me a better writer, and writing them makes me a better listener."

He uses anecdotes and sharp descriptions (see Chapter 5 for ways to make your writing vividly descriptive) to paint a picture for the audience. "When people listen they'll get lost—or fall asleep—if they can't 'see' what you're talking about. If a speech is about drug arrests, it should describe one of the arrests. People listen when they get involved in the story."

When a first draft is done, it goes again to conference. "Teaching speechwriters has taught me some things about how to give feedback in the unit. Since we have to work together and since I want people to be creative, I have to be able to keep a writer's confidence high—and yet be able to tell him or her that a speech needs changing."

How does Gladis do this? "We try to follow a sequence: first, we praise the speech for the things we like—that's crucial; second, we ask questions about whatever seems confusing to us (there's always something confusing in every first draft); third, we offer help—our suggestions—where we think they're needed." Two ideas work simultaneously: consideration for the writer's morale and responsibility of the team to the director, the Bureau, and the audience. "If something in the draft is inaccurate or misleading or poorly said, we have to say so—and the writer, me included, has to pay attention to the criticism. I don't expect speechwriters to write perfect first drafts, but I do expect them to revise."

The revised draft is sent to the appropriate divisions for review: Are the details accurate? Does the message adhere to agency policy? After further revision, the draft goes to the director for comments.

The director's comments lead to final revision. "The last draft we send to the director is our 'documented draft.' This means that we footnote statistics and examples; it also means that we attach to the draft the letter or the report that was our source for the footnote. Sometimes the attachments are longer than the speech itself."

Steve Gladis doesn't claim that his system is the best; he's always looking for ways to improve as a writer and as a manager. "I talk a lot with other speechwriters; I read the speechwriting magazines. I also write in my journal about what works and what doesn't." He has not yet found a reason to take shortcuts with the process of planning, drafting, and feedback. "I keep hearing complaints from speechwriters at other places—'I really sweated over this speech, and then the boss said it was exactly what he *didn't* want.' In every case, they could have avoided the disaster if there'd been communication between the writer and the speaker. Sometimes it's the speaker's fault, for not allowing access by the writers. But sometimes the writer just doesn't seem to realize how successful writing gets done."

✍ **EXERCISE:** Like other managers in business and government, Steve Gladis writes documents and speeches that someone else will sign or speak. Imagine writing a speech that someone else will give (or writing a letter that someone else will sign). If you can think of a time when you have done this, recall the experience in your journal. What problems did you face? How did you handle them? If you had it to do over again, what would you do differently?

If you have never had this experience, hypothesize about what you would do. ∎

✍ **EXERCISE:** From this chapter, it should be clear that writing is collaborative; its success depends on people working together. For your "History of a Writer," write about yourself as a collaborative writer. How have you relied on others for advice and feedback on your writing? How have others relied on you? What has been difficult about these interactions? ∎

✍ **EXERCISE:** The opposite of the collaborative writer is the solitary writer, romanticized in figures such as the brooding, misunderstood genius or the secretive diary keeper. Before you read this chapter, did you think of writing as primarily a social or a solitary process? Why? How do you feel now? In what ways is the collaborative writer solitary? How is even the most secretive writer collaborative? ∎

✍ **EXERCISE:** Write a story, like that of George Jenkins or Margaret Ellis, that conveys something important about writing for others. Show a draft to someone whose opinion you value. Formulate questions for this reader that will give you information to make the story better. ∎

⚜ PROJECTS FOR WRITERS

Write Your Own. In this chapter, I've focused on the transition from writing for the self to writing for others, with the mental gear shifting that this transition implies. Considering the skill, craft, art, sport, or other activity that you focused on in the Write Your Own sections of previous chapters, write about the difference between performing that skill for yourself and for others. If you're an athlete, write about the difference between practice and the actual game; if you're a painter, writer about the difference between experimenting in your studio and doing a painting for someone else; and so on. Write to give advice to someone who's interested in your skill but who does not know it as well as you do.

You might create a case study like Ellis's or Jenkins's. How do you, in learning to perform your skill for others, adapt your talents? You might describe an occasion when you had to adapt to difficult conditions or strange expectations.

Share your writing with others; get appropriate feedback; revise.

Connecting with Fellow Writers. Read biographies or autobiographies of two or more people who are experts in the skill, craft, art, sport, or other activity that you particularly enjoy. (If necessary consult Chapter 7 for tips on using the library.) Try to find as many examples as possible of ways in which the expert copes with performance anxiety, with hostile audiences, or with skeptical critics. How did the person cope? How did the person learn to take advantage of performance situations? Where do you see evidence that the expert learned how to get feedback to improve the skill?

As you read, make notes about what you find. Draft an informal report on your findings. Share your work with fellow investigators. Revise.

Free Experiment. Central to this chapter is the idea that writers grow from fear of their readers to cooperation with them; they make readers their allies in the process of writing. To show this, I experiment with different forms and formats: the fictional case studies of

Margaret Ellis and George Jenkins, the interviews with Ray Chapman and Steve Gladis, the hypothetical invitations to the office picnic, even the mathematical formula Form = Time + Practice. Play with diverse forms and formats to communicate your own message about personal growth. You may come up with a comic strip, a mathematical model, a piece of music, a series of sketches, a board game or computer game that would award points for learning within a hostile environment (isn't this what most computer games are about?).

After you've experimented, bring others into the act. Use their responses for further experiments.

Chapter Checklist

First write for yourself, then revise for others

Use the three-step method
Ask advice
Find good examples
Get feedback

In getting advice, ask questions about format and form
To learn format:
    Ask questions (length, items to include, order, and so on)
    Study appropriate samples (check the files)
To learn form:
    Be patient
    Practice different types of writing for different readers
    Get regular feedback from knowledgeable readers

To use models in learning form
Dive in and swim around:
    Use your own "history" as a reader, writer, talker
    Read many examples of the form you're trying to write
    Read widely among various kinds of writing

To get good feedback
Make your reader your ally, your advisor
Use the natural way of getting feedback
Write first, then ask the reader questions about the writing

Ask questions that your reader is qualified to answer
Take the initiative, don't wait for an invitation
Try to establish mentor relationships with trusted readers

Words to Write By

Writing to other people means working with other people.

If you don't know what a reader wants, it's your job to find out.

We don't expect writers to be perfect the first time, but we do expect them to be willing to revise.

4 Writing for the Teacher

I got a B+ on my first paper and a B+ on my second paper. I'll get a B+ on my third paper, no matter what I do.

　　　　　—Diane Hudson
　　　　　History graduate student, May, 1990

I was wrong. I got an A.
　　　　　—Diane Hudson, June, 1990

BAD WRITERS AND REAL HELP

We've all had this experience. A teacher gives a writing assignment: a research paper, a critical book analysis, a lab report. We feel tense, wary. We know that we will be judged by our writing and we suspect that the assignment is a minefield designed to destroy us.

How do we make our way through this minefield? Many of us just take our chances. Out of our narrow experience as writers, we put together something that sounds good and hand it in, hoping for the best. Others believe that somewhere, in the teacher's head, in the heads of our fellow students, or maybe in a book, a map of the minefield exists that, if we possessed it, would lead us smoothly across. The catch is that the teacher, if he or she has the map, keeps it from us and makes us guess what it says. We try to think of the strategies to find out from the teacher what he or she wants in the assignment. But our strategies don't work, so we, too, wind up just taking our chances and hoping for the best.

Most students eventually come to feel that they will never be good writers. I don't know how many times I've heard people say that they can't write. Strangely, however, many of these people are writers! On the job, in their homes and communities, and in school, these people write letters, memos, applications, reports, budgets, personal notes, and term papers. They may find writing painfully confusing and slow; they may be afraid to show their writing to others. Still, they write.

Often, the writing is beautiful. I think of the family friend who writes exquisite poetry, but who rarely has the courage to show this writing to others. I think of the student whom I praised for his stunning cancer research report, but who had always received D's on his high school writing and had put off taking his college composition course for two years. I hear these stories constantly and I am consistently amazed by the honesty, clarity, and richness of writing done by people who say that they can't write.

Where does this sense of inability come from? Sure, we can blame parents. Everyone's parents make them feel inadequate in some, or many, ways. Sure, we can blame our consumer society. Anyone feels like a failure when he or she is incessantly told by advertisers that success and happiness should be just as easy as buying dandruff shampoo and drinking a certain beer. And sure we can blame schools. Whatever else they may be, schools are competitive: they are in the business of giving rewards and punishments. How are the winners and losers determined? Often, through writing. Since all competitive systems have few winners and lots of losers, most people wind up feeling that they can't write.

Figuring Out Writing in School

The first thing to learn about writing in school is that it is not supposed to be a guessing game. School is supposed to help all students to learn and grow. Competition in school is supposed to make everyone work harder and learn more. Competition is not supposed to make people feel like losers and stop trying, though that frequently happens. If people fail, they are supposed to learn from their mistakes, try again, learn some more, and so on. Learning is the reward, and learning is supposed to be difficult, often painful, and time consuming. Success in school, as in anything else, is supposed to be a feeling, a sense of accomplishment, that comes after hard work. Unfortunately, schools do a bad job of conveying this idea of success. Teachers often try to make us feel that it is easy to be successful and that if we fail, we will be losers for the rest of our lives. That is why we treasure those rare people who stick with us through our pain, people who show us that failure leads to learning and that learning brings success.

The second thing to learn about writing in school is that there is no map of the minefield. Rather, there is no single map. In theory, there are an infinite number of ways to write anything, including a school paper assignment or an essay question on an exam. In fact, a key rule of writing is that my essay must be different in some ways from yours; if it isn't, then one or both of us is cheating.

What is the reason for this rule? Simply, the purpose of school is learning, and the purpose of writing in school is learning. Sometimes, in the incessant competition for high grades, this purpose gets lost, and it seems that the purpose of writing is to have, not try for, the A paper. All too often, the grading system ignores our effort, our pain in failing, our fear, and our gaining the courage to try again. All too often, teachers forget that students want to learn; instead of recognizing effort and growth, they reward only the demonstration of knowledge. They reward the students who enter the class already knowing the course material and methods. Similarly, students often think that paying tuition and buying books buy them knowledge. In these ways, both teacher and student subvert the purpose of school.

If the purpose of school is learning and the purpose of writing in school is learning, that explains why it's so hard to find out what a teacher wants in a piece of writing. If my map of the minefield has to be my own, and if I have to struggle through the minefield inch by inch in order to draw my map, then how could the teacher tell me what he or she wants? The teacher might show me someone else's successful map from the previous semester (I've sometimes used A papers as models), but by itself it doesn't teach me anything about how to cross a minefield, or about writing. Like it or not, the only way to get your money's worth out of any course of study, including writing, is to pack your first aid kit and start off into the unknown.

Some Tools for the Quest

Although we can't ask our teachers for maps, our teachers can help us to learn to write their assignments. The third thing to learn about writing in school is that teachers are writers, too. Like most of us, most teachers feel that they can't write. That is, most of them do write, many of them write beautifully, and almost all of them share our fear of being embarrassed by our writing.

This shared fear means that they can teach us. It's not likely, however, that we'll be in many classes where the teacher will talk freely about his or her fear of writing; unfortunately, our culture frowns upon the person in authority who admits weakness of any kind, so it's likely that the only teachers who will admit their fear of writing are those who have achieved success in writing. Moreover, in many of our classes, particularly those which are not primarily writing classes, the teacher, even if a successful writer, may feel that there is too little time in the course and too much material to cover to allow him or her to spend time talking about the painful process of writing. So, if you don't hear from your teachers about their own struggles as writers, at least you're hearing about them here.

Why should we care that our teachers share our troubles with writing? First, it means we have something in common, and that's important in any relationship. Second, it proves that our writing difficulties are normal and that these difficulties do not mean that we are less intelligent than others. Third, it can help us ask the teacher questions that can help us get through the minefield. You might ask the following questions:

1. If you were going to write this assignment, what's the first thing you'd do?
2. What problems am I likely to encounter in doing the research for this paper?
3. I've done some thinking about a topic for the paper. Would you tell me your reaction to my idea?
4. I've done some brainstorming for a first draft of the paper. Would

you look at my notes and tell me if I'm on the right track? What should I do next?

5. I've written a first draft of the paper. What's the most important thing I need to do in revising it?

You may look at these questions and say, "I might be able to ask a couple of my teachers questions like these, but I wouldn't dare ask Professors _____ and _____. They'd make me feel like I'm wasting their time and they might take it out on my grade." Or "I'd just be letting them know how stupid I am." I know those excuses because I've used them; I still use them when I'm anxious about approaching someone with an idea or a request that they might not like.

There's just enough truth in those complaints to convince us not to summon up the courage to ask for help. There are a few teachers who don't want to be bothered by students or who will peremptorily label any student question stupid or impertinent. But there are only a few, and we hear about most of them from students who may or may not have tried to talk with them. More valid is the common complaint of teachers that students don't visit them during office hours. It's possible that some teachers unconsciously put off students by their attitude in class, but more often, the students just don't take advantage of this opportunity for learning. I'm always amazed at the number of students who apologize for imposing on me by asking for some comment on their paper idea or their rough draft. I respond by regularly reminding the class about my office hours and my availability after class. This works for many students, yet there are some who feel that using this time is asking me to work overtime. It isn't; colleges and universities require faculty to set aside time (usually at least one hour a week per course) to meet with students outside class. This is precious little time, so it is all the more amazing that so many teachers find it unused.

Overcoming Teacher Anxiety

I know, from my own student years, that another reason students don't approach their teachers for help is fear of criticism. Asking for help implies that I need help, and my pride, my ego, won't let someone in authority tell me that I'm not perfect, even though I know I'm not. Many people, myself included, would rather suffer a bad grade (or a publisher's rejection) than find out what to do to avoid it. It's easy to make up excuses: "she never gives A's," "he doesn't like me," "my teacher [my boss, that editor, that customer] is a jerk." It's hard to ask, "How am I imperfect? How can I improve?" It's hard to risk hearing that the idea you've sweated about and that you think is good may be superficial, headed in the wrong direction, or inaccurate.

Nevertheless, without that risk, without swallowing one's pride, nothing is learned or achieved, particularly in writing. Every good idea will offend someone who thinks differently about it. Every interesting piece of writing is interesting because it tells some truth that would offend someone. Thinkers who play it safe don't think; writers who play it safe are dull, to others and to themselves.

Learning to Ask the Right Questions

Happily, when we risk asking for help (what teachers and parents call *constructive criticism*), we are almost always met with a smile, and with help, if we ask the right questions. What are the right questions to ask about writing? You can answer this by putting yourself in the teacher's position. Imagine that someone asks you for help to do something that you requested or that you are proficient at.

🖎 **EXERCISE:** Briefly visualize such a scene, in writing. Then read on. ■

The person does not ask you to do the job for him or her, but needs to know better how to perform it. You, as the teacher, want to say something useful so that (1) you won't have to do the job yourself and (2) the person will be able to do the job at another time, when you aren't available. But you don't know what the person needs to know. If the person asks you the wrong question, you may give information that won't be useful. If the person asks too general a question, you may be overwhelmed by how long it would take to answer.

🖎 **EXERCISE:** Jot down a wrong question and a too general question that the person in your scene might ask you. ■

The right question gives you information about (1) what the person has already done and (2) what sort of problem the person is having. The questions suggested in Some Tools for the Quest fit this form. All of them focus on one part of the writing process for a particular assignment and three of the five ask for comments on specific aspects of the assignment.

✍ **EXERCISE:** Jot down two or more right questions that the person in your scene might ask. ■

Keep in front of you the scene you've visualized; try to imagine your reaction to the two right questions. What makes them seem right to you? They seem right because (1) the person shows respect for you by thinking and maybe doing some other work before coming to you for help and (2) you'll be able to give the person a fairly clear answer. Even if you're tired or busy, you are willing to take time with the person because you feel that the question is manageable and you appreciate the questioner's respect.

When you ask your teacher a question about your writing, make sure that it's the question you want answered. Don't be embarrassed to ask what you think is a trivial question. For example, when you're editing your revised draft, if you need to know how to punctuate a particular sentence, show it to your teacher and ask for the advice. Don't ask, "Do you know of a grammar book I could read to brush up on my punctuation?" Your teacher may know of such a book (including this one, Chapter 8), but it won't tell you about your sentence as quickly and as surely as your teacher can. Most teachers like to answer such easy questions. Furthermore, there's no need to be embarrassed; every writer has questions like this from time to time.

Don't fail to ask a question just because you've never heard anyone else ask it. For example, if your teacher assigns your class to write an essay on the differences between high school and college and you would rather write a story on the topic, ask if a story would be permissible. Even if the answer is no, the teacher will probably explain the answer in a way that will help you understand the assignment, saying for example, "It's important that you not invent anything. I want you to remember the details of your typical high school day and compare these with college. As a matter of fact, you might telephone a former classmate or visit the school to help your memory." If you feel that you can meet the teacher's requirements and still write in the form of a story, go ahead and say this. At the very least, by pursuing a line of questions that you want answered (as Margaret Ellis did in Chapter 3), you will get even more helpful information. Besides, if your teacher is like me, he or she will be impressed by your interest and originality.

Three Common Questions and When They Are Right

Instead of asking the questions they really need answered, writers frequently ask questions that they've heard other people ask. These are good questions only when the writer really wants these questions answered. Here are three such questions and occasions when they would be pertinent questions or inappropriate questions:

1. How Long Should the Paper Be? Ask how long your paper should be if you suspect that the teacher wants to read a certain number of words. If minimums and maximums are important to the teacher, knowing length can help you to narrow or expand your subject and to decide what details to include. However, asking how long a paper should be will not tell you how important an assignment is, what to write about, or what form—report, story, or essay—to write in. Don't estimate the amount of work involved based on suggested length. Sometimes a short assignment can be more crucial and time-intensive: "your contest entry should be no longer than ten lines of copy," "your proposal should not exceed two single-spaced, typewritten pages." Ask about length, but don't let this question substitute for others.

If you have a lot to say about an idea and want to exceed the suggested length, ask the teacher. I've yet to meet a teacher who thinks a word limit is more important than the thorough exploration of an interesting idea.

2. How Important Is Spelling in This Paper? The question "How important is spelling in this paper?" is like some other common ones, such as "How important is good grammar in this paper?" and "Do I have to type this paper?" Since you've read about the writing process in Chapters 1 and 3, you know that these are appropriate questions in considering what I like to call the deadline draft, the one you submit to a teacher for a grade. (I don't like the term "final draft," because all writings can be revised further.) The typing question is good; because some teachers don't mind reading strange or difficult handwriting, they won't require a typed deadline draft.

The spelling and grammar questions should be asked, too, if the teacher's instructions haven't already answered them. However, these are tough questions for most teachers to answer. Most teachers don't want to say something like "I'll lower your mark one letter grade for each word misspelled or every misplaced comma" because they realize that the quality of research and the logic and originality of thinking are more important than mechanical correctness. They don't want students to feel that the correctly spelled paper is better than the one with brilliant ideas and a few errors. However, most teachers, like most readers, have trouble seeing the brilliance of students who frequently misspell words and use punctuation incorrectly. For instance, every time I have to stop my reading to figure out what word your trying to use or where you're sentence is supposed to end. I lose my concentration. (See what I mean?) If your paper contains many errors, I'll never realize the beauty or logic or excitement of your work. A songwriter would not want his songs recorded by bad musicians; an architect would not want her plans drawn by poor drafters. I wonder if Shakespeare would have been recognized as a genius if his plays had not first been performed by England's best acting company.

Ever since my sophomore year in college (when I had the shocking experience of having an international relations paper graded only on the number of typos), I've assumed that whatever paper I submit, to anyone except my closest friend or relative, should be correctly spelled, punctuated, and proofread. If typed (or word-processed), the paper should be carefully scrutinized for typos at least twice.

Nevertheless, you might ask your teacher about the importance of spelling and grammar if you worry about these aspects of your writing. It's common for teachers to disregard spelling and usage errors in journals and logs. Even on more formal work, you might find that your teacher really isn't bothered by occasional errors, so you can relax a bit. You might find that he or she will overlook errors on one assignment, but will be more critical on another project. Of course, you might find that the teacher is a real stickler for correct spelling and grammar. (I wish that I'd asked if my international relations teacher was!). It is important to know this so you can plan a way to avoid anxiety that could keep you from doing the work. (See Chapter 8, Getting Help with Editing.)

Your teacher can be a valuable resource. If your fear of writing comes from fear of spelling and grammar, consider telling this to your professor. As an English teacher, I discover again and again how fearful most people, including some teachers, are about their inability to spell and use correct grammar. If you confide in your teacher, you will find that he or she will empathize and will, if you ask, give you advice for improving your writing, or at least your state of mind. Remember, the teacher would rather have you complete the work of the course than be stymied by your fear of the language.

Don't wait until you get your paper or exam back with a lowered grade to start thinking about spelling and grammar questions. Many writers have been surprised to find, as I was in my first years of college, that sometimes the most strict graders of English mechanics are the faculty in departments other than English. Over the years, teacher after teacher, from history to engineering to music, has told me of the angry student who has complained, "How can you count off for spelling? This isn't English class." Perhaps no one has told this writer that one purpose of the English course has been to prepare him or her for the writing requirements in courses to follow. Perhaps no one has told the writer that the teacher's concern for precise usage comes from the knowledge that anyone, regardless of major, who goes into a profession must write. Perhaps, finally, the student has been misled by other teachers who have not required careful prose, or any writing at all. The student may have mistakenly imagined that careful, mechanically correct writing was important only in the English class and to the English teacher.

3. Do I Need to Summarize the Book? The question "Do I need to summarize the book?" (or the plot, the lecture, or the experiment) with its implied second part, "or should I assume that you know what I'm talking about?" is a great question, because many assignments require writers to relate information from their reading, lectures, or experiments to other reading, lectures, or experiments. It's a great question, because your teacher may not be aware of what you know and may want you to demonstrate your knowledge by summarizing the material. It's a great question, except that it's almost impossible to answer clearly.

As a teacher, I cringe when I hear this question, because how much a writer should say depends on what he or she does say. Suppose you say to me, "You should go outside and look at the sky. It looks like it's going to rain any minute." Chances are I'll know how you came to that conclusion, so I won't ask you to summarize what you saw and how you analyzed it. On the other hand, if you say to me, "You should go outside and look at the sky. It looks like it's going to rain tomorrow," chances are that I'll ask you to tell me what you saw and how you arrived at your prediction.

The answer to the question also depends on who you are. In other words, my answer to the student depends on what I already know about the student. In Chapter 3, I stressed the point that your writing is part of a network of communications by which you build relationships with people. The same is true here. Indeed, it may be more true of the writing you do for teachers. As I get to know the writers in my classes, as I read their writing and hear them speak in class discussions, I build expectations about how well they'll write and about how much they know. By the end of the semester, when I read their last essays, stories, or reports, I have a pretty clear sense of what I can assume about each person. So if your speaking and your writing have consistently shown that you are articulate and that you've read and thought conscientiously, then even before I begin reading your final paper I assume that you know what you're talking about. Conversely, the writer who hasn't contributed to discussion and whose writing has been superficial or inaccurate will have to show me more on the last paper.

This may not sound fair; it isn't. But it is a fact that none of the people to whom we write, teachers, friends, relatives, editors, bosses, public officials, clients, personnel directors, and so on, make the same assumptions about every person who writes to them. We always demand more proof from some writers than from others.

So instead of asking the teacher how much will be assumed

about your knowledge of the reading, the lecture, or the experiment, show the teacher that he or she can safely assume that you know a lot and want to know more. Do the reading and do it well (see Chapters 2 and 6), add your ideas to class discussion, and ask thoughtful questions to create a climate in which your writing will be well received.

Putting Your Best Questions Forward

A better way to find out what your teacher will and won't assume is to ask the process questions on page 128, questions 2, 3, and 4 in particular:

- What problems am I likely to encounter in doing the research for this paper?
- I've done some thinking about a topic for the paper. Would you tell me your reaction to my idea?
- I've done some brainstorming for a first draft of the paper. Would you look at my notes and tell me if I'm on the right track? What should I do next?

Generally, the advice you get from a teacher, or any other reader, will be more specific if the reader has something definite to respond to, whether it's a written statement of your topic, your written thoughts (brainstorming), or your initial draft. If you're concerned about how much the teacher assumes about your knowledge, ask the question you need answered (such as "Do I need to describe the stages of precipitation here?" or "Do I need to state why Polonius is hiding?")

   Showing the teacher a piece of your writing and getting feedback about it is so important to writing successfully in school that it should be stated as a golden rule of writing:

WRITE FIRST; SHOW THE WRITING TO YOUR READER;
ASK THE QUESTIONS YOU NEED ANSWERED.

EXERCISE: Think of some other common questions that writers ask about their writing or about school writing assignments. For each, consider when it might be a pertinent question, when it might be inappropriate, and when it might be too general. (The objective is to improve your questioning, to get better feedback from your reader.) ∎

GETTING HELP FROM FRIENDS, RELATIVES, AND FELLOW STUDENTS

But my parents liked it.

—The author after receiving a D
on a freshman literature paper

In most school situations, we write when the teacher tells us to and hope to win the teacher's approval. I've devoted the first pages of this chapter, "Writing for the Teacher," to your understanding of the teacher's role as a source of help. However, if the main goal, as I said earlier, of school writing is learning, then the long, frustrating, creative hours you spend on your writing must give you personal satisfaction apart from the teacher's approval. As you become more confident in your writing, approval from others will mean less, because the most important person, you, will approve. Indeed, writing with confidence means that personal enjoyment and understanding become your goals, whether your readers agree with your views or enjoy your language.

Ironically, as we grow less dependent on others for our self-esteem, others tend to like us, and what we create, more. The Little League players who turn their heads to see if their parents are smiling or frowning miss the pitch, while the players who concentrate on the ball hit it and win the smiles. The same is true of writing. Indeed, one can't mature as a writer unless he or she grows quite fearless of disapproval or antagonism from others. As I noted before, interesting writing always risks offending someone. This doesn't mean that the writer deliberately looks for a fight, by taking a sarcastic, belligerent tone. It means that your or my view of the truth, no matter how carefully objective we strive to be, will inevitably conflict with someone else's.

I mention this here because maturing as a writer in school means that sooner or later you will have to risk conflicting with a teacher's views. If you've read my suggestions about how to get guidance from your teacher, you may have imagined yourself in the obsequious position of pleasing the professor to get a high grade. However, no matter how conscientiously you seek your professors' advice, no one will ever take notice of your writing unless you tell the truth as you see it. You'll never enjoy your writing unless you express yourself freely and you'll never learn by writing unless you feel this freedom.

Freedom can be terrifying and lonely if it only means opposing others. Fortunately, the ideal of most colleges and universities is to foster freedom within an atmosphere of tolerance. People openly debate opposing political and religious views; they suggest and explore different methods of teaching, building bridges, and analyzing the movements of the stars; they measure achievements by different standards of excellence. Within free universities set up on a scientific model, faculty are trained to tolerate many points of view, to test all of them fairly but rigorously, and to draw conclusions based on evidence, not on the imposed will of anyone. Most teachers practice these principles; thus, when they criticize an essay, it is not the position or conclusions that they consider but the care and precision with which the writer gathers, thinks about, and uses information to establish a point of view. Most college teachers, regardless of their fields, will tell you, "I won't lower your grade because of your views, but I will lower your grade if your reasoning isn't logical or you don't provide evidence." One of the most exciting discoveries of college is that scholars hold widely different convictions on important issues, such as nuclear disarmament or social equality, but still respect the care and thoroughness in one another's work. From my own college days, I recall the lengthy and heated debates about the fighting in Southeast Asia and about the students' right to protest, sometimes violently, against U.S. foreign policy. I now treasure the freedom to debate and I try as a teacher, as do all the other teachers I know, to preserve this freedom for students.

Of course, because no one can be completely objective, no teacher can *always* regard all arguments with equal favor, even if each viewpoint is presented with equal care for logic and evidence. It is likely that if you express yourself honestly you will conflict with at least one of your teachers. If you do, you will need to call on other resources to sustain your confidence.

The Helping Reader

What do other writers do? Every good writer I know of turns to at least one other person, usually another writer, for good advice, for the push to keep writing amidst distractions, and for comforting words to cope with rejected manuscripts, rejected proposals, and bad reviews. This advisor should have two traits: first, the ability, including the courage, to help the writer improve a manuscript, and second, the sensitivity to understand the type of response the writer needs on a given day. Unfortunately, very few people are trained as constructive writing critics because only recently have schools begun to pay attention to how successful writers work. So, if you want the advantage of a good reader's advice and moral support, you'll have to take the initiative and train your friend, parent, co-worker, or classmate to be the reader you need.

First, you have to train yourself. It's just as fine an art to know how to ask for and react to help as it is to know how to give it. In the old story, a writer says to a friend, "Would you read my paper and tell me what's wrong with it? Don't worry; you won't hurt my feelings." But when the friend says, "I don't understand your main point and I think your conclusion could be stronger," the writer exclaims, "How do you know? You're not so great a writer your-self!" Whereupon the friend yells, "So get someone else to read your stupid paper," and stomps out of the room. The point is that we have to know what we want from a helping reader and, again, ask the right questions. Beyond this, we have to listen to our reader, so that we don't hear more or less than is said. And above all, we have to remember that we asked for the criticism. Happily, most writing groups are mutual support groups: there's an unspoken agreement to read each other's work. Whether we talk about my writing or yours we learn more about how to ask for, give, react to, and use help.

Asking for Help

Though we focus again on asking the right questions, getting help from a writing group differs from getting help from a teacher in that we expect the group to give moral support. On a day when the words won't come and the deadline is looming, we can't expect the teacher to agree that the assignment is silly, the course is crazy, and the deadline should be extended. But we can expect our group members to listen to our gripes patiently and to say a few kind words such as "How can I help?" After all, we'll listen to them on their down days and work with them through the hard task of revision.

Moral support is the first job of the helping reader. Take it for granted that anyone who asks you to read and comment on writing wants some form of support, if only specific ideas for improving the piece. The reader in the little story didn't realize this, just as the writer didn't admit that he or she wanted praise. Try to give praise that doesn't sound empty or patronizing—we all know how it feels to hear "That's good" as if it includes "OK, now don't bother me anymore." Remember how much harder it is to come right out and ask for praise. We usually won't do this unless we're desperate: "Isn't there anything you like about it?"

Most teachers of writing are taught that every piece should be praised specifically in some way so that the writer knows what strengths to build on. This is good advice for helping readers. Keep this in mind, because, as the well-known teacher and writer Peter Elbow points out in *Writing Without Teachers*, we have a cultural tendency to criticize first and praise later, or never. Finding features to praise may be difficult at first, but it gets easier with practice. Actually, if you are willing to find something positive, finding it is simple. The reader in the story could have begun the critique positively by saying, "Your conclusion seems right on target. In fact, I'd make it even more emphatic," instead of negatively saying, "Your conclusion could be stronger." The statement would have been no less honest, it would have been more helpful, and it would have made the writer feel good.

The writer's role is to ask directly for moral support. You needn't say, "Praise me! Praise me! All I want is praise!" To get some sugar with your medicine, say something like "What's working well in this draft?" or "What's strong here? What can I build on?" Never tell your helping readers just to be critical, because (1) you probably don't want only criticism, (2) you deprive your friends of something they like to do, which is give praise, and (3) you imply that you don't trust praise they've given before.

Besides moral support, what every writer wants from a group is ideas. Depending on the stage in the writing process, the writer wants ideas for topics, for getting unstuck, for connecting A with B, for the right word in the key sentence. Here the reader's role is closer to the teacher's, so the right questions are largely the same as those discussed earlier (p. 128). However, don't rely on the group's advice in place of the teacher's merely because the group is more accessible or more supportive. The quotation at the beginning of this section illustrates a mistake that I made as a freshman when I shared drafts of papers with my parents. As constructive critics, my parents were at a disadvantage because I told them nothing about my professor and little about my assignments; and I asked them only the worst and most general question: "What do you think of this?" I should have listened to the little voice inside telling me that I was looking for an excuse to avoid revising. Instead, I basked in the praise I knew they'd give: "I can't believe how smart you are. Look at all the big words you can use." If I'd listened carefully to what they said, I would have been concerned that my big words got in the way of my meaning, and I would have been able to learn from their response. But I didn't follow up with the right questions and, more important, I didn't realize that I should have been asking the professor questions as well.

🖎 **EXERCISE:** Write about your own experiences seeking praise and/or constructive criticism. What methods have you developed (or do you admire) to get the encouragement and advice you need to hear? What keeps you from asking for the help you need? ∎

The Other Trap and How to Avoid It

In asking for help with ideas, beware of the other trap into which you can fall. The purpose of the group is to stimulate your thinking, to give you benefit of others' knowledge and unique ways of looking at something. But the group is not there to do the work for you, nor to make you throw away your ideas in favor of theirs. That's why it's essential to bring to every group meeting (1) something you've written, and (2) an open, but discriminating mind.

Something You've Written. Something you've written can be as much as a full draft or as little as a few free-written notes. Bringing a piece of your text, no matter how small, assures your helping readers that you have made some investment of thought, if not time, in the project. Moreover, as it does for the teacher, the sample text gives the readers something concrete to respond to and gives you something concrete to ask your reader questions about.

An Open, but Discriminating Mind. You must have an open mind, but you also must be discriminating about suggestions you receive. If you bring nothing for your helping readers to read and have only vague images about an idea that you might like to write about, don't be surprised if your helpers, if they have good imaginations, take off with your vague idea in their own directions leaving you confused by their sincere attempts to help. The best thing your helping readers can do is to tell you to write down your thoughts and bring your writing to the group. The second best thing is to keep you talking about your idea so that you begin to give some shape, some words, to your idea. If you do bring some text to the meeting, good readers will give some advice that you can use and much that will be confusing or that might work for them and not you. Moreover, every helping reader will give you somewhat different, sometimes contradictory advice. (I recently took part in a writing group meeting in which a member and I told a colleague to cut a certain sentence. A fourth member, who arrived late, told the writer that that sentence was the best one in the entire draft!)

Remember, although the helpers give you their ideas, you are not obliged to use them. Remember, too, that most readers' comments are spontaneous, sincere, but not tested. The best that happens in writing groups is that someone says something that sparks your imagination ("Aha!" you'll think, "that gives me an idea for how to start the paper" or "Yes, the meaning is clearer if I switch the third and fourth sentences"). Readers don't expect that you'll follow all their advice, nor do they want that kind of responsibility for your work. In years of training and working with writing groups, I've found that readers are flattered if anything they say to a fellow writer makes its way, in any form, into a future draft. People won't be offended if you don't use their suggestions, and you shouldn't be offended if they don't use yours.

You must also bring a third thing to your helping reader or group: persistence. Many students I know find that their group meetings are a waste of time because they don't push their readers to talk. They give up on their group or on certain members because the words don't come easily. But giving good feedback is hard work: it takes imagination to think of other ways to phrase a thought, other angles to explore, and other facts to bring in. It takes tact and caring to give constructive criticism without injuring the writer's confidence. In essence, it takes concentrated time to read other peoples' manuscripts. Since most of us like to avoid hard work, we have to show that we really want the other person's comments. For example, if your reader's comments are vague (such as "I really like what you've done so far"), ask precise questions: "Would you show me one sentence you really like? Why do you like it?" Or share with the reader a concrete problem you're having and ask the reader how he or she would solve it, for example, "My professor said that we had to show original thinking in this paper. I'm worried that my conclusion is off the wall. Can you help me figure out how to show that my conclusion follows from what I've already written?"

Sometimes a reader doubts his or her competence to comment on your writing, saying perhaps, "I don't think I'll be able to help. I haven't taken that course. Besides, I'm not that good a writer myself." Whether readers put these fears into words or not, they all feel them from time to time, so it's a good practice for you to let them know why you value their feedback. Perhaps they know the teacher well; perhaps they have written papers on a similar topic or in a similar form; or perhaps you just respect their conscientiousness and judgment. Moreover, you can and should assure the readers that you won't blame them if their advice isn't exactly what you need.

Some Starter Questions for Helping Readers

Besides the questions noted throughout the chapter, here are some others that can help you get started. I include them because they are frequently used with success for school paper assignments. All of them assume that the reader has a piece of your writing to look at. All ask the reader to say something without demanding whether your writing is good or bad.

Note that the questions require more than a simple yes or no answer. This is crucial; yes or no answers provide no information. The reader can answer a question such as "Do you think my writing is clear?" with a safe, vague, "Yes." If you rephrase the question and ask, "Where is my writing most clear to you? Where is it less clear?" you force the reader to give you definite information.

1. What do you feel are the two or three main ideas in this writing? Which one seems to be the most important?

2. What knowledge or experience do I assume my reader has? Show me one or two places where I might need to explain or describe something more.
3. What's the most vivid (or surprising) statement (or phrase or word) in my draft? Why does it stand out?
4. From reading this draft, what do you think might be a good title for the paper?
5. I'm really concerned about the flow of this paper. Would you point out a place where I need to strengthen the connection of ideas?
6. If I were going to write another paper on this topic, what would you like me to write more about?

These questions are good because they push the reader to read closely and to perform concrete, clear tasks; they are bad because they're not specific to any particular paper. Your questions will have the same virtues, but they'll be better because they'll relate directly to your assignment, your audience, and your words.

🖎 **EXERCISE:** Read through your latest draft of an assignment. (If you haven't written anything yet on the assignment, take the time now to do some focused freewriting.) As you read, mark places where you have some concern about accuracy, clarity, logic, or grammar. Formulate a question that pertains to each of the marks. Formulate each question as if you were going to ask it to a helping reader. Make sure that each question (1) draws the reader to the actual text, (2) doesn't ask for a good or bad judgment of your writing, and (3) can't be answered with a simple yes or no. ∎

SOME SPECIAL CONDITIONS OF COLLEGE WRITING

The writing done in college is similar to the writing done anywhere else. It is no more real or unreal than the writing done anywhere else. College teachers are no more or less sympathetic to you as a writer than are the bosses, clients, editors, public officials, friends, and relatives that you write to. However, the college environment offers special conditions and situations that you are not likely to encounter elsewhere. I'll describe some of these and suggest ways to think about and cope with them.

Large Classes

The larger the class, usually the less comfortable students feel about approaching the teacher with questions. In a large class, the teacher is less likely to invite students to bring their drafts in for review and even less likely to set up a schedule of individual conferences for this purpose. This does not mean, however, that the instructor is unwilling or too busy to take time with individual students.

Not surprisingly, most teachers dislike large classes because they do not know whether they are reaching people with whom they can't converse. Because of the problem of communication, many large classes turn into lectures, in which the professor speaks or reads notes and the students copy down what they hear. Although the teacher may ask for questions about the lecture, usually no questions are asked, even though the students may not understand a key point or how the material applies to anything else. Students would ask questions if they felt that the professor would respond approvingly. But the lack of a student-teacher relationship in large classes make such a feeling unlikely.

Because of the greater distance between teacher and student, reader and writer, in a large class, it's especially important for you, the writer, to bridge the gap. Otherwise, you may experience feelings of isolation and confusion that will inhibit your writing and studying.

If a student doesn't bridge the gap, it's likely that any writing the student does will be safe writing; that is, reporting back to the teacher what has been said in the lecture or the textbook. This strategy works only if an assignment asks for straight reporting. (Essay questions on tests can be like this; for example, "State and define in one sentence each of the five institutions that are common to all reproducing societies.") But a safe writer will stumble if an assignment asks the writer "to draw your own conclusions," "state your opinion of this article and provide evidence to support it," or "show the similarities and differences you perceive between these two interpretations." Many students get angry with such questions because they have no idea what conclusions or opinions the teacher might find acceptable. They often search their notes and assigned reading to paraphrase the teacher's or the author's opinions. But the teacher wants the writer to think originally, to learn, so the safe strategy is really unsafe. The student-writer who follows the questioning approaches outlined earlier in the chapter has the advantage.

Bridging the gap in a large class requires courage. If no one else asks questions, it's hard to ask the first one. When everyone else assumes that the teacher is unreachable and doesn't want to be bothered, it's hard to make an appointment. Groups tend to build strong myths about why conditions can't improve. However, people in large classes learn to write successfully and confidently either because they won't tolerate the isolation and anxiety or because they have the mutual support of a few friends, perhaps their helping readers.

✍ **EXERCISE:** Write about your experiences writing in a large class. Did you bridge the gap between student and instructor? How? Were you confident about your writing in that class? Why or why not? ∎

Teaching Assistants and Graders

You may be surprised to discover, as I did in my first year in college, that much of your writing is graded by someone other than the professor, usually a graduate student who is earning money—and gaining valuable job experience—as a teaching assistant or grader. Sometimes the assistant has other course responsibilities, including lecturing or leading of discussion groups. Frequently, however, the assistant is paid only to grade tests and papers, and is anonymous, sitting in class, taking notes like the rest of the students. (I know, because I did this as a graduate student.) A teaching assistant (TA) will not read your paper the same way your professor would; TA's exercise independent judgment and their standards may differ significantly from the professor's. So, if your writing is being judged by a TA, approach the TA as you would the teacher, with ideas and drafts, plus questions to help you think and revise. Like professors, TA's have office hours. Use them before the deadline draft of your paper is due.

✍ **EXERCISE:** Have you written in classes in which a TA, not the professor, graded your writing? Describe your writing process in these classes. How did you get advice and feedback? ∎

Cheating and Plagiarism

Although only some colleges maintain formal honor codes, by which students agree not to cheat and to report the cheating of others, all schools depend for their success on the students' and teachers' honesty. We can't learn without thinking for ourselves, using our imaginations, and struggling as writers and speakers to express meaning in our own words. This does not mean that we can't discuss our papers or the results of our lab experiments with our fellow students. After all, the major premise of this book, and the major premise of schools, is that we learn best together, sharing our discoveries and our successful ways of learning. Whenever we write to others, we share. Moreover, when we write, even for ourselves, we depend on other people's ideas and words. We do this consciously when we quote other authors or paraphrase, report in our own words, what other people say; we do it unconsciously when we use an idea that we have heard somewhere or that may have come from our own thinking. Sometimes we make tacit use of other people's ideas. Throughout this book, for example, I write about ideas that others have written about in other books, in professional journals, or in handouts they've prepared for their students. Indeed, you might not be reading this book unless a teacher or committee had found it very similar to their own ideas about writing. We call these shared ideas common knowledge or current thinking. We don't consider use of them cheating or plagiarism because they are not the exclusive property of a single writer.

In business, plagiarism, or infringing on a copyright, is a matter of law. Courts decide claims and there are no easy rules. In school, the usual definition of *plagiarism* is "passing off someone else's work as your own"; but where do you draw the line between the help a helping reader has given you and plagiarism? Because colleges do not maintain forces of plagiarism police to regulate your asking of help, monitoring your use of ideas is ultimately up to you, with the help of your teachers and fellow students.

Here are some general rules to follow:

1. *Always credit your sources.* If any of your data or any of your opinions about data come from a printed source or from a person whom you consult, give that printed source or that person credit

in your paper. Footnote as frequently as you need to. (There are many footnoting styles; see Chapter 7, p. 302.) If you're worried about over-footnoting or about the need to give credit for a particular statement, ask your instructor a specific question. Also, don't hesitate to credit nonprofessional sources such as your friends or your parents. If their data are reliable and if you are presenting ideas they've contributed, credit them.

2. *You usually need not credit the help you get with organizing your paper or with editing the paper for spelling, punctuation, and grammar, but check with your instructor.* It is customary in large companies and in government, especially when documents are to be published, that documents be reviewed and edited by someone other than the author. It is clearly not plagiarism for writers to get help with organization and style from anyone they can. In school, however, the rules are sometimes different, particularly in a writing class. Most writing teachers, especially in courses that meet the English composition requirement, will evaluate your work based in part on your ability to apply the rules and conventions of Standard Written English (see Chapter 8). If you rely heavily on another person to spell and punctuate your language or to correct your errors in use of Standard Written English and if your teacher does not know of this help, you may be misrepresenting yourself. Check with your instructor, regardless of the level of the course or the department in which you are taking it.

   Note: Teachers often suspect plagiarism of those students whose papers contain better spelling and syntax than their in-class exams and other writing assignments. It is very important for teachers to know if their students receive substantial help with this type of editing.

3. *Always remember that the primary goal of writing in school is learning.* The help you get from any person, group of helping readers, or published source should stimulate your thinking and your writing. If you copy large chunks of someone's article into your text, or if you let a helping reader write large chunks of your paper for you, you are not learning from your writing, and you are probably plagiarizing as well.

Grades

Becoming a slave to grades is one of the easiest and most dangerous traps to fall into for the writer. Certainly every writer in college is grade conscious. Even when a writer loves to write, grades give the writer incentive to meet deadlines, to read that difficult article or book, and to ask helping readers to look at the manuscript one more time. Grades give students the incentive that promotions or profits give the professional writer.

But grades must be kept in perspective. Assigning a piece of writing a letter or a number is inappropriate to the purposes of writing. As described in Chapters 1 and 2, writing is communicating and thinking. As communication, writing is valuable to convince readers to do or feel what the author wants them to. As thinking, writing is valuable to push the writer to see things in new ways, as more exciting or beautiful. The real grade of a written work, whether a memo, research paper, poem, or diary entry, is the effect it has.

Consequently, every writing teacher I've ever met admits to having difficulties assigning grades. Most give grades because the educational system requires them. But most teachers believe grades hurt more than help the development of writers. People tend to think that the writing process is finished when a grade is given; whereas they should think of writing as a part of an infinite process of thought and building relationships. Students often look at their grades and ignore the reader's comments about how to improve the paper; yet it is through the comments and in conference that communication occurs. In the job world, the memo writer would never ignore the reader's comments because those comments can tell the writer how to change office policy, improve sales, build morale, and so on.

Moreover, grades mislead a student into thinking that there is some perfect A+ paper against which this one is compared. They also mislead students into thinking that there must be a clear list of criteria that define the differences from A to F. When students ask to see a model paper no wonder they are disappointed when the A paper doesn't show them how to write their own papers. If the interest in grades were replaced by an understanding of writing as communicating, students would not make this request and would avoid the disappointment.

Because grades can lead students to make simple, drastic judgments about themselves as writers teachers often give high grades so the students won't become so discouraged that they stop writing. Teachers often give low grades to other students who seem pompous or complacent and no longer use their writing to develop their thinking. Grades given under these circumstances have nothing or little to do with the value of a given piece of writing.

Finally, grades cause writers to focus on the piece of writing rather than on the skill or craft of writing. Because the grade appears on the so-called final draft (note the illusion that the process of writing comes to an end), writers are misled into thinking that this document, in itself, is more important than the notes, the freewriting, the questions, the revising, or the comments by helping readers that have gone into it. Even worse, the document appears more important than the learning and the experience achieved through the process, though it is the learning and the experience, regardless of the grade, that is valuable for future class assignments or in one's career.

Teachers try to correct the wrong impressions grading causes. Some give no grades except a final grade. Others give a grade on each step of a writing process; for example, they mark students for discovery drafts or for participation in helping groups. More and more teachers use portfolio grading, by which students receive one grade at the end of the term, for all or a selected portion of their writing.

Whatever methods of grading are encountered, it is vital that the students be independent of other people's imprecise or misleading judgments. Ultimately, you'll write if you enjoy it, and you'll write successfully if you enjoy it.

EXERCISE: Select a brief essay from any printed source (such as a newspaper editorial, a report in a weekly news magazine). Note every statement that is directly quoted from another source; note places where the writer credits another source for a statistic or an opinion. Of the remaining statements in the essay, which do you feel are original? Which seem to be from other sources but not credited? Do these seem to be common knowledge or current thinking? Can you identify uncredited statements that you think should have been credited to someone? ■

✍ **EXERCISE:** Freewrite about your own grade-consciousness. When has a grade boosted your confidence? When has it inhibited you? When has a grade been irrelevant to your incentive to complete a project? Consider a time when your pleasure and incentive did not depend on someone's approval or disapproval. Where did the pleasure and incentive come from? ■

✍ **EXERCISE:** Freewrite about conditions in your writing environment that inhibit your ability to write well and confidently. Consider each condition; brainstorm one or two reasons why it causes a problem. Then, speculate on possible solutions involving either a course of action or a change of attitude on your part. (If possible, share your freewriting and brainstorming with other writers and exchange suggestions.) ■

Case Study: A Successful College Writer

Ann Jeffries began classes at the local public college one semester after completing high school. Three and a half years later, one semester short of receiving a history degree, she married and moved from Virginia to Illinois, where her first son was born. While in Illinois, she began a diploma program in obstetric nursing, a field about which she had become intensely interested after the birth of her son. Three years later, halfway through the nursing program, she moved with her family back to Virginia. She completed the final semester of her history degree and began a Bachelor of Science program in nursing, aiming to practice as an obstetric nurse. By transferring some of her science credits from the Illinois school, Ann was able to complete her nursing degree in three years. Since receiving her degree, she has worked as a psychiatric nurse, an obstetric nurse, and a childbirth educator. In addition to raising her four children, she writes professional articles and fiction about childbirth, family life, and education and serves as contributing editor of a magazine for young families. Of writing she says, "I can't imagine anything more important, if you value the life you live."

As an eighteen-year-old college student, Ann recalls, she did not lack confidence in her writing. She credits a high school English teacher for helping her achieve self-esteem: "She was an interested reader. I remember her spending time with me after school to go over my papers, because she felt that I had promise." She also recalls a sixth grade teacher, who taught her something about revision, though this was years before teachers commonly spoke about the process of writing. "Mr. Robins of Cooper School—we always wrote two drafts of our book reports for him—a 'pencil' copy and an 'ink' copy. He'd go over our 'pencil' copies, write a suggestion, and mark our spelling and punctuation errors. Then we had a chance to add things and correct our errors. Only then would he give us grades."

Despite her confidence as a writer when she entered college, Ann found that writing papers for English and history classes was largely a guessing game. "That was a few years before teachers began emphasizing revision, and teachers never encouraged us to ask questions about assignments or to bring in drafts. No one that I knew had ever heard of students considering one another's papers. We were just given the assignments and the deadlines. Then we were on our own. It never dawned on any of us to use the teacher as a resource during paper writing, because the teacher never offered." She does recall asking for help on one occasion: "My English professor had assigned us to write a critical paper on the Greek play *Medea,* and I was totally blocked. So I took my notes to my teacher and asked him for comments on my idea. I don't recall exactly what he said, but I do know that the conference definitely helped me get through the paper."

Fortunately, that same English teacher introduced her to journal-keeping, which gave her a way to play with ideas and styles without having to fear the teacher's disapproval. "I loved writing my journal because of the freedom to explore my theories about the books we were reading and to relate what we were doing in class to other books and to events. He read the journals totally differently than he read our papers. There were no grades on the journals, except for just doing it, and he wrote questions and comments that showed his interest. I felt able to 'talk' with him in the journal in a way I could not in the papers."

The journal reinforced her confidence. When she reached upper-level courses in her major, she stopped worrying about how her professors might react to her writing. "No one had ever taught me 'how' a person is 'supposed to' write a paper—all that about thesis statements and body paragraphs and transition words. I learned to write strong papers by reading a lot of history and essays, and by writing a lot about what I read. That taught me. I'd revise and revise my papers until, to me, they sparkled. I can't tell you how I knew, but I knew that they were good. I don't mean to say that my professors always agreed with me (though they usually did), but I didn't worry about their reactions, because I felt good about my work. I had revised until I had discovered something meaningful to me in the reading or the lectures; I then revised some more until I felt that I had expressed that meaning."

When she began her nursing studies, Ann found the writing to be constant and enjoyable. "I'd entered nursing school out of my joy over the birth of my son, and out of my desire to help other mothers experience that joy. I considered all the writing an opportunity to learn and a further opportunity to express my excitement. I had no doubt that all my teachers would love my care plans and research papers, because I knew that my excitement would show through in the amount of work I did, the kinds of questions I'd ask, and the ideas I'd discover. And I was right!"

This did not mean that all of the writing was easy. Her efforts to make her data precisely accurate and her writing sparkle sometimes meant days of revision or successions of phone calls and library explorations to track down a detail that existed in a back issue of an obscure medical journal possessed by only one hospital library miles away. But this, too, was fun. "I'd call a library expecting the staff to be indifferent to my request, and find that the librarian would get as intrigued by the 'puzzle' as I was. Sometimes they'd discover in their own libraries resources that they didn't know they had." Other times Ann would run into roadblocks, such as the discovery two days before a project was due that the article most essential to her topic had been stolen from the library. "Usually I could track down something almost as useful, but I recall once having to change my topic just enough so that I wouldn't need the article I'd counted on."

As a meticulous reviser, Ann would, and does, cover page after page with longhand paragraphs to which she adds cross-outs, marginal notes, winding arrows, and notes to herself between the lines. Sometimes she switches to the typewriter for a later draft, "in order to get a different perspective." Recently, she has begun to do her later drafts on a word processor, which makes it possible for her to revise just as much, and to avoid having to retype into final copy.

While in nursing school, Ann remembers, her confidence was such that she never felt the need for another student's views on her work. Nevertheless, she would spend considerable time on the phone with fellow students, two in particular, exchanging ideas about the kinds of data the teacher might find important. They'd give another kind of help, too: "One of the requirements of our assessment and treatment papers (written about patients we had worked with) was that we include citations from articles or books to back up our opinions. If time was short, and it usually was, we'd ask each other for good quotes to use. Of course, I knew that getting this kind of help defeated the purpose of the requirement—which was to get us to read the literature—but it was an easy way to finish this part of the work. Luckily, the most important work for these papers—giving nursing care and designing care plans—we always did completely on our own. From these papers and diaries I kept as a student, I learned to be precise and full in my observations. This was one of the most important skills I learned for nursing—and for writing."

While still a nursing student, Ann wrote pieces that would become her first publications. "In my senior diary in psychiatric nursing, I wrote a poem, called 'Someone of Significance,' about one of my patients, a teenage boy. I wrote it really for my professor, as a kind of gift, because I knew she would like it. She did, and encouraged me to send it to a nursing journal, *Perspectives in Psychiatric Care*, that sometimes printed poetry." Also in her senior year, she followed up on another teacher's enthusiasm for her survey of patient attitudes toward midwives and obstetricians. "I took my professor's suggestion that I write a much-shortened abstract of the study for the research section of *The American Journal of Nursing*. I'd never written an abstract, so I had no idea how to proceed. Thankfully, the people at the magazine knew exactly what they wanted—they sent me a detailed format that I filled in with data and conclusions from the study. Even so, it went back and forth several times, with their asking questions and my making revisions, until I got it the way that they wanted it. But that's what writing's all about. If it hadn't been for my teachers' encouragement, I don't know how I would have learned these lessons, or had the inclination to try to get my writing into print."

After graduation, when Ann took her first professional job as a psychiatric nurse in an adolescent unit at a private hospital, she learned other hard lessons about writing. She found that her college writing experience had both prepared her and misled her. "As a student, I'd had maybe two patients a week to work with and write about, and usually a few days to get my assessment-and-treatment papers done. Suddenly, here I was on a 3:00-P.M.-to-11:00-P.M. shift, in charge of twenty-three to twenty-nine patients whose charts had to be accurately updated. Because I'd be so busy during the shift, I'd never get to my share of the charts until 11—when I was supposed to be off work! My endless papers in the nursing program had taught me how to observe closely and how to analyze what I'd seen, heard, felt, etc. But they hadn't prepared me for the caseload or the exhausted condition in which I'd be writing. It was on the job that I learned speed; I learned to identify the few most important facts that the next shift had to know about each patient. Because I had so many patients, I also learned to take quick notes during the shift (I kept the notes in my pocket), so I wouldn't forget important things. Needless to say, I also pretty quickly learned the jargon and the shorthand that would communicate with the other staff members— it's pretty unintelligible to anyone else. And I always had to keep aware that what I was so hurriedly writing could be used as evidence in court, in the event of a malpractice suit—so I couldn't afford too many shortcuts." She says that as a student she had noticed how brief the professional nurses' notes were in comparison with the detailed plans she was taught to write, but she realizes that she could not have learned the professional style except on the job. "Like any other kind of writing, you learn to do it with practice. I was slow at it at first, but if you write enough charts and read enough charts, it's amazing what you can learn to do."

The confidence and practice Ann gained as a college writer and later on the job have helped her in the types of writing she has done recently. In the past two years she has written biographical sketches, charts and handouts for her childbirth classes, lyric poems, questionnaires, reports of surveys, personal essays on family life, research articles, interviews, and, most recently, short fiction, not to mention letters to friends and diaries she is keeping for her children. "There's probably nothing I'm not willing to try. I know I can do well eventually at anything I undertake." Moreover, she sees close connections among all the forms and topics she tries. For example, her interest in history, her first college major, is more intense than ever even though she has not for years written what most people would call historical articles. "Everything I write comes out of my need to capture the present, to save it and to savor it. If I don't write, I'm depressed, because I feel that events are being lost." She feels that the discipline of observation she practiced in her nursing papers and course diaries has helped her meet this need. "The most important writing I do is my diaries for the boys, and the writing is very concrete, full of ideas of all kinds: the exact time, the clothes we are wearing, the color of the sunlight on the walls. I am writing the diaries for the boys to read when they are grown. In my mind, I can see them reading the diaries and I want them to feel, 'Oh, yes, I remember exactly how it was!' " As she did as a nurse during her shift, she is always making notes to herself of items, new achievements, tender moments, to include in the diaries. "I like calendars with big spaces for each day, so I can jot down words, phrases, and milestones."

She also feels that she has a common purpose for all her writing, from the diaries to the interview articles to the screenplay she is planning to attempt: "That's easy—I want my reader to think! It's getting harder and harder for all of us to keep from being swept along by fads and mass ideas. Whatever I've written about, whether midwifery or patients' responsibilities or parents' teaching their children at home, I've always wanted my reader to know that there's more than one way to feel, more than one way to do things. I suppose one could define writing that 'sparkles' as writing that makes one think. That was what I loved about the books that I read in literature classes and that I wrote about in my English journal.

That's still what I look for in my reading and what I want to achieve in my writing."

If she writes to preserve the present and if the purpose of her writing is to make her readers think, then the fun in her writing is its promise of discovery and learning. "Writing forces me, but it also frees me, to think. Writers have to keep growing. I get tired of writing the same types of articles. I've begun writing short stories both because it gives me a new way to reach readers and because it's a tremendous challenge." She seeks the reactions of fellow writers and she reads other short fiction to learn what she wants to emulate and what she wants to avoid. "I know I'm not confident at this yet, so I ask all the questions I can. People whose opinions I respect have been saying very nice things about my stories, but I haven't written enough or read enough yet to know when I'm good. And I'm the one I have to please."

✍ **EXERCISE:** This section is titled "Case Study: A Successful College Writer." In what ways, do you feel, has Ann Jeffries been successful as a writer? Are there other meanings of *successful* that have not been dealt with here? Write some questions that you would ask Jeffries to determine for yourself her degree and kinds of success in writing. Finally, write reflectively about your own goals as a writer. What successes do you feel you would need to achieve in your writing in order to be as confident and enthusiastic as Jeffries? ∎

✍ PROJECTS FOR WRITERS

Write Your Own. No matter what work you most love, doing it well includes working closely with a teacher or perhaps many teachers. Anyone who succeeds can point to at least one person who was a mentor, as Ray Chapman describes this person in Chapter 3.

As part of your ongoing project about your favorite skills, craft, art, sport, or other activity, write a chapter about your relationship with teachers. You need not name names, but you should identify for your reader, as I have tried to in this chapter, the most common features of teacher-student relationships, how to handle them, and how to get the most from the teacher's expertise. Don't be afraid to tell stories about yourself that illustrate whether you did this poorly or well.

Depending on the skill you describe, your teachers may be coaches, parents or other relatives, employers, older friends, and so on, whoever has explicitly taught or tried to teach you. If you can, bring into your discussion good advice for working with these teachers that you've picked up from other students.

If you've had experience teaching this skill, even if that teaching has been informal, of a younger sibling perhaps, use this experience to help your reader understand the teacher's perspective.

Connecting with Fellow Writers. Take part in a collaborative project in which each participant studies and reports on the writing environment in each course that he or she is currently taking (if you are not in school, study and write about the writing environment of your workplace or of another situation in which you write). For reference, you might read a similar study in the February 1990 issue of *College Composition and Communication* by Susan Miller and several of her students at the University of Utah. (See Chapter 7 for strategies on using the library to find such articles.)

Write a separate report about each class. Use this chapter for ideas of features to look for: teacher's attitude toward and advice about writing, how students talk with (or don't talk with) each other and the teacher about writing, how students discover the teacher's expectations, and so on. What do you do differently in each class? What standard procedures have you developed?

In particular, try to apply to each class the advice given in this chapter. What happens? Describe as closely as you can what you, the teacher, and fellow writers do in response to these techniques.

Share your reports in your group. Discuss the various observations. What consensus does the group reach for the most useful strategies?

Free Experiment. Either as follow-up to the above project or as a free-standing experiment, imagine that you make the policies for your college or university (or work environment) about how writing is taught, assigned, responded to, and evaluated. You have been assigned to write one of the documents that state the policies or put them into practice. Typical documents include course syllabi, guides or instruction sheets for faculty, memos from the program director to the faculty, rules and procedures in the college catalog, and so forth. In deciding what to write and how to write it, follow the advice of Chapter 3 for studying writing environments. Collect enough sample documents from teachers, fellow students, and program leaders to help you with format. Ask questions of appropriate sources. When you have a draft, share it with other members of your group, comparing your goals and assumptions.

If you are writing policy for a work environment, be aware that the assumptions about writing may not be written down (don't assume this, however). You may be the first person to realize that there should be explicit suggestions for bosses and employees about how writing should be taught and responded to. Your policy statement should consider the specific nature of your business or agency. Refer back to the studies of Jenkins, Chapman, and Gladis in Chapter 3 and to the study of Ann Jeffries in this chapter for examples of ways that writing is used in specific work environments.

Chapter Checklist

To use your teacher as a resource for your writing
Realize that the teacher is also an insecure writer
Frame specific questions to ask the teacher
Ask for feedback on your notes for the assigned writing
Ask for feedback on a discovery draft

To frame the right questions
Identify exactly what you need to know, no matter how basic
Ask for feedback on specific passages in your notes or draft
Use the Three Common Questions only when appropriate
Avoid general questions that will receive a vague answer

To train your helping readers
First, train yourself to set an example, by
   Asking good questions
   Giving specific praise to other writers

Giving specific, respectful responses to other writers' concerns
Reacting maturely to comments from others
Ask the right questions of readers whose judgment you respect
Ask specific questions about a writing that you bring to the
reader(s)
Use the six Starter Questions if needed
Avoid general questions such as "What do you think of this?"
Avoid questions with yes or no answers
Invite readers to be imaginative
Be persistent in getting the response you need for revising
Push for precise responses

Adapt to special conditions of college writing
Large classes
Break down isolation by talking with the teacher
Ask for feedback from the teacher
Avoid safe writing
Rely on helping readers
Teaching assistants and graders
Find out who is reading your work
Treat that person as you would the professor
Cheating and plagiarism
Find out school and course policies
Ask about freedom to use helping readers
Give credit (through footnotes) to all sources you use
Avoid quoting large chunks of others' texts
Learn to paraphrase (Chapters 2 and 6) through using reader-
response log
Remember that the main goal of writing is learning, not grading
Inform teacher if you need help with editing or proofreading
Grades
Keep them in perspective, subordinate to real feedback
Seek feedback, never be satisfied with a symbol
Never let a grade shortcircuit your writing process
Never let fear of grades shortcircuit your desire to grow as a writer

Words to Write By

Write first; show the writing to your reader; ask the questions you
need answered.

5 Four Common Tasks for College Writers

My endless papers in the nursing program had taught me how to observe closely and how to analyze what I'd seen, heard, and felt.

—Ann Jeffries

If an assignment is vague, use it to your advantage. Instead of asking the professor to be more specific, write out your idea for the paper, then propose it to the professor. If you take ownership of the project—if you show that you've done some thinking—the teacher will usually respond positively. Besides, you'll have much more fun doing the project in a way that challenges and excites you.

—Christine Sorge

A WARNING

This chapter gives specific advice about four typical tasks that writers face in college courses in all disciplines. The tricks and hints in this chapter assume that you have already read and practiced the basic strategies in Chapters 1 through 4. If you have not learned how to get started and stick with it, write to discover, experiment, and know, get advice, find examples, and get feedback, and write for the teacher, you will misunderstand this chapter. On the other hand, if you feel confident and skilled in these basics, then this chapter may give you some useful tips for writing in many college writing situations.

A FURTHER WARNING

This chapter deals with only four typical college writing tasks. You will find that these cover a lot of territory, but they are not meant to cover everything that you may encounter. Remember, as we saw in Chapters 3 and 4, every writing situation is different and it's your job to determine the necessary format and form. Furthermore, you can read about other typical writing tasks in other parts of this book. Chapter Two showed how to write summaries, to take notes, to keep many different kinds of journals, and to perform other tasks common to college classes across the disciplines. In Chapter 3 Margaret Ellis handled an assignment for a personal essay about an event in her life. All of Chapter 6 deals with writing about reading, including writing critical papers about literature; Chapter 7 discusses research projects, including using libraries and doing interviews.

A THIRD WARNING

This chapter deals with four typical college writing tasks:

- observing and describing
- taking in-class, timed essay tests and exams
- drawing a conclusion (making a point, supporting a thesis)
- making a plan of action

These are complex tasks that take much practice to do well. Moreover, a student is likely to encounter them in situations that will require other skills and different kinds of knowledge. So this brief chapter suggests a few basic ways to handle these tasks. Don't expect to find an example that precisely illustrates your assignment. In fact, don't even expect that your teacher will use the same terms that I use. For example, in a chemistry lab report, you will be expected to observe and describe the experiment and draw a conclusion about what you observe. But the teacher may never use the words *observe and describe* or *draw a conclusion.* The teacher may ask you to "state a hypothesis" or "report your results", or may merely say, "Write a report on the experiment." It's your job to find out, using the techniques from Chapters 3 and 4, what the assignment requires; never assume that you won't need to perform the tasks discussed in this chapter just because the teacher doesn't name them the way I do.

Finally, remember that any assignment will probably require that you perform more than one of these tasks. These tasks overlap all the time in real writing situations. Typical lab reports require at least two of these tasks; a case report requires at least three (observing and describing, drawing conclusions, and making a plan of action); writing a computer program requires four (the three that writing a case report requires plus analyzing existing programs); analyzing a short story on your English final exam requires at least three; and so on. You may never in your life, except in this chapter, have to just observe and describe or draw a conclusion. You will put these tasks together throughout your life as a writer in school, on the job, and in the community.

OBSERVING AND DESCRIBING

> I know it like the back of my hand.
>
> —Familiar saying

Try this experiment. On a clean sheet of paper, draw an accurate picture of the back of your hand without looking at it. No excuses and no cheating; just draw. When you're finished (or give up), compare your drawing with your hand. What's missing? What's wrong? Think about it: have you ever really *seen* the back of your hand? Think about this: how much more do you know about your hand just by doing this exercise?

Try this experiment. For a few seconds, watch something, anything, happen. Now, describe it in words. Pretend that you are writing this description for someone who did not witness the event. Read over your description. What have you left out? Rewrite the description so that your reader will feel that he or she witnessed the event.

Read over your revised description. Pretend that your reader is one of the following:

blind
deaf
less than ten years old
lives in another country

And pretend that the reader hates to read anything unless it's about one of the following topics:

politics
sports
romance
scientific discoveries
famous people
crime

After you give your reader one of the four traits and one of the six topics, rewrite the description so that your pretend reader will understand it and find it exciting. What must you add to your rewritten description? What should you take away? What else changes?

One purpose of these experiments is to show that what we observe is limited by our ability to observe, and most of us are not trained to observe well. In this chapter, I'll give some tips to improve observation.

Another purpose is to show that how and what we describe depends on the reader we are describing for. Not only that, how we observe and what we observe also depend on the needs of our reader. As you imagined different traits for your reader, you probably replayed the event in your mind and tried to observe it as your reader would.

Clearly, to be a good observer and describer in any field you have to be able to imagine your reader's needs and to adapt to different readers. Fortunately, there are well-known techniques to practice and keep in mind as you observe and describe.

Using All the Senses

When asked to describe something most of us think of how it looks; we visualize, then describe what we see. But we experience life with all our senses so when we describe something the only way to bring that experience to life for someone else is to use all our senses in the description. Note the difference in what you imagine as you read these two descriptions of a park:

> The leaves change color as the branches move in the breeze. They turn bright green, almost yellow, in the sun, then dark in the shadow. Patterns of light and dark move across the grey trunks.

> The leaves change color as the branches move. They turn bright green, almost yellow, in the sun, and dark in the shadow. Patterns of light and dark move across the grey trunks. Smells of cold earth, sweet wet grass, and the last marigolds of the year are carried on the sharp breeze. The traffic beyond the park and the occasional jets overhead cannot drown out the fresh rush of the blown leaves.

Note how the senses are used in the second description. Using the senses forces the writer to be aware of more things to describe and it becomes easier for the reader to feel part of the scene. Note also how much more about the place is communicated.

Of course, a description using all the senses will be longer than one that is only visual. If a certain situation demands brevity, the writer will have to choose which sensations to include and which to leave out. But observing with all the senses gives you choices that the visual-only observer will not have. The person who sees a plant as only green or brown, or tall or short, does not observe or describe as thoroughly as the person who is also aware of brittle or tough, sweet or peppery, hairy or smooth.

Training and practice in observation and description is invaluable in all fields for many different writing tasks. Lab reports, clinical observations in nursing and medicine, case studies of business environments, and reports of criminal investigations are among the types of writing that require multi-sensory (using all the senses) observation.

Using Comparisons: Analogy, Metaphor, and Simile

Before continuing, stop to describe something difficult such as the taste and appearance of an exotic dish at an international food festival; the sight, smell, and movement of what you found under a rotten stump in your garden; or the expressions and mannerisms of an interesting person you recently met. Imagine you are doing this for a reader who has never eaten that food, dug up a rotten stump, or met that person.

Even if you write a multi-sensory description, you will probably find that you run out of adjectives to get your meaning across. *Spicy* and *sweet, dark red* and *sticky* may not describe exactly what you ate; *stinky, whitish green,* and *wiggling* might not do justice to the underside of the stump; *twitching* and *scratching* may only begin to describe the person you met.

As you search for the right words, try comparing what you encountered to something else you know. In Chapter 1, I wrote that the only way we can know something is by comparing it with things we already know. In Chapter 2, I mentioned that comparisons help us understand something new because they let us see how the new thing is like and unlike something else. So it is natural to make comparisons.

When it comes to describing something to someone else, comparisons are useful, but also treacherous. For example, it may be accurate to say about the person you met: "He kept wrinkling his nose and scratching his head just like Uncle Charlie does." However, the analogy between the person and Uncle Charlie won't make sense to anyone who doesn't know Uncle Charlie. You may choose one analogy for your biology professor: "The larvae on the stump were twice as dense and much lighter than those we grew in the lab," and another for your cousin in the city: "Pulling up that stump reminded me of the time we looked for the buried treasure in Gibson's basement, but the stump smelled a little better than the dead rat we found." Comparisons not only make your observing and describing more precise and lively, but also force you to consider your reader.

One good way to check on the effectiveness of your writing is to draw your reader's attention to the comparisons. If, for example, you write in a history essay, "John F. Kennedy seemed like a movie star to many people," you can ask your helping reader what the simile *like a movie star* means to him or her. If your reader says, "To me it means 'superficial' and 'unreal'," and if you wanted it to mean "handsome" and "awesome," then you may want to find a different comparison.

Note that comparisons convey much more in a few words than whole strings of descriptive words can. A simple metaphor can stimulate our senses, can stir up years of memories, and provoke powerful feelings. Advertisers, for example, love comparisons to *homemade* because any reader or listener immediately imagines the familiar warmth, good smells, beloved faces, and happy times associated with home.

On the other hand, comparisons can be unpredictable. A reader who sees a product advertised as having homemade flavor may remember that other products advertised as homemade turned out to be stale, flavorless, or saturated with chemical preservatives. This is another reason why feedback is so vital when we write. We cannot know how our language will affect what readers remember and imagine; we have to check.

Using Numbers

Observation in many fields requires use of statistical measurement. When we use numbers to describe what we observe we draw an analogy between the information we get through our senses and the standards that readers can understand. For example, if I say a tree is twenty-seven feet tall or twice as tall as a two-story house, it is easy for most people to visualize the tree. My description might not be as lively as "the tree was too tall for the little girl to climb but it was much shorter than her imagination," but the numbers are precise and meaningful. Observing and describing with numbers is essential for many types of writing, for example, recipes, floor plans, circuit diagrams, construction manuals, medical prescriptions, inventories, financial reports, lab reports, projected budgets, and musical scores.

Observing with numbers does not substitute for using all the senses or using analogies, metaphors, and similes; all methods can be used together to give readers different and more kinds of information. Numbers never tell the whole story, but they can give information that no other method can provide. For example, one way to describe that exotic dish at the international food festival would be to write a recipe for it. The quantitatively minded observer would think in terms of "how much pepper?" and "when do I add the coconut milk?" and "how long should I cook the peapods?" Similarly, you could observe the rotten stump quantitatively, especially if you were writing it up in a lab report: "I counted an average of seven larvae per square inch on the undersurface."

Quantitative observation is particularly useful when we want our reader to reproduce or recreate what we have described, such as the exotic dish. Numbers may lack the emotional or provocative power of metaphor, but they are indispensable for precision.

Because of the frequent need in many fields for a reader to reproduce results, writers should practice quantitative observation even in cases that don't usually require it. For example, my earlier multi-sensory description of the trees in the park could be looked at quantitatively:

> There are forty-seven trees within the borders of the kidney-shaped park, which comprises about one acre. More than half are varieties of oak, five are dogwood, four are silver maples, and the remaining are hickory, sumac, honey locust, and other types with which I'm not familiar. The oaks range from forty to roughly seventy feet in height. None have leaves less than fifteen feet from the ground. Although today is the eighth of October, the temperature (at 10:30 A.M.) is 38°F, and there is a brisk breeze of about 20 mph, there has been no noticeable change from the summer green of the oak leaves and no more than a few leaves have fallen in fifteen minutes of observation.

While this description lacks the sensory fullness of the other, it would allow an observer to make quantitative comparisons over time (perhaps in a scientific notebook). It would also allow an artist to sketch fairly accurately some details of the park. Remember, how you observe and describe depend on your reader and your reason for writing.

Using Change, Place, and Purpose

We often tend to think of description as frozen in time, like a photograph. But we can observe further if we think of what we observe as changing, if we look at what is around it, and if we think of the purposes it serves in its environment. Let's say that you describe yourself in a job application. You may include a picture of yourself, talk about your current job, or list any degrees, certificates, or awards you've received. If you think of yourself as a dynamic, changing person, you will also talk about how you came to be the person you are and write about your goals and expectations. After all, these are just as much a part of who you are as your height, weight, and hair color.

You can use place when you observe and describe something. Imagine that you are writing an advertisement for a new housing project. Describing features of the house won't make your ad stand out from all the others for similar houses. How can you make your project sound special? Look at your project on the map: how close is it to schools, parks, shopping, rapid transit? To most home buyers, location is at least as important as the house itself. (Conrad Hilton once said, "There are three things that determine the success of a hotel: location, location, and location.") Describing your project's relationship to its environment can make the difference to a potential buyer.

Purpose is an important part of observation and description if you realize that our whole idea of something broadens and deepens when we consider what it does or might be capable of doing. How does it function in its environment? What are its purposes? Look at what happens to the description of the park when we observe with purpose in mind:

> To everyone who looks out on this autumn day, the oaks, dogwoods, maples, and other trees present a soothing scene of shifting light and color. The fresh sound of the breeze-blown leaves mutes the roar of traffic just a quarter-mile away and the occasional jets overhead. Squirrels, gathering for winter, scamper up and down trunks and leap from tree to tree high above. Chipmunks dart through the undergrowth, and millions of other creatures do their invisible work in the damp, black earth. Here and there a jogger plies the bikepath; parents sit on the benches by the play equipment and chat, while keeping one eye on the preschoolers who swing, slide, and climb through plastic tunnels.
>
> In March and August, the quiet creek that winds through the park swells above its banks with the heavy rains, but the grass, vines, and massive roots of the trees hold fast the soil. The houses that hold the gentle slopes above the park remain dry in the wettest weather.
>
> The neighborhoods that border the park appreciate its gifts. Long-time residents remember the developers' petition to rezone the land for townhouses; they recall the later plan to run a four-lane highway through the park. They speak proudly of their own petitions to save the park, their impassioned speeches at the open hearings. When they enjoy the quiet, the birdsong, and the summer breezes, they know in the back of their minds that, as the city grows, they will have to fight for the park once again.

🖎 **EXERCISE:** Experiment in your journal with observing and describing the same object, person, or event for two or three audiences and purposes. For example, describe the same object (e.g., an arrowhead, a seashell) for three different courses you have taken, say science, history, and art. In your descriptions try to use the four techniques for observing and describing illustrated in this section. (Note: A group project could be to assign different purposes and pretend readers to different members of the group. Imagine the array of writings that would be produced from a single topic!) ∎

🖎 **EXERCISE:** As you read textbooks, novels, or newspaper articles observe how the writers use description. Do they use all the senses? Comparisons? Numbers? Change, place, function? Choose several passages of description and revise them, using the four different techniques to create different effects. ∎

TAKING IN-CLASS, TIMED ESSAY EXAMS

Surveys of college writing requirements across the curriculum show that the in-class essay exam is the most common form of writing. If you write nothing else (besides your class notes) in a course, you will probably write a final essay and perhaps a midterm.

Timed essays test your writing ability and confidence as much as how well you have studied. When you write a timed essay, you can't ask for feedback and you rarely get a chance to revise. Because of this, you have to make the most of the advice and feedback that is available before the timer starts running. It is important to learn to:

1. be a careful reader of exam questions
2. ask good questions about exam questions
3. use writing as a thinking and planning tool
4. divide your time into planning and revision stages

Becoming a successful essay test writer doesn't happen by good luck. Good test takers work hard at it, and they start long before the day of the test. Here are some suggestions to help you prepare, including some training techniques.

Start from Day One

Teachers give tests to see what we know. Why do they give essay tests? Every teacher will give a somewhat different answer. One common reason is that they want to see how we use what's been presented in textbooks, lectures, labs, and so on. They want to see how we think about the material. They want to see if we can make connections among ideas in the course, compare one idea with another, draw conclusions that are our own and that make sense to the teacher. They want us to think and express ourselves, which we cannot accomplish in a short-answer or multiple-choice test.

Note how close this reason is to the purposes for writing explained in Chapter 2. It's no coincidence that people who effectively use writing to discover, experiment, and know also write strong timed essays. People who keep journals to respond to their reading or to summarize, reflect on, and speculate on class lectures or films are trained to work with ideas or apply them to new situations on essay tests.

Hence, if a person uses the techniques described in Chapter 2 from day one of a course, that student will be prepared for the midterm or the final. The student will have practiced thinking and writing skills and also will have learned the course material in a full, personal way that cannot be achieved by cramming from haphazard notes or by highlighting the textbook.

Despite stories about the mythical student who got an A on a final essay in a course he did not take, good writing is always about something. The best writing has a strong base in knowledge. The student who is well-practiced in writing to discover, experiment, and know has the best chance on an essay exam. In William Perry's famous essay about the mythical student, he makes the same point, though in different words. While arguing that the mythical student is a master of bull, he says that *good bull* shows that the writer has thought deeply about a subject and understands the complexity of ideas, even if he or she can't repeat word for word a textbook definition or a list of details from a lecture. Perry says, moreover, that colleges ultimately reward understanding with higher grades than they reward memorization and repetition because understanding is knowledge, whereas repetition is only . . . repetition.

Train Yourself to Read Essay Questions

Not preparing from day one is the number one reason why students do poorly on essay exams. The number two reason is not knowing how to read essay questions. Teachers complain endlessly about students who seem to know something about the course, but whose exam answers don't fit the questions. You can improve your reading of such questions by using Planning to Read suggestions and the instructions for the reading response journal in Chapter 2. In Chapter 6, I describe other techniques for analyzing what you read.

Here I draw your attention to some common traits of exam questions and how they determine your essay writing strategy.

Look for the Action Words. Every question contains one or more action words that tell you what to do with the requested information. Consider this question from a comparative government exam:

> Name and define five types of nation-state government in Africa. Discuss one example of each. (1 hour)

The action words are the imperative verbs *name*, *define*, and *discuss*. You cannot answer the question unless you are sure what they mean. It isn't always easy to be sure; after all, it's no secret that teachers often write unclear exam questions. The rub is that it's your grade that suffers if you don't understand. So let's try to clear up the vagueness.

Name seems pretty straightforward. *Define* seems pretty clear, too. If you know five types of nation-state government in Africa and if you know what they mean, you shouldn't have much trouble with the first part of the question.

"Discuss one example of each" reads the second part. *Discuss* is one of the most common action words in exam questions and one of the vaguest. In this case, it could mean "describe the details of," "explain the working of," "summarize the history of," or many other things. You have one hour to answer this question, so it's pretty clear that you're supposed to do more than just list an example of each. But what are you supposed to do?

You know what my answer is: ask. Often, the use of *discuss* is a tip-off that the teacher doesn't have a clear idea of what he or she wants and is waiting to see what you come up with. If you ask what *discuss* means, the teacher can think more clearly about the question and discover what he or she wants. Write down what the teacher says because it can give you a format for your answer.

If the teacher gives a vague response, then it's up to you to suggest some possible meanings. When you encounter a vague action word, brainstorm (see Chapter 1) some possibilities. If there's time, suggest these to the teacher. Again, this can clarify the question for you and for the teacher. If there isn't time for this dialogue, use the brainstorm to give you an outline for your answer. If you think that *discuss* in this case means "explain the workings of" and "summarize the history of," then you can fill in the data. If you follow these steps for each of the five examples, you'll write an organized essay and you won't waste time worrying about the vagueness of the action word.

Read for Structure. Most essay questions give you some information about what format to follow. The clearer this information, the more easily you can plan your essay. If the information isn't clear, you can try to make it clear for yourself by asking.

In this example, the format seems clear because the question is clearly divided into two parts and the number of subsections is exact. Your format might look like this:

Types of Government
> Type One + Definition; Type Two + Definition;
> and so on.

Examples of Types
> Example of Type One + Discussion, and so on.

A logical alternative might look like this:

> Type One + Definition + Example + Discussion; Type Two
> + . . . and so on.

Which alternative you choose is not important; using a systematic format that fits the question is. If you don't find any help for structure in the question, ask. If the teacher does not have a structure in mind, you can brainstorm to come up with a format and ask the teacher for a response. This is a quick way to get feedback that can save you anxiety and that can help you plan and fill in the data. Your essay will be clearly organized and easier to read.

Read for Criteria. What are you going to be graded on? Read the question for grading criteria. In the sample question, *name, define, discuss, five types,* and *one example of each* are all key criteria terms. You'd better include all of them if you want full credit. If any of the terms is unclear to you, follow the ask-brainstorm process.

What other criteria might there be? Another secret (which you know from Chapters 3 and 4) is that people who assign writing tasks are never aware of everything they want (remember Mr. Pemblechook?). For essay exams, these questions are often appropriate:

- "Will you take off points for mistakes in spelling and grammar?" (If so, proofread the final draft before handing it in.)
- "Is it all right to include information that isn't in the textbook or the lectures?"
- "Is it all right to disagree with the author? What should I do to support my opinions?"
- "How much knowledge should I assume my reader has? For example, can I assume ——— (some instance you provide)?" (See my discussion of this question in Chapter 4.)
- "I plan to write an outline (or mindmap, brainstorm, discovery draft, and so on) before I write my final draft. Can I hand this in with my final draft?"

Think of other questions you might ask as well. Remember, a writer doing an assignment is responsible for meeting all the criteria, even the ones that aren't listed. So ask.

Plan Time and Organize

Looking for action words and reading for format and criteria help us to plan our exam essays. The minutes we spend planning the format save us time drafting and revising because we avoid anxiety and confusion as we write. In addition, the draft you submit will be clearly organized so that your reader can follow your explanation and won't be confused by information that is thrown in or tacked on because you failed to plan.

Planning Your Time. How much of your allotted answer time should be used for planning? You need to see the essay in three stages—planning format, drafting, and revising.

As you become practiced in reading exam questions, you'll be able to use the question to help you format, as we saw in the preceding discussion. This takes a few minutes. Of course, if the question has vague action words or if you have to ask about criteria, you'll have to allot more time. (Note: Practiced question readers can spot vagueness right away, before the clock starts running. They ask their questions and get the teacher's answers without losing any writing time.)

Designing your format determines how you'll spend the rest of your answer time. Let's look at the comparative government example again and assume you have one hour to complete the exam. Let's say you choose this format:

Type One + Definition + Example + Discussion; . . . ;
Type Five + Definition + Example + Discussion.

If you spend five minutes asking questions and planning format, you are left with fifty-five minutes for drafting and revision. Skilled writers know, of course, not to shortchange themselves on the vital task of revision; so you plan to reserve at least fifteen minutes for the third stage. This leaves forty minutes for drafting, or about eight minutes for each of the five sections. A classmate might choose another schedule for the fifty-five minutes: allotting three minutes for brainstorming or mapping the data for each section (fifteen minutes total), twenty-five minutes for drafting the full answer, and fifteen minutes for revising. Different writers are comfortable with different techniques, but all benefit by planning.

Drafting. We organize for two readers: ourselves and the other person. On essay exams, we plan the format and write a draft (or plan the format, brainstorm, and draft, as our classmate did) so that we, ourselves, keep from being confused by the data and worried about the time limit. In the third stage, revision, we look through our other reader's eyes, as best we can, at what we've written. (Can I add anything to make my meaning clearer or more vivid? Have I met all the criteria? Is my handwriting legible? And so on.)

Why is this distinction between readers important? If we try to skip the second stage, drafting, and move to the third, revising, we apply inappropriate criteria (such as neat handwriting) to what is really the time for writing to discover and experiment. There's no way to skip the writing-for-yourself stage, though many people delude themselves into thinking that they can. Every teacher has read many neatly written exams that don't make sense to anyone but the writer. Indeed, these exams might not even be good writing-to-discover pieces, because the writer was thinking more about neatness than about understanding the information.

When we organize for ourselves, we have to be messy before we can be neat, just as someone organizing a closet has to pull everything out and spread it around in order to see what to keep and where to put it. This means that in the drafting stage, the exam writer should use whatever techniques, including any of those in Chapters 1 and 2, that allow him or her to generate as much pertinent information as possible in a short time. If you can't fit all your second stage writing in the exam book, use whatever other paper is available.

Revising. Planning your format and drafting with the format as your guide brings you most of the way toward completing an organized essay that makes sense to your reader. The third stage, revision, lets you review to make sure that the organization, which is clear to you, will be clear to the reader. As you revise your essay in the short time left, ask yourself the following questions:

1. "Can my reader immediately see my format?" Don't make your reader guess how you'll answer the question. Remember, the teacher reading exams for a whole class is like the executive reading a stack of memos. There is little time to read each one and no time to waste searching for the writer's plan. If necessary, add a short introduction that tells the reader what to expect. For example, "I discuss five types of nation-state government in Africa: constitutional monarchy, tribal federation, representative democracy, dictatorship, and oligarchy. I define each in turn, giving an example of the type and summarizing its history in that country."

2. "Is there anything crucial left out?" Even though time is short,

rereading the essay slowly can help you remember other details that you want to include. If you do find something of this sort, don't be afraid to insert it into the text. I've heard students say that they didn't want to add anything because it would make their exams messy or confusing to the teacher. On the contrary, adding good information in the appropriate place always helps. Credit your reader with the intelligence to realize the role of revision. Likewise, don't be afraid to delete. If you want to get rid of something, cross it out neatly.

3. "Can my reader read this?" In the final analysis, neatness does count for something. Teachers who assign timed essays realize that they'll have to read lots of hurried handwriting, so they're usually quite accepting. But if you have reason to believe that even a handwriting expert would have trouble deciphering your scrawl, make sure that your final draft rises above your usual standard of neatness. Again, this is one good reason why it's crucial to separate your writing-for-yourself from your revising stage. Many people, including me, write neatly when they don't have anything else to think about, but scribble crazily when they're writing to discover. If you try to do both at the same time, you won't do either very well.

🖎 **EXERCISE:** Practice some timed writings. Ask a fellow student to compose an exam question (including a time limit) for a course you are taking. Follow the outlined sequence in this section, from reading the question to revising your answer. If possible, do this exercise with others and compare your answers and your techniques. ■

🖎 **EXERCISE:** Write about your experience as an exam taker. What techniques have worked for you? How might you change your exam-taking practice based on your reading in this section? ■

DRAWING A CONCLUSION

"What is the point?" "What does it mean?" "So, what's the bottom line?" "What do you make of all this?"

We draw conclusions all the time: we see dark clouds blotting out the sun and conclude it's going to rain; we see interest rates fall and conclude that it's a good time to buy a house or car; we see a gregarious friend acting strangely quiet and conclude that he or she is sad or worried, or perhaps angry.

Much of the time, our conclusions are not systematically thought out. We react on reflex—the batter lunges away from an inside fastball. We react by habit—our friend has that look and we immediately ask, "Now what did I do?" We jump to conclusions on partial or false evidence—we overhear our name in a conversation and conclude that we're being criticized.

Almost all teachers want their students to learn how to draw conclusions through systematic reasoning. Most of your school writing assignments are practice in systematic reasoning, also called *logical thinking.* Your teacher expects you to show in these assignments that you can think logically. Every subject stresses this, though the formats are different. Mathematicians demand that you show your work, not just report your answer. Science lab reports require that you create a hypothesis, design an experiment, report your procedures, observations, and calculated results, and explain what the results mean. Business and legal case studies require that you ask systematic questions about people and events and that you compare these cases with previous cases. Psychological and medical cases work the same way. Artists study the systematic structures of sonnets, symphonies, and ballets. The legal brief, the math solution, and the symphony appear different from one another, but all are based on systematic, logical thinking.

Thinking vs. Reporting

If you reread Chapter 2 with this idea of logic in mind, you'll see that the techniques, questions, and exercises are little logical systems for thinking. If you reread the section Observing and Describing in this chapter, you'll see that my suggestions for ways to observe are also logical systems. These systems are meant to make us aware, conscious, of parts of life that we usually miss. They are also meant to allow us to focus our awareness on different parts of life at different times. All logical systems help us to focus. If we are aware of many little systems, we have many alternatives for our focus. We can think about things in many different ways, not just a few.

Keep in mind, however, that thinking logically is not the same as writing so that someone else thinks that we are logical. The excerpt from Charles Darwin's *Red Notebook* (Chapter 2, p. 71) is a good example of logical thinking, even though it looks like non-sense. My son Jimmy's steppingstones (Chapter 2, p. 74) are also logically thought out, although they don't look logical because he doesn't explain why he chose those particular events. When we write to discover, experiment, and know—that is, when we write to think—we use powerful logical systems. However, we should not fool ourselves into believing that a piece of writing that helps us to understand (my colleague Anne Wotring calls this "think-writing") will necessarily make sense to someone else. It might, but we can't assume it will. Making your conclusion understandable to someone else means that you must revise your think-writing. How should you revise? What format should you follow?

As I suggested earlier, formats vary from discipline to discipline, ranging from showing your work on math homework to filling in a lab report section by section to writing a poem that makes a point to writing a letter to a senator about your view of foreign policy. To a great extent, you can answer the format questions by asking your teacher, your boss, or whomever else gives you the assignment (see the discussions in Chapters 3 and 4 about asking the best questions).

Nevertheless, when we report our thinking and conclusions, one of our goals is to be convincing, so that the reader agrees with our conclusion. This common goal means that all these formats, despite their great differences, have several elements in common:

1. a thesis statement, your main point
2. evidence that the reader will understand
3. your awareness of other possible conclusions and reasons why you believe in yours

Depending on the format that the teacher assigns or that you choose, these three elements can appear in any order. Some examples of different arrangements follow later in this section of the chapter.

Convincing Your Reader

The evidence you present to your reader depends not only on format, but also on what you are trying to convince your reader of and how willing the reader is to be convinced. The reader may already agree with you, may be undecided, may be dead set against you, or may not care about your topic. If you can figure out the reader's position by asking questions, good for you. Sometimes you just have to, as they say in advertising, "run it up the flagpole and see if it flies," that is, get feedback. If the reader's (or helping reader's) reaction to a draft is negative, you can choose how and if to revise.

When getting feedback, find out if the reader objects to your conclusion or to your format or to your evidence. If a teacher expects the thesis statement in your first paragraph and you put it at the end, the teacher will object to your format. If a teacher agrees with the results of your experiment but finds your description of procedures too brief, the teacher will object to your evidence. If, on the other hand, a teacher disagrees with your bottom line, even if he or she finds no fault with your argument, the teacher will object to your conclusion. The only way we can know how to revise is by getting specific answers to specific questions.

Drawing Conclusions: Three Formats

I mentioned earlier that the three key elements that make your conclusions convincing—thesis statement, evidence, and awareness of other possible conclusions—could be arranged in any order, depending on the assigned format. As an exercise, or an effective reading technique, try marking where these three elements appear in articles that you read in newspapers, popular magazines, advertising, etc.

If you are not assigned a specific format, you may still find it interesting to experiment with different formats. To illustrate three formats, I choose a topic that I used for illustration in Chapter 2: homelessness. Let's assume that I have gone through the writing-to-learn techniques in Chapter 2 and have generated lots of ideas and details to work into a draft. Let's also assume—a huge assumption that I'm making just for this illustration—that my reader is an open-minded person willing to be persuaded by sound evidence.

My think-writing has led me to the following conclusion, which I'll use in my draft as a tentative thesis statement:

> Many homeless people are members of the working poor, people who have jobs but who can't afford to pay the high rents in the cities and suburbs.

In my think-writing, I had also included the following details, among others, which I might be able to work into my draft as evidence:

> The minimum wage of $3.80, even for a full-time worker, barely covers the rent of a substandard apartment in the city and leaves almost nothing for food, clothing, transportation, or anything else.

> At the suburban shelter, many of the people are construction workers who come to the suburbs because there is work but get the lowest pay and have no job security. Rents in the suburbs are even higher than in the city, there is almost no subsidized housing, and public transportation is expensive and slow. The shelter director told me of families who live in their old cars.

> The *Times* printed an article about George, a man who lives in the woods near here and works when he can as a day laborer. But living outside, he is frequently sick and can't work. The director of the soup kitchen where he gets his supper said that men like George can't get steady employment because employers don't want to hire people who don't have a fixed address. "It's an impossible dilemma," she said.

When I begin to deal with other possible conclusions, the third element of my essay, I find that I have not discussed them in my think-writing. So I do a second think-writing to speculate (see Chapter 2, pp. 63–67) some other conclusions from the evidence:

> There doesn't seem to be a way around the simple economics of their plight: the wages are too low and the prices are too high (more evidence: all the fast-food restaurants with help-wanted signs; the work is there, but people can't afford the transportation and they can't afford the rents, so they can't take the jobs.) The only people who can make it on such low wages are those who are part of families in which everyone is old enough to have a job and all money goes into family subsistence, with always a little put into savings. (I'm thinking of my Chinese friend, who says Americans always waste their money on things that lose value, like cars and clothes. I wonder if our consumerist culture is making us unable to live on a little and to delay gratification. Maybe it's little wonder that the number of homeless people, especially families, is growing so rapidly.) I'll have to find out more about this.

Using my two think-writings for a discovery draft, I try out three formats for arranging my three key elements of thesis, evidence, and other possible conclusions. The following opening paragraphs (newspaper and magazine writers call these *leads*) show these variations in format:

(Thesis lead) Homeless people are often stereotyped as jobless men and women who either can't or won't work. If they had jobs, so the theory goes, they could afford a place to live. However, more and more homeless in the United States are members of the working poor, employed people receiving such low wages that they cannot afford to pay the high rents in cities and suburbs.

(Evidence lead) George, who takes his supper at a soup kitchen run by volunteers from local churches, had work today as a laborer on a townhouse construction project. He will have work tomorrow, and for as long as the job and his health hold out. His health concerns him, because George must live outside, in a tent in the woods. His wages aren't enough for the cheapest rental apartment in this wealthy suburban county. He wishes he could live in a cheaper area. "But there's no work there," he says. "There's plenty of building here, but none of it is for housing that a man like me can afford."

(Possible conclusions lead) The economics seems simple: on minimum-wage pay with no job security, a person in an urban or suburban area cannot afford to rent even a substandard apartment, to pay for transportation to the job, and to buy food and clothing. But most people with low-wage jobs are not homeless, even though the numbers of working homeless are increasing. What are the characteristics of the working homeless? What factors enable some to get by on very low income?

These variations are not just simple rearrangements of the identical material. Varying the lead changes the reader's sense of what comes next, changes *expectations*. The reader of the first lead will probably expect that evidence backing up the thesis will follow, followed in turn by the other possible conclusion. On the other hand, the reader of the second lead will expect a thesis to follow the story about George. When we start an essay with a detail, we encourage the reader to ask, "So, what's the point?" After we state the thesis, then we give more evidence, and then introduce the other possible conclusion. Finally, the reader of the third lead is given two questions at the end. If you are the reader, you'll expect an answer to both questions, in order. (Note: By ending the paragraph with questions, I give myself a clear organizational format for the rest of the essay. Readers appreciate this, because it lets them know what to expect. My job as a writer is to meet those expectations.)

Using Revision to Revise

Don't be surprised if revising your think-writing into a draft for a reader causes you to change your conclusion. As Chapter 2 asserted, every time we write we are testing what we think we know. Let's say, for example, that I decide to write my draft using the third lead as my opening. Those two questions at the end force me to look for more evidence than I have in my think-writings. I may discover that I know little about what enables people to get by on a very low income. Chances are that if I do more research on this question, talk to people, read articles, I'll discover more than I had imagined. If I am an honest writer, I'll have to modify my conclusion to reflect the new information. My writing will be better, but I have to be ready to give it time and thought. This is the risk, and the adventure, of writing to draw a conclusion.

Incidentally, this is another reason why we have to plan and schedule our writing. Review the section Sticking with It in Chapter 1 that deals with scheduling your time.

EXERCISE: Find an entry in your journal in which you come to a conclusion about any question or issue (it need not be something as political as homelessness). Does it contain the three elements: thesis, evidence, and other possible conclusions? If it does not, do another think-writing with these elements in mind. Use your think-writing to compose a draft for a reader (before composing the draft, be aware of the reader's stance on the question and what you'll have to do to be convincing). Try out more than one lead for the draft. When you get one you like, use it. Point out gaps in your knowledge that you may have to fill in by reading and talking with people.

Carry on this process as long as you wish beyond this point. Ask questions and get feedback as needed. (Note: This is an excellent method to get started on a research project. See Chapter 7 for details on using libraries and personal interviews for research.) ∎

MAKING A PLAN OF ACTION

Often the college assignment asks us to go a step beyond drawing a conclusion about some set of information. Many disciplines, particularly in the natural, behavorial, and social sciences, require the writer to evaluate information and recommend or design a plan of action. The laboratory scientist presents experiment conclusions and then may be called on to design other experiments to test these findings. The nursing student charts the physical and emotional condition of a patient, evaluates the current treatment, and recommends further action. The information systems student observes a communications environment and recommends ways to move information more quickly to more people. The business marketing student analyzes a business and suggest ways to improve advertising and promotion. Indeed, there is not a field in which a student is not asked from time to time to recommend, design, suggest, or plan in response to a conclusion that the student has drawn.

Such writing is great professional training. Much of the writing done by professionals conveys a plan of action; these plans take many shapes and formats. In Chapter 3, Ray Chapman's proposals convey complex, step-by-step plans for solving problems; George Jenkins's financial projections also fit into this category. Even the simple note to a co-worker describing the key procedure for a computer operation or setting the agenda for a brief meeting relies on our skill to design a plan and convey it to a reader.

Making a plan of action involves two essential elements that must occur in sequence: designing a plan that makes sense to you and writing the plan so that your reader understands it.

Designing a Plan That Makes Sense to You

The professional training you receive in any course of study is meant to teach you to observe situations, to draw conclusions, and to make plans or decisions. If a training or degree program does not give you practice and feedback in these three tasks, then what is it for? Each discipline has its own methods for teaching these skills (though many of these methods overlap from field to field), so I won't discuss this part of plan-making. But since writing is such an important tool for designing (systems, procedures, plans) and problem-solving, I'll talk about how some of the writing-for-planning techniques from Chapters 1, 2, and 3 can help.

Speculative Writing. Such techniques as "What if?", Pros and Cons, and Big Wish (Chapter 2) train your mind to plan in an imaginative, organized way. Let's say you've been asked to go a step further on the homelessness project, to recommend community action to help the working homeless. Big Wish can help you create a firm set of goals and to distinguish between short-term and long-term objectives. Once you have speculated on a tentative plan, Pros and Cons can alert you to problems with the plan and help you weigh the benefits against the costs. "What if?" helps you imagine situations that will test your plan. All three techniques help you avoid superficial analysis and snap judgments. They force you to look at your ideas critically and to imagine a more refined plan that can meet potential problems.

Writing to the Limit. In my think-writing on the working homeless, I discovered ideas that I needed more information about before I could draw a conclusion. I can write to the limit to get more information on a plan of action. For example, I can ask myself "What other plans have been tried elsewhere? In what places? With what results?" If I write to the limit on this question, I'll probably discover examples that I can use in my report and the gaps that I need to fill in.

Storyboarding, Mindmapping, and Other Graphic Techniques. Sometimes it helps our planning to use space to give us a sense of what we face and what we can do. (Using spatial, graphic tools can also help our reader understand our plans. See my discussion of this in the next section, Writing a Plan for a Reader.) The proposal writer uses the storyboard (Chapter 3) to map out the sections of the proposal and fill in the subsections. The proposal writer, indeed any kind of planner, also needs a timetable or timeline to mark off the stages of a project or a completion schedule (also see Chapter 1 for using this technique to plan writing projects). In my experience, I find timelining valuable in planning meetings, workshops, and long-term projects. I spread out on a page the activities that I need to cover, in the order I want them to occur. Since the exercise forces me to think clearly and imaginatively, I often find that I think of more things to do or that I want to revise the order or change some of the activities. This is easy to do because there is space for the insertions (it's exceptionally easy on the word processor). Moreover, when I've completed the timeline to my liking, I've got a draft of the schedule that I can give to the people involved.

Recall that mindmapping (Chapter 1) shows relationships among ideas in a graphic way with connecting lines or spokes of a wheel across a page. To help them see relationships, planners in diverse fields use similar graphic devices such as blueprints, computer flow charts, circuit diagrams, organization charts, account books, and communications networks. Opportunities abound. Let's say that you want to get a clearer picture of how you might design a community action plan for the working homeless. You might brainstorm community groups across the page (leaving room to add more as you think of them):

Media   Shelters   Churches   Schools

Social Services   Employers   Transit

Under each, you might list actions that are already being done to help, that could be done to help, and that should be avoided. Under Schools, for example, you might say, "Reading-writing assignments on hunger and homeless in community" or under Employers, you might say "Pay transportation for workers who can't afford to live in local area." If ideas in one group relate to those in other groups, use lines to suggest connections and possible cooperation between groups; for example, a community education project on the working homeless sponsored by the media, the schools, and local churches.

Graphic planning tools work because they use the whole page and they leave spaces that can be filled in as we discover more information.

EXERCISE: Practice one or more graphic tools to help you picture a plan of some kind. If you have a favorite method of using space to help you plan, write about what you do, and how it helps, in your journal. ■

Writing Your Plan for a Reader

Again, the best way to understand what your reader wants and how to provide it is to follow the three-step process outlined in Chapter 3: ask advice, find good examples, and get feedback. In addition, let me make two other suggestions for conveying a plan of action to a reader.

Give Your Reader a Sense of Options. In the previous section, Drawing a Conclusion, I stressed the need to describe other possible conclusions besides the one you envision. Readers—especially teachers, whose job it is to get students to think, and business managers, whose success depends on being prepared for the unexpected—like to see writers come up with more than one way to think about an issue.

How does this relate to writing up a plan of action? The same idea holds true. Considering only one plan in a situation usually shows the teacher or the executive a lack of imagination. Thus, most plans you write for a reader will have to discuss options. A useful way to include them in your draft is to imagine yourself in conversation with your reader about the plan you are suggesting (remember Dialoguing from Chapter 1?). You can usually anticipate the questions that a smart reader will have about your plan. You can use these questions to organize your written presentation (Note: In some cases, you might even use these questions to format your writing. See Chapter 3 about how to format your writing for a reader.):

1. What is the problem the plan addresses? Why is it a problem?
2. What is your plan? Describe it in its parts or steps.
3. What are its potential benefits?
4. What are its costs likely to be? (Remember Pros and Cons.)
5. What are potential problems with the plan? Who is likely to object to it? Why? What could go wrong?
6. How would you respond to these problems and objections?
7. How could the plan be changed without seriously hurting its potential?
8. What are one or two alternative plans and why did you reject them? (Note: You need not reject any alternative. Your plan can sometimes include several equal alternatives.)

If you've used the writing-for-planning techniques described earlier, you'll already have written with questions like these in mind.

You might consider using this list of questions as a tool for your planning. You can also use this list of questions to get feedback on your draft from your reader or from a helping reader (see Chapter 4). If you find yourself on a team or committee designing a plan or making a decision, the group can use these questions to brainstorm ideas, analyze them, and work them into a report (see also Chapter 1 for brainstorming guidelines).

🔊 **EXERCISE:** As a think-writing exercise, brainstorm a problem (or find one that you've written about in your journal). Use the eight questions to generate a plan and give a sense of options. You might try storyboarding the exercise by spreading the eight questions over several pages and filling in the spaces. (Note: Answer the questions in order. Don't move to the next question until you've written something thoughtful about the current one.) ■

Be Graphic—Let Your Reader See Your Plan. If the storyboards, flowcharts, timelines, and so on help you keep the details straight, you know that they'll help your reader. Of course, the big difference between the graphics you use for yourself and the ones you present your reader is that the latter have to be understandable to someone who doesn't know your shorthand of lines, circles, symbols, and abbreviations. Charts and graphs are not helpful to a reader who has to wade through a page of explanation in order to make sense of the hieroglyphics. Remember, the purpose of graphics is to make relationships between ideas clear at a glance. For example, $3/4 = 6/8$ is a graphic way of saying "three and four are related in the same way that six and eight are related, in terms of proportion." This graphic helps the reader as long as the reader understands the symbols. If I don't understand the slash and the equals sign, the graphic doesn't help me. If you, as the writer, want me to understand the relationship, you'll have to design a different graphic. How will you know what I understand? The only sure way is to get my feedback. Hence, you need feedback on your graphics as much as you do on your words.

Nevertheless, there are a few common graphic tricks that most readers understand that can be useful in writing your plans for a reader:

Blank Space: People see connections between things that are placed together, differences between things that are separated. If you want each group to keep straight what it is supposed to do, you might try this:

Duties for Working Homeless Education Project

Media: public service announcements, newspaper series on
  the problem
Shelters: press releases, open house for visitors and school
  groups
Churches: organize volunteers for soup kitchen and emergency
  shelter
Schools: discuss selected articles and films, organize visits to
  shelter
Social Services: press releases, send speakers to schools and
  church groups
Employers: advertise social services to employees, cooperate
  with media
Transit: post public service announcements in buses, subways

Indentation: Readers infer organization of information by its placement on a page; usually, if information is indented, we understand it to be part of or classified under the information above it. For example:

Committees for Project

Public Service Announcements
  Joanne
  David
  Kevin

Press Releases
  Lenore
  Vince
  Kathleen

Volunteer Clearinghouse
  Mitch
  Kim
  Andre

Calendars and Other Grids: Calendars and other grids can be useful for writing schedules, organizing statistical information, or comparing information within categories. For example:

	Monday	Tuesday	Wednesday	Thursday	Friday
9:00 A.M.					
10:00 A.M.					
11:00 A.M.					

Evaluation of Working Homeless Public Service Ads

	Poor	Adequate	Good	Outstanding
Clarity of Ideas				
Visual Effectiveness				
Pace				
Technical Competence				
Effectiveness of Text				

Contributions to Education Project

	Plastech, Inc.	Hometown Foods	Apex Manufacturing	Amalgamated Industries
10,000				
7,500				
5,000				

Visitors to Shelter

Week	1	2	3	4	5	6	7	8	9	10	11	12
300												
250												
200												
150												
100												
50												
0												

Number Order and Alphabet Order: People tend to classify by these systems when sequence is important. For example, sequence is important in the questions in the previous section about giving the reader a sense of options. If your plan calls for a definite sequence of steps, this is a good way to keep the sequence clear to the reader.

A well-known variant of the number order system is the formal outline, in which numbers and letters are used to show categories and to distinguish between large and small divisions. Formal outlines are a useful way to give your reader a picture of the overall format of your report. Long proposals or reports and books of rules or laws often present formal outlines at the beginning of the text so that readers can see how the work is organized and can easily refer to a particular section. For example, laws are often referred to by numbers and letters: Section II.B-2c of the Code.

(Note: You may have been taught to use a formal outline as a planning tool for your writing. But, as with any planning tool described thus far, you may find one tool more useful or comfortable than another. Formal outlines help some writers to think and to organize as they write. Remember, however, that the formal outline is mainly a graphic way to present your format to a reader. Most writers do not create a formal outline until they have a final draft. When you are writing for yourself in the planning and drafting stages, it's better to use informal outlines, mindmaps, brainstorms, and so on as graphic aids.

✍ **EXERCISE:** Read through a few pages of today's newspaper. Find and mark some of the graphic devices used to show relationships between ideas at a glance. How do these devices use space and symbols to communicate? Do they do so clearly? How much explanation of each graphic is given so that you can understand the symbols and abbreviations? What kind of reader would have trouble understanding the graphic? How could you revise the graphic so that it would communicate with that reader? ■

✍ **EXERCISE:** Find several examples of action plans, such as the Recommendations section of a civic report; a regimen of diet and exercise in a fitness manual; practice plans in magazines for musicians, writers, weightlifters, and so on. How are these presented so that the plans seem logical, justified, convincing? Do they give a sense of options? If you were asked to evaluate these plans, what questions would you ask? ■

✍ PROJECTS FOR WRITERS

Write Your Own. If you have been doing the Write Your Own projects to this point, you are well on your way to a book about your favorite skill, craft, sport, or other activity. If this is your first Write Your Own assignment, it's a perfect place to start.

For this project, try, as I have for writing in college, to break down your skill into major subskills. You may find this difficult, as I did with college writing, because your skill, like writing, isn't made up of separate actions but is a blend, a coherent, smooth action. Nevertheless, you may be able to describe parts of the skill that a learner can practice. If the subject you choose is as complex as writing, your toughest task may be limiting the major subskills to four or five.

For each subskill you describe, also include one or two appropriate exercises.

Connecting with Fellow Writers. Make a list of your favorite books of any kind on any subject. Select one. Find a section in the book where the author (or a character) achieves one or more of the three tasks: description, drawing a conclusion, making a plan of action. How does the author write about this or the character achieve this? Use the appropriate sections of Chapter 5 to help you understand how this task is accomplished. For example, when your author or character describes, does he or she use all the senses? Analogies? Location? Function? In drawing a conclusion, how is the writing organized? Thesis first? Evidence? Other possible conclusions?

Make notes as you read, then draft an informal report of your findings.

Free Experiment. 1. Write a series of descriptions of the same place, object, or event. In each description, limit yourself to one sense, as if you were all ears, all eyes, all nose, all skin, or all tastebuds. Then, continuing with the same subject, write two multi-sensory descriptions that are as different from one another as you can possibly make them. Hint: review Comparisons in the section Observing and Describing.

2. Choose a single, recent, historical moment, such as a controversial court decision, the approval or defeat of legislation, or the final contest of a major championship. Study the newspaper files in your library (either in print, on microfilm, or on-line; ask your librarian or see Chapter 7 about how to use newspaper files) to find as many accounts of the moment as you can. Read at least three reports. Note how each writer describes and draws conclusions. Then write your own version of the story, using any of the options in Chapter 5 that you wish.

Chapter Checklist

Use Chapters 1 through 4 as necessary background.

Review Chapters 3 and 4 for strategies on finding out form and format in specific assignments.

Compare your specific assignments with the four tasks and check which tasks fit assignment.

Assume that most assignments will require more than one of the tasks.

To observe and describe
Use all the senses
Use comparisons: analogy, metaphor, simile
Match your comparisons with your reader (get feedback)
Use statistical measurement
Use change, location, and purposes
Let reader's needs and your purpose determine descriptive strategy

To prepare essays on exams
Start from day one with Chapter 2 techniques
Train yourself to read essay questions
      Look for action words
      Read for structure
      Read for criteria
Plan time and organize
      Use format to help you plan time (stage one)
      Allow time to write for yourself (stage two)
      Revise for the reader (stage three)
      Allow time for format and criteria review (stage three)

To draw a conclusion
Distinguish between logical thinking and logical reporting and divide the process
Revise to include the three common elements
      Thesis statement
      Evidence
      Other possible conclusions
Arrange elements to suit you and the reader
Get feedback with questions on thesis, format, evidence
Experiment with formats
      Thesis lead
      Evidence lead
      Other conclusions lead
Allow revision process to change your thesis and spark further study.

To make a plan of action
Divide the process into planning and reporting stages
To plan
      Use speculative writing techniques

Use writing to the limit
Use storyboarding, mindmapping, and other graphic techniques
To report your plan to a reader:
Use the three-step process (Chapter 3) to understand reader
Give the reader a sense of options (8 questions)
Use presentation graphics
Blank space
Indentation
Calendars and other grids
Number order and alphabet order
Formal outline

Words to Write By

First we write for ourselves; then we revise for a reader. If we try to do both at the same time, we won't do either well.

6 The Writing Reader

Persons attempting to find a motive in this narrative will be prosecuted; persons attempting to find a moral in it will be banished; persons attempting to find a plot in it will be shot.

> —Mark Twain, Notice before page 1,
> The Adventures of Huckleberry Finn

HOW TO USE WRITING TO MAKE YOU A BETTER READER

Let me count some of the ways to use writing to make you a better reader by referring you to the appropriate sections in Chapters 2 and 7. In Chapter 2, you may want to read Planning to Read, Listen, and See; Writing to Summarize; and A World of Journals (specifically, using the journal to respond to books, magazines, and newspapers). In Chapter 7, you may want to read The Research Log and Reflective Note-Taking.

Moreover, in every chapter, several of the Exercises call on you to write about something that either you or someone else has written. In the first chapter, for example, I ask you to write about the six reasons students have problems writing; in Chapter 3, I ask you to compose your own story about a writing event using the case studies of George Jenkins and Margaret Ellis as models. My ultimate purpose is to help you become a stronger, more confident writer; but the immediate purpose of the exercises is to focus your attention on the reading. Studying the cases of Jenkins and Ellis can help you understand your own growth as a writer. When you write about the six reasons and about the cases, the writing forces you to pay attention to the reading. Put most simply, that's what good reading is all about.

If you have not yet read the appropriate sections of Chapter 2, I suggest you do so before continuing with this chapter. The techniques described there give you many ways to get more out of your reading through different kinds of writing. Everything we read is like a multi-faceted jewel; each time we change our angle of vision, we see a different face, a different way it catches the light. The different techniques in Chapters 2 and 7 shift the angle of our reading, so that we find more to gratify our sight, more that we can apply to our own craft.

EXERCISE: As you proceed through this chapter, keep a reading response log, as described in Chapter 2. Try out some of the roles described there; do some planning to read; experiment with summarizing all or part of the chapter. Do some reflective writing about what happens to your reading when you write in these ways. ∎

HOW TO WRITE SUCCESSFULLY ABOUT WHAT YOU READ

If you are keeping the reading response log, you are already writing about what you read. Moreover, if the log, as intended, deepens your understanding of what you read, you are already achieving an important kind of success. Further, if the log is increasing your confidence that you have something interesting to say to others about your reading, you are well on your way toward successful writing about what you read.

You will need that confidence when you turn from the reading response log to situations in which you write about your reading to meet the expectations of others, such as when you:

• write an analytical paper in a literature class
• write a review of several articles in your major field
• do a written evaluation of a proposal on the job

• interpret books, articles, or manuals so that others in your field may understand them

In this chapter I'll focus only on analyzing literature, for brevity's sake and because the analytical skills you apply to this common college task can be easily applied to the other tasks. I'll ask you to apply them through several of the exercises.

ANALYZING LITERATURE

Don't be thrown off by the imposing terms *analyze* and *literature*. Many people are terrified of literature because a well-meaning teacher or two expected them to say brilliant things about famous authors, such as Shakespeare. To these terrified people analyzing literature means chiseling beneath the hard surface of a play, poem, or novel to discover a deep hidden meaning. If you've tried to read literary criticism, even something that's supposed to be easy, like *Cliffs Notes*, you're likely to be intimidated by how easily the writers seem to come up with those deep hidden meanings. Many people are so intimidated that they wind up writing so-called analytical papers that are just bunches of quotes pulled out of *Cliffs Notes* or out of a critic's introduction to the book they are supposed to be analyzing. If you think that analyzing literature means trying to sound as learned and as definite as a literary critic, then the logical thing to do is copy someone who sounds learned and definite.

But that's not what *analyzing literature* means. Analysis means

> deciding on something (or more than one thing) to look for in your reading and then studying the text to see what you find.

Anyone can do that. You do analysis every time you read anything purposefully; for example, when you scrutinize the brochures for several different kinds of stereo equipment, life insurance, or college education to find which has the best features at a price you can afford. The problem with analyzing literature is that the purpose, something we want to look for, is not as easy to recognize as the purpose for reading the product brochures. The problem is motivation: "What am I looking for when I read a novel, an essay, a poem? Why should I look for it?"

Literary scholars don't have this problem because they enjoy the challenge of understanding more about the writings they love and the people who wrote them, just as mechanics love to study every facet of an engine or gardeners love to scrutinize every petal of a rose and compare brands of fertilizer. What do you love? What would you spend unlimited hours doing?

EXERCISE: Write about something you really enjoy doing, something that you steal as much time as you can for, something that you get up early for and stay awake late for at night. Why do you love it so much? Do people ever wonder why you spend so much time on this? What do you tell them? ■

Your answer to these questions will probably be similar to that of the literary scholar. No matter what we love, whether it's reading, roses, or rock music, we'll encounter skeptics who'll wonder if we could spend our time more wisely and who'll force us to justify our love. You and the literary scholar probably have more in common, too. More likely than not, what you love to do most has something to do with reading.

EXERCISE: Does this love of yours involve reading? Think about this. If you read as part of this enjoyable work, why do you read? What are you looking for? What are your favorite things to read in this field? Do some writing about this. ■

If you read anything about the work that you love to do, you are analyzing literature. You may not have thought of your favorite reading as literature, with all that term's connotations of prestige and difficulty. But all writing, regardless of who writes it or how much prestige it has, possesses that quality that literature scholars write about: form. If you're not sure what form is, review the discussion in Chapter 3 where I talked about how one learns the form of any type of writing to perform that writing.

Remember Jenkins and Ellis? Remember Ray Chapman and Steve Gladis? All four learned to write office reports, personal essays, proposals, and speeches by reading a lot of them, trying to write their own, asking good questions of helping readers about their reading and writing, and doing more reading and writing. To write their own memos, essays, proposals, and speeches, they were forced to pay attention to, to study—to analyze—what they had read. The more they read and wrote and reread and rewrote, the better they became not only in writing and reading, but also in their ability to analyze. Moreover, and here's the pertinent point, they could teach others how to read and analyze memos, essays, proposals, and speeches. Chapman and Gladis became managers of proposal-writing and speech-writing teams. Jenkins and Ellis, by their reading-writing experience, could teach others.

EXERCISE: Imagine that you've been asked to write an article for your favorite publication in the field you most enjoy. Draft a page or two. If you need to, reread a couple of the pieces in your favorite publication and note features of style or organization that you want to follow in your piece.

When you've written this draft, write a short piece, one or two pages, that describes all the features of form and format that characterize the articles in your favorite publication and that you tried to include in your draft. After you've done this, revise this description, imagining that the person who'll be reading your writing is someone who's interested in your response, but who does not know as much about the field as you do.

Whatever you come up with through this exercise will be a piece of literary analysis. You have been able to write it because you know what you're looking for in your reading, and you have a strong purpose for your reading. ∎

WRITING ANALYTICAL PAPERS ABOUT WORKS YOU DON'T KNOW WELL

If you can analyze literature that you know well, you can analyze literature that you don't know well. You need the two qualities you brought to the previous exercise: purpose and something to look for. You need purpose in order to give you incentive, motivation. You need something to look for in order to give your analysis focus and organization.

Finding Purpose

If we're lucky enough to be in a class about our favorite subject, we have all the motivation we need to write analytically about our favorite reading. Often, however, we're asked to analyze works for which we have no enthusiasm. How can we find motivation where we think there is none?

Somehow we have to make the work we are analyzing ours. Christine Sorge, one of the success stories portrayed in Chapter 9, says that she always finds something in her school assignments to make them interesting to her. She does this by trying hard to make a connection between her subject and some purpose or experience that has meaning for her. This takes imagination and hard work. Meaningfulness, value, and relevance are not qualities that jump out of the page and grab you so that you can't wait to write your assignment about that poem or essay. We have to want to find meaning and value; we'll find that value if we try hard to make that connection between ourselves and what we've been assigned to study.

MAKING THE CONNECTION: AN EXPERIMENT

Assignment: write an analysis of the following poem by Gwendolyn Brooks:

kitchenette building

We are things of dry hours and the involuntary plan,
Grayed in, and gray. "Dream" makes a giddy sound, not strong
Like "rent," "feeding a wife," "satisfying a man."

But could a dream send up through onion fumes
Its white and violet, fight with fried potatoes
And yesterday's garbage ripening in the hall,
Flutter, or sing an aria down these rooms,

Even if we were willing to let it in,
Had time to warm it, keep it very clean,
Anticipate a message, let it begin?

We wonder. But not well! not for a minute!
Since Number Five is out of the bathroom now,
We think of lukewarm water, hope to get in it.

Imagine that you have been given the assignment in this example. The wording of the assignment doesn't give you much to go on. You'll want to use the strategies in Chapter 4 to find out from the teacher more information about what is expected. Let's say that the teacher says that you can focus on anything in the poem that interests you and that your goal is to explain to the teacher what the poem means to you, and how the poet conveys that meaning.

OK. This gives you something to work with, at least something to base a draft on. Once you have written the draft, you can ask the teacher for feedback.

You're supposed to write about what interests you. What if nothing is of immediate interest to you? Here are some ideas, which you can try out on Brooks's poem, for making the connection:

- *key word:* reread the poem. Circle a word that strikes you, that seems relevant to your life, your emotions. Circle several, if you find them. In your reading response log, freewrite, brainstorm, or mindmap (see Chapter 1 if these terms confuse you) to understand more deeply the meaning of each key word.

- *"this reminds me of":* reread the poem. If you think you understand the situation or the emotions of the writer, freewrite about a similar situation or set of feelings in your own life. Explore this experience until you've made sense of it for yourself, increased your understanding of it. Now, do a focused freewrite in which you compare the writer's experience to yours.

- *note your confusion:* reread the poem. Read as far as you can until something, anything, confuses you. It may be a word, it may be punctuation, it may be sentence structure; it may be that you just can't get the idea clearly. Write about your confusion. Note where your understanding stops. What's causing the block? What words could you substitute that would make sense to you?

- *write your alternative:* reread the poem. If you think you've got some idea what the poet is talking about, but the poem doesn't interest you, write about that. How could the poet make it interesting? If you were going to write about this subject, what would you say? What would make it interesting to you?

- *dialogue with the writer:* don't be passive. Imagine that the writer is speaking directly to you and that you're expected to reply. What will you say? What questions would you ask? Carry on the dialogue. How would the writer respond to you?

Of course, feel free to try out some of the roles and other techniques suggested for the reading response log in Chapter 2. Any of these is likely to trigger your motivation to write about the assigned work.

Finding Something to Look for

Recall that your goal is to explain to the teacher what the poem means to you, and how the poet conveys that meaning. You have in this assignment a structure that you'll encounter again and again in writing both in school and in your career. It's a version of the drawing conclusions assignment discussed in Chapter 5 as one of the four common tasks for college writers. (You might review the section Drawing a Conclusion now, if you don't recall it.) Whenever you receive such an assignment, you are expected to present three elements to your reader:

1. a main opinion, or thesis
2. evidence to back up the thesis
3. other possible theses or conclusions

You begin by studying your data and discovering, through writing, several possible theses or main ideas. Then you continue this discovery writing to find which thesis you like best, which one best fits the data (evidence). After studying the data and discovering your thesis, you reorganize (revise) your writing so that it makes sense to your reader. Review Drawing a Conclusion in Chapter 5 for suggestions for organizing (revising) your discovery writing so that it makes sense to a reader. Pay special attention to the three formats for organizing the draft you'll submit to the reader.

Suggestions for Studying the Data

Let's not jump ahead to theses and revision before discussing the most important task, studying the data. When literature, such as Brooks's poem, is your data to be analyzed, there are some standard elements to look for. Read through each of these elements. Before going on to the next one, answer the questions or try out the techniques described for the element on the poem "kitchenette building." Use your reading response log for your writing. See what discoveries you make.

The Writer's Sense of a Reader. How much knowledge of the subject does the writer assume the reader has? Do you find terms that you can't understand, and that are not explained in the text? Do you find other terms that are defined, but that you think don't need to be defined? In "kitchenette building," for example, you might ask what's implied by "dry hours" or "white and violet" or "Number Five." Can we figure out the meaning of these terms by reading more carefully? Or do we need more information, a context outside the poem, to make sense of the terms? Imagine the writer talking to you. What does she assume you are familiar with?

The Writer's Format. How is the book, article, poem, software package, and so on organized? What information comes first? Second? Why do you think the writer follows this order? How is it organized: chronologically (events one after the other in time)? Spatially (things next to one another in a place)? Associatively (by the order in which the writer thinks of the images or ideas)? Or in some other pattern? Also, how does the writer use features such as headings, outlines, and so on? About this book, for example, you might say, "The author uses many lists of techniques to try. Every chapter ends with the checklist format." Brooks doesn't use headings. What does she do to mark divisions in the text? Why?

The Writer's Voice and Tone. In Chapter 3, I stressed that voice and tone are hard to perceive until we have had a lot of experience reading different kinds of material. *Voice* and *tone* are speaking terms, not writing terms; we can't really "hear" them in our reading until we've read enough to imagine clearly how a book or article would be spoken to us. This doesn't mean, however, that voice and tone are so subtle that we can't write about them for another reader. There are a few things we can look for.

To write about voice, we can ask whether the writer uses *I*, *me*, and *you* frequently (first and second person) or avoids writing about *me* or *you*. What is the effect of this choice? Where does the writer use active voice; that is, where does he or she write about people doing and saying things? On the other hand, where is passive voice used; that is, where does the writer emphasize what was done rather than who did it? Compare these examples:

Professor Jones and I decapitated the rats in the experimental group and collected their blood. (*Active Voice*)

The rats in the experimental group were decapitated and their blood was collected. (*Passive Voice*)

Even in this short passage, you can see how change of voice dramatically affects our response to the writing. What can we say about the effect of an entire piece of writing if the author consistently uses the active voice, or vice versa? In "kitchenette building," how does Brooks use voice? You can get a sense of voice in a work by reading it aloud. How does the sound of the poem affect your response and understanding? Is Brooks's poem mainly active voice or passive voice? Where does she emphasize the "who," where the "what"?

To write about tone, we can ask what mood the writer seems to be creating. What tone of voice do we imagine the writer would have if speaking and not writing to us? Is humor used? Does the writer use description to create an atmosphere or a feeling? If you characterized the tone of "kitchenette building," which words and lines would you cite to back up your opinion? If you wanted to change the tone of the poem, which words would you change, which ideas would you cut out or revise? Some common words used to describe tone include *friendly, relaxed, serious, gloomy, forbidding, carefree,* and so on.

When reading to observe tone, you have to stay aware of how the text makes you feel as you read and how it would sound if the writer were speaking to you. Then, when you write about these feelings and sounds, you have to avoid being impressionistic, that is, just stating vague feelings. Instead, you have to mark clearly in the text what makes you feel a certain way, for example:

The second line of Yeats's "Song," "Because a fire was in my head," made me feel the pain of the narrator's confusion.

I think that potential users might be scared off from the software by the technical terms in the first menu. It's intimidating and misleading to have the "help" screens called the "Error Prevention and Potential Oversight Module."

Point of View. Every piece of writing is limited by the writer's point of view. No writer can see from every angle and no writer can imagine every possibility. We all see certain things and ignore everything else. We can improve our powers of observation (see, for example, the section Observing and Describing in Chapter 5), but we will never see exactly what another person sees and we will never think about it exactly the same way.

Learning to understand a writer's point of view challenges the reader. While some writers, such as novelists, deliberately choose a particular point of view, most of us are not aware of the limitations of our view when we write. Only by reading a lot of writing by a broad range of people, and only by hearing a lot of different views, can we become aware of our limitations and overcome them. In the section Drawing a Conclusion in Chapter 5, I stress the value of showing readers more than just one way to look at an event or an issue by discussing other possible conclusions.

Because we are usually not well aware of our point of view, we don't make it clear in our writing. Our readers have to read between the lines to figure it out. When we read, we have to do the same thing. If we read a lot, especially if we read about the same topics by different people, we can detect point of view by comparing one writer to another. For example, you might say, "One writer of an article about legalization of drugs writes from a legal point of view. She takes her examples from court cases and focuses on the legal language of legislation. The second writer, an economist, looks at the impact legalization would have on the price of drugs and the number of people who make their living from the drug trade." Such comparisons are the best means to detect point of view. Asking imaginative questions like the following can teach us something about the underlying viewpoint of the writer:

1. "What if this piece were written by another writer; how would it be different?" (See Chapter 2 for more on "What if?" questions.)

2. "Where does the writer get examples or evidence? What evidence or examples are left out?" (For example, experiment with details from your experience that you could use to create a mood similar to that in "kitchenette building." How does the poem change? What does it gain and lose?)

3. "What seems to be the purpose of this writing? What is the writer trying to get me to do or feel? Why does the writer want me to read this?"

4. "Does the writer show any awareness of other viewpoints on this topic? What might someone object to in this piece?" (Again, imagine someone in dialogue with the speaker in "kitchenette building," perhaps someone in the same setting who looks at the details of life from a different point of view.)

5. "What statements in this piece are treated as fact? Would everyone regard them as true?"

ANALYSIS BY COMPARISON

Whenever you read or hear a review of a book, movie, TV show, record album, and so on, the reviewer always compares the work to something else, to other albums by the same group, other spy novels, other movies about Vietnam, other articles about the stock market. The reviewer does this because (1) we can only talk about something new in terms of something that we already know, and (2) the reader can't understand what *good* or *bad* or *4 Stars* or *Gag!* mean unless the reviewer compares the new work to something the reader already knows about.

The same is true of reading analysis that you do for another reader. If you write about a new spreadsheet software package, it's meaningless just to tell your teacher that it's "easy to use." To be convincing, you have to compare its procedures to others that are easier or harder to use. Similarly, if you write an essay about your favorite magazine, you'll want to compare a few articles before you tell your teacher that your format and style are typical of the work in that magazine.

What we say about any piece of reading is usually determined by what we compare it to. What we think about our reading depends on the context in which we place it. For example, read these six analytical statements about Mark Twain's novel *Huckleberry Finn* and note the context in which each statement is made:

1. One test of a book's greatness is how much controversy it arouses. *Huckleberry Finn* was banned in Boston because it was thought to be a bad example of behavior for youth. It's been reviled by segregationists for its treatment of whites and by civil rights groups for its treatment of blacks. It's been preached against in pulpits for its satire of churches and scorned by athe-

ists for its "naive" religiosity. (*Context:* analyzing the novel by
looking at what critics have said about it in the century since it
was published. Note: If you wondered why Twain wrote the
Notice that opens this chapter, the reason is that he was annoyed
at moralistic critics, whom he felt did not really read his books,
but saw in them ideas they didn't like.)

2. Most scholars see *Huckleberry Finn* as a greater book than *Tom
Sawyer* because of the maturity that Huck achieves through his
ordeal. The Huck who carries good luck charms at the beginning
of the story is very different from the Huck at the end who risks
hell to save Jim. In *Tom Sawyer,* neither Tom nor Huck become a
wiser person. (*Contexts:* comparison to another of Twain's books
and comparison of two events in the novel.)

3. Twain made a sincere attempt in *Huck Finn* to capture the different dialects of people from Missouri to Louisiana. Unfortunately,
without phonetic spelling Twain could only do a rough job of
reporting these variations. Needless to say, if he had used phonetic spelling, only linguists would have wanted to read the
novel. (*Context:* comparison of Twain's use of dialects to books
that use phonetic spelling.)

4. I like Huck Finn because he acts like a real boy. Sometimes I wish I
could run away like Huck did. I'm glad my father isn't like his.
(*Context:* comparison of Huck's life to the life of the person writing about the book.)

5. The book *Huckleberry Finn* is very different from the Hollywood
movies that have been based on it. The movies feature the pranks
of Huck and Tom and the clownish antics of the King and the
Duke. They don't portray the cruelty, hatred, and stupidity that
are shown again and again in the book. (*Context:* the same story
told in different media.)

6. The entire tale is told from Huck's point of view. If Twain had
used a third person narrator, he could have told the reader how to
think about people and the events. By using Huck as the narrator, he gives us insight into the thoughts of a boy at a particular
time and place, and he challenges the adult reader to be a careful
judge of the characters and what they do. (*Context:* use of first
person compared to use of third person.)

EXERCISE: It's obvious that using some contexts requires more outside knowledge than using others. One can't analyze *Huck Finn* in the context of other books or other movies without having read the other books or watched the other films. But two of these six contexts use internal comparisons, either between characters or point of view. Reread "kitchenette building." Brainstorm several contexts in which statements about the poem might be made. Note which of these contexts are internal, that is, comparisons you can make within the poem, and which are external, those for which you need outside information. ■

The point of the *Huck Finn* examples is that comparisons, contexts, are almost limitless. Depending on the context we choose, we focus on a different aspect of the reading and, therefore, we write about it in different ways. Granted, *Huckleberry Finn* is a rich and varied work; but that doesn't mean that you can't find just as many contexts for a lesser work, say an advertising brochure for a new car:

- from what you know about photographs, you could write about the quality of the pictures
- from what you know about language, you could write about the current slang used in the copy
- through research in *Consumer Reports* or other consumer magazines, you could compare the claims in the ad with performance results
- through research among your friends, you could evaluate how people interpret and respond to the ad
- you can apply to the ad questions about point of view, tone, voice, sense of the reader, and format

All it takes is a bit of imagination.

EXERCISE: Choose a piece of reading that you have been assigned recently (or that you're doing for fun). Write statements about the reading that focus on the categories described in this section, including:

- writer's sense of a reader
- writer's format
- writer's voice and tone
- point of view

It necessary, use the questions in each subsection to help you analyze the piece. ▪

✍ **EXERCISE:** Choose the same or a different piece of reading and use different contexts to help you focus on different aspects of the text. Think of at least five contexts in which to make statements about the text. If you wish, imagine yourself looking at the text from the different roles described in Chapter 2 in the section about the reading response log. ▪

✍ **EXERCISE:** Choose one of the statements you made in the previous exercise. Let this serve as the thesis of a short essay analyzing the piece of reading you chose. Apply the process of the Drawing a Conclusion section in Chapter 5 toward composing the essay. Remember to cite specific evidence from the piece of reading; imagine and explain at least one other possible conclusion. Be ready to modify your thesis depending on the evidence you find. ▪

HELP WITH ANALYSIS FROM YOUR HELPING READERS

Once you have discovery-drafted your analytical essay and revised it to reflect one of the three organizational formats in Chapter 5 (under Drawing Conclusions), take it to your helping readers for comments. The questions you ask your readers will be determined by the format of your essay. Since you will have stated a thesis somewhere in your essay, depending on the format you've chosen, you can ask your readers to identify your thesis and your most convincing pieces of evidence. You can also ask which evidence strikes your readers as less convincing or unclear. Remember, always ask questions that require more than a simple yes or no answer.

In choosing readers, include at least one person who read the text. This person can point out sections of the text either that you have not covered in your analysis or that your helping reader has interpreted differently. This is not to say that one of you is right and the other is wrong. Depending on the context we choose and the questions we ask of a text, we derive different, but equally enlightening interpretations. The benefit of different interpretations is that someone else's insight can make our own view richer.

⚓ **EXERCISE:** After you have discovery-drafted and reorganized your essay for a reader, write a list of questions for your helping readers. Make slightly different lists for those readers who are familiar with the text and those who are not. ■

ANALYSIS AND RESEARCH: LOOKING AHEAD TO CHAPTER 7

You'll find that much of the research process described in the next chapter depends on the analytical skills described here and in Chapter 2. Besides sections on the research log (a specialized version of the reading response log) and on reflective note-taking, Chapter 7 also includes several analytical exercises that call on you to observe closely the features of four sample research essays, each quite different in theme, tone, and the other aspects we've discussed here. When you read the four essays, you might want to test your own analytical ability by writing your own analytical paper. Let me assure you that for your efforts at probing these texts you will be neither prosecuted, banished, nor shot. You'll just find yourself becoming a more skilled reader and a more versatile, confident writer.

⚓ PROJECTS FOR WRITERS

Write Your Own. Two of the exercises in this chapter ask you to focus on a subject or activity that you love, just as you have been doing in the Write Your Own projects in previous chapters. Where the second exercise asks you to identify the typical features of articles in publications about your favorite subject, this project asks you to recommend to your reader the most useful books and periodicals (magazines and newsletters) for someone interested in this subject.

On the assumption that you already know several worthwhile publications in this field, fill in your knowledge with further reading, enough so that you can recommend at least four sources. In your writing, specify why you recommend each source, what it includes that the others do not. What does it do particularly well? What does it not do as well as the others? How would you character- ize its point of view and tone? How can your reader obtain a copy or a subscription?

Connecting with Fellow Writers. 1. Choose a favorite book, not necessarily a recent book. Using library sources such as the *Book Review Index* and *The New York Times Index* (see the section The Reference Room in Chapter 7), track down as many reviews of the book as you can. Take notes on each review, noting features such as point of view of the reviewer, context (the sorts of comparisons the reviewer makes), and tone of the review. Write a summary of the reviews, including your assessment of each of the features.

2. As a group project, let each person write an analysis of the same work (a poem, a piece of software, an historical essay, and so on), using a personally meaningful point of view, tone, and context. Share the analyses among the group members. Take notes on the distinctive features of each analysis you read.

Create a group anthology of the analyses. If the group wishes, members may vote for the best four or five analyses that should then be reread. Discuss the features that make these stand out from the rest.

Revise your own analysis, incorporating the best qualities that emerged during the discussion.

Free Experiment. When I read really good writing, I am often inspired to write something in the same voice, tone, and point of view (writers call these features, collectively, style). On the other hand, I am sometimes inspired to write something on the same subject but with different style. For instance, after reading Alice Walker's story "The Child Who Favored Daughter," I wrote about a similar theme but used the style of Genesis in the Old Testament.

Try an experiment of one or both types. For example, you might try interchanging the styles of two authors you admire, writing on a theme of one author in the style of the other, and vice vera.

Share these with a group if possible. You'll be amazed at your creativity.

Chapter Checklist

To use writing to make you a better reader
Practice the reading response log (from Chapter 2)
Write to summarize (from Chapter 2)
Plan to read, listen, and see (from Chapter 2)
Practice the research log (from Chapter 7)
Practice reflective note-taking (from Chapter 7)

To write successfully about what you read
Practice techniques in Chapters 2 and 7
Don't be intimidated by critics
Don't be thrown by the terms *analysis* and *literature*

To analyze literature
Use techniques to find purpose
    Key word
    "This reminds me of"
    Note your confusion
    Write your alternative
    Dialogue with the writer
Find something to look for
    The writer's sense of a reader
    The writer's format
    The writer's voice and tone
        Read aloud for sound
        Avoid impressionistic comments
    Use point-of-view questions
        "What if another writer . . . ?"
        "Where does the writer get evidence?"
        "What's the writer's purpose?"
        "Is the writer aware of other viewpoints?"
        "What is the writer's sense of facts?"
Analyze by comparison
    Try different contexts
        Compare the critics
        Compare with other books by the same writer
        Compare one character with another
        Note changes that occur: characters, setting, tone
        Compare the character or the situation to your own

Compare works on the same topic
Imagine a different point of view for the speaker
Try different roles as an analyst
Use the reading response roles (from Chapter 2)
Use your different types of knowledge to give you different perspectives on the work
Be willing to go outside the text for information—research

To write your analysis for a reader
Use the three-step process (from Chapter 3)
Write for yourself (discovery)
Reorganize for others (Use the formats described in Drawing Conclusions (in Chapter 5)
Seek feedback from helping readers
Choose at least one reader who studied the text
Ask questions that probe your thesis and evidence
Seek out different interpretations to enrich your own

Words to Write—and Read—By

Writing about reading forces you to pay attention—that's what good reading is all about.

To analyze literature, you don't need to sound like a literary critic. All you need is motivation and good questions to ask of the text.

7 Writing for Research

When I was asked if I would be willing to write a book on death and dying, I enthusiastically accepted the challenge. When I actually sat down and began to wonder what I had gotten myself into, it became a different matter. Where do I begin? What do I include? How much can I say to strangers who are going to read this book, how much can I share from this experience with dying patients? How many things are communicated nonverbally and have to be felt, experienced, seen, and can hardly be translated into words?

—Elisabeth Kübler-Ross
Preface, On Death and Dying

. . . One day, several years ago, a friend gave me a small volume of Tocqueville's travel diaries, his notebooks translated from French into English for the first time in the 1930s. They were a working reporter's notebooks, complete with questions and answers . . . .

I was in awe. I was looking at the notes for what was probably the best book ever written about my country, my people. I decided then that, whatever else I did, I would try to take those notes and recreate Tocqueville's journey: travel the same roads, see the same things or what had replaced them, talk to the modern counterparts of the men and women he questioned.

—Richard Reeves
Preface, American Journey

RESEARCH: WRITING BEYOND THE LIMIT

I keep running up against the stone walls of my ignorance. When I write to the limit (see Chapter 2), I reach the limit very quickly. In Chapter 5, as soon as my think-writing gave me the idea of the working poor who are not homeless, I saw that I needed to find out more about how the 30 percent of people in the United States just above, at, or below the poverty line manage to survive. I decided that I had to read more and talk with people; that is, in order to draft an essay that I would be satisfied with on the "working homeless," I'd have to do research.

Sometimes students in writing courses get the idea that the research paper is a special breed of writing, an exotic pet that requires special paraphernalia, such as boxes of index cards, footnotes, and complicated rules for formatting. The research paper is the assignment that means you have to go to the library, whereas the rest of the writing in the course doesn't require you to go anywhere, except into your own thoughts and memories. In the research paper, so the myth goes, you have to cite facts and figures and you have to quote other people's opinions; in the rest of your writing, you can say pretty much anything you please, and to back it up you need only cite your experience.

But the myth is pure chimera. Whatever your experience may have been, real writing forces us to seek more than we know, and real research is not a few perfunctory trips to the library nor a stack of index cards, but the response that we make to the need to find out what we don't know. Reread the passages that begin this chapter. Kübler-Ross and Reeves write of enthusiasm and awe. What inspires them? Each is filled with the quest to learn: most of Kübler-Ross's sentences are questions, while Reeves is awed by Tocqueville's question-filled journals. However much they must read, however many people they must talk with, both are ready because they have the thirst to know.

Because their research is undertaken with such strong desire to know, it's no wonder that their resulting books convey enthusiasm to a reader. A person with the notion that research writing has to be unimaginative and impersonal might not recognize as research passages such as these:

(from *On Death and Dying*)   Watching a peaceful death of a human being reminds us of a falling star; one of the million lights in a vast sky . . . .

(from *American Journey*)   Big Talk is the genius of American democracy. Loud talk. Crazy talk. Free talk.

Thorough, devoted research, rather than stealing liveliness from our writing, makes it even more alive because finding the answers to our questions gives us confidence to assert what we believe.

This chapter will address mainly two questions that have to do with writing for research:

1. How can writing help me meet the need to find out more than I already know?
2. How can I write so that other people learn from my research and feel my enthusiasm?

These questions reflect the sequence that is central to the previous four chapters: first, we write for ourselves, then we write for others. Even if the assignment comes from another person, we first have to make the writing our own before we can make it interesting and persuasive to someone else. The suggestions in this chapter are meant to help you with both stages of the process.

EXERCISE: Write about your experience with research. Recall a time when you were filled with the quest to learn something. What or who inspired you? How did you go about your search for information? Were there surprises? Difficulties in finding information? Great discoveries? How did you communicate your excitement and your information to someone else?

Relate this experience to your thoughts about the research paper. What have you done (or could you do) to make someone else's assignment your own? ■

Using Writing-to-Learn Tactics

If you have not reviewed the techniques in Chapter 2 for writing to discover, experiment, and know, this would be a good time to do so. Your reading response journal, your reflective-speculative writing, your learning log can each be the source of the idea—the question—

that you'll want to pursue through research. Pay particular attention to the section Writing to the Limit (pp. 46–51); the series of
writing steps helps you accomplish the researcher's most basic task,
to focus on a question that you really want answered. The researcher's best tool is a specific question. Once you've identified
what you really want to know, you can design the experiment,
design the questionnaire, plan your reading, or plan your interviews, whatever you must do to answer the question.

Developing Questions

Some research writing guides tell us to start with a *topic*, defined as
"something to write about." Indeed, when we get the urge to write
(or when someone gives us a writing assignment), that urge or that
assignment may come to us first as a topic, say homelessness or the
recent stock market crash or the manufacture of microchips. The
urge may come to us as an image or a feeling: the man in a slightly
rumpled business suit asking you for spare change, the graph in the
newspaper showing the falling stock market, the technician peering
through a microscope to craft a circuit on a chip. These images are
topics to write about, but they are vague. What can you say about
them? Without a question on which to focus your research, you may
find yourself leafing through articles in the library and jotting down
random bits of data about your topic, but lacking any sense of how
to work those bits into an essay that will sound logical or interesting
to a reader.

The Chapter 2 discussion of writing to the limit gives you an
extended way to identify what you don't know (plus what you do
know) and to turn your doubts into questions for research. The
following exercise can quickly turn your sense of a topic into a
question that can give focus to your research and a logical plan to
your essay.

EXERCISE: Think of something that you've wanted to know more
about, but that you've never had time to pursue. (You might freewrite or brainstorm to come up with several things.) With this topic
in mind, freewrite to discover one or more questions that you have
about this topic. As you freewrite, you may find that you write
several related questions, each question following from the previous one.

Now review your questions. Focus on one that seems the most important or interesting to you. In a second freewrite or brainstorm, speculate about where you might begin to find answers to the question:

Can you begin with something you've read or a book you've seen on a library shelf?

Do you know anyone who could give you some data or tell you whom else to talk with?

Do you know of some other source—a public agency, a business, a private collection—that might have some information?

Can you travel, perform an experiment, get a particular job to add to your information? ∎

This exercise can, in a few minutes, give you a focus and a few places to begin. Although you are just starting and the leads you discover may turn out to be unhelpful, chances are that at least one will turn up a person, article, or public record that will be a gold mine. The research process is very much like Ray Chapman's proposal-writing process described in Chapter 3. It depends on asking questions of a variety of people, reading around in different places, and getting feedback. Starting off with a question that interests you gives you the initial push, but most researchers find that their energy increases as they discover more, often in surprising places.

Here are some of the questions to get started generated by a writing class embarking on a research project. The writers chose their own topics using the previous exercise:

What caused the 1987 stock market crash?

How do the poems of John Keats reflect incidents in his life?

What are some causes of the economic decline in Bangkok?

Have American blacks advanced economically since the 1960s?

How can lasers be used in medicine?

Is astrology valid for predicting human behavior?

Why did the German invasion of Russia in World War II fail?

Should PAC's (political action committees) be allowed to contribute to campaigns?

Should I or shouldn't I use steroids?

Using the same exercise, students in a comparative cultures course produced these questions, among others, for a research project about China:

> What are the common procedures of acupuncture and on what theory are they based?
>
> How was the Great Wall built, how long did it take, and what were the costs?
>
> What are the history and future prospects of the Chinese missile program?
>
> What is the current state of Chinese-U.S.S.R. relations? Why?
>
> How has Western music been received in China since the Cultural Revolution?
>
> How did the Opium Wars in nineteenth century China affect Maoist attitudes toward the use of drugs?
>
> What is life like for the typical Chinese college student?
>
> How is the Chinese New Year celebrated in different parts of the country?

Diving In and Collecting

Once you've found a compelling question and brainstormed a couple of places to begin looking for information, you can dive into the search, somewhat like the diver seeking buried treasure. Since you don't yet know what information will prove important or even trustworthy, you should assume at the start that everything you find is potentially valuable; hence, you should keep track of it.

Writers use many methods to record what they find. Some use index cards, on which they summarize an article or a conversation, often quoting word-for-word passages that particularly strike them. The advantage of index cards is that they can be filed in any way that the writers choose, such as by author, title, or subject of the article. When the writers reach the drafting stage, they can pick out cards and pull certain ideas together.

Some writers may prefer to keep a spiral or looseleaf notebook that may be less cumbersome than a file box and that allows the writer more space for quotations, summary, or personal comments (a sample notebook page follows, later in the chapter).

The writer who is comfortable with word processing and computerized filing can easily insert new notes into existing files and pull together similar pieces of information when drafting the re-search report. (Though this option is still unavailable to many writers who do not yet know the technology, there are writers who do know filing programs but who have not considered their poten-tial as a research tool.)

When we dive into the process of research, every item of information we collect influences our thinking about the focus ques-tion. As I read a newspaper article on the working poor, the article, no matter whom it pictures or what point of view it supports, shapes my thoughts about the homeless. If tomorrow I read an-other article that cites different statistics and draws a different conclusion, then my thinking changes even more. Inevitably, I compare each new article or conversation with the others that have gone before. Gradually, I build up a sense of how each source can contribute to my project; I also learn, by comparison, which articles or talks are more useful than others. When I investigate several sources and compare them in this way, then I find that an idea emerges for a possible answer to my question.

During this gradual process of discovery and understanding, it's important to have a means of comparing our sources and reflect-ing on what we take from our research. Writing can provide that means through the research log, a type of journal, and reflective note-taking.

The Research Log. The research log is a variation of the logs and journals, including the scientific notebook, described in Chapter 2. Reread the excerpts from the scientific notebooks of Darwin and of Lewis and Clark (pp. 71–72) to see two ways in which a writer might keep such a log. Note that Darwin's "Red Notebook" cryp-tically records his thoughts about the tertiary formation he has recently seen. He compares it with another formation which it resembles. He also uses his new observation to evaluate an article he has read: "In De La Beche, not sufficient distinction is given to angular & rounded." This entry in the log is brief, but it allows Darwin to note comparative-reflective observations that he does not want to forget.

The Lewis and Clark log is more descriptive than Darwin's. Note how the researchers use the aurora borealis entry to describe a complicated event. Note how they use the prairie fire entry to compare two interpretations of another event. While they use this log for the same reason Darwin does, they also write with awareness of another reader, who is not present at the events. Lewis and Clark, therefore, also use the log to try out ways of expressing their observations to a reader, as a preliminary draft of a future research report that they will write.

At a certain point in the research, one can use the log to begin to summarize and draw conclusions about one's observations. After five months of travel in the young United States in 1831, the French official Alexis de Tocqueville wrote in his journal these preliminary conclusions about the nation he had been sent to study:

Causes of the social condition and present political organization of America.

1. *Their origin,* fine starting point, intimate mixture of religion and spirit of liberty. Cold and reasoning race.
2. *Their geographical position.* No neighbors.
3. *Their activity,* commercial and industry. Even their vices are now helpful to them.
4. *The material happiness* which they enjoy.
5. *The religious spirit which reigns.* A Republican and egalitarian religion.
6. The diffusion of *useful* education.
7. Very pure morals.
8. *Their division into small states.* They are incapable of a great state.
9. The lack of a large capital where everything is central. Care in avoiding such a place.
10. Communal and provincial activity, which enables everyone to find employment at home.

When Tocqueville wrote his famous book *Democracy in America* (see Richard Reeves's comments on this work at the beginning of this chapter), he incorporated many ideas from his log, though in greatly revised form. When we use the research log to begin to draw conclusions, it can become a preliminary outline of the report we eventually will write, as it did for Tocqueville.

✍ **EXERCISE:** My description of the research log notes several kinds of work the log can perform, among them:

- describe people, places, things, events
- compare anything with anything else
- evaluate ideas and opinions
- summarize
- draw conclusions and test them
- let the writer experiment
- let the writer draft for a reader.

Your "History of a Writer" is a kind of research log in which you are the subject. Leaf through your "History" and locate entries in which you do the kinds of work that the research log accomplishes. Consider how your "History" might serve as the research tool for a substantial essay on you the writer. ∎

Reflective Note-Taking. Because much of the research process involves diving into printed sources, you'll need an effective system for taking notes and keeping them organized. Don't think of your notes as a substitute for the research log; you'll use the log to do the expansive thinking that helps you make sense out of all the notes you've taken and to practice expressing your ideas for your readers. Conversely, you can use your notebook not only to record what you find in sources, but also to do a little of the reflecting and speculating that you'll expand in the research log.

The notes you take during your research, as you read, talk with people, and observe events, can take three different forms:

- verbatim statements (the exact words a speaker or writer uses)
- paraphrases and summaries
- your own reflective or speculative comments and questions

Sometimes writers are taught that note-taking consists only of verbatim statements, paraphrases, and summaries. But, as we see in the notebook excerpts of Tocqueville and Darwin, we do some of our most important thinking as we read, listen, and observe; there is no reason why reflective note-taking should not help this thinking along.

Besides, once you get into research, you will find that there is no clean break between the research phase and the writing phase. The searching inspires thought and the thought inspires more searching.

You may handle these three types of notes in whatever way you find comfortable. You may wish to keep them all together in your notebook, writing your comments and questions as they come to you. Or you may prefer a version of the double-entry format I described in Chapter 1, with verbatim statements and paraphrases on the left and reflections-speculations on the right. The following are examples of the all-together notebook format and of the double-entry format. Only the format is different (note how I distinguish between verbatim statements, paraphrases, and my own comments in the all-together example—it is important to make these distinctions to avoid confusion about which statements are yours and which come from someone else when you write your draft):

All-Together Notebook Format (verbatim statements from Richard Reeves's *American Journey*)

p. 322   "Information was power in the America I was traveling through—and that was becoming more true as the amount of information expanded."

L. Clinton Hoch's map of what he calls the "real United States"—just a grid of 500-mile squares with 100-mile subdivisions. State boundaries meaningless in the age of information.

p. 323   Jerry Brown—people as "children, dependent beings who look to the elites for their central thoughts."

(But compare this to what Ed Koch says about the new entrepreneurs. Are there really individuals, in Tocqueville's sense, anymore, or is the presence of ethnic minorities, especially new immigrants, the best chance for individualism that the country has?)

Double-Entry Notebook Format

322 "Information was power in the America I was traveling through—and that was becoming more true as the amount of information expanded."

L. Clinton Hoch's map of the "real United States"— just a grid of 500-mile squares with 100-mile subdivisions. State boundaries meaningless in the age of information.

323 Jerry Brown—people as "children, dependent beings who look to the elites for their central thoughts."

(But compare this to what Ed Koch says about new entrepreneurs. Are there really individuals, in Tocqueville's sense, anymore, or is the presence of ethnic minorities, especially new immigrants, the best chance for individualism the country has?)

I prefer the all-together style because it is more natural for me to spread my thoughts out across the page; but the double-entry style allows one to add comments and questions on the right side when reviewing the notes. For example, when I review, I might want to comment on Hoch's map, comparing his views to those of local officials who think political boundaries are important for tax purposes.

Whatever method you choose, remember that the goal is to use writing to aid your thinking as you study. The format you follow depends on which best suits your convenience and efficiency.

(Note: In taking notes on any source, don't forget to list the author, title, date and place of publication, and where you found it [including the call number for a library source]. You may need to find the source again to check your notes.)

EXERCISE: Take notes on a page or two of a book of your choice. Practice (1) citing statements verbatim, (2) paraphrasing or summarizing (the statement on Hoch's map is a paraphrase), and (3) reflecting-speculating-questioning. Try out the all-together and double entry formats.

Consider yourself a note-taker doing research. What system makes sense to you? ■

FINDING INFORMATION—WHO, WHAT, WHERE

It's great to have systems for keeping a journal and reflective note-taking, but the writer needs to find good material to take notes about and reflect on. Countless are the times that my students brainstorm terrific topics, only to say later, "I can't find anything." I always assure these students that there is something, usually much too much to deal with, on any question that a person chooses, but that the searcher needs skill to find the treasure. We explore ways to unearth the gold.

(Incidentally, a main reason why academic programs require research is to teach students how to access hard-to-find information. It's a maxim of academia that the measure of educated people is not whether they know the answer, but whether they know where to find the answer. Knowing where and how to look is often more useful than knowing any number of discrete details.)

Experienced researchers do all kinds of things to track down information. Successful searching requires imagination, persistence, and the ability to tolerate failure. It usually requires some courage and a sense of adventure.

You may not need to look far for your data, like the travelers Darwin, Lewis and Clark, Tocqueville, and Reeves, nor may you have to be as persistently brave as Kübler-Ross in her interviews with the terminally ill, but you will have to overcome fears of calling a source who does not want to be bothered or who is suspicious of your questions. You may risk the embarrassment of asking questions that show your ignorance. No doubt you will have to overcome the frustration of locating the perfect source in the library catalog, only to discover either that it was stolen from the library or that an interlibrary loan will take two weeks. And sooner or later you'll have to work around breakdowns in computers or photocopying machines, on the one day in the week that you have free for library work.

The discussion that follows includes some suggestions for finding information in the three sources most commonly used by college writers: libraries, personal interviews, and public documents and records.

A Plan of Attack for the Library

All libraries, like all readers, are different. Just as the writer must ask for advice and feedback from readers, the researcher must take the initiative to get to know the library. Don't assume that any library has exactly what you're looking for and never assume that it doesn't. Particularly now, when libraries are rapidly acquiring computer hook-ups and massive databases on microfiche, your local library is in large part the local terminal of a vast network of information.

Most libraries publish a brochure listing their services and outlining their holdings. When beginning a project, or even just getting acquainted with a facility for future use, review this publication. Take a walking tour of the library; ask the library staff questions about services. If the librarians are busy, be patient.

Catalog of Books—Card Catalog, Microfiche, and Computer Database. Many libraries have replaced the traditional card catalogue with books of microfiche (sheets of film) or with computerized filing systems. All three systems allow you to access books by author, title, or subject.

Since most of us begin our research with a subject in mind, we try to access books by subject first. However, since subjects are less definite than authors and titles, we can't be sure that expression of a subject matches the subject categories in the library catalog. For example, to pursue my study of the working homeless, I expect that "working homeless" is too new a term to be a subject category. However, "homelessness" and "work" should produce results, though most entries in these categories will not be relevant to my specific topic. Yet, they should lead me to books I can start reading, and the reading will give me clues to other categories and sources.

The Library Stacks. The catalog will give you call numbers of books in the collection. Even if the catalog does not at first seem to have a book specifically on your topic, it will show you where the useful sources are likely to be. Walk to this part of the collection and browse. Look for titles that seem relevant. Read the Table of Contents and look through the index. Experienced researchers often have stories of the great source they discovered by accident, but they really found it by systematic browsing. For example, when I was looking through the university library's collection of books about exploration to find an excerpt from the Lewis and Clark journals (see Chapter 2), I browsed through a book on the Antarctic expeditions and came across the harrowing story of Robert Falcon Scott, whose final journal entry so moved me that I included it in the chapter.

Library of Congress Subject Headings. Most libraries in the United States use the subject categories of the Library of Congress. *The Library of Congress Subject Headings* (*LCSH*) is a two-volume reference tool (many libraries have the *LCSH* on-line) that not only lists all the headings in the library, but also directs you to the actual headings when you've made a wrong guess. For example, if I look in the *LCSH* for "homelessness," the entry reads

> *sa* [see also] Children, vagrant
> Domiciles in public welfare
> Homeless women
> Housing—effect of war on
> Migrant labor
> Poor
> Refugees
> Relief stations (for the poor)
> Rogues and vagabonds

Runaway children
Runaway youth
Tramps
xx Cost and standard of living
Housing
Poverty
Social problems
Law and legislation (*Indirect*)

Not only can this list of subtopics and related topics help me to make my way through the card catalog or the computer database, but it also can give me new ways to think about my topic. Recall that my brainstorming in Chapter 2 did not mention "migrant labor" or "runaway youth," although these are important aspects of my topic.

The Reference Room. Browsing through the library reference room awakens many a tired researcher. It invariably sparks the imagination. In the reference room, every subject is represented. It contains encyclopedias, dictionaries, *Who's Whos*, bibliographies, indexes, lists, and statistics of all kinds. These books give the researcher enough information about any subject to lead to other, more detailed sources. These books can't be borrowed because they are constantly in demand. Becoming familiar with the reference room gives one an idea of what's in the entire library. The next paragraphs describe some of the reference tools usually found in the reference room.

Bibliographies and Indexes to Periodicals. These are compiled yearly (or more frequently) and list, by subject, articles published in journals and magazines. Most bibliographies and indexes refer to journals of a scholarly rather than popular nature; that is, magazines that are used by specialists for research, rather than magazines that feature articles for the general reader. Scholarly journals set higher standards of accuracy and fairness than popular journals; consequently, research by professionals and college research assignments, which usually stress accuracy, demand familiarity with bibliographies and indexes.

The following indexes are a small sampling of the hundreds available for particular fields:

Art Index
Abstracts in Anthropology
Applied Science and Technology Index
Business Periodicals Index
Computer Literature Index
Current Law Index
Education Index
Energy Research Abstracts
General Science Index
Historical Abstracts
Humanities Index
Index Medicus
Mathematical Reviews
Physics Abstracts
Public Affairs Information Service Bulletin
Psychological Abstracts
Social Sciences Index

There are also general indexes such as

American Statistics Index
Biography Index
Book Review Index

Note that some of these indexes are called "abstracts." Abstracts are summaries of books and articles. An abstract can often tell you whether the book or article is relevant to your subject. Almost all fields of study publish at least one yearly book of abstracts for major books and articles.

Like the book catalogs, indexes and bibliographies use subject headings from *The Library of Congress Subject Headings* (*LCSH*). Consult the *LCSH* if you can't find your subject in an index.

If you are searching for articles in popular magazines, such as *Time, The New Republic, Popular Mechanics, Psychology Today,* or *Scientific American,* use *The Readers' Guide to Periodical Literature.*

Computerized and Microform Indexes. Find out your library's holdings of indexes that are on-line or on microfiche. For example, more and more libraries are acquiring *Infotrac,* a computerized index to over 800 journals and magazines in government and social science. Most of the students with the research questions listed on page 219 were able to find at least several useful references using

Infotrac. Almost every discipline now has on-line or microfiche indexes, though the number of indexes varies. So ask.

The Periodical Room. Let's say that I find a reference in the *Social Sciences Index* to a 1987 article about homelessness in the April issue of the *American Journal of Orthopsychiatry.* I can't read the article until I find the magazine, but how do I know if my library carries that journal? Most libraries have a list of their periodical holdings in published form or in a central location, perhaps at the reference desk or in the periodical room. This list tells you which journals the library carries and how far back they go. Once you find that your library carries the periodical you need, you may find that it is available not in print, but in the space-saving form of microfilm or microfiche. Many libraries keep their microform collections in separate rooms, while others keep them together with print issues.

Typically, periodicals, in any form, may not be borrowed from the library, so allow time for reflective note-taking at the library.

Newspapers and Newspaper Indexes. Most libraries carry newspapers, including current copies of many and continuing collections of several. Large national papers such as *The New York Times, The Washington Post, The Chicago Tribune, The Christian Science Monitor,* and *The Wall Street Journal* publish computerized or microform indexes (sometimes as far back as the mid-nineteenth century) that they sell to libraries.

Newspapers are invaluable sources of historical and current events topics. Since newspapers deal with the present, whenever that might have been, they show us the temper of the times as no other source can.

Interlibrary Loan and Consortial Agreements. What if my library doesn't have the book or periodical I need? Almost all public and college libraries have the means to find out the nearest location of the work you're seeking, so ask the librarian. For a fee, libraries can usually get you the book or article through interlibrary loan, though you may have to wait more than a week for it. (This is another reason to start your research well before the deadline.)

Libraries also tend to have consortial agreements with other libraries in the area, which means that you can use your library card to check out books and use services at all libraries in the consortium. Your library may also have access via computer to the book and periodical catalogs at the other libraries.

Audio-Visual Services. In thinking of possible sources, don't forget videotapes, films, records, and audiotapes. As these resources proliferate, more and more libraries are building substantial collections; and audio-visual sources are showing up more frequently in bibliographies in many fields. (Ask your teacher whether you are allowed to use these sources.) If you plan to use audio-visual sources, prepare yourself by doing the exercises in Chapter Two under Planning to Listen and Planning to See.

Special Collections. Your library and other nearby libraries may have special collections donated by individuals or organizations that have to do with local history or the special interest of the donors. If you have the freedom to choose a topic for your research, you might investigate such collections; they are usually much deeper though far less broad than the rest of the library's holdings. Such collections may have their own librarians to answer your questions. Usually they are given their own rooms, so they may not be noticed by the casual library user.

EXERCISE: Describe an experience in which you used a library to do research for an assignment. What went well? Why? What didn't? Why? What aspects of the library environment would you mention that are not noted in this chapter? What advice would you give a fellow researcher? ■

EXERCISE: Take a leisurely tour of your local library. Check where each of the services discussed in this section is located. Note additional services not mentioned here. Note differences between my description of the typical library and what you find on your own tour. ■

How to Do Personal Interviews

Talking with the right people can give your research report vividness and authority. The strong remark by an expert can be just what
you need to liven up your style and make your point with a reader.
At the very least, asking the right questions of a person can lead you
to other, better sources. Remember, for example, Ray Chapman's
advice in Chapter 3 about talking with people to get feedback on a
proposal and to find out whom else to consult.

Doing interviews well takes planning, good listening, the ability to think on your feet (or sitting down), and courtesy. Let me go
briefly through these four essentials.

Planning the Interview. Go into an interview with a few questions
written down and with the tools to take notes. You may think that
you can keep questions and responses in your head, but experienced interviewers know that written questions can keep an interview from drifting to irrelevant topics, even though they may be
interesting. Taking notes forces the interviewer to pay attention. If
you don't have questions prepared and take notes, you may fall into
the common trap of thinking about your next question instead of
listening.

You can use a tape recorder to capture the entire interview, but
don't let taping substitute for taking notes. Taping is a recording
process; notetaking is a thinking process. They serve different
purposes.

Plan a follow-up interview. When you begin to write up your
notes, putting them into prose for your research article, you'll
invariably discover that there are other questions you want to ask
and that you're not sure of some things you heard. This doesn't
mean that you planned poorly. It only means that you can't make
complete sense of a conversation while you're conversing. Revising
the notes shows you what you missed. Hence, plan for follow-up in
your schedule. If at all possible, make an appointment with your
interviewee to go over what you've written, for accuracy. Besides
helping you do a better job of research, follow-up shows your
interviewee that you care to use quotations honestly and fairly. Few
interviewees, no matter how busy, would be unwilling to grant you

the extra time. For example, Ray Chapman and Steve Gladis, whom I interviewed for Chapter 3, suggested substantial changes in my reports of their interviews, changes that showed me where I had reported inaccurately. (Unfortunately, follow-up interviews are rare for the deadline-conscious journalist. People who are interviewed for TV, radio, and newspapers often take it for granted that they'll be misquoted and misunderstood.)

Listening Well. Bad interviews happen all the time. The following two examples illustrate behavior to guard against:

1. Smith interviews the Mayor already believing that the Mayor is 100 percent right (or 100 percent wrong) about the issue under debate. Smith listens only for good quotes to back up the opinions in his article. Smith doesn't hear anything else.

2. Johnson takes a list of questions into the interview with the visiting expert. Johnson asks question 1, scribbles down the response, asks question 2, scribbles down the response, and so forth. Johnson does not ask any questions in response to anything the expert says and does not ask for more detail. The expert sees that Johnson only wants to get through the list and that Johnson doesn't care whether what is said makes any sense.

The good listener wants to understand. Therefore, the good listener (1) pays attention and (2) asks follow-up questions for clarification and further detail. The planned question list keeps the conversation from drifting, but it should never force the interviewer to move too fast from question to question. Be flexible; stay with a conversation that takes off in an interesting direction. Glance at the list to remind yourself of ground you still want to cover.

If understanding is your goal, then don't ignore most of what your interviewee says as you search for good quotes. Writers who conduct interviews only to back up their own points of view with lively statements from experts are not doing research; they are only getting testimonials for their preconceptions.

You can listen to understand by using questions that challenge your interviewee. Ask your questions not in an aggressive way but out of the desire to learn. If there is controversy about an issue ask for the interviewee's response to the diverse points of view. For example, if I interview a town council representative about a motion to rezone the neighborhood park, I may read the opposition's opinion to my informant and ask for a response. I may have already formed my own opinion, but asking challenging questions keeps my mind, and ears, open.

Sometimes, of course, I look to my interviewee to let me know what the issues are. The good interviewer always listens for differences of opinion and asks questions to probe the controversy. (You can be sure that every topic worth researching has some controversy attached to it, though it may not be obvious. If an interviewee tells you that everyone agrees about the facts of a topic, be skeptical.) A simple trick is to ask directly, "What things do people disagree about?" The response can give you perspective on the topic and point you toward interviewees with other ways of thinking.

Thinking on Your Feet (or Sitting Down). The good interviewer listens, asks questions, writes, and, therefore, thinks all the time. Remember, the advantage of an interview over a book or article is that you have someone in front of you who can think, struggle with a tough question, change an opinion, and show emotion, whether excitement, anger, confusion, or amusement. The thinking interviewer, who listens to learn and asks probing follow-up questions, makes the interviewee think; and the interview teaches both people. Indeed, don't be surprised if a good interview causes the interviewee to ask you some questions, about your research, about your interests, and so on. While you don't want the interview to turn around and lose its focus, it's only natural for a good interview to become a good conversation. You always have your list of questions to fall back on, and it's all right for you as the interviewer to shift the focus back to your subject. Be flexible.

Showing Courtesy. Interviewing etiquette consists of a few simple rules by which we show our respect for the interviewee. Following these rules also makes our research more productive and accurate.

- *Set a time and place at the interviewee's convenience.* Most interviewees prefer to have you come to them and although this may mean some inconvenience to you, you should honor this request because you want your informant to feel at ease. Besides, meeting your interviewee on his or her own ground lets you see and feel the person's environment and can spark other good questions. Phone interviews are generally a bad idea unless you know the informant well, because unfamiliar informants tend to be less open over the phone. Don't use phone interviews unless it's impossible to meet in person.

- *Show the interviewee that you are prepared.* Having a list of questions, even if you vary from it, shows that you've spent time preparing. If your questions are informed by the reading you've done or by other interviews, the interviewee will see that you've done some homework. Also, be ready to tell the interviewee how you obtained his or her name (it also helps to pass along any words of praise you might have heard).

- *Ask permission to record the interview.* If you want to tape record, be up front: no hidden recorders, no phone mikes; most interviewees are not put off by recorders; some are flattered; if someone should object, smile and just proceed without the tape.

- *Be honestly curious and interested, not aggressive or sneaky.* We've all seen on TV the microphone-in-the-face, search-warrant style of interviewing. But you're trying to learn, not make headlines or dig up bodies. On the other hand, you need not apologize for your research; good interviewees like to answer challenging, thoughtful questions. If someone gets defensive about a question or just wants to keep the interview on a surface level (like the public official who keeps repeating the official policy and won't give a personal opinion of it), it's better to back off than to get angry or create a clever question to trap the informant into making an unguarded statement. Such answers may look flashy in newspapers, but they are unreliable research.

- *Offer to let your interviewee check your write-up.* Ask the interviewee to check the accuracy of any quotations or paraphrases that you want to use in your research report. Not only is this fair, but it also protects you against the inevitable mistakes you'll make in interpretation. Should you wish to pursue your research, you'll want the interviewee to trust you later on. A remote possibility is that a person may request that you not use the interview in your report. If leaving out the interview is only an inconvenience, grin and bear it. Remember that you still learned from the experience, and the interview might have led you to other, better sources. Professional reporters often face the tough question of including or deleting the words of someone who may be angry or afraid. The reporter has to weigh the readers' needs against the interviewee's request. Fortunately, you will not be confronted with this type of ethical dilemma in most of your research.

✍ **EXERCISE:** Tell the story of an interview you have done. How did it go? What was the best thing that happened? What would you do differently (perhaps based on suggestions in this chapter)? ■

How to Use Public Records (and Other Nonlibrary Documents)

Maybe the most neglected sources for research (especially by students) are the hundreds of public records files, historical collections, and files of pamphlets and reports kept by special-interest groups. Some years back, I decided to do a study of the history of the land on which my apartment building stood. My eldest son, who was six at the time, asked me if Indians ever lived there; his question made me curious about how long ago that might have been and what happened to the land since then. I went to the local historical society, where an interview with the director led me to an interview with the official county historian, who in turn told me to study the land records, the files of deeds and sales, in the county courthouse.

The time I spent in the records room was enthralling. Having done almost all my research as a student and teacher in libraries and by interview, I learned to appreciate many other sources that had previously escaped my attention.

In the records room, with a bit of assistance from the staff, I did, in effect, what real-estate people call a "title search." I traced back the ownership history of the property for more than two hundred years, to the beginning of record-keeping by the British colonists in the area. I came across deeds, wills, bills of sale from public auctions, reports by surveyors, and maps. The words and signatures were those of men and women whose names I had only known

from the names of the streets, towns, and neighborhoods. The
maps showed long-forgotten roads, corn fields where now stood
oak woods, sprawling farmhouses where now stood honeycombed
condominiums. The wills and deeds hinted of families gone bank-
rupt, children disowned, feuds between neighbors. Back through
time, the print and paper changed: black type gave way to faded
brown ink from a quill pen; wood pulp gave way to parchment. I
encountered strange words: land measured in "chains," not feet;
days termed "instants."

   While the public library could give me a few historical summaries of the local area, only through the courthouse records could I
uncover the documents about my little patch of living space. Moreover, these were what scholars call "primary materials," original
sources, writings that have not been changed by the interpretations
of other researchers. College, school, and public libraries carry few
of these in proportion to the number of "secondary materials,"
books and articles about the primary materials. Public records files
and historical collections contain mainly primary materials.

   The discussion that follows contains suggestions for using public records and historical collections, plus the files of pamphlets and
reports kept by special-interest organizations.

Public Records. The key word is "public." The public is allowed
access to most documents that people are required to submit to local
jurisdictions, including, deeds, wills, bills of sale at public auctions;
marriage, business, and all other types of licenses; birth and death
certificates; transcripts of court cases; minutes of town or city council meetings; laws proposed, passed, and defeated. Though public
records files seem labyrinthine to the inexperienced researcher,
records rooms employees can answer the researcher's questions.

   These rooms also have rules. Because public records do not
circulate, to protect public access, records rooms may strictly regulate the number of files that may be searched at one time, whether or
not files may be photocopied, and who is authorized to take them
off the shelves. Some records rooms, just like some libraries (including the Library of Congress), require you to request a few materials,
which are then brought to you by the staff, the only people with
direct access to the files. Rooms may allow access only to those at or

above voting age; they may charge substantial fees for photocopying, or they may require you to use a pencil for notetaking, since ink can permanently mar a record.

Historical Collections (Including Museums). Every state, county, and city (and almost every town) is blessed with people who treasure history and establish historical societies. Sometimes these historical societies are based in impressive buildings. Sometimes they have just a few people who meet occasionally in a member's home and who keep documents, photographs, and other memorabilia in a spare room of the town hall. Sometimes they consist of a lone individual, a long-time resident or the editor of the local newspaper, who keeps bits of history such as photographs, family diaries, or the brass doorknob from the first city hall in an office closet or boxed in the attic. What the members of these historical societies share is the desire not only to preserve but also to educate. They want to talk about history with others and nurture historical interest.

In smaller towns, you might have to ask around to find out who the local historians are. In larger towns, the library or the town hall would be a good starting place. In cities, you can usually find the historical society in the phone book.

Historical societies are often ignored by researchers because the word "library" is not in their name. But since so many historical collections are largely made up of documents, they are, in effect, libraries, where researchers can study. For example, I had the good fortune in 1980 and 1981 to spend several days in the reading rooms of the Maryland Historical Society in Baltimore, reading old, old newspapers, maps, and theatrical playbills for a book chapter I was writing about the history of Shakespearean plays in America.

Museums, too, are libraries. While we tend to think of museums as displays of paintings, machines, or dinosaur bones, remember that every museum, behind the public galleries, contains rooms, often whole departments, of documents. The next time you're in a museum, find the library and ask about the use of materials for research.

Every topic or question for research has its historical dimension, even if that history goes back only a few years. Historical societies and museums are just as devoted to today and yesterday as to the more distant past. If my topic in 1980–1981 had been soil erosion along Chesapeake Bay or corruption in two recent political contests, instead of Shakespearean play performances in Maryland before the Civil War, I still could have found abundant primary sources at the Maryland Historical Society. It's only our narrow view of history that keeps us from realizing the broad usefulness of these resources.

Publications of Special-Interest Groups. You're sitting in a dentist's office waiting to have the pain in your jaw checked out. To get your mind off your troubles, you take some colorful pamphlets from the rack in the waiting area. You read the titles: "Dieting and Dental Care" and "Baby's First Tooth Brush." The pamphlets don't advertise; they summarize current research and describe recommended procedures. They provide helpful information.

You note that the pamphlets come from a special-interest or professional organization, such as the American Dental Association. The pamphlets may include a short bibliography or an address to write for more information.

You might not think of the pamphlets as research material, but special-interest group literature can give you a place to start, and often more than that, on many topics. For example, the brochure "Dieting and Dental Care" might spark a research question on the effect of certain fad diets on teeth; in summarizing the research, the pamphlet can tell what the issues are, why experts disagree, and where to start looking for more data.

There are two kinds of special-interest publications: (1) books, magazines, and short articles to keep the members and the public informed, and (2) pamphlets and brief reports that argue for the official position of the group on political issues. Because the two kinds of publications are different, we have to use them very differently.

The first category includes scholarly journals and indexes that are published by professional and special-interest groups to keep their members well-informed about new ideas and discoveries in their fields. In these works, different opinions are aired and controversial issues are addressed. Readers and writers rely on these sources for accurate, carefully-researched information.

The second category includes literature that is produced by professional and special-interest groups to win favorable votes from members, the public, and elected officials about certain ideas. These groups are often formed for political lobbying. Even though a pamphlet or brochure speaks for or against certain legislation, we should not exclude it from our research. But we should handle it carefully. If, for example, I research the sale of handguns to citizens, I may come across literature about the stand taken by a national association of police chiefs. Instead of disregarding this literature as political, I'll do some reflective note-taking on their argument and their evidence; I'll seek out literature with an opposing viewpoint from the National Rifle Association; and I'll do some reflective note-taking on that. I won't base my conclusions on either or both groups' views (after all, there are usually more than two sides to a story), but position statements of both groups may appear in my report.

EXERCISE: This section asks you to take a broad view of what might be useful research material. Brainstorm some other unconventional sources. Choose one or two of these. How would you evaluate their usefulness in research? For example, can a candidate's campaign letter be good research material? How? How not? ∎

WRITING YOUR RESEARCH FOR OTHERS—SOME NOTABLE SEARCHES

When people really love searching, it comes through in their writing for others. It says, "Listen to me. Pay attention. I've learned something you'll want to know."

This section presents the writings of four researchers. One is a research paper for a college course; three are excerpts from books. The styles differ; the subjects differ greatly; the research materials are also very different. But all four share the writer's deep interest in the search. Note how this comes through in each sample. Note that all four spend some time talking about themselves: their reactions, their problems, their methods of doing research. But also note that all focus most of their attention on what they are studying and on what they found.

As you read, keep in mind that you are both a reader of research and a writer. When we read as writers, we read not only for information or entertainment, but also to see "how the writer does it." What do these writers do that might help us to write our own research for another reader?

The "How" Questions to Analyze Research Writing

The following questions can help us to focus our study of these writers' techniques.

How do you know that the research is important to the researcher? Find sentences or paragraphs that convey the researcher's involvement in the work, even if the researcher doesn't plainly say, "I really love this."

How did the writer do research? Reading? Interviews? Personal observation? As you read, mark pieces of information that have come from the writer's research.

How does the writer work the research material into the essay? In well-written research, quotations and paraphrases always make a point or explain an idea. Good research writers tend to use few direct quotes and many paraphrases because the paraphrases blend better with the writer's train of thought. Inexperienced research writers who have not done enough reflective note-taking don't develop a structure of their own thinking into which to fit their research; as a result they often quote lots of material from their sources. I've read many research papers that are just strings of quotes from different books and articles. Without a strong research question, and without a research log or reflective note-taking, it's easy for writers to lose control of their research.

How does the writer show awareness that you, a thinking person, are reading the essay? Well-written research always shows awareness that the reader needs to understand and be convinced. That is, good research writing describes clearly and uses research material as evidence for the conclusions it draws. The thoughtful research writer knows that the reader needs to understand important terms and needs more than one point of view in order to form an opinion on a controversial issue. (Reread the sections in Chapter 5, Observing and Describing and Drawing a Conclusion. Use the recommendations there to help you analyze the work of the four writers.)

How does the writer show that he or she is indeed trying to answer one

or more questions? Look for questions or at least a questioning attitude in the piece. Note where and how the writer expresses the goal
of the research. Note where and how the writer shifts the focus of
the essay after answering one question or part of a larger question. If
new questions are phrased, the writer should always show why he
or she is moving on to another part of the topic. This facet of writing
is called *transition*. Note how the writers make transitions, especially as they end one paragraph and begin another.

How does the writer document the sources? A scholarly book or
article usually uses a system of formal documentation (notes and
bibliography) to show when a source has been used and the identity
of that source. Formal documentation is required in some college
research assignments. In reading the sample essay that uses this
method, mark which information is noted by number. Why do you
think these data are noted? Are there other statements that you feel
should indicate reference to a source? While it isn't possible or
desirable to attach source numbers to every statement in a scholarly
essay, a good rule of thumb is that you should note every opinion
from another source and every piece of evidence that comes from
your research. To decide whether or not to note a statement, ask
yourself, "Will my reader wonder where I got his idea?" (See A
Note on Formal Documentation, later in this chapter, for more on
systems of documentation.)

Most research writing does not use formal documentation.
However, newspaper reports, magazine articles, and nonfiction
books, if the writers are careful, try somehow to let readers know
where the evidence comes from. Good research writing doesn't cite
opinions and statistics without giving credit to sources. The good
writer knows that the good reader will always ask, "How does he
know? Where did she get that idea? Is that source reliable?" Note
carefully how the writers indicate their sources. They usually try to
do this in a way that doesn't interrupt the flow of the essay.

Ali Ghobadi, "Elementary Particles of Relativistic Quantum Mechanics" (1987)

A freshman majoring in systems engineering, Iranian-born Ali
Ghobadi wrote this paper to fulfill the requirement of a brief library
research paper in his English composition class. As he told me in an
interview, he used this assignment both to delve into a topic he

wanted to know much more about and to experiment with writing about a highly technical subject for nontechnical readers. Because of his intense interest, the five-page assignment turned into a twenty-page revised draft, part of which I include here. Note his English professor's comments and questions (in cursive handwriting) and Ghobadi's responses to them (printed). As an intelligent writer, he uses the feedback to spur further thought that will be incorporated in his next revision.

Consider also his printed comments about his page of notes at the end of the excerpt. Because, as he admits, he did not carefully record the bibliographical data when he took notes on his sources, his draft of the reference page omits some bits of data that he'll have to go back to his sources to reconstruct.

See the character sketch of Ali Ghobadi among the success stories in Chapter 9.

ELEMENTARY PARTICLES OF RELATIVISTIC QUANTUM MECHANICS

I. Introduction

It's said that seeing is believing, but, at the same time, you can't always trust your eyes. It may be more accurate to say that understanding is believing, and sometimes that is where the difficulty really begins. To report on a set of particles that you can't see and give a set of statistics would accomplish nothing towards the goal of really understanding the phenomena, which is what I shall try to explain. Particle physics has been developing steadily since the discovery of the atom and its constituents, and in this report, I will attempt to be up to date. Scientists who are involved in this field are asking questions that defy the mind: what is everything in the universe made of and why does it interact in specific ways? To answer these questions, scientists often use extremely abstract mathematical ideas to express reality in precise equations. This fact and the nature of the problem itself makes the subject difficult to comprehend and difficult to explain.

This report will be a journey into a world that is on the smallest scale imaginable, and the information given may at times seem confusing. It would take years to ~~achieve a~~ *learn enough* physics to understand *convey?* the principles through their actual equations. Instead, the material will be presented in a loosely organized manner with the emphasis being on ~~a final~~ understanding ~~of~~ the subject rather than ~~a~~ superficial knowledge *ly* *ing* of the equations. The journey into the sub-atomic world will begin at the atomic level and progress into the more elementary states. While many aspects may appear unclear, I will attempt to answer questions *in order the readers' when* as they *are most likely to* arise, or will treat them in detail at a later stage. I believe that informality is necessary in understanding the concepts to come, and patience will be required as well. What seems unclear at first, will ~~be~~ *I try to* explain~~ed~~ at a time when it is most comprehensible. ~~While some topics may not seem to fit in a particular category, they are present to make things more understandable as a whole.~~ Now, let's ~~begin and~~ take a look at what our universe is made of.

Not clear as to how they "arise"

Could cut

II. Hadrons

Atomic structure was determined by Ernest Ruther-
ford in 1911, and it was the first major step in understanding the atom. He found that atoms had a tiny,
positively charged core, or nucleus, that was then
surrounded by a swarm of negatively charged
electrons. The nucleus is only about one ten-thou-
sandth the size of the atom, but it contains almost all
the mass. Scientists knew that enormous energy interactions were taking place there, and radioactivity, the emission of particles from the nucleus, was

James Chadwick

who?
evidence for it. In 1932, an English physicist discovered the neutron, which was similar to the positively
charged proton in the nucleus, but had no charge.

To what can this strength be compared?
It's rather incomparable.
So it became clear that nuclei were composed of
protons and neutrons bound tightly together by im-
mensely strong nuclear forces. *that keep the universe from flying apart.*

With the emergence of the first generation of
particle accelerators, physicists determined that
protons and neutrons were arranged into definite
energy shells in the atomic nucleus.[1] All the different atoms have different nuclear shells and their
energy levels were hundreds of times greater than
those of electron energy levels outside the nucleus.
Consequently this strong nuclear force was much
stronger than the electromagnetic field that binds
the electron to the nucleus. H. Yukawa, a Japanese
physicist, suggested that the nuclear force had an

associated quantum particle that interacted strongly with protons and neutrons.[2] It was already known that the electromagnetic force had its associated quantum particle—the photon. Photons are particles of light; when something glows, it is because electrons lose energy, and when they drop to a lower energy shell they emit photons which our eyes detect. Anyway, Yukawa's nuclear particle was experimentally found in cosmic rays and was called a pion, or pi-meson. Mesons eventually became a family of particles, and cosmic rays are kind of like high powered radioactivity from space.

A more exciting discovery came ~~around~~ ? in late 1952, and this was nucleon resonance, the fact that the proton and neutron could be energetically transformed into a new state of matter.[3] Think of resonance as a normal nucleus in an excited, vibrational state, like a guitar string being plucked, through the input of energy. Well, the nucleon resonance was unstable and decayed into a proton, neutron, and pion; ~~but it~~ the discovery was important because it meant that there were other quantum states of matter besides the neutrons, protons, and pions. When the next generation of accelerators was introduced, many new particles were identified and they were collectively called "hadrons," from the greek word for strong, since they all had strong nuclear interactions.

Einstein's theory of relativity, $E = mc^2$, among other things, shows that energy can be converted into matter. New accelerators supplied the energy needed to create other hadrons by smashing protons against other particles. These other hadrons were highly unstable and decayed into more stable hadrons such as the familiar proton in less than a billion-billionth of a second. Yet the hadrons all had a definite extension into space; they took up area. Also, hadrons had electric charge, magnetic properties, and they could spin. It was the spinning that led to the first principle of their classification. The spin of the hadron could take on only certain values (it was quantized) such as 0, $1/2$, 1, $3/2$, 2, etc., so it was either an integer or half-integer value.[4] The hadrons which had integer spin were called mesons while those with half integer spin were called baryons. The proton and neutron with spin $1/2$, for example, are baryons. Mesons and baryons behave differently in hadronic interactions. For example, the number of baryons entering a collision is equal to the number leaving; this is the law of baryon number conservation. But there is no law of meson conservation. The hadrons also had other charges besides electric, such as strangeness and isotopic charge, and always the same charges existed before and after a collision.

In 1961, Murray Gell-Mann, a physicist at Cal-

Tech, noticed a pattern based on mathematical symmetry which incorporated the conversation of charges. This was called the eightfold way and grouped hadrons in families with a definite number of members. All the members would have identical spin, but different electrical, isotopic, and strangeness charge.[5] The proton and neutron were members of a family called the baryon octet. The other six particles had already been discovered in the accelerator labs. They were lambda, three sigmas, and two xi particles.[6] Many properties of a given family of particles, such as their different masses, could now be related using mathematical symmetry. Proof for the eightfold way came when Gell-Mann predicted a particle, omega -. He did so because that particle was the only one remaining in a family of ten. Its discovery in 1963 brought a classification for hadrons, but it also raised some questions. To answer the question of how the eight-fold way worked, Gell-Mann introduced a set of really elementary point particles which we shall next examine, and it was these particles inside the hadrons that were being conserved.

III. Quarks

The particles that Gell-Mann theorized were called quarks, and they existed as point quantum particles similar to electrons with the same $1/2$ spin, but with a fractional electric charge. Supposedly, there would be three quarks, called up, down, and strange. These three quarks, like all particles, had antimatter partners, the antiquarks. The quarks were denoted u, d, s, and the antiquarks $\bar{u}$, $\bar{d}$, $\bar{s}$. So these particles bound together with strong forces to create hadrons. It is known as the SU(3) model and the baryons are made out of three quarks, qqq. Antimatter baryons are made out of three antiquarks, $\bar{q}\bar{q}\bar{q}$, but the mesons are made out of a quark and an antiquark, $q\bar{q}$.[7] In making hadrons, the quarks will always combine so that the total electrical charge is an integer (see quark table in appendix). The reason you can build so many hadrons from three quarks is that quarks orbit each other inside the hadron, and each different type of orbit corresponds to a different hadron. At the same time, the more energetic quark orbits also explain the resonances that quickly decay.

So the quarks explained hadrons and the eightfold way, because by using rules for combining quarks, you would end up with hadrons in the same groupings that the eightfold way required. The differences in the quarks are in the different fractional electric charge referred to earlier, and differences in mass. The u quark is only slightly more massive than an electron, and the d quark is about three times more massive than the u, but the s quark is fifty times more massive. The differences in masses is an unsolved problem (remember that these masses are extremely small—see appendix). Experimental evidence for quarks came around 1968 when the two-mile long linear accelerator at Stanford began operation. Experiments conducted there using very high energy photons revealed that the proton's electric charge was concentrated in

¶ pointlike structures. ~~At this point~~, physicists began trying to account for the motion of quarks inside the hadrons. One well known model was the "bag model" proposed by Kenneth Johnson at MIT. He proposed the hadrons to be like bags or bubbles containing quarks. In a hadron collision, the bubbles could overlap for a short time, and in the process, quarks could be exchanged. Then the bubbles separated again and each may be a different hadron.

Another problem was that free quarks had never been found. One theory to account for this is known as string theory and it says that pulling quarks apart is like pulling a band that constantly increases, thereby requiring an infinite amount of energy to break it. But before it would be broken, the energy input would be transformed into a quark-antiquark pair anyway, and so free quarks cannot be created. Yet, quantum chromodynamics, the theory of the interaction of quarks, does not strictly forbid the existence of free quarks, and the search for them continues.

Yes, but remember $E = mc^2$. Energy and mass are convertible. C is the speed of light squared, so in this equation, a tiny amount of mass is equal to a huge amount of energy.

do this because quarks are energy.

Around 1973, theoretical physicists postulated a fourth quark, called charmed, based on mathematical symmetries. In 1974, teams at Stanford, at Brookhaven, and in Germany independently discovered a new meson made out of a charmed quark and antiquark $(c, \bar{c})$.[8] The family of mesons created by these became known as charmonium. So the charmed quark was added to the other "flavors" of quark and in 1976, new mesons combining it with other quarks were created. Nevertheless, the charmed quark worked in quark model theory and was basically the same *as what? As the up quark.* except it had higher mass, which is why it had not been discovered sooner (no accelerator could create the energy necessary).

The hunt is not over yet, because another quark was added to explain the discovery of a high mass meson in 1978 at Fermilab near Chicago; this was the bottom quark. An even more massive quark, the top quark, is now postulated, and probably awaits discovery at higher energies. While there are now many fundamental quarks, they truly seem to be the end of the road. To see if this is true, we have to wait and let the future decide. With the quarks we have reached the end of one road, but now we can look outside the nucleus and find some more elementary particles, as well as look at the forces that control all we have seen and all those to come.

IV. Leptons

Here we have a class of particles that are not unfamiliar; it even includes the electron. All leptons have $1/2$ spin, and the other members of the class are the neutrino, muon, and the tauon. Leptons are different from other particles in that they do not experience the strong nuclear interaction, but only weak interactions.[9] Better yet, leptons do exist in a free state, and they really are all over the place. Now let's examine the leptons and some of their properties.

The electron was discovered way back in 1897. Since then, technology has put it to use in the form of electricity (electrons moving through a conducter) and civilization has been transformed accordingly. Paul Dirac, one of the founders of quantum theory, tried to devise a quantum theory which agreed with the theory of relativity. He tried to apply a mathematical theory to the electron wave, since the electron's properties were known and he could compare his results. The solution to Dirac's equation did predict the known properties of the electron, but it also gave a negative solution. The other solution described a positron, or an antimatter electron. But this was just one example of combining quantum theory with relativity; what was really discovered was the existence of antimatter. Antimatter really exists and tho only difference between it and ordinary matter is that electric charge is reversed. Laws of physics state that for each particle, an antiparticle also exists, and therefore, particles can be created and destroyed, since the meeting of matter and antimatter results in a total annihilation of both and an incredible release of energy. Today, Dirac's theory is incorporated into a theory called quantum electrodynamics, and this predicts the interaction of electrons very accurately.[10] It seems that the electron is the lightest particle with electric charge, and since electric charge is believed to be conserved, there are no particles for the electron to decay into. The electron seems to be another of the fundamental particles along with the quarks.

Another lepton, the muon, was discovered in cosmic ray experiments around 1937. The muon seems to possess the same properties as electrons, but its mass is about 200 times greater. The muon is also specified by quantum electrodynamics, and like all leptons, it is only affected by the weak nuclear force.

In the 1930s, studies of radioactivity showed that there was more energy before a nucleus was split than after. Mass-energy conservation cannot be violated, so Wolfgang Pauli suggested that a new particle had taken the energy. These particles became known as neutrinos, and unlike electrons

and muons, they have no electrical charge (neutrino means little neutron). Neutrinos are much
lighter than electrons in mass (they may not have
any mass) and have only weak interactions with
other matter.[11] Neutrinos are hard to stop; one
could pass through a billion miles of lead before
hitting something. There's also a lot of neutrinos
around, since they are the result of many decays;
there are probably billions of neutrinos passing
through your body right now. Strangely, there are
two types of neutrino, one which is associated with
the electron, the other being associated with the
muon. So there is both an electron neutrino and a
muon neutrino. [The strangest feature of the neutrino, and most difficult to understand, is that neutrinos are only "left-handed." Actually they have
$1/2$ spin, but only in one direction. This is a violation
of parity conservation (if a particle exists, its mirror
image can also exist). Experiments were conducted by Yang and Lee that proved it to be true,
making the neutrino an odd particle indeed.]

No doubt!

unnecessary?

In 1976, electron-positron collisions at Stanford
pointed to the existence of another lepton, the tau,
and its mass was about 3,500 times the electron
mass. This lepton probably has its own neutrino
also, and the reason for its existence are presently
unknown.

All the leptons behave as point particles like

It's really hard to understand these experiments without knowing how an accelerator works.

If you have time, I'll explain it, but to make a complex field impossibly short, it's done with magnets.

the quarks, and so seem to be equally elementary or fundamental. Whether or not more leptons exist will probably be answered by the next generation of accelerators. Having our fundamental groups, the quarks and leptons, we can now see how they interact.

V. Gluons

Understanding the gluons requires thinking about forces and fields in a different way, because it is the gluons that cause fundamental quantum interactions. These are the gravitational interaction, the weak nuclear interaction, the electromagnetic interaction, and the strong nuclear interaction. These interactions were presented in order of increasing strength, and each has *an* associated gluon of related strength. To put gluons in a proper perspective, you must think in the "quantum" way. Instead of thinking of an atom as a proton particle and electron particle bound together by an electric field, think of them as discrete quanta (an amount of something) exchanging another quanta—the photon. For example, if we are playing catch, you and I would be quanta, and the ball would be the quanta that keeps us together, so interactions (or forces if you must) are themselves quanta called gluons. Each gluon is responsible for a certain interaction, and we shall examine them all.

Gravitational interaction is the weakest inter-

Excellent analogy

Would the game be the gluon?

The ball.

action, yet it operates over very long distances. It only seems strong because when there are very large concentrations of matter (planets and stars, for example) so ~~there's enough of an~~ *the* effect ~~to be~~ *is* noticeable. The gluon for gravity fields is the graviton. Remember to think of a gravity field such as the sun's or the earth's as quantized into an infinite number of gravitons. This way, through the exchange of gravitons, the earth and sun are bound together. Unfortunately, graviton interaction is far too weak at the level of quantum interaction to be detected, so it is unlikely to be seen.

Electromagnetic interaction is also long range, but it is billions of times stronger than gravity. The source of electromagnetic fields are electrically charged particles that are either positive or negative, so the electromagnetic force can be either attractive or repulsive (like fields repulse and unlike fields attract). While large quantities of matter are usually neutral, their constituent atom's particles are charged, and almost all the properties of ordinary matter can be understood by the quantum and electromagnetic properties of atoms. The gluon of electromagnetism is the photon, or light particle, and it was postulated way back in 1905 by Albert Einstein. Experiments have detected recoiling electrons hit by photons, making it the only gluon confirmed experimentally. The theory de-

scribing the interactions became known as quantum electrodynamics, and it was the first example
of relativistic quantum field theory.[12] It was so because it incorporated relativity and quantum mechanics and related them to electromagnetic
fields. Quantum electrodynamics raised much
hope that all interactions were related to gluons.

The effects of the weak interaction are best
known by radioactivity, the disintegration of heavy
atomic nuclei. Most quantum particles are unstable
and decay into the few stable ones, which are the
electron, photon, neutrino, and proton. The decay is
caused by a special weak interaction. This interaction obeys a physics proportionality that requires
more massive particles to be effective over a
shorter distance (the graviton and photon, having
no mass, are effective over infinite distances), so the
weak interaction is very short ranged. The theory of
the weak force is that the interaction is mediated by
massive "weak gluons" (these are the latest experimental confirmation in the field; W and Z "bosons"
were discovered at CERN in Geneva). The way that
weak gluons cause decay in hadrons is that they
change the "flavor" (type) of quark. Through their
interaction, the charmed and strange quarks can
be changed into normal up and down quarks. Ultimately, this means that all hadrons will decay into
the stable proton. This same effect can also be carried over and effects the leptons.

Give whole title

The last of the interactions is the strong force which binds the quarks. The theory that explains the strong gluons is called quantum chromodynamics and it presents gluons so strong that quarks do not become separated. In this theory, the idea is that all the quarks also come in three "colors," which are just a way of labeling them. To go with the quarks, there are eight colored gluons. Since both the quarks and gluons are colored, the gluons stick to the quarks and bind them together. The gluons also stick to each other, so they do not become unglued either (this nuclear force is really strong).

Who came up with the "colors" categories? Why?
The colors were invented by scientists as a classification scheme that can be used to identify hadron forms.

Some colored quarks and gluon combinations, however, are neutral in color (for example, two shades of gray creating a white) and it's these neutral combinations that form the hadrons.[13] This theory, I think, is the most difficult to understand, but the ideas are well supported by quantum chromodynamics, so be it as it may.

Explain more.
This sounds more like theology than physics.

The four interactions have now been presented and so have their gluons, but what is really fascinating *to me* is that physicists today believe that the four interactions become unified as one universal interaction at the highest energy levels. At these highest energy levels, the universe was perfectly symmetrical. Today's reactions are the asymmetrical remnant of that past universe. It was the breaking of the symmetry that has allowed life to exist and our universe to be what it is today.

Actually, I think the report can stop here, because the rest may be more confusing than it is informative.

not needed here.

This paragraph, though, seems clear to me.

VI. Understanding Some Consequences of Relativistic Quantum Mechanics

We have now come to the end of the road in identifying the particles and forces that control all we see and fail to see around us. Already identified are the quarks, leptons, and gluons, and some of their properties. But I cannot end this report yet without trying to explain some of the consequences of what has been examined above. While I hope that some questions may be cleared, I also understand that some questions may be further compounded. Nevertheless, I hope the ideas can be accepted on the basis of an open mind.

First, let's tackle the field concept of quantum theory. What I will try to say is that fields, such as electromagnetism or gravity, have a physical existence. Keep in mind that relativity states that matter and energy are convertible (mass is just bound energy). Next, quantum theory states that particles and fields are not different, but particles are just the quanta of various fields. Material reality is only the transformation and organization of field quanta—nothing else. So, the intensity of a field is the statistical probability of finding the associated quanta present. Field and particle interactions are just interactions of associated quanta. Think of each field as an infinite lattice made of rubber bands or springs infinitely small. The plucking of spring or band would represent quanta (vibrations) such as electrons or quarks, etc. Now imagine the gluons connecting the fields (gluons may be springs or bands as well). The interactions of the vibrations are our material reality.

For me, this was the most fascinating thing to learn, but again, too vague without further lengthy explanation.

Next, let's examine the mind‾bending idea of virtual quanta. There is a physics principle called Heisenberg's uncertainty principle. At the quantum level, it means that if we measure the energy of an electron, for example, over a short time interval, there is a degree of uncertainty in the measurement inversely proportional to that time interval. So, for very short periods of time, the laws of energy conservation can be violated, and quanta can come into being and then disappear into oblivion.

This is hard to understand.

These virtual particles could become real if they are supplied with energy, and this has actually been observed in the laboratory. *What?* It can be thought of as the creation of a particle and antiparticle that immediately annihilate each other. While this

How? Do you mean approximate?

seems truly bizarre, it illustrates the statistical nature of reality. Also, it is the way that quarks were discovered, by pulling them out of the virtual vacuum. Indeed, the universe itself may be the product of a vacuum fluctuation (virtual until energy was added) called the big bang.

Finally, the discussion concludes with symmetry and gauge field theory. The result of the theory was

Ali, To me this is really opaque. Does it really contribute to the overall paper?

Unfortunately, this paragraph does not apply well to the paper, but it describes the current aim of physicists. I think the problem is that I don't understand it well enough to explain it clearly. It takes a lot of math and a lot of physics.

the unification of the weak and electromagnetic forces, and to understand it, symmetry must be first examined. Unfortunately, it takes too long to explain symmetry completely, instead I will provide an example. The theory basically states that a spontaneously breaking symmetry gave rise to the differences between the weak and electromagnetic interactions. Where originally there were four massless gluons, the broken symmetry left one massless gluon, the photon, and the others acquired mass. They are the W +, W −, and Z weak gluons. To imagine the symmetry breaking, think of people around a table with plates on both sides. The situation is perfectly symmetrical until one person picks a certain plate. If he picks the right, everybody else must do the same, and the opposite is also true with the left. Anyway, the evidence for the weak gluons was recently discovered at CERN and this lends great credibility to the electroweak unification.

While the physics does not end here, this report must end somewhere. Using higher symmetries, theories have risen using gauge symmetries that unify the strong force as well. *[Could resume here.]* In the future, it is reasonable to expect a theory uniting all the universal interactions. I realize that it is difficult to end a discussion on the subject as it has been presented because only intermediary conclusions can be drawn. In the quarks, leptons, and gluons, the forces of the universe are present, and at this point, accounted for, and it is these quanta which are the fundamental building blocks of all reality.

If this report has been at times difficult to comprehend, I apologize, but state it was just as difficult to produce. For all the questions that remain, either I am not educated enough to answer them, the average reader is not educated enough to comprehend them, or they have no explanation yet. The length of this report represents an attempt to make the subject comprehensible, but I hope that if it has accomplished anything, it has caused an awareness of the incredible and fantastic universe that we are a part of.

[handwritten] Energy = mass · (speed of light)^2
C = 186,000 miles per second, approximately.

Appendix

[handwritten] Measurement of mass using E = mc^2 where m = E/c^2

mass of electron	9.11×10^{-28} grams *[handwritten: -28]*
	.5110034 MeV/c *[handwritten: What is this?]*
mass of proton	1.67×10^{-24} grams *[handwritten: -24]*
	938.2796 MeV/c

			QUARKS
		$\leftarrow$ electron $\leftarrow$	proton
Name	Symbol	mass	charge
up	u	2	2/3
down	d	6	− 1/3
strange	s	200	− 1/3
charm	c	3000	2/3
bottom	b	9000	− 1/3
top	t	n/a	2/3

GLUONS		
Name	Quanta of	Role
Graviton	mass	gravity
Photon	electric charge	electromagnetic
Weak Gluon	weak, flavor	decay
Colored Gluon	colored charge	quark binding

These notes are horrible. I had a hard time re-finding anything when I tried to continue the revision. (Good experience. Now I know I must keep more accurate bibliography.)

Notes

1. Kenneth Ford, *The World of Elementary Particles:* (Blaisdell Pub. Co., 1963), p. 20~~-36.~~

2. Laurie Brown, "H. Yukawa and the meson theory," *Physics Today,* Dec. 1986, p. 55.

? 3. Axe, Nicklow, "Neutron Scattering...," *Physics Today,* Jan. 1985, p. 26.

4. Steven Weinberg, *The Discovery of Subatomic Particles,* (Scientific American, 1983) pp. 170–182.

5. L.B. Okun, *Particle Physics...,* (Harwood Academic, 1985) pp. 88–93.

6. Okun, p. 90.

7. Y. Nambu, *Quarks: frontiers in elementary...,* (World Scientific, 1985).

8. Nambu, p. 36.

9. Randall G. Hulet, "Electrons and atomic physics," *Physics Today,* Jan. 1987, p. 23.

10. Hulet, p. 23.

11. "Weighing the neutrino," *Science News,* 11 May, 1985, p. 293.

12. Hulet, p. 23.

13. I.S. Hughes, *Elementary Particles,* (Cambridge University Press, 1985), p. 286.

Ali, this is a wonderfully ambitious project. I feel that I understand, partially, small bits of it, but much that is basic is incomprehensible to me. What stymies me is the statement, "observed and verified in the laboratory." Since I don't know physics labs, I can't visualize the experiments. How can these hypotheses be "observed" to be true? Excellent work at trying to make such difficult stuff available to an uninitiated reader.

✍ **EXERCISE:** Imagine that you, like Ali Ghobadi's professor, are one of his helping readers. Imagine that he has asked you to read his essay and to comment specifically on what seems clearest to you and what seems least clear. Write your response. Remember to focus on specific passages and to be aware of your tone. (Review Chapter 4, if you need to, on the kinds of responses that are most helpful to writers.) ■

James Witkin, from *Bicycling New York City* (1987)

I'm no cyclist. Therefore, as Jim Witkin's advisor in our Professional Writing and Editing program, I could give Jim good feedback on his thesis, a guide to "prepare newcomers to the sport to face the challenges of bicycling in New York City." If his book made sense to me, we reasoned, it would probably make sense to everyone else who didn't know his derailleur from his Presta valve, but who wanted to learn.

With advice on everything from buying a bike to cleaning it to finding the best rides around New York, Witkins's book shows that a how-to manual can be written with wit and a sense of adventure.

This excerpt includes Witkin's introduction and the final two sections of his guide. These show the roots of his commitment to the sport and to the research. They also show how he uses his research

material—books, public records, interviews, and street experience—
to handle some hotly debated issues.

INTRODUCTION

My fascination with the bicycle began fifteen years ago when I left
New York to attend college in Washington D.C. Living on a student's
budget, which didn't include a car, I depended on my bike for
inexpensive and reliable transportation. But I soon discovered that
biking was more than just practical; riding my bike was like taking
a vacation. My daily commute was short; but even for just that hour,
I could relax and unravel the day's complications. This daily dose
of freedom inspired me to keep pedaling and learn more.

After graduation, I rode my bike as a messenger on Capitol
Hill. I spent so much of my spare time in the local bike shop that they
finally offered me a job as a mechanic and salesperson. A year
later, two friends and I opened a retail store, The Bicycle Exchange.
For the next six years, I rode the quiet, suburban streets of Fairfax,
Virginia. I started to write about bicycles while teaching a course in
bicycle maintenance for the Fairfax County Adult Education Program.

Because of a career opportunity I moved back to New York in
1984. Besides some rusty, urban cycling skills, all I brought with me
was my experience in selling and fixing bicycles. I collected the
other information in this handbook to help me meet the challenges
of cycling in New York.

The facts I provide here only introduce the subject. I've covered what I thought every bicyclist who ventures out onto the streets
of New York should know, including where to learn more. I've
organized the material for quick reference, so you can read this
book from start to finish or just each section as needed. The chapters are complete but not so detailed that you'll spend more time
reading than riding.

DO MESSENGERS GIVE THE SPORT OF BICYCLING
A BAD NAME?

You're out in your car for a drive. You hear police sirens and look in
the rear-view mirror to see a police car right behind you. You pull
over but can't imagine what the problem is, maybe that yellow

light a few blocks back. The officer asks for your driver's license. You search your pockets, but just this once you left all your ID at home. Before you have a chance to offer any explanation, you're in handcuffs and on your way to jail. Does this sound like a punishment that fits the crime?

Don't worry. You can't go to jail just for forgetting your driver's license. But if the original version of Local Law 47, the law regulating commercial cyclists, had passed, messengers who were caught without their ID would have received jail terms, demonstrating, I think, the hysteria generated by the bicycle messenger issue.

It's no wonder motorists and pedestrians are mad. They're having too many close encounters with bike messengers, those suddenly-appear-from-nowhere, two-wheeled demons whom Russell Baker called the "one menace of New York that nobody ever warns you against."

The number of bicycle messengers has grown steadily over the first five years of this decade (from an estimated 500 in 1980 to over 4000 by 1985) because they are practical: In this traffic-clogged city, there is no faster way to transport documents. They're faster than foot messengers and unaffected by gridlock; their bicycles are easy to park and impossible to tow.

As their numbers grew, though, so did the complaints about their reckless habits. The city government first tried issuing more tickets, which was a step in the right direction. But because messengers were not required to carry identification, they simply gave fake names and addresses to the police officers. The solution: Local Law 47, which passed on July 6, 1984, after several rewrites to remove the cruel and unusual penalties attached to some of the crimes. It requires:

• messengers to display a number plate, each messenger receiving a unique number;
• messengers to wear a jacket or vest with their company's name;
• messengers to carry a picture ID card
• messenger companies to keep a log of all their riders' activities.

The maximum fine for violating any of these regulations is $250.

So the Answer Is Yes

Bicycle messengers are giving the sport a bad name. Even Commissioner Ross Sandler of the Department of Transportation, who generally encourages bicycling in the city, admits that the messengers "have taken the gloss off the whole biking experience in New York City." But they're guilty with an explanation.

Everyone agrees that if bicyclists break the law, they must be ticketed. But this should be true for everyone who uses the streets. Increased enforcement over the last few years has concentrated on bicyclists and has completely overlooked a much larger group whose habits can be just as careless—pedestrians. "They have a habit of sleepwalking," explains James Lehman, a rider for Cycler Service Messengers. Much of what pedestrians call cyclists' reckless behavior is really cyclists' struggle for their right-of-way.

Also, the pressure of working on commission encourages riders to hustle and sometimes break the law. Messenger Humberto Hudson says, "Time is money to us. We get paid by piecework, not by the hour. We can't take time to stop for red lights all the time."

Taxis, another group that works on commission, have their fees standardized and adjusted by a city agency. But messenger services must compete with each other by keeping their prices low. Most messengers I talk to feel that if they obeyed every traffic signal, they couldn't make enough money to justify the hard labor and high risk that comes with riding a bike for eight hours a day on congested, unfriendly urban streets.

But the messenger problem, most importantly, suggests a more serious condition. The increase in the demand for bike messengers is a direct result of the increase in traffic congestion, and this is the issue that I think needs attention, especially because New York City presently violates federal ozone levels.

The city must reduce traffic congestion. We need more dependable mass transit, cabstands to keep the taxi business from the middle of the street, and the elimination of all unnecessary motor vehicle traffic, such as the mobile billboards that are gaining in popularity.

Instead of fighting each other, bicyclists and pedestrians should join together, as they do in several European countries, to work toward the common goal of reducing motor vehicle traffic. In

Germany, an environmental group called the Greens have adopted the slogan, "Don't trust anyone over 30 (kilometers per hour)" to draw attention to the problems of congested roads. Concerned pedestrians in Switzerland have organized their own "pedestrian-friendly" automobile club.

Manhattan Borough President David Dinkins agrees that "the greatest danger to pedestrians and bicyclists alike is motor vehicles." But New York has only one pedestrian advocacy group, Pedestrians First, and their primary focus now is anti-bicycle. We need groups whose ideas reach much further.

THE FUTURE OF BICYCLING IN NEW YORK CITY

The future depends on the outcome of several issues, which advocates from the bicycling community and officials of the city government are working on together. On the issues, the City of New York's official policy, as voiced by the Department of Transportation, "is to encourage the safe use of bicycles and to provide facilities for this mode of transportation as needed." Within the DOT exists a Bicycle Advisory Committee whereby members from such groups as Transportation Alternatives, Bicycle Transportation Action, and the New York Cycle Club meet with officials of the city government.

If Only the Bureaucracy Were as Easy to Fix as a Bicycle

The replacement of the unsafe, parallel sewer grates provides a good example of how slowly the bureaucracy moves. The Mayor in November, 1980, suggested that bicycle-safe grates be used when possible. To test new designs, the Department of Environmental Protection took $3^{1}/_{2}$ years. When they finally approved a new design, the engineer in charge of ordering the new grates submitted drawings to the manufacturer with the wrong dimensions. The new grates finally arrived but each one had to be modified to fit.

Because the city has a policy of avoiding sole-source contracts, another grate from another manufacturer must go through the same process of testing and approval. Of the thousands of unsafe grates in use, the city has replaced less than 200 in the six years since the problem was first recognized.

The bureaucracy is slow, but it's the only process available for effecting change. However, the process doesn't move by itself. The fuel that keeps the system rolling comes from the cyclists who get involved. Change can only come if concerned members of the bicycling community constantly remind the city government of the issues that need attention.

Many legislators are sympathetic but say they rarely hear from the cyclists in their districts. These officials can't work to improve matters if they don't know what the problems are.

The future of bicycling in New York depends on your involvement. Write to the Mayor at City Hall, New York, NY 10007. Write to the Transportation Commissioner at 40 Worth Street, New York, NY 10013. Get involved with one of the advocacy groups (see Chapter 9). You may even have some issues of your own, some particular pet peeves or ideas, which aren't currently being discussed.

The Current Issues

Most of the pressing issues facing cyclists today were addressed at the last meeting of the Bicycle Advisory Committee, held in November 1986. I've gathered these issues under three headings—engineering, education, and enforcement—and have included their current status.

Engineering. These issues cover the city's responsibility to replace, install, build, or repair something. They are usually the hardest issues to resolve because they demand the greatest expenditure of time, money, and effort by the city.

• *Replace dangerous, parallel sewer grates:* Every street has metal sewer grates by the curb (the part of the street used by bicyclists) to allow water to drain. Almost all grates are constructed with parallel bars set a few inches apart. A bicycle tire can easily fall through the space between the parallel bars, bringing the bicycle to a sudden stop and throwing the rider off. The city has been testing new sewer grate designs and has begun installing bicycle-safe sewer grates.

• *Install secure bicycle parking facilities:* Bicycling advocates argue that more people would commute by bicycle if their office buildings would provide a safe place to lock a bicycle. Two of the best places in the city to lock a bike are the World Trade Center and Rockefeller Center. Ironically, the new Jacob Javits Convention Center, which now hosts the annual International Bicycle Show, provides no facilities for locking bicycles.

- *Build new bikeways along new or refurbished street and highway projects:* A Westside bikeway is being planned into the current Westway project.

- *Improve access on bridges to encourage bicycle commuting:* An excellent bikeway now connects Brooklyn and Lower Manhattan over the recently refurbished Brooklyn Bridge. The city is looking at plans to improve bicycle access on the Queensboro and Manhattan Bridges, two targets of upcoming reconstruction.

Education. Finding the best ways to reach the most people is the challenge of educating the public.

- *Educate cyclists about safety and the importance of obeying the traffic laws:* One such program already exists. In 1973 the state legislature passed State Education Law Section 806:

  The regents of the University of the State of New York shall prescribe courses of instruction in highway safety and traffic regulation which shall include bicycle safety to be maintained and followed in all the schools of the state.

- The state can withhold funds if a school does not comply with the law. Roger Herz of Bicycle Transportation Action reports that even though few students in the New York City school system receive any instruction in bicycle safety, the President of the Board of Education signs a certificate of compliance every year.

- *Educate motorists and pedestrians of the rights and responsibilities of bicycles:* Transportation Alternatives is currently working with the Metropolitan Transportation Authority to teach bus drivers how to deal with bicycles on the road.

- *Create an Office of Bicycle Programs within the Department of Transportation:* To resolve many of the issues mentioned in this chapter often requires the involvement of more than one city agency. The DOT's Bicycle Advisory Committee provides an opportunity for representatives from different city agencies to meet and hopefully to coordinate their activities. But at the present time, the Bicycle Advisory Committee has no regular meeting schedule.

Members of the bicycling community feel that an Office of Bicycle Programs could orchestrate the actions of the different agencies, and it would serve as a central ear for all complaints. Critics of this idea argue that adding another office to the bureaucracy will not increase its efficiency.

- *Provide maps of all five boroughs specifically for bicyclists, which indicate the best commuting and recreational routes and bridge access points:* Transportation Alternatives has just completed a Brooklyn Bicycle Map.

- *Encourage the use of helmets:* Assemblyman Edward Sullivan is promoting a state law which would require cyclists to wear helmets on all public roads.

Enforcement. Everyone agrees that the law enforcement agencies must ticket anyone—cyclists, motorists, or pedestrians—who violates traffic laws.

- *Increase the number of police assigned to the "bike patrol," officers whose primary duty is to ticket cyclists who break the law:* The statistics show the value of increasing the size of the bike patrol. In 1985 two officers issued summonses to 6,578 cyclists. That year there were 5,401 bicycle-motor vehicle accidents and 24 fatalities. In 1986 the bike patrol, after growing to ten officers, issued 20,820 summonses. The number of accidents and fatalities dropped to 2,629 and 7 respectively.

- *Enforce Local Law 47:* This law requires bicycle messengers (see Chapter 10) to display an ID number and their company's name. The law also requires that companies keep a log of all their messengers' deliveries.

Some think the law should be extended to require all cyclists to carry identification. For example, if I'm ticketed for violating a traffic law, I can give a fake name to the officer. Not only am I not required to carry identification, but there is no penalty for giving a fake name.

What's Next?

Will conditions on the streets improve, stay the same, or worsen? What does the future hold for New York's bicyclists? Get involved. It's up to you.

✍ **EXERCISE:** Jim Witkin wrote a manual on a subject he knew well for people who were relatively new to it. On what subject could you write such a manual? Freewrite on this topic. Then draft a one-page description of your manual, similar to Witkins's introduction. Ask for feedback on this draft from your helping readers. ∎

Annie Dillard, from *Pilgrim at Tinker Creek* (1974)

This book taught me a world about writing, and living. When I ponder well-written research, I think first of *Pilgrim at Tinker Creek*. One of America's most celebrated essayists, Annie Dillard epitomizes for me the writer whose reading, talking, sensing, and thinking spring from her love of the quest to know. She writes modestly, "I am no scientist. I explore the neighborhood"; but, as this excerpt shows, she possesses the scientist's persistence and imagination commingled with the poet's dedication to the word.

What is *Pilgrim at Tinker Creek*? She tells us in Chapter 1: "I propose to keep here what Thoreau called 'a meteorological journal of the mind,' telling some tales and describing some of the sights of this rather tamed valley, and exploring, in fear and trembling, some of the unmapped dim reaches and unholy fastnesses to which those tales and sights so dizzyingly lead."

II

Learning to stalk muskrats took me several years.

I've always known there were muskrats in the creek. Sometimes when I drove late at night my headlights' beam on the water would catch the broad lines of ripples made by a swimming muskrat, a bow wave, converging across the water at the raised dark vee of its head. I would stop the car and get out: nothing. They eat corn and tomatoes from my neighbors' gardens, too, by night, so that my neighbors were always telling me that the creek was full of them. Around here, people call them "mushrats"; Thoreau called them "Musquashes." They are not of course rats at all (let alone squashes). They are more like diminutive beavers, and, like beavers, they exude a scented oil from musk glands under the base of the tail—hence the name. I had read in several respectable sources that muskrats are so wary they are almost impossible to observe. One expert who made a full-time study of large populations, mainly by examining "sign" and performing autopsies on corpses, said he often went for weeks at a time without seeing a single living muskrat.

One hot evening three years ago, I was standing more or less *in* a bush. I was stock-still, looking deep into Tinker Creek from a spot on the bank opposite the house, watching a group of bluegills stare and hang motionless near the bottom of a deep, sunlit pool. I was focused for depth. I had long since lost myself, lost the creek, the day, lost everything but still amber depth. All at once I couldn't see. And then I could: a young muskrat had appeared on top of the water, floating on its back. Its forelegs were folded langorously across its chest; the sun shone on its upturned belly. Its youthfulness and rodent grin, coupled with its ridiculous method of locomotion, which consisted of a lazy wag of the tail assisted by an occasional dabble of a webbed hind foot, made it an enchanting picture of decadence, dissipation, and summer sloth. I forgot all about the fish.

But in my surprise at having the light come on so suddenly, and at having my consciousness returned to me all at once and bearing an inverted muskrat, I must have moved and betrayed myself. The kit—for I know now it was just a young kit—righted itself so that only its head was visible above water, and swam downstream, away from me. I extricated myself from the bush and foolishly pursued it. It dove sleekly, reemerged, and glided for the opposite bank. I ran along the bankside brush, trying to keep it in sight. It kept casting an alarmed look over its shoulder at me. Once again it dove, under a floating mat of brush lodged in the bank, and disappeared. I never saw it again. (Nor have I ever, despite all the muskrats I have seen, again seen a muskrat floating on its back.) But I did not know muskrats then; I waited panting, and watched the shadowed bank. Now I know that I cannot outwait a muskrat who knows I am there. The most I can do is get "there" quietly, while it is still in its hole, so that it never knows, and wait there until it emerges. But then all I knew was that I wanted to see more muskrats.

I began to look for them day and night. Sometimes I would see ripples suddenly start beating from the creek's side, but as I crouched to watch, the ripples would die. Now I know what this means, and have learned to stand perfectly still to make out the muskrat's small, pointed face hidden under overhanging bank vegetation, watching me. That summer I haunted the bridges, I walked up creeks and down, but no muskrats ever appeared. You must just have to be there, I thought. You must have to spend the rest of your life standing in bushes. It was a once-in-a-lifetime thing, and you've had your once.

Then one night I saw another, and my life changed. After that I knew where they were in numbers, and I knew when to look. It was late dusk; I was driving home from a visit with friends. Just on the off chance I parked quietly by the creek, walked out on the narrow bridge over the shallows, and looked upstream. Someday, I had been telling myself for weeks, someday a muskrat is going to swim right through that channel in the cattails, and I am going to see it. That is precisely what happened. I looked up into the channel for a muskrat, and there it came, swimming right toward me. Knock; seek; ask. It seemed to swim with a side-to-side, sculling motion of its vertically flattened tail. It looked bigger than the upside-down muskrat, and its face more reddish. In its mouth it clasped a twig of tulip tree. One thing amazed me: it swam right down the middle of the creek. I thought it would hide in the brush along the edge; instead, it plied the waters as obviously as an aqua-plane. I could just look and look.

But I was standing on the bridge, not sitting, and it saw me. It changed its course, veered towards the bank, and disappeared behind an indentation in the rushy shoreline. I felt a rush of such pure energy I thought I would not need to breathe for days.

That innocence of mine is mostly gone now, although I felt almost the same pure rush last night. I have seen many muskrats since I learned to look for them in that part of the creek. But still I seek them out in the cool of the evening, and still I hold my breath when rising ripples surge from under the creek's bank. The great hurrah about wild animals is that they exist at all, and the greater hurrah is the actual moment of seeing them. Because they have a nice dignity, and prefer to have nothing to do with me, not even as the simple objects of my vision. They show me by their very wariness what a prize it is simply to open my eyes and behold.

Muskrats are the bread and butter of the carnivorous food chain. They are like rabbits and mice: if you are big enough to eat mammals, you eat them. Hawks and owls prey on them, and foxes; so do otters. Minks are their special enemies; minks live near large muskrat populations, slinking in and out of their dens and generally hanging around like mantises outside a beehive. Muskrats are also subject to a contagious blood disease that wipes out whole colonies. Sometimes, however, their whole populations explode, just like lemmings', which are their near kin; and they either die by the hundreds or fan out across the land migrating to new creeks and ponds.

Men kill them, too. One Eskimo who hunted muskrats for a few weeks each year strictly as a sideline says that in fourteen years he killed 30,739 muskrats. The pelts sell, and the price is rising. Muskrats are the most important fur animal on the North American continent. I don't know what they bring on the Mackenzie River delta these days, but around here, fur dealers, who paid $2.90 in 1971, now pay $5.00 a pelt. They make the pelts into coats, calling the fur anything but muskrat: "Hudson seal" is typical. In the old days, after they had sold the skins, trappers would sell the meat, too, calling it "marsh rabbit." Many people still stew muskrat.

Keeping ahead of all this slaughter, a female might have as many as five litters a year, and each litter contains six or seven or more muskrats. The nest is high and dry under the bank; only the entrance is under water, usually by several feet, to foil enemies. Here the nests are marked by simple holes in a creek's clay bank; in other parts of the country muskrats build floating, conical winter lodges which are not only watertight, but edible to muskrats.

The very young have a risky life. For one thing, even snakes and raccoons eat them. For another, their mother is easily confused, and may abandon one or two of a big litter here or there, forgetting as it were to count noses. The newborn hanging on their mother's teats may drop off if the mother has to make a sudden dive into the water, and sometimes these drown. The just-weaned young have a rough time, too, because new litters are coming along so hard and fast that they have to be weaned before they really know how to survive. And if the just-weaned young are near starving, they might eat the newborn—if they can get to them. Adult muskrats, including their own mothers, often kill them if they approach too closely. But if they live through all these hazards, they can begin a life of swimming at twilight and munching cattail roots, clover, and an occasional crayfish. Paul Errington, a usually solemn authority, writes, "The muskrat nearing the end of its first month may be thought of as an independent enterprise in a very modest way."

The wonderful thing about muskrats in my book is that they cannot see very well, and are rather dim, to boot. They are extremely wary if they know I am there, and will outwait me every time. But with a modicum of skill and minimum loss of human dignity, such as it is, I can be right "there," and the breathing fact of my presence will never penetrate their narrow skulls.

What happened last night was not only the ultimate in muskrat dimness, it was also the ultimate in human intrusion, the limit beyond which I am certain I cannot go. I would never have imagined I could go that far, actually to sit beside a feeding muskrat as beside a dinner partner at a crowded table.

What happened was this. Just in the past week I have been frequenting a different place, one of the creek's nameless feeder streams. It is mostly a shallow trickle joining several pools up to three feet deep. Over one of these pools is a tiny pedestrian bridge known locally, if at all, as the troll bridge. I was sitting on the troll bridge about an hour before sunset, looking upstream about eight feet to my right where I know the muskrats have a den. I had just lighted a cigarette when a pulse of ripples appeared at the mouth of the den, and a muskrat emerged. He swam straight toward me and headed under the bridge.

Now the moment a muskrat's eyes disappear from view under a bridge, I go into action. I have about five seconds to switch myself around so that I will be able to see him very well when he emerges on the other side of the bridge. I can easily hang my head over the other side of the bridge, so that when he appears from under me, I will be able to count his eyelashes if I want. The trouble with this maneuver is that, once his beady eyes appear again on the other side, I am stuck. If I move again, the show is over for the evening. I have to remain in whatever insane position I happen to be caught, for as long as I am in his sight, so that I stiffen all my muscles, bruise my ankles on the concrete, and burn my fingers on the cigarette. And if the muskrat goes out on a bank to feed, there I am with my face hanging a foot over the water, unable to see anything but crayfish. So I have learned to take it easy on these five-second flings.

When the muskrat went under the bridge, I moved so I could face downstream comfortably. He reappeared, and I had a good look at him. He was eight inches long in the body, and another six in the tail. Muskrat tails are black and scaled, flattened not horizontally, like beavers' tails, but vertically, like a belt stood on edge. In the winter, muskrats' tails sometimes freeze solid, and the animals chew off the frozen parts up to about an inch of the body. They must swim entirely with their hind feet, and have a terrible time steering. This one used his tail as a rudder and only occasionally as a propeller; mostly he swam with a pedaling motion of his hind feet, held very straight and moving down and around, "toeing down" like a bicycle racer. The soles of his hind feet were strangely pale; his toenails were pointed in long cones. He kept his forelegs still, tucked up to his chest.

The muskrat clambered out on the bank across the stream from me, and began feeding. He chomped down on a ten-inch weed, pushing it into his mouth steadily with both forepaws as a carpenter feeds a saw. I could hear his chewing; it sounded like somebody eating celery sticks. Then he slid back into the water with the weed still in his mouth, crossed under the bridge, and, instead of returning to his den, rose erect on a submerged rock and calmly polished off the rest of the weed. He was about four feet away from me. Immediately he swam under the bridge again, hauled himself out on the bank, and unerringly found the same spot on the grass, where he devoured the weed's stump.

All this time I was not only doing an elaborate about-face every time his eyes disappeared under the bridge, but I was also smoking a cigarette. He never noticed that the configuration of the bridge metamorphosed utterly every time he went under it. Many animals are the same way: they can't see a thing unless it's moving. Similarly, every time he turned his head away, I was free to smoke the cigarette, although of course I never knew when he would suddenly turn again and leave me caught in some wretched position. The galling thing was, he was downwind of me and my cigarette: was I really going through all this for a creature without any sense whatsoever?

After the weed stump was gone, the muskrat began ranging over the grass with a nervous motion, chewing off mouthfuls of grass and clover near the base. Soon he had gathered a huge, bushy mouthful; he pushed into the water, crossed under the bridge, swam towards his den, and dove.

When he launched himself again shortly, having apparently cached the grass, he repeated the same routine in businesslike fashion, and returned with another shock of grass.

Out he came again. I lost him for a minute when he went under the bridge; he did not come out where I expected him. Suddenly to my utter disbelief he appeared on the bank next to me. The troll bridge itself is on a level with the low bank; there I was, and there he was, at my side. I could have touched him with the palm of my hand without straightening my elbow. He was ready to hand.

Foraging beside me he walked very humped up, maybe to save heat loss through evaporation. Generally, whenever he was out of water he assumed the shape of a shmoo; his shoulders were as slender as a kitten's. He used his forepaws to part clumps of grass extremely tidily; I could see the flex in his narrow wrists. He gathered mouthfuls of grass and clover less by actually gnawing than by biting hard near the ground, locking his neck muscles, and pushing up jerkily with his forelegs.

His jaw was underslung, his black eyes close set and glistening, his small ears pointed and furred. I will have to try and see if he can cock them. I could see the water-slicked long hairs of his coat, which gathered in rich brown strands that emphasized the smooth contours of his body, and which parted to reveal the paler, softer hair like rabbit fur underneath. Despite his closeness, I never saw his teeth or belly.

After several minutes of rummaging about in the grass at my side, he eased into the water under the bridge and paddled to his den with the jawful of grass held high, and that was the last I saw of him.

In the forty minutes I watched him, he never saw me, smelled me, or heard me at all. When he was in full view of course I never moved except to breathe. My eyes would move, too, following his, but he never noticed. I even swallowed a couple of times: nothing. The swallowing thing interested me because I had read that, when you are trying to hand-tame wild birds, if you inadvertently swallow, you ruin everything. The bird, according to this theory, thinks you are swallowing in anticipation, and off it goes. The muskrat never twitched. Only once, when he was feeding from the opposite bank about eight feet away from me, did he suddenly rise upright, all alert—and then he immediately resumed foraging. But he never knew I was there.

I never knew I was there, either. For that forty minutes last night I was as purely sensitive and mute as a photographic plate; I received impressions, but I did not print out captions. My own self-awareness had disappeared; it seems now almost as though, had I been wired with electrodes, my EEG would have been flat. I have done this sort of thing so often that I have lost self-consciousness about moving slowly and halting suddenly; it is second nature to me now. And I have often noticed that even a few minutes of this self-forgetfulness is tremendously invigorating. I wonder if we do not waste most of our energy just by spending every waking minute saying hello to ourselves. Martin Buber quotes an old Hasid master who said, "When you walk across the fields with your mind pure and holy, then from all the stones, and all growing things, and all animals, the sparks of their soul come out and cling to you, and then they are purified and become a holy fire in you." This is one way of describing the energy that comes, using the specialized Kabbalistic vocabulary of Hasidism.

I have tried to show muskrats to other people, but it rarely works. No matter how quiet we are, the muskrats stay hidden. Maybe they sense the tense hum of consciousness, the buzz from two human beings who in the silence cannot help but be aware of each other, and so of themselves. Then too, the other people invariably suffer from a self-consciousness that prevents their stalking well. It used to bother me, too: I just could not bear to lose so much dignity that I would completely alter my whole way of being for a muskrat. So I would move or look around or scratch my nose, and no muskrats would show, leaving me alone with my dignity for days on end, until I decided that it was worth my while to learn—from the muskrats themselves—how to stalk.

The old, classic rule for stalking is, "Stop often 'n' set frequent." The rule cannot be improved upon, but muskrats will permit a little more. If a muskrat's eyes are out of sight, I can practically do a buck-and-wing on his tail, and he'll never notice. A few days ago I approached a muskrat feeding on a bank by the troll bridge simply by taking as many gliding steps towards him as possible while his head was turned. I spread my weight as evenly as I could, so that he wouldn't feel my coming through the ground, and so that no matter when I became visible to him, I could pause motionless until he turned away again without having to balance too awkwardly on one leg.

When I got within ten feet of him, I was sure he would flee, but he continued to browse nearsightedly among the mown clovers and grass. Since I had seen just about everything I was ever going to see, I continued approaching just to see when he would break. To my utter bafflement, he never broke. I broke first. When one of my feet was six inches from his back, I refused to press on. He could see me perfectly well, of course, but I was stock-still except when he lowered his head. There was nothing left to do but kick him. Finally he returned to the water, dove, and vanished. I do not know to this day if he would have permitted me to keep on walking right up his back.

It is not always so easy. Other times I have learned that the only way to approach a feeding muskrat for a good look is to commit myself to a procedure so ridiculous that only a total unself-consciousness will permit me to live with myself. I have to ditch my hat, line up behind a low boulder, and lay on my belly to inch snake-fashion across twenty feet of bare field until I am behind the boulder itself and able to hazard a slow peek around it. If my head moves from around the boulder when the muskrat's head happens to be turned, then all is well. I can be fixed into position and still by the time he looks around. But if he sees me move my head, then he dives into the water, and the whole belly-crawl routine was in vain. There is no way to tell ahead of time; I just have to chance it and see.

I have read that in the unlikely event that you are caught in a stare-down with a grizzly bear, the best thing to do is talk to him softly and pleasantly. Your voice is supposed to have a soothing effect. I have not yet had occasion to test this out on grizzly bears, but I can attest that it does not work on muskrats. It scares them witless. I have tried time and again. Once I watched a muskrat feeding on a bank ten feet away from me; after I had looked my fill I had nothing to lose, so I offered a convivial greeting. Boom. The terrified muskrat flipped a hundred and eighty degrees in the air, nose-dived into the grass at his feet, and disappeared. The earth swallowed him; his tail shot straight up in the air and then vanished into the ground without a sound. Muskrats make several emergency escape holes along a bank for just this very purpose, and they don't like to feed too far away from them. The entire event was most impressive, and illustrates the relative power in nature of the word and the sneak.

Stalking is a pure form of skill, like pitching or playing chess. Rarely is luck involved. I do it right or I do it wrong; the muskrat will tell me, and that right early. Even more than baseball, stalking is a game played in the actual present. At every second, the muskrat comes, or stays, or goes, depending on my skill.

Can I stay still? How still? It is astonishing how many people cannot, or will not, hold still. I could not, or would not, hold still for thirty minutes inside, but at the creek I slow down, center down, empty. I am not excited; my breathing is slow and regular. In my brain I am not saying, Muskrat! Muskrat! There! I am saying nothing. If I must hold a position, I do not "freeze." If I freeze, locking my muscles, I will tire and break. Instead of going rigid, I go calm. I center down wherever I am; I find a balance and repose. I retreat—not inside myself, but outside myself, so that I am a tissue of senses. Whatever I see is plenty, abundance. I am the skin of water the wind plays over; I am petal, feather, stone.

III

Living this way by the creek, where the light appears and vanishes on the water, where muskrats surface and dive, and redwings scatter, I have come to know a special side of nature. I look to the mountains, and the mountains still slumber, blue and mute and rapt. I say, it gathers; the world abides. But I look to the creek, and I say: it scatters, it comes and goes. When I leave the house the sparrows flee and hush; on the banks of the creek jays scream in alarm, squirrels race for cover, tadpoles dive, frogs leap, snakes freeze, warblers vanish. Why do they hide? I will not hurt them. They simply do not want to be seen. "Nature," said Heraclitus, "is wont to hide herself." A fleeing mockingbird unfurls for a second a dazzling array of white fans . . . and disappears in the leaves. Shane! . . . Shane! Nature flashes the old mighty glance—the come-hither look—drops the handkerchief, turns tail, and is gone. The nature I know is old touch-and-go.

I wonder whether what I see and seem to understand about nature is merely one of the accidents of freedom, repeated by chance before my eyes, or whether it has any counterpart in the worlds beyond Tinker Creek. I find in quantum mechanics a world symbolically similar to my world at the creek.

Many of us are still living in the universe of Newtonian physics, and fondly imagine that real, hard scientists have no use for these misty ramblings, dealing as scientists do with the measurable and known. We think that at least the physical causes of physical events are perfectly knowable, and that, as the results of various experiments keep coming in, we gradually roll back the cloud of unknowing. We remove the veils one by one, painstakingly, adding knowledge to knowledge and whisking away veil after veil, until at last we reveal the nub of things, the sparkling equation from whom all blessings flow. Even wildman Emerson accepted the truly pathetic fallacy of the old science when he wrote grudgingly towards the end of his life, "When the microscope is improved, we shall have the cells analysed, and all will be electricity, or somewhat else." All we need to do is perfect our instruments and our methods, and we can collect enough data like birds on a string to predict physical events from physical causes.

But in 1927 Werner Heisenberg pulled out the rug, and our whole understanding of the universe toppled and collapsed. For some reason it has not yet trickled down to the man on the street that some physicists now are a bunch of wild-eyed, raving mystics. For they have perfected their instruments and methods just enough to whisk away the crucial vein, and what stands revealed is the Cheshire cat's grin.

The Principle of Indeterminacy, which saw the light in the summer of 1927, says in effect that you cannot know both a particle's velocity and position. You can guess statistically what any batch of electrons might do, but you cannot predict the career of any one particle. They seem to be as free as dragonflies. You can perfect your instruments and your methods till the cows come home, and you will never ever be able to measure this one basic thing. It cannot be done. The electron is a muskrat; it cannot be perfectly stalked. And nature is a fan dancer born with a fan; you can wrestle her down, throw her on the stage and grapple with her for the fan with all your might, but it will never quit her grip. She comes that way; the fan is attached.

It is not that we lack sufficient information to know both a particle's velocity and its position; that would have been a perfectly ordinary situation well within the understanding of classical physics. Rather, we know now for sure that there is no knowing. You can determine the position, and your figure for the velocity blurs into vagueness; or, you can determine the velocity, but whoops, there goes the position. The use of instruments and the very fact of an observer seem to bollix the observations; as a consequence, physicists are saying that they cannot study nature per se, but only their own investigation of nature. And I can only see bluegills within my own blue shadow, from which they immediately flee.

The Principle of Indeterminacy turned science inside-out. Suddenly determinism goes, causality goes, and we are left with a universe composed of what Eddington calls, "mind-stuff." Listen to these physicists: Sir James Jeans, Eddington's successor, invokes "fate," saying that the future "may rest on the knees of whatever gods there be." Eddington says that "the physical world is entirely abstract and without 'actuality' apart from its linkage to consciousness." Heisenberg himself says, "method and object can no longer be separated. *The scientific world-view has ceased to be a scientific view in the true sense of the word.*" Jeans says that science can no longer remain opposed to the notion of free will. Heisenberg says, "there is a higher power, not influenced by our wishes, which finally decides and judges." Eddington says that our dropping causality as a result of the Principle of Indeterminacy "leaves us with no clear distinction between the Natural and the Supernatural." And so forth.

These physicists are once again mystics, as Kepler was, standing on a rarefied mountain pass, gazing transfixed into an abyss of freedom. And they got there by experimental method and a few wild leaps such as Einstein made. What a pretty pass!

All this means is that the physical world as we understand it now is more like the touch-and-go creek world I see than it is like the abiding world of which the mountains seem to speak. The physicists' particles whiz and shift like rotifers in and out of my microscope's field, and that this valley's ring of granite mountains is an airy haze of those same particles I must believe. The whole universe is a swarm of those wild, wary energies, the sun that glistens from the wet hairs on a muskrat's back and the stars which the mountains obscure on the horizon but which catch from on high in Tinker Creek. It is all touch and go. The heron flaps away; the dragonfly departs at thirty miles an hour; the water strider vanishes under a screen of grass; the muskrat dives, and the ripples roll from the bank, and flatten, and cease altogether.

Moses said to God, "I beseech thee, shew me thy glory." And God said, "Thou canst not see my face: for there shall no man see me, and live." But he added, "There is a place by me, and thou shalt stand upon a rock: and it shall come to pass, while my glory passeth by, that I will put thee in a clift of the rock, and will cover thee with my hand while I pass by: And I will take away mine hand, and thou shalt see my back parts: but my face shall not be seen." So Moses went up on Mount Sinai, waited still in a clift of the rock, and saw the back parts of God. Forty years later he went up on Mount Pisgah, and saw the promised land across the Jordan, which he was to die without ever being permitted to enter.

Just a glimpse, Moses: a clift in the rock here, a mountaintop there, and the rest is denial and longing. You have to stalk everything. Everything scatters and gathers; everything comes and goes like fish under a bridge. You have to stalk the spirit, too. You can wait forgetful anywhere, for anywhere is the way of his fleet passage, and hope to catch him by the tail and shout something in his ear before he wrests away. Or you can pursue him wherever you dare, risking the shrunken sinew in the hollow of the thigh; you can bang at the door all night till the innkeeper relents, if he ever relents; and you can wail till you're hoarse or worse the cry for incarnation always in John Knoepfle's poem: "and christ is red rover . . . and the children are calling/come over come over." I sit on a bridge as on Pisgah or Sinai, and I am both waiting becalmed in a clift of the rock and banging with all my will, calling like a child beating on a door: Come on out! . . . I know you're there.

And then occasionally the mountains part. The tree with the lights in it appears, the mockingbird falls, and time unfurls across space like an oriflamme. Now we rejoice. The news, after all, is not that muskrats are wary, but that they can be seen. The hem of the robe was a Nobel Prize to Heisenberg; he did not go home in disgust. I wait on the bridges and stalk along banks for those moments I cannot predict, when a wave begins to surge under the water, and ripples strengthen and pulse high across the creek and back again in a texture that throbs. It is like the surfacing of an impulse, like the materialization of fish, this rising, this coming to a head, like the ripening of nutmeats still in their husks, ready to split open like buckeyes in a field, shining with newness. "Surely the Lord is in this place; and I knew it not." The fleeing shreds I see, the back parts, are a gift, an abundance. When Moses came down from the clift in Mount Sinai, the people were afraid of him: the very skin on his face shone.

Do the Eskimos' faces shine, too? I lie in bed alert: I am with the Eskimos on the tundra who are running after the click-footed caribou, running sleepless and dazed for days, running spread out in scraggling lines across the glacier-ground hummocks and reindeer moss, in sight of the ocean, under the long-shadowed pale sun, running silent all night long.

EXERCISE: Dillard writes in this excerpt that atomic particles are "free as dragonflies." So, too, seem her thoughts, which move from idea to idea, image to image, source to source, with dizzying speed. In response to the question, "What is this essay about?" one might respond, "Everything!" Nevertheless, I want you to try to find what you feel is the main idea and write a summary of it for a fellow student who has also read it. Remember from Chapter 2 that a summary is not a list of items, but your attempt to make sense of what you observe.

Share your summary with others in the group and listen to theirs. What have you seen that they have not? What have you missed that they have seen? After the discussion, write reflectively in your journal about ideas and feelings produced in you by the reading, the writing, and the talking. ∎

Victoria Rader, from *Signal through the Flames* (1986)

Sociologist Victoria Rader is known to several thousand students as one of the most brilliant professors at George Mason University. As one of the many colleagues who admire her as a teacher, I have been inspired by her efforts to raise community awareness of social injustice, especially toward the homeless. *Signal Through the Flames*, her first book, details the courageous work of many years of the Community for Creative Non-Violence (CCNV) led by the charismatic Mitch Snyder on behalf of the growing homeless population of Washington, D.C.

This excerpt, the Introduction to her book, makes clear her desire and her goal, while boldly showing us the world in which the CCNV works. Just as the CCNV flourishes through the cooperation of many people, so Vickie Rader, like other honest writers, acknowledges the helping readers on whom she relied:

> This book has been a labor of love, the concrete love of many people. Mary Ellen Hombs always found the time to read a chapter draft and sit down to talk. Each of these colleagues has read parts or all of the text and offered valuable suggestions: B. Wardlaw, Fred Millar, Dave Kuebrich, Karen Rosenblum, Lois Horton, Max Schleuter, Tom Dietz, and Marc Jacobs. . . . I was so lucky to find Eleanor Gerber, the imaginative, sensitive, and competent editor who moved the manuscript gracefully through the rough spots. . . . Bill Bennett, Robert Butler, Joe Scimecca, Thomasina Borkmann, and Doug McAdam expressed their faith in my work at very crucial times and helped me learn to take my own work seriously. I will always be grateful.

INTRODUCTION

My first night on the streets was Christmas Eve, 1983. The Community for Creative Non-Violence (CCNV) had arranged to use the soon-to-be demolished Presidential Hotel as an emergency shelter over the holidays and, with the wind chill plummeting to 31 degrees below, I was asked to drive through the city offering transportation. My husband Dave and I packed a thermos of hot coffee, made some ham sandwiches, and rushed over to pick up CCNV's Rich Miller. Rich was spending this winter on the streets himself, so he knew where to find the homeless. Once you knew where to look, they were hiding everywhere, huddled in abandoned buildings, wrapped in plastic behind hedges, curled up under bridges, in back alleys, garages, doorways, phone booths. The first person we escorted was a pencil thin black man trying to get some relief from the cold in an abandoned car. He was frightened of freezing to death in his sleep, as two of his buddies had the winter before.

Huddling around a fire barrel on "S" Street, three young men were bundled up like mummies, stoking the flames with broken two by fours. They wouldn't come but tried to convince an old man with painful arthritis to go with us. The man had something in a supermarket cart which he refused to leave. The younger men softened him up, gently joking, and swearing to guard the cart till morning, and the old man finally gave in. While the street men helped "Pops" to the car, I stole a glance into the cart and wished I hadn't. The treasure was a bloody pile of raw chicken parts; kidneys, necks, feet—the works.

After we dropped the old timer off at the hotel, we headed to the Ellipse, a massive grassy expanse between the White House and the Washington Monument. Proclaiming itself a center of attraction, the National Christmas tree glittered for attention off in the distance. But tonight there was no one; no cars passing by, not even a determined jogger. The frozen desolation was interrupted only by steam clouds erupting from the steel mesh grates connected underground to the heating system of federal buildings. Rich and I trekked along in silence from one empty heat grate to another, until we finally approached the last one, close to the Christmas tree. Then the steam cleared away from the metal frame, revealing a folded body.

It did not move when we called. We squatted nearby, and Rich touched one arm. Suddenly a man lurched up, sending me reeling backwards to the ground. The grate man laughed and helped me up. He had a white beard, flowing hair, and skin as loose and crumpled as a baked potato. He said he couldn't come with us, but he slurped our steaming coffee gratefully since the cup he had hidden in the bushes that afternoon had frozen solid. We said good night. Someone would freeze to death tonight, Rich predicted (correctly,) but probably not anyone protected by the dank warmth of a steam grate.

Rich went to help in the shelter while Dave and I checked the Metro stations. Down by the foot of the "I" Street escalator, four men slept together for warmth, but it was only a matter of time until police would chase them out. We offered to take them two at a time to the shelter in our small Honda and they accepted. That's when I saw Angelina. A tall blanketed figure stood hidden in the shadows and, approaching apprehensively, I offered a ride. The army blanket opened a crack and a young black woman with a gaunt face looked me straight in the eye, shook her head, no, and closed the blanket back around her. We dropped the first two men at the hotel and hurried back for the others. I spoke again to the woman, pleading as the weather worsened; we could take her to a women's shelter. It would be no trouble. But the crack did not open. We escorted the last two men to the hotel and returned.

This time, I stood with her in silence. After awhile, I told her a little about myself, about CCNV. If the women's shelters were full, I offered finally, we would drive her back to this exact spot. She pulled the army blanket more closely around her and moved toward the car. She had no belongings with her, but she carried herself with dignity.

Dave drove to Luther's Place women's shelter on 14th Street, and the volunteer let us in. She said we had arrived past their curfew and there were no more beds. I was shocked by the rejection in this cold and started to argue, when Angelina interrupted us both, saying her first words of the evening.

"Do you have showers? I would like a shower," she requested.

"No, we don't" the volunteer smiled pleasantly. "Now what are your names?"

We gave them and the shelter worker disappeared. What is she checking our names against? (Later, I would learn that there is a list of women barred from the shelter.) When she rounded the corner of the hallway again, she was still smiling.

"There are two beds left at Calvary," she explained. "I called and told them you were coming. Why don't you go over there?"

When Angelina reached for the car her hands were bare, so I

gave her my gloves, and we began to talk a little. She had owned some brown wool mittens, but they were stolen last week, along with everything else she owned. The shelter was on the other side of town and we took some wrong turns, circling around endlessly, it was late and getting even colder and there were many more people who needed transportation. Finally we found the church, but there were lots of doors and no signs of a shelter. Irritated now, I ran up the church steps to the most likely looking door and started knocking with my bare knuckles. Angelina climbed the steps and stood beside me. I switched to pounding, shouting now, "Hello! Hello! Let us in! Please, let us in!" There was no response. I tried the next door. Then the next. Running from door to door now, I circled the entire church, pounding and bellowing for help, tears of frustration streaming down my face. When my knuckles turned raw, I banged with my feet. They knew we were coming! Where in the hell were they!

"Let's go back," Angelina said calmly when I circled back around. No wonder she hadn't walked to these shelters by herself! As we started down the stairs, I missed a step and stumbled, and when Angelina grabbed for me, her blanket slipped off. "My God, you're pregnant," I gasped under my breath. She nodded, fear flashing across her face and then disappearing as quickly as it had surfaced. I thought of the burlap banner hanging in CCNV's living room. It simply says, "No room at the inn."

We found Angelina a bed for the night, but this first evening on the streets left me with a new question to ponder. As a concerned human being, I had identified deeply with the courageous attempts of Ethiopians to survive the war and famine in the Horn of Africa. I had protested in outrage at the insanity of the nuclear arms race, the butchery occurring in Central America and the savage oppression of apartheid. But before this Christmas Eve I had never really seen the suffering right in front of me. Nor had I developed a sense that, by my own actions, I could save lives. How do we become aware of human suffering, and where do we develop our capacity to respond?

My study of CCNV involved a lot of interviewing, of past and present members, of friends, supporters, detractors and opponents. I also talked with media representatives who covered the issue. I spent a lot of time analysing the change in news coverage over time and pouring through CCNV's extensive archives. But the most significant insights invariably came the hard way—while scavenging through supermarket dumpsters knee deep in tomatoes; lifting countless 50 pound boxes of food (CCNV feeds 1500-2000 people a day); by sitting through interminable court trials and tense, late night meetings; and participating in actions of civil disobedience. Most importantly, I volunteered in CCNV's soup kitchen and shelter and reduced my own distance from the poor. I was a sociologist interested in social change, not a Christian activist, but my experience with CCNV has changed me. Maybe they are also changing America.

Is something very different happening in this country, with two to three million "new homeless" living on our streets? I wanted to know who these people were. Where did they come from and what did they need? The Community for Creative Non-Violence (CCNV) has a lot of these answers. When they stumbled onto evicted families over 12 years ago, they opened up their living room, then storefronts, church basements, deserted school buildings, a railroad station, even tents when they thought it necessary. In fact, the group was instrumental in increasing D.C. shelter space from 174 beds in 1974 to over 1800 beds in 1986. CCNV created model infirmaries, daytime drop-in centers, clinics and soup kitchens. They galvanized a nationwide network of advocacy groups for the homeless, compiled the first reliable national statistics, wrote the first book, and organized the first Congressional hearings on national homelessness since the Depression. So I asked them, "Who are the homeless?" and they sent me out on Christmas Eve.

I had other questions. While their fifteen years of unwavering service is impressive, it is CCNV's dramatic acts of protest that capture the public's attention. The dramatic confrontations. The illegal occupations of buildings. The pray-ins, eat-ins, cage-ins, jump-ins and even laugh-ins. And most of all, Mitch Snyder's fasts. The danger of his condition, the size of his risk has captured the nation's attention and pricked our conscience about a group of people Americans didn't see, and didn't want to see.

Syndicated columnist Colman McCarthy writes regarding Snyder: "History looks kindly on the mad ones—Gandhi and his fasts, Paul and his seething, Joan and her voices." Snyder does seem mad in his stunning abrasiveness. "He's a lot like John the Baptist," commented a former friend. "People couldn't stand John the Baptist, either, but the world needs people like that." Others aren't so sure. The strident leader has alienated more people than he can count, including his natural allies and those at the top of *The Washington Post,* who called him a power hungry publicity hound and a fanatic.

The second time I went out on the streets was New Year's Eve. My guide this evening was Monroe, an amiable young vet with six months on the streets after his Army discharge. We ducked into a hamburger stand in Georgetown to look for his friend and discovered an entire encampment of homeless under Key Bridge. When we parked in front of the hotel which was being used as a shelter, after our last run, Monroe introduced me to Flimflam, a local con artist, and the Professor, a quick-witted, light-skinned black man from New Orleans. Both men were full of amusing stories about panhandling. Where's the sense of urgency I had felt the other night? This evening's shock came when we went inside.

The small hotel lobby was jammed with over 250 men glad to get in out of the cold. There were a few young black men, nattily dressed, carrying shoulder bags, and many middle aged black men looking perfectly normal. Most noticeable were the older looking men—both black and white—who appeared totally destitute in dirty clothes and rough beards, with snot running down their noses, frozen in their mustaches. They carried ripped satchels, suitcases, and sacks. I recognized two men from Christmas Eve and sat down with them on the lobby steps. They had been drinking, which eased their talk about missed families and past lives, and how miserable the last year had been. A wife dying of cancer; an eviction notice in between jobs with a seven-to-ten year waiting list for public housing. Beside us, several people were talking out loud to themselves, while others withdrew, hugging the lobby walls.

At the front desk, CCNV staff were handing over blankets, trying to give them out fairly but overwhelmed by the confusion. Some men had no covers while others had collected two or three new quilts, donated by Woodward & Lothrop Department Store as their Christmas gesture. The 80 quilts were brand new, shiny and soft, a lush pink satin. A few men sported them like capes around the lobby, while others sat or learned against theirs protectively. Two old men had them carefully folded on their laps.

At about 9 o'clock there was a commotion at the lobby doors. Mitch Snyder walked in with a white guy about 25 years old who had styled hair and a California tan, beaming a sunny smile. Who is that? Men jabbed one another, but no one knew. Cameramen and reporters followed the two inside and were hastily backing into and stumbling over street people as they pushed their way along with the two celebrities, making their way through the crowded lobby. Snyder called for the men's attention and proudly announced: "Hey. Guess who this is? It's Potsy from *Happy Days*! He's here because I told him a lot of you guys are his fans. You watch him every day on the re-runs." For a moment, the men were completely quiet. Finally, a few started yelling, "How ya doin' Potsy?" "We watch *Happy Days*" "Right On!" They were hooting and hollering now. Potsy looked distracted. Snyder had met the actor on a talk show the day before and talked him into coming down to the shelter to create a little publicity. After five or ten minutes, the TV star made a dash for the door, and Snyder passed out paper hats, New Year's blowers, and streamers. Most of the men felt too wiped out to fool with them. CCNV staff passed out Roy Rogers chicken and the famous bean soup from Dominique's Restaurant. The clock struck twelve and the cameras clicked on: Here were the hungry and destitute in the Presidential Hotel, wrapped in pink satin, smacking their lips on golden fried chicken, wearing party hats and throwing confetti. CCNV had made the news again.

Is Mitch Snyder a genuine shepherd of the poor or the ultimate flim flam man? After this New Year's Eve encounter, I wasn't so sure. But Snyder doesn't work alone. He's part of a very unique community. The media often refer to it as a rag-tag collection of teen-age college dropouts, middle-aged ex-convicts, ex-alcoholic street people with a few radical Catholics thrown in. Can this be? Where do they come by their dedication and how did these individuals arrive at CCNV? You don't often hear about these other Community members.

The rain dripped down. It was just cold enough for six CCNV members and myself to bunch together intimately while we talked about Tex's funny looking rain poncho and how some of our own families lived in large, nondescript suburban houses almost like the one we were huddling in front of now.

There was no media invited, no signs hastily painted, no dramatic scenes to stage. It was December 12, 1983, and we were the second shift in CCNV's 48 hour vigil in front of the home of White House Advisor Edwin Meese. To be honest, we were a motley looking crew. Jan, a religious Jew returning from nine months in India, was wearing a pierced nose ring. Justin, Yale University dropout, looked more like a high school student, with a young face and oversized raincoat. Wendy looked pale and awful, burned out from overwork and constant worry for her homeless friends. Eddie was small, with a shy crooked smile. Tex was stocky with a bushy beard that covered almost his entire face. He had created his raincoat out of a green plastic garbage sack. Then there was Angie, bright-eyed and energetic; she was new to CCNV.

The stars were clouded over, and it was dark except for the front yard lamp post and our meek little candles in plastic cups which kept flickering out. Coming out in the early evening, Mrs. Meese brought coffee and left the front door open so we could use the bathroom. Finally at midnight, a dark chauffeur-driven car turned onto the private drive and proceeded slowly toward us. Meese got out with his arms stacked high with papers and the chauffeur covered him with an umbrella until he reached the door. "See you at six tomorrow morning then?" queried Meese. The chauffeur assented and drove away. Meese said hello and disappeared inside, but he came back out in a couple of minutes and invited us in to talk.

Standing there in his tastefully appointed suburban home, I began to understand how this presidential advisor could have informed the American public a few days ago that people in soup lines were freeloaders, that the number of hungry people in America was exaggerated. Such statements were typical of officials distant from the poor, and it was typical of CCNV members to try to educate them. I felt the urge to abduct Meese bodily and carry him down to the CCNV kitchen or to Martha's Table to meet the children who eat their one meal a day there.

We talked instead. Justin was articulate, describing the conditions which cause people to turn to the soup lines. The others chimed in. Meese defended himself, saying that his statements had been taken out of context. "You guys know what that's like, right?" Everyone chuckled politely. Then Meese recounted stories he'd heard of cheating in the soup lines and the smiles disappeared. "I'd like to invite you to come down to the soup kitchen," Wendy intervened. She had lived with the homeless for over two years and knew almost everyone in the CCNV soup line. "If you saw for yourself, you couldn't say the things you did." I thought Wendy was shy, but she spoke up boldly now, describing individuals in the soup line, how many walked all day looking for jobs, how many had severe physical and mental disabilities, how all of them struggled just to survive.

"Well, maybe that's true in your soup line. I've heard about your group. But in other places, it's different," said Meese, authoritatively.

"No," replied Wendy, "It's not different in other soup kitchens. It's pretty much the same across this whole country. I would invite you to come and see for yourself. No cameras, no protest, just an honest visit."

Meese said he would consider it, and we talked a few minutes more. Then Tex offered him CCNV's book on the homeless, and we all shook hands and said good night. Gathering up our thermos and candles, we returned down the long windy drive to our cars.

"Well, he sure was cordial," Angie said. "Do you think he was open to what we said?"

"It's worth the effort," Justin answered, sounding exhausted now. He'd been up since 2 a.m., beating the pig farmers to the dumpster food, working in the free food store, and serving dinner at the soup kitchen before coming here. Two days later, we read what Meese had been doing that night, before he came home and spoke with us. Entitled "HO HO HO" in the Washington Talk section, *The New York Times* reported:

> If Edwin Meese 3rd, the White House counselor, had been embarrassed by his recent remarks on hunger and soup kitchens, he does not show it among friends. On Monday night, Roy Pautch, a wealthy Reagan stalwart, gave a Christmas party for 380 guests, most of them Republicans, at the Folger

Shakespeare Library, and after a dinner of smoked trout, prime rib of beef and plum pudding, accompanied by three wines, Mr. Meese presided as Santa Claus . . . Then he closed the party by saying "I want you all to sing 'Jingle Bells' so I can make a dignified exit and get back to the soup kitchen.' The diners laughed appreciatively.

CCNV members weren't as cynical as I was when I read *The Times* report. "We sow, we don't always reap," shrugged CCNV member Mary Ellen Hombs.

But they reap as well. The following fall, I watched Snyder begin a fast that he vowed to continue until the President of the United States agreed to renovate a dilapidated federal building that CCNV was running as a shelter. It was right before the 1984 Presidential elections and Snyder's chances didn't look very good. "LANDSLIDE PREDICTED: PRESIDENT MAY WIN EVERY STATE" read the newspaper headlines. American voters were affirming Reagan's economic policies and their hopes for renewed prosperity. The fast was hardly turning the nation around. In fact, after 48 days of starving himself, there was still no coverage of Snyder's fast in the media, with the fanfare of last minute election campaigning dominating the news.

Mitch's health was deteriorating rapidly and no one seemed to care. Sitting around CCNV's Euclid Street House, there was a sinking sensation of being nowhere, certainly not in the center of history, not even in the thick of battle. Columnist Colman McCarthy came by for a visit. He was writing Snyder's obituary.

I marched with shelter residents to the White House two days before the elections and we listened to some speeches, sang some hymns and trekked back slowly to the shelter. We brought our dinner over to the TV and huddled together to watch the 6 o'clock news. There was the President, talking to yet another cheering crowd; he looked pleased with the way things were going. Then Mondale's face replaced the smiling Reagan. Mondale was grinning too, walking briskly with advisors, shirt sleeves rolled up. Now he and Ferraro were raising their arms and clasping hands together in a gesture of victory for the supportive crowd below them. As Mondale faded out, a new story came on. A snapshot of Mitch

Snyder appeared on the screen, and the shelter residents murmured in concern. Snyder looked so small now, lying in his bed. Bare chested, his ribs poked out grotesquely, and his face sank in like an old man's without teeth. There was no smile, no crowds cheering him on. "Well, he ain't gonna be elected no President, lookin' like that, " someone noted sympathetically. The news commentator reported that Snyder was in critical condition after a 51-day fast. He was starving himself to death until the President showed some concern for the homeless. The shelter women agreed, things seemed pretty hopeless.

Then the snapshot was replaced with a video of two uniformed men, placing Snyder on a gurney, strapping him in, carrying him out of his house on Euclid Street down the crumbling steps into a waiting ambulance. Was he about to die? No, the reporter consoled us. Mitch Snyder had won. From aboard Air Force One doing some last minute campaigning, the President sent these instructions: Let Snyder have his model shelter.

How did CCNV claim such attention and get its way with the most conservative American president in recent history? Could anyone fast for a deeply felt cause and achieve such notoriety? Probably not. My recounting of CCNV's success raises serious questions about the source of the Community's power and the meaning of their victory.

I have spent three years studying this small community, recounting the day by day efforts of a group of ordinary individuals who act with extraordinary courage on the basis of their faith. I have tried to show how much their work matters in individual lives. So I have written this social history primarily from CCNV's point of view. Although I have tried to represent the viewpoints of outside observers and opponents at controversial junctures, my major interest has been to understand the experience of CCNV members and the ways they see themselves and relate to the world.

At the same time, I want to distill an analysis which extends beyond these particular people and events. CCNV's story is a concrete example of the general process by which a "private trouble" can become a "public issue" in modern America. Why was homelessness "discovered" in the middle 1980's and not before or after? And how is the problem being interpreted and framed? It's still too early to evaluate CCNV's long term impact on the alleviation of homelessness, but we can explore the short term achievements, by examining the Community's history. It's a remarkable story, and it's not over yet.

✍ **EXERCISE:** Good research is always inspired by strong feelings and passionate interest in a subject. Surely this is clear in Victoria Rader's writing. Yet, as a social scientist, Rader has been trained to strive for objectivity, to give fair consideration to conflicting views of a situation. Reread this excerpt to determine how she tries to be objective without losing her sense of conviction. How well does she succeed? From rereading her account, what research experiences seem responsible for giving her the beliefs she most strongly holds? ■

✍ **EXERCISE:** On July 5, 1990, Mitch Snyder, leader of the CCNV, was found dead, an apparent suicide. Writing in the *Washington Post* (July 6), authors Chris Spolar and Marcia Slacum Greene noted that "Associates of Snyder said yesterday that he . . . had been disheartened by the rejection of Initiative 17, the emergency shelter law that had been recently weakened by the D.C. Council." Using the newspaper indexes and files available at your library, locate several reports about the death of Mitch Snyder or about other events in his career as an activist for the homeless. Observe the methods of the writers: which sources do they use? How do they use quotation and paraphrase in citing their sources? Compare the reports in terms of tone and point of view. ■

A SEARCH OF ONE'S OWN: THE SEVEN STEPS

The following sequence of exercises applies sections I through III of this chapter. Use these exercises to complete projects that you have chosen or that you have been assigned.

Step 1: Create the Research Question. Do the exercise on page 218 for something you've wanted to know more about. Treat this as a freewriting exercise to discover a research question. If you keep a learning log or any other type of journal, use that as an additional source for questions.

If you are assigned a topic, freewrite to turn that topic into a question that you can research. As you freewrite, you'll probably discover several related questions you're interested in. Keep writing until you come up with a question you're comfortable with.

Don't discard any of your questions at this point. As you research you may find that you can answer several questions and that your focus will shift as you learn more.

Step 2: Write to the Limit. As a preliminary answer to your research question, do the exercises for writing to the limit in Chapter 2. These will help you generate ideas and tell you the difference between what you know and what you think you know. Indeed, you may find that these exercises cause you to shift the focus of your research. That's why I recommend them at this early stage.

Step 3: Scope the Project. If you've conscientiously followed steps 1 and 2, you'll have a solid foundation on which to begin your research, including names of books, people, and other sources.

At this point, try to scope the project. Draw a time line. Include in the time line the following activities:

- Writing in your research log (remember to include time for this as part of each element of the project; see Step 4)
- Library searching (plan slack time for dealing with unavailable sources, broken machines, or interlibrary loan)
- Interviewing: setting up appointments, writing questions, conducting the interview, and following up
- Searching other sources (again, plan slack time for the unforeseen)
- Discovery drafting (see Step 5)
- Asking for feedback from helping readers (see Step 6)
- Further searching, based on feedback (see Step 6)
- Revising of draft (see Step 7)
- Asking for feedback from readers
- Further searching and subsequent revising, as needed

Allot time from now until the deadline. Recall from Chapter 3 that Steve Gladis and his team at the FBI spread out their research and writing over two months in preparation for a major speech by the director. You'll find that what takes most of your time is not the actual reading, writing, and sharing with readers, but unforeseen delays, waiting for appointments for interviews, waiting for inter-library loan documents, and making room in your schedule for all other daily activities.

The fortuitous part of all this waiting is that you can incubate in your mind all that you've studied, so that you can really understand it (see Chapter 1, A Brief Look Inside the Brain).

Of course, sometimes you are given an immediate deadline of a few days or overnight. The same advice applies: space out the elements of the research process, even though each space may be small. Don't be fooled into thinking that just because the assignment is not due until next month, that you have plenty of time before you need to get started.

Step 4: Keep the Research Log. Consider your exercise responses as the first entries in the research log and go on from there. As described on pages 221–223, the log can be the place to reflect on your sources. The log can also include all your reading notes, interviews, or field work, if you use the all-together or double-entry forms of reflective note-taking.

Using the log to reflect makes the next job easier: writing a discovery draft of the entire project. The more you read, talk with people, write, and so on, the more well-informed your log entries become. As you carry on this process, your writing tells you when you've accumulated enough information to put it together in a draft for someone else. As a matter of fact, you can write this draft in the log. When you've written it, you can take it to a helping reader for feedback.

Step 5: Write the Discovery Draft. The discovery draft, whether or not it's part of your log, is the piece that takes you from writing for yourself to writing for others, the focus of your subsequent drafts.

Here you begin to deal with the questions of format, form, and reader's expectations that we talked about in Chapters 3–5, while continuing to write to experiment and know. For example, when Ali Ghobadi wrote his discovery draft, he confronted the problem of communicating to a reader who had not studied quantum physics some data that he himself only partly understood. If the discovery draft succeeded, it would help him understand leptons and gluons better and find out if someone else could understand them as well. Before writing his discovery draft, his notes had been only for his own benefit; after, his revisions were mainly for the benefit of his readers (although, I remind you, even the final revision can teach the writer something new).

Before writing this draft, find out the format specifications for your reader (if necessary, reread the format questions in Chapter 3 and read sample documents). However, remember that this is a discovery draft; if you suddenly realize something new about your subject, write it down for yourself. Come back to it later to reshape it for your reader or include it in a subsequent draft. In your discovery draft, you want to think about your reader, but you shouldn't ignore your own understanding.

Remember as you write this draft that you will get feedback. I often find myself bogged down in questions like "Will my reader understand me if I say it this way or would it be better to say it that way?" You can always ask your helping readers such questions.

To help you focus on your reader's needs, you may want to review the advice in Chapter 5 about describing, planning a course of action, and drawing conclusions. Most research writing, in school or on the job, involves one or more of these activities.

Step 6: Ask for Feedback from Helping Readers. Use the suggestions in Chapters 3 and 4 for choosing your helping readers and designing appropriate questions for them. Use the "how" questions (pages 242–243) to analyze the four selections and your own draft. You may wish to show these questions to the reader analyzing your draft.

Good feedback on the discovery draft will probably include questions about the accuracy of your statements and suggestions for other sources to consult. Be sure to seek out readers who are qualified to give you this type of feedback. You'll probably want to follow up these questions and suggestions by doing more research. Getting good feedback is one of the main reasons for writing the research discovery draft and if you've planned time for further searching, you won't be tempted to ignore your readers' comments.

By all means, if a reader does recommend a source, ask for help tracking it down. People who suggest sources often have access to them.

Step 7: Revise the Draft. Be guided by your readers' suggestions and your further searches. Repeat the feedback-search-revision process as many times as feasible.

A NOTE ON FORMAL DOCUMENTATION

Less experienced research writers often wonder about the right way to set up notes and bibliographies. There is no single right way. Not only are there several well-known documentation systems (listed below), but many periodicals and publishers use their own systems.

The system you use depends on your reader. When you ask your format questions, ask about documentation. If possible, check sample documents.

If your reader and sample documents are no help, use one of the style manuals listed below. Your library reference room should carry them and perhaps more:

- The *MLA* (Modern Language Association) *Style Sheet* (used mainly in the humanities)
- Kate Turabian's *Writing Term Papers, Theses, and Dissertations*
- The *APA* (American Psychological Association) *Publications Manual* (used in the natural and social sciences)
- *The Chicago Manual of Style* (published by the University of Chicago)
- *The Campbell-Ballou Guide to Style in Theses, Reports, and Term Papers* (Boston: Houghton Mifflin)

You may be confused by what seem to be small, arbitrary differences among these guides. My advice is to choose one system and use it consistently. If you get hung up on whether to put a comma after the author's name or two spaces after the colon, remember that the mechanics of documentation is less important than making sure that your reader knows what your source is, who wrote it (if this is known), who published it, and when. You want your reader to be able to track down your sources.

If a style guide doesn't tell you how to document a certain kind of source, say an interview or an old letter in a family collection, ask your reader's advice. If the reader can't help you, remember that for interviews, the crucial information is the interviewee and the date; for sources such as the letter, the essential data are the author, the letter recipient, the date, and the letter's present location. Use common sense: if you were reading the research paper, what information would you need to find the source?

Caution about style guides: these often include much other information about format. Although you might find this interesting, it might be inappropriate for your project. Check with your reader.

PROJECTS FOR WRITERS

Write Your Own. In this part of your growing work on your special skill, craft, art, or other activity, inform your reader about how to learn more, to do research. You may refer to the sources you recommended in the Write Your Own assignment in Chapter Six, but your goal here is to discuss fully how a devoted searcher can deepen and broaden knowledge of this subject or skill. For example, if your subject is playing the guitar, you might want to include how guitar players find out about the best guitars: do they go to libraries for information? Do music stores help? Should they visit factories? Must they ask performers at concerts? And so on. Be prepared to use the advice in Chapter 7 to do whatever research it takes to write your own research chapter.

In your chapter, be sure to include at least one brief example of a search that you conducted.

Connecting with Fellow Writers. Design and conduct interviews with two faculty members in your college or university or with two persons who conduct research in your place of employment. Review this chapter to help you brainstorm a list of questions. If you do this project with others in a class, compare your question lists and then revise your list.

Use the interviewing suggestions to help you conduct the

interviews. Use the interviews to deepen your awareness of the tools and methods used by successful researchers. These tools and methods will vary significantly from person to person and field to field, but you may find some surprising similarities. Write up your findings and report them to others in your group.

Free Experiment. "Seek and ye shall find." One of the fundamental themes of literature in all ages and cultures is the search. We are enthralled with searching, whether for the misplaced house key, for the mystery substance that all science has yet to find, or for love, happiness, or riches. Choose two or three of your favorite books, movies, or other works. How is the search a theme? What is being sought? What methods does the searcher use? What helps? What hinders?

Write about these questions in your journal. Then, using any form you choose, such as story, painting, song, video game program, and so on, express what you've discovered about searching in these two or three works.

As an alternative, experiment in one or more of these forms with capturing a search of some kind that you have been part of. Share your work with others and then revise it.

Chapter Checklist ─────────────────────────

To write for research
Develop a question, not a topic
  Use your journal as a source
  Use writing to the limit
Brainstorm potential sources
  Books and articles
  Persons to interview
  Public records, historical documents
  Special-interest literature
  Field experience (labs, travel)
Dive in and collect, using
  Index cards
  Notebooks
  Computerized filing

Keep a research log, to
  Compare sources (for connections and distinctions)
  Evaluate your sources
  Summarize and draw conclusions
  Write a discovery draft for a reader
Use reflective note-taking
  Try the all-together format
  Try the double-entry format

To find information
Use library sources, including
  Catalog of books (in different forms)
  Library stacks
  LCHS
  Various holdings of the reference room
  Bibliographies, periodical indexes, and periodical abstracts
  Computerized and microform indexes
  Periodical room
  Newspapers and newspaper indexes
  Interlibrary loan and consortial agreements
  Audio-visual collections
  Special collections
Do personal interviews
  Plan interview questions
  Take notes
  Ask detail and clarify questions
  Be flexible
  Be courteous
  Arrange follow-up appointment
  Ask for feedback from the interviewee
Use public records
Use historical societies and museums
Use publications of special-interest groups

To write your research for others
Study sample articles of varying styles and purposes
Study specific samples for your audience
Ask format questions

Use "how" questions to analyze form of samples
Follow the "seven step" method
  Create the research question
  Write to the limit
  Scope the project
  Keep the research log
  Write the discovery draft
  Ask for feedback from helping readers
  Revise the draft

To use formal documentation
Consult intended reader for preferred format
Consult specific sample documents
Use a style guide
Be consistent and use common sense

Words to Write By

Real writing always forces us to seek more than we know.

Good searching always requires imagination, persistence, and the tolerance of failure. It usually requires courage and a sense of adventure.

Research writing need not be dull. Research should give us the confidence to say what we really believe.

8 Getting Help with Editing

All morning I worked on the proof of one of my poems,
and I took out a comma; in the afternoon I put it back.
—Oscar Wilde

NOW THAT WE'VE PRACTICED THE BASICS . . .

I've focused to this point on the basics:

• writing to discover, experiment, and know
• learning how to write for others
• learning how to revise

We've seen that the writer's best tools are writing itself, asking questions, and using others' sample writings as models. If you feel comfortable with the strategies described, that is, comfortable with the challenges that always face the writer, then you can keep in perspective the role editing plays in the writing process. Editing, the final stage of the revision process, comes after you have revised the piece in answer to the questions asked in Chapters 3 through 6. Depending on the writer and the situation the editing process may be called "fine tuning," "proofreading," "making sure the i's are dotted and the t's are crossed," "checking for grammar, spelling, and punctuation," or "making sure everything's in order." Companies that depend on writing for their image and communication hire editors. Copy editors, technical editors, proofreaders, design-layout-printing specialists, expert word processors and typists all are concerned primarily with that part of writing that comes after the text has been written and revised.

For much of our writing, we have to be our own editors. Part of this chapter teaches you to be your own editor by noting things to check for as you edit and by describing some common traps for careless editors (plus ways to avoid them). The final section of the chapter provides sources of editing help, and advice on how to use these helps and to avoid misusing them.

TWO EDITING RULES

Rule One: Never Edit Too Soon

There are only two absolute rules for the writer-editor. The first rule is that you should never edit too soon. Give yourself as much time as you need to write and revise before you focus on whether or not all the words are spelled correctly and all the commas are in the right places. The worst mistake is to start editing as soon as you start writing. The writer who is terrified of being sloppy or of misspelling words will not overcome the blank page.

If your writing becomes bogged down by such fears, try free-writing, mapping, or any other strategies described in Chapters 1 or 2. Remember, if you don't keep editing in its place, you won't have anything to edit.

Since so many budding writers have been smothered over the years by a teacher's or parent's criticism of their spelling, it's crucial to keep spelling in perspective. If you consider yourself a poor speller, don't let that stigma paralyze your writing. Write, revise, then edit for spelling using the proofreading tips in this chapter, computerized spell-checkers, and the help of others.

Rule Two: Nothing Is Always Correct

The second rule for the writer-editor is that nothing is always correct. What to check for as we edit depends on the particular format of the piece we're writing. The format questions in Chapter 3 suggest elements to check for. Remember to learn the format by studying samples and asking questions before editing.

Some elements pertain to most formats. Correct spelling, for example, is one, so proofreading for correct spelling is an obvious task. But even this task somewhat depends on the particular format. For example, when may you use abbreviations or acronyms? Should any words always be capitalized, any never? May you use contractions? How about colloquialisms? If you quote someone who uses a different dialect or language, may you quote the person in that dialect or language? Later in the chapter there is more information on spelling and format. The point here is to illustrate how little we can assume about what to look for when we edit.

EDITING BY FORMAT: A CHECKLIST OF THINGS TO LOOK FOR

Chapter 3 lists basic format questions for revising to meet others' expectations. That list is supplemented here by descriptions of several categories in which format is likely to change from task to task.

Spelling

As noted earlier, most spellings stay the same from situation to situation. Still, some formats follow different spelling conventions. Here are a few ways in which spelling might vary from format to format:

1. **Abbreviations.** Some formats allow common abbreviations (such as *dept.* for "department," *&* for "and," *Sept.* for "September"). Some don't, especially in addresses.

2. **Acronyms.** Government and industry have created an alphabet soup by using initials to abbreviate the names of companies, agencies, products, chemicals, and many other things. Sometimes these acronyms form related words (such as, *MADD*, "Mothers Against Drunk Driving"); most are used by people who are familiar with the full names (USDA, DNA, IBM). Check sample documents for their use of acronyms. Remember that not all readers will understand the acronyms. To inform readers you can write the name in full the first

time you mention it (such as *deoxyribonucleic acid*) and follow it by the acronym (such as *DNA*) in parentheses. You can then use the acronym in the rest of the piece.

3. Capitalization. Generally, all proper names, plus names of specific places, businesses, and institutions, are capitalized. But businesses and other organizations sometimes capitalize other terms that are not usually capitalized (such as, *Company, Client, Sales Manager*).

4. Contractions. Formal writing does not use contractions (such as *don't* instead of *do not*). Informal writing uses more contractions, which sound more like casual conversation. Check format.

5. Dialect Spelling. In essays, biographies, stories, plays, and poems, writers often try to write the way words are actually spoken (such as, *I'm gonna go now,* or *It'll prob'ly rain*). Some formats allow you to take this liberty with conventional spelling; others don't. (Mark Twain was a great innovator in dialect spelling. Note his handling of dialects and the practices of other fiction writers such as Bret Harte, Alice Walker, and Carolyn Chute.)

Be sensitive to national differences in spelling. While *favourite* and *jewellery* are correct in England and Canada, *favorite* and *jewelry* are used in the United States. Be alert to these differences in the books you read.

Vocabulary

Is there anything more dangerous than a word? Saying the same word to two people may produce two different reactions, reactions that you can't often predict. There's no better reason for diving in and swimming around in sample documents than to learn which words are preferred, how different people use the same words, and which words should never be used in that place or with that person. Learning the language of an environment takes time and practice (see Chapter 3), including the inevitable mistakes. You may save time by learning some common ways in which acceptable vocabulary differs from format to format:

1. "I." Some technical publications still have a rule that articles not include *I* or *me*. However, this rule is disappearing as editors realize that avoiding the first person does not make an article more scientific and does not enhance the quality of the research. As you read documents that avoid the first person, note how the writer does this. For example, instead of *I interviewed fifty people*, the author might write, *Fifty people were interviewed* or *This researcher interviewed fifty people*. The event is the same, but the tone changes.

Note that company correspondence may also avoid the first person in some documents. As you read business documents, consider possible reasons why this policy is followed. Conversely, why might companies deliberately use *I* in some circumstances?

2. Colloquialisms. This is a fancy word for "everyday language." Generally, it refers to words that you'd be more likely to hear in casual talk than to see in print (*ain't* is the classic example). A word that's surprising in one context may be natural in another: *hell* and *damn* would sound strange in a research report on the potential growth of pumpkins grown in different types of light, but they wouldn't sound strange in a character sketch of your uncle who used to swear at the pumpkins he tried to grow in the basement.

In short, there are no words which are never appropriate. The context is the indicator and the only way to learn context is to dive in and swim around.

3. Fancy Language, Pompous Talk, Fifty-Cent Words. After a little bit of swimming around in scholarly journals, legal documents, or government reports, people often infer that they have to use long words to sound intelligent or to be good writers. They start writing *utilize* instead of *use, develop* instead of *build, activate the system* instead of *flip the switch*. Again, no words are always right or always wrong. When you read sample documents, note such things as the length of words, the average number of syllables, the simplicity or complexity of the language. You'll find, among other things, that these features vary greatly from situation to situation and among types of writing. The good writer is one who can vary language according to context, who can use the short, everyday word and the long, uncommon word equally well, depending on the situation. (As an exercise, reread the selections from Ghobadi, Witkin, Dillard, and Rader in Chapter 7. Note how these writers vary their vocabulary; Dillard, for one, has been recognized as a master of this.)

4. Gender. How does the writer refer to the gender of people in the document? Before feminist writers alerted us to the sexism in much of our use of language, it was conventional in published writing for both sexes to be referred to as *man* and *he*, as in the phrase *the history of man* and the sentence, *Every student should work as hard as he can.* Some writers still follow this convention, but most published writing now tries to handle gender reference differently.

Look at part of the sentence in the previous paragraph, *The good writer is one who can vary language according to context.* Following the older convention, I might write, "The good writer is *he* who can vary *his* language according to context." However, to avoid gender reference, I'll change *he* to *one* and remove the unnecessary adjective *his.* Another way to avoid gender reference is to use plurals rather than singulars: "Good writers are *they* who can vary language according to context."

Throughout this book, I use *he or she* with the singular verb: "The writer may do as *he or she* wishes." Although it's easier for a reader to picture *he* or *she* rather than *they,* there are two drawbacks to this alternative: (1) *he or she* sounds clumsy to many readers (maybe only because they are not yet accustomed to it) and (2) the pronoun order puts one sex before the other and so may still be considered sexist. Writers try variations: *she or he, s/he,* or even replacing the conventional *he* with *she,* as in "Every student should try as hard as *she* can."

While gender reference is a complex topic, I would like to point out that one other aspect to think about when you edit is gender assumptions about job titles. Though many titles carry no obvious gender association (such as farmer, engineer, nurse, teacher, professor, doctor, lawyer, secretary, politician), convention causes us to associate a gender. More and more writers avoid these conventional associations. For titles that carry obvious gender denotations (such as fireman, stewardess, actress, salesman, saleswoman), writers are substituting job-specific terms (such as firefighter, flight attendant, actor, salesperson).

As when you use colloquial language, your treatment of gender reference can lead to various, often unpredictable reactions by readers. Being aware of some of the options can help you avoid needlessly antagonizing readers.

Punctuation

While this book will not give you a complete refresher course in punctuation, later in the chapter I'll describe a few frequently broken rules and suggest some sources that can answer your questions about commas, colons, quotation marks, and so on. The discussion here concerns several common ways in which punctuation varies according to format and environment, though punctuation, like spelling, varies little compared to vocabulary.

When you edit a text for punctuation, remember above all that punctuation serves two basic purposes: (1) it separates one piece of text from another (the way the period does between sentences), or (2) it shows a logical relationship between two pieces of text (the way the colon in this sentence indicates that ideas will follow to explain the statement before the colon). Note also that some punctuation does both (for example, a semicolon separates two statements that could stand alone as sentences, but it also shows that the two statements are related ideas).

When you study any format, note how the writer uses space to separate text and show relationship. For example, instead of using ordinary punctuation, the poet might separate ideas by skipping lines

and show relationship by running four words together withnospacesbetween. A textbook or proposal writer might emphasize related ideas by indenting them in blocks and using a good deal of white space around them.

When you think of punctuation in this broad, basic way, the options proliferate.

After noting space, be alert to the variety of punctuation used. Note these three variants, each of them correct grammatically:

Winds sang. Leaves flew. November.

Winds sang; leaves flew. November.

Winds sang, leaves flew: November.

The first example uses only the period. The writer does not tell us how to relate the statements. In the third example, the comma shows the equality in importance between the first two sentences and the colon shows that *November* somehow explains the wind and the leaves. All three versions follow the rules, but the writers give us different ways to interpret their writing through the punctuation they choose. (As an exercise, review a few pages of the selections in Chapter 7. How would you characterize the variety of punctuation used by the four writers?)

Finally, study examples to see how different writers use punctuation to show emphasis or emotion. How frequently do they use exclamation points? Underlining? Boldface print? Dashes? Since questions change the way a reader mentally hears a text, they can show emphasis: how often is the question mark used for this purpose?

You'll find that some writers use these marks frequently. On the other hand, many newspapers reject almost all punctuation marks except the period, comma, quotation marks, and question mark. You may want to read through some current papers to check this. With such little variety of punctuation, how do newspapers achieve emphasis?

Graphic Design

See Chapter 5 for ways in which writers use graphics to enhance their texts. One role the editor can play is to imagine graphic devices to liven up or clarify a piece of writing. See also the discussion of space in the preceding section about punctuation.

Syntax

Syntax is commonly referred to as "sentence structure" or "grammar." Just as this book is not a complete handbook for punctuation, it is not a handbook of grammatical rules. The next section does go over a few of the errors commonly made by inexperienced writers at the college level and later sections describe sources of help for various aspects of editing, including editing of syntax. Here I note some major ways in which writers vary syntax. Knowing this variety can increase your options as you edit your own or others' writing.

Simple, Compound, and Complex Sentences. Look at the following three samples:

(simple sentence structure) I came. I saw. I conquered.

(compound sentence structure) I came and I saw and I conquered.

(complex sentence structure) After I came, I saw, then I conquered.

As you read, try this exercise for understanding tone and rhythm: see how these three types of sentence structure are used. (The most interesting writers vary the types to change rhythm. Changing rhythm keeps you slightly off balance, so you don't get lulled to sleep as you read.) Try this exercise on your own sentences.

Note that the complex sentence tells you more than the simple or compound sentences. Conjunctions such as *after* and *then* tell you how the ideas are related. Simple sentences force you to create the relationships.

Verbs, Nouns, and Participles. Consider the following three examples:

(verb-dominant sentence) The conferees *seek* to *eliminate* intermediate-range ballistic missiles.

(noun-dominant sentence) The *goal* of the *conference* is the *elimination* of intermediate-range ballistic missiles.

(participle-dominant sentence) *Eliminating* intermediate-range ballistic missiles is the goal of the conference.

Many style guides urge writers to make their writing more verb-dominant than noun-dominant. Why? Not only do verb-dominant sentences save words, but they also convey more action. Active verbs, say the rhetoricians, show more life than being verbs like *is* and *are*. The noun-dominant sentence forces the writer to use being verbs rather than action verbs and to use *of* and *the* more often, which add baggage to the sentence. Note that the participle-dominant sentence eliminates some of this baggage by substituting the participle *eliminating* for the noun phrase *the elimination of.*

On the other hand, each of the three sentences has a distinctive tone. You might read the first in a newspaper report; you'd more likely read the second in an official government announcement of the conference. (I'm not saying that government announcements should pile up noun phrases; they just do.)

Many inexperienced writers fall into the noun-dominant format because they haven't practiced verb-dominant writing. They pile up "ises," "ares," "ofs," and "thes" in essays and reports that should sparkle. Writers who know why they are writing and whom they are writing for use these different structures to create different moods.

Sentence Length. Study yourself as a reader. Do you pause at the end of a sentence before reading the next, like a singer taking a breath before the next measure or like an eater chewing and swallowing before the next bite? Most readers do. People who study readability, the ease with which we understand a text, agree that readability improves as sentence length decreases. The smaller the bite, the better your digestion. (Length is only one factor in readability.)

As you study formats, note how sentence length affects your ease of understanding and your level of attention. Don't observe only the number of words between periods. Longer sentences can be easy to read if there are rest stops along the way. Read, for example, this sentence from Dillard's book:

> The heron flaps away; the dragonfly departs at thirty miles an hour; the water strider vanishes under a screen of grass; the muskrat dives, and the ripples roll from the bank, and flatten, and cease altogether.

The semicolons and commas let us take quick breaths without losing touch with the whole sentence.

The writer's choice involves rhythm as well as readability. As you edit, try reading the text aloud. Listen to the rhythm of your reading. Does your voice drone on like the sleep-inducing hum of the heating system? Do you stop every five or ten seconds like the steady rise and fall of the waves against a sleepy beach? If so, try varying the sentence length. The sentence by Annie Dillard just before the one above is a short one: "It is all touch and go." Good writers learn to vary the rhythm as they compose; they surely keep it in mind as they edit.

Standard Written English and Other Dialects. Some teachers, employers, and publishers say that they expect you to write using "correct English," "good English," or "good grammar." This usually means correct spelling, punctuation, and syntax. We've already seen that what one person might mean by "correct" can differ greatly from what another person means. One teacher might want students to use *I*, while another might think it incorrect; one publisher might permit contractions, while another wouldn't, and so on.

Nevertheless, recent research suggests that all those who require use of good English do agree on some things. Spelling is one; Standard Written English is another.

What is Standard Written English (SWE)? Basically, SWE is a system of syntax rules that makes it slightly different from other systems, or dialects, of English. Linguists disagree about the exact differences among dialects, but all experienced users of SWE agree that some sentence constructions are "wrong," that is "nonstandard." For example, I might say, "Me and Tom run the office," and few people will complain about the syntax. But a written report with the same sentence will bring protests. In fact, the same person to whom I casually said, "Me and Tom," will think me illiterate if I write "Me and Tom" instead of "Tom and I." Similarly, speakers of Black English, a recognized dialect, would say, "He go to school," rather than "He goes to school." Any experienced user of SWE would consider the construction nonstandard if the sentence appeared in writing.

While many of the rules of SWE or any other dialect can be described, most dialects are too complicated to list neatly all their rules. Many of the rules are not part of a logical system, but are *idioms*, constructions that have become correct through common usage. For example, most Americans say "standing in line" while the British say "standing *on* line." Americans say, "I was in *the* hospital" while the British say, "I was in hospital." There are countless distinctions among dialects, none of which can be explained except by common usage.

Despite the vast number of idioms, we all manage to learn at least one, and often several, dialects. However, no one is born knowing any dialect, and if we don't do a lot of reading and writing, none of us will learn SWE. Remember, a written dialect has spelling and punctuation marks; spoken dialects do not. Moreover, spoken dialects are embellished by hand gestures and facial expressions, plus changes in loudness and tone of voice. We learn SWE the same way we learn form: time + practice (+ learning from our mistakes).

Keep in mind that SWE is not a style: it isn't about using long or short sentences, everyday or scholarly words, a casual or an official tone. None of these are issues of correct English; they are issues of format, situation, and the writer's choice. People will sometimes try to convince you that good English means making one kind of stylistic choice, but if you've read different kinds of works and tried writing in different styles and forms, you can correct their error.

Sometimes writers of SWE will deliberately include examples of other dialects. There's no reason why you can't, as long as you give the reader a reason for it. Indeed, using other dialects can bring life to writing that describes people's daily lives. To learn how to use other dialects in writing, study writers who do so, including playwrights such as Sean O'Casey, Tennessee Williams, and Lorraine Hansberry; novelists such as Mark Twain and Toni Morrison; essayists such as James Baldwin, J. W. Dillard, and Studs Terkel.

SOME COMMONLY BROKEN RULES

The following is a brief troubleshooting guide to help you edit your own and other writers' work. I try to cover some of the most frequent spelling and SWE syntax and punctuation errors made in college writing.

Spelling

The most frequent problems are with *homophones* (words that sound alike but are spelled differently) and with common terms that are often spoken differently than they are written (*phonetic spellings*).

Homophones. Though most college writers know the distinctions between the words in the following list, writers often misspell them when composing, because they are writing for meaning, not correctness. Editors need to be aware of this tendency. (Note: These errors are among those that computerized spell-checkers will not pick up.) If you are in doubt about any meanings, use a dictionary.

its, it's
their, there, they're
lose, loose (not homophones, but frequently confused)
who's, whose
tale, tail
undo, undue
bore, boor
fair, fare
foul, fowl
hear, here
desert (verb), dessert

A special subcategory is the mistaken use of apostrophes to form the plurals of nouns. Most English plurals are formed by just adding s to the singular (for example, *room, rooms*). Often writers mistakenly place an apostrophe before the s. Watch for this as you edit. People do this frequently when they pluralize family names (for example, *the Smiths,* not *the Smith's*).

Phonetic Spelling. Though English has some rules for spelling, those rules, unfortunately, have little to do with how words are pronounced. Most writers in this rich language learn early that the only way to learn English spellings is through reading, reading, reading, and writing, writing, writing. We often criticize ourselves and others for our inability to spell; in fact, we should congratulate ourselves and each other for the great number of words we can spell, despite the lack of help we get from pronunciation.

When we're not sure how to spell a word and no dictionary is handy, we try to sound it out, usually with poor results. Fortunately, we tend to remember the words we wondered about, so we can correct them in editing. (An editor must have a dictionary handy; an editor without a dictionary is like a batter without a bat.)

Some common misspellings occur when we hear a different word from what is actually said. Two examples I continually come across are in the phrases *used to* and *supposed to*. Writers write these as *use to* and *suppose to* because they don't hear the *d*.

> *Incorrect*: I'm *use* to this weather.
> *Correct*: I'm *used* to this weather.
> *Incorrect*: He was *suppose* to arrive at noon.
> *Correct*: He was *supposed* to arrive at noon.

Another common error is writing *then* instead of *than*. *Then* refers only to sequence in time; *than* is used to compare one thing with another.

> *Incorrect*: She made higher scores *then* he did.
> *Correct*: She made higher scores *than* he did.

Other such errors I run across occasionally include *bran new* for *brand new* and the substitution of *in* for *and* in common sayings, for example, *now and then, nip and tuck, touch and go*.

Vocabulary

Everyone has pet peeves about misused words. For example, I am outraged by the phrase *center around,* as in "The discussion centered around the recent firing of the chief of police." A center is a point, I argue; how can it be around anything? Friends of mine won't tolerate other errors that don't bother me at all: "You can't say, 'Bring the child home'; you have to say, 'Take the child home.'" "You can't say, 'The senator inferred that he would run for president'; you have to say, 'The senator implied that he would run for president.'" "They can't say, 'The city council condemned the action of the landlords'; they should say 'criticized' or 'voted to disapprove.'" I once knew a writer who said she felt ill whenever she heard the common question, "How come?" (Unthinkingly, I replied, "Oh? How come?")

The most frequent objection I hear is to the word *hopefully*, as in "Hopefully, the snow will melt by Saturday." Critics complain that *hopefully*, as an adverb, must modify the verb in the sentence. Since hopefulness is not a property of melting, I can't use *hopefully* in that sentence. To be proper, I'd have to say, "I hope the snow will melt by Saturday,'' even though everyone would know what I meant if I said it the other way.

Some style manuals, such as Foley and Gordon's *Conventions and Choices* (Heath, 1986), devote forty or more pages to lists of common errors in usage. These are useful for editors. Still, they barely begin to account for all the conceivable errors readers may find in our work. Writers should be prepared for readers' objections to certain words and phrases. Part of your job as a writer is to listen to these objections and decide whether the reader is right. Don't hesitate to make a change if the revision doesn't really violate your meaning.

If you are editing someone else's work, be careful about questioning the writer's vocabulary. Don't let your pet peeves get in the way of judicious reading. Ask yourself, "Does this word really obscure the meaning? Will this word mislead or anger the reader?" If you do suggest a change, do it respectfully. Rather than crossing out the word you don't like and writing in your choice, underline the word in question, then write your preference above it with a question mark beside it:

Morgan <u>continuously</u> *continually?* wondered if he were not too attached to the world. He found himself absorbed in the <u>sensual</u> *sensuous?* nature of things: not only rich meals and delicately perfumed women, but even the upholstery of his furniture and the sound of the traffic in the boulevard.

Punctuation

Studying the punctuation in your reading is the best way to learn how to punctuate. SWE punctuation follows relatively standard rules from publication to publication. As with spelling and syntax, the rules are not always logical, but they are pretty much agreed on. I'll attempt here to answer several of the most common questions about SWE punctuation.

1. When Is a Question Not a Question? Use a question mark after a sentence that is a question.

But how do you know it took four hours?

Use a question mark after a quoted sentence that is a question.

"But how do you know it took four hours?" I asked.

Do not use a question mark after a statement that only implies a question.

Watson wondered why the journey took four hours.
Watson asked Holmes why the journey took four hours.

2. Does Punctuation Go Inside or Outside Quotation Marks? At the beginning of a quotation, all punctuation comes before the quotation mark.

Holmes turned to me and said, "Come quickly, Watson, we must get to Anderson's and search Penwether's room."

At the end of a quoted passage, all punctuation that is part of the quotation goes inside the quotation mark.

"Because he feared being recognised by some fellow traveller?" I asked.

"Here!" he exclaimed. "The most recent one, and at the correct time. That accounts for all seven robberies, by my calculations."

If the quotation ends with a period or a comma, the period or comma always goes inside the quotation mark.

Holmes stated that there were no pigeons of a type called "Brewster."

"Mr. Holmes," he replied solemnly, "I come on a matter of the utmost delicacy concerning the security of our nation."

However, if any punctuation other than a comma or period follows a quoted passage, that punctuation goes outside the quotation mark.

Ledgard and Singer's *Elementary Pascal* contains hundreds of uses of the word "I"; it's written in the style of a Sherlock Holmes mystery.

Holmes and Watson rely on Babbage's "Analytical Engine": this machine led directly to the modern computer.

Why did Holmes say, "I can tell a Moriarty when I see one"?

3. How Do I Punctuate with Parentheses? First, no punctuation goes before the opening parenthesis within a sentence.

> After mitosis (cell division), the daughter cells reform their peripheral processes.

> Looping circuits center on the hypothalamus, which regulates the activity of glands and smooth muscle (such as the involuntary muscle of the viscera).

Second, only punctuation that is part of the parenthetical expression goes inside parentheses.

> The September 1979 issue of *Scientific American* (a marvelous issue!) summarized years of research about the brain.

> Did you read the September 1979 issue of *Scientific American* (about research on the brain)?

Third, if a parenthetical expression is an entire sentence, the final punctuation goes inside the closed parenthesis.

> Some readers are confused by the common terms *axon* and *fiber.* (*Axon* and *fiber* are synonymous in neuroanatomical usage.)

4. How Do I Punctuate with Conjunctions? Some conjunctions, including *and, but, if, though, although, when, then, because, since, after, before,* and *whenever,* among others, are usually preceded by a *comma* (sometimes by no punctuation) and followed by no punctuation.

> The Wisconsin senator could be engaging in the Victor McClaglen manner, *and* the ambassador even perhaps saw the campaign against this fighting Irishman as one more outlet for the anti-Catholic sentiment which had so long oppressed the Irish-American community. Moreover, Robert Kennedy worked for a time on the staff of the McCarthy Committee, *though* he soon found himself in disagreement with the Committee's procedures and resigned.

Sometimes conjunctions such as *and* and *but* may be used to begin sentences, though some editors and teachers object to this.

> One might have hoped that Kennedy, another Irish Catholic senator and a genuine war hero, would have seen himself in a particularly strong position to challenge McCarthyism. *But* there were perhaps deeper reasons for his lack of involvement.

He always served as sponsor for ADA's annual Roosevelt Day dinners in Boston. *And,* if he kept out of the public debate, he did not hesitate to intervene privately.

Conjunctions such as *still, however, nevertheless, nonetheless, moreover,* and *furthermore* may begin sentences; within sentences, they are usually preceded by a semicolon. They are almost always followed by a comma.

> *Nonetheless,* Kennedy's silence on McCarthy contrasted with Stevenson's eloquent defense of civil freedom.

> Arthur Schlesinger's *A Thousand Days* is perhaps the best-known book written about the Kennedy presidency; *however,* it is only one of several written by men and women who were close to the President.

5. When Do I Have to Use Commas? Commas are the most frequently used punctuation marks, yet there is great disagreement about where they have to be used. I once knew a person who was so confused by commas that he just stuck one in after every five words!

Because commas can go so many places and because people do disagree about where they must go, the best way to learn commas is by, guess what, reading. I haven't done a systematic study of this, but from observing what I read I think that writers choose to put in commas, or to leave them out, for two reasons. First, they use the comma as a signal to the reader to pause briefly, before going on with the rest of the sentence. The comma says, "Digest this first, then go on." The second reason is for clarity: writers put in commas wherever they think a reader would be confused if the comma were left out. For example, in the first sentence of this paragraph, I wrote, "The best way to learn commas is by, guess what, reading." I put the commas around "guess what" because I thought the reader would be confused by "The best way to learn about commas is by guess what reading."

People leave out commas whenever they feel that a comma will break up the smooth flow of a sentence or whenever the comma itself will cause confusion. For example, read these two sentences without commas:

> After the victory the players celebrated in the locker room. Still they worried in the backs of their minds about the upcoming game.

Inserting commas changes the flow, or pace, of the writing, though the syntax is not affected:

> After the victory, the players celebrated in the locker room. Still, they worried, in the backs of their minds, about the upcoming game.

A comma might cause confusion in instances such as the following:

> The Kimballs' daughter, Ann, just applied to veterinary school.

Using commas in such instances implies that the Kimballs have only one daughter. If the Kimballs have more than one daughter, the sentence would have to be written

> The Kimballs' daughter Ann just applied to veterinary school.

Note, also, the following:

> People who write regularly for themselves usually write well for others.

If I insert commas, the meaning changes:

> People, who write regularly for themselves, usually write well for others.

The commas indicate that the "who" phrase applies to all people. Leaving out the commas implies that a specific group of people fit the description.

Notwithstanding the optional nature of much comma usage, commas are mandatory in some circumstances to avoid confusion. For example, when directly addressing a person:

> It is true, Simmias, that man does not exist before he is born, is it not?

> Quick, Agathon and Simmias, get my bags. I must be going.

Many writers confuse their readers by leaving out the second comma:

> Quick, Agathon and Simmias get my bags.

Remember that whenever we use commas to set off one portion of text from the rest, we should use one comma at the beginning of the passage and one at the end, unless the passage comes at the beginning or end of the sentence.

Kugelmass, a professor of humanities at City College, was unhappily married for the second time.

Plus she had a few bucks, which is not in itself a healthy reason to marry a person, but it doesn't hurt.

Kugelmass made a face and, grunting, climbed into the cabinet.

I can't believe this, thought Kugelmass, staring at the doctor's beautiful wife.

"Last night at dinner, Mr. Personality dropped off to sleep in the middle of the dessert course."

Woody Allen's *Side Effects*, a collection of parodies and short stories, is particularly funny to people who have studied literature and psychology.

Syntax

We can get away with more syntax errors in speaking than we can in writing. Why? First, because most people tolerate everyday speech as a kind of discovery draft, in which we don't know what we'll say until we say it. Second, because our spoken words disappear as soon as we say them, people can't study our mistakes. Third, we use our hands, our faces, body language, and the people and objects around us to make our meaning clear. When we write, our words (plus punctuation and white space) do all the work. It would be correct to say, "Which do I like better, this Rembrandt, this Vermeer, or this Van Dyck? I think this one." The statement makes sense because I have the three paintings before me and I have my hand to indicate "this" one. But if I write such a statement, my editor should immediately note my obscure pronoun reference; which of the paintings is "this one"? Similarly, if I ask, "Did everyone bring their ticket?" I can be pretty sure that no one will notice that "their" is plural and "ticket" is singular and that the two words shouldn't be used together. But if I write, "Did everyone bring their ticket?", my editor will, and should, mark the error.

While many syntactical errors are possible (and a full handbook would deal with them), I want to concentrate on four kinds of frequent errors: errors of agreement, errors of obscure reference, sentence fragments, and run-on sentences. If you can be alert to such errors in your editing, you'll catch most of the syntactical errors writers make.

Agreement. Grammarians specify two major types of agreement in syntax: agreement of tense (time) and agreement of number. "Their ticket" is an example of disagreement of number.

Agreement of Number: People get confused about singulars and plurals for a logical reason. If you write, "Did everyone bring their tickets?", you might wonder, logically, "Why should I say 'tickets,' when each person had only one ticket?" Note, however, that it's no more logical to say "their ticket"; in fact, "their ticket" implies that everyone had the same ticket. By convention, therefore, not logic, we say that the pronoun should agree with the noun: either "their tickets" or "his or her ticket" or "a ticket."

Note: The pronoun *everyone* causes many problems of agreement. By SWE convention, it is considered singular and therefore takes a singular verb, as in:

Everyone *has* a key to the office. (*not* Everyone *have* a key to the office.)

Though we find it more natural to say, "Everyone has a key to *their* office" (grammatically incorrect), rather than the correct "Everyone has a key to his or her office," remember to follow the SWE convention.

Another pronoun that causes similar confusion is *none*, which is also considered singular. Watch out for other number disagreements. Read this sentence:

The biggest problem at this plant are people who arrive late and leave early.

The correct syntax would be, "The biggest problem at this plant *is* people who arrive late and leave early." By SWE convention, the verb agrees with the subject; hence, if I turn the sentence around, the sentence correctly reads this way:

People who arrive late and leave early *are* the biggest problem at this plant.

The following is another incorrect example:

In the ideal hospital, the team of professionals solve problems.

The sentence should be:

In the ideal hospital, the team of professionals *solves* problems.

The singular subject *team* takes the singular verb *solves*. The phrase *of professionals* describes the subject, *team*. Remember, the verb must agree with the subject.

Agreement of Tense: When writers describe actions (narrate), they often, unconsciously, shift tense. This shifting happens most frequently when writers write about something from the past as it if were occurring now, but forget, as they compose, to keep the tense consistent. Read, for example, my mangled version of a passage from Edith Hamilton's *The Greek Way*:

> In the conversation that followed, it appears that he can do all the things young men admire most, the world over. "He can drink any quantity of wine," said Alcibiades, "and not get drunk." This declaration was made in humorous despair, after he had insisted on Socrates' draining a two-quart wine jar, which Socrates did with entire composure. Alcibiades himself, when he first appears at the door, "crowned with a garland of ivy and violets," asks, "Will you have a very drunken man as companion?"

Editors should note that such shifting is common in discovery drafts. The editor needs to decide in which tense the writing sounds best. The important element is consistency. Hamilton, who summarizes a famous essay (written in dialogue form), *The Symposium* of Plato, chooses the present tense:

> In the conversation that follows, it appears that he can do all the things young men admire most, the world over. "He can drink any quantity of wine," says Alcibiades, "and not get drunk." This declaration is made in humorous despair, after he has insisted on Socrates' draining a two-quart wine jar, which Socrates does with entire composure. Alcibiades himself, when he first appeared at the door, "crowned with a garland of ivy and violets," had asked, "Will you have a very drunken man as companion?"

Note that the verbs in the final sentence are in the past tense (*appeared*) and past perfect tense (*had asked*). This use of the past is consistent here because Hamilton wants to show that Alcibiades' arrival had occurred before the events she describes as occurring now. My version is inconsistent because it mixes present and past with no regard for the order of the events.

Reference. When I say the word *this*, I can point to a specific object or I can make a sweeping gesture to include an entire room or landscape. When I write the word *this*, my reader has to be told to what I'm referring. When we write quickly, we often throw in a *this* or a *which* that refers to several ideas at once. Our reader doesn't know what we're referring to. For example:

> In 1591, Londoners faced large groups of poorly-educated soldiers returning from war, possible revolt by religious dissidents, and, most alarming, the threat that the Queen would die with no English successor. This became subject matter for many plays and pamphlets.

The alert editor will question the meaning of *this*. Does it refer to the threat of the Queen's death without an heir or to all three of the problems? Writers can quickly clarify by adding an appropriate noun after *this*:

> This *group of problems* became subject matter for many plays and pamphlets.

> This *threat* became subject matter for many plays and pamphlets.

When *which* is the obscure referrent, confusion occurs:

> Building the outdoor theaters coincided with a rise in the number of deaths from the plague, which made many of the opponents of the theater happy.

Did plague deaths make those people happy? The sentence seems to say so, because readers associate the pronoun *which* with the nearest noun. The writer is trying to use *which* when it's necessary to use more than one word. Note this editorial change:

> Building the outdoor theaters coincided with a rise in the number of deaths from the plague. This coincidence made opponents of the theater happy.

Which is acceptable when the reference is obvious:

> The year 1592 saw a sharp increase in the number of plague deaths, which caused London officials to close the public theaters.

Editors should also watch for obscure reference caused by dangling modifiers. For example:

In 1588, the smaller British ships defeated the huge Spanish Armada, *receiving the aid of violent storms from the southwest.*

With storms having blown them far off course, the British fleet never received the full force of the Spanish galleons.

Readers associate modifying phrases with the nearest noun. In each sentence above, the placement of the modifying phrase (in italics) confuses the reader: in fact, the British fleet was aided by the winds and the Spanish ships were blown far off course. It is easy for writers to make these errors in the course of composition.

Editing of dangling modifiers requires moving them close to the appropriate nouns:

In 1588, the smaller British ships, receiving the aid of violent storms from the southwest, defeated the huge Spanish Armada.

The British fleet never received the full force of the Spanish galleons, with storms having blown them far off course.

Sentence Fragments. A sentence fragment is part of a sentence written as if it were a complete sentence, with capitalization at the beginning and a period at the end. For example:

The British fleet never received the full force of the Spanish galleons. *With storms having blown them far off course.*

Young William Shakespeare might have come to London around 1587. *Though there is no proof of his having been there before 1592.*

Big Talk is the genius of American democracy. *Loud talk. Crazy talk. Free talk.*

Sentence fragments are not always errors in SWE. Experienced writers use them, as in the third example above (by Richard Reeves), to emphasize words and phrases. Reread the third example. Note how the fragments work, as in poetry, to set off the phrases and create a strong rhythm as you read.

The fragments do not work this way in the first two examples; they seem merely to be broken-off pieces of the sentences. There is not a clear reason, as there is in the third example, for these clauses to be set apart.

Why then do writers write such purposeless fragments? Usually, use of fragments signals lack of experience with complex sentences in reading and writing. As people gain experience, they learn that the writer has at least three correct ways to handle complex structures. The problem in the Shakespeare example could be solved in three ways:

> Young William Shakespeare might have come to London around 1587, *though* there is no proof of his having been there before 1592.

> Young William Shakespeare might have come to London around 1587; *however,* there is no proof of his having been there before 1592.

> *Though* young William Shakespeare might have come to London around 1587, there is no proof of his having been there before 1592.

If the editor wants to emphasize the idea about proof, a dash could be used to set it off:

> Young William Shakespeare might have come to London around 1587—there is no proof of his having been there before 1592.

Each of the options uses punctuation besides the period. Regular reading and writing also teaches one how to use a variety of punctuation to achieve options in building sentences.

Run-On Sentences (Plus Comma Splices). Other common errors made by writers learning to express complex ideas are run-on sentences and comma splices. A writer makes these errors when trying to express more than one idea in a sentence without using the correct punctuation or conjunction. The following two examples are run-ons:

> People who criticize others for something often do the same thing themselves I don't know why.

> One city had 10,000 persons per square mile another city had only 1,500.

In each example, the writer probably saw a close connection between two ideas and wanted to show that closeness by combining the ideas in a single sentence. With correct punctuation and conjunctions, connections can be shown without confusing the syntax (and the reader). The editor who has learned these forms has options:

People who criticize others for something often do the same thing themselves; I don't know why.

People who criticize others for something often do the same thing themselves, though I don't know why.

I don't know why people who criticize others for something often do the same thing themselves.

A comma splice uses a comma to do the work of a conjunction or of correct punctuation. Again, the writer is trying to show a relationship but does not know the options:

People who criticize others for something often do the same thing themselves, I don't know why.

One city had 10,000 persons per square mile, another city had only 1,500.

The following are correct options:

One city had 10,000 persons per square mile, while another had only 1,500.

One city had 10,000 persons per square mile; another city had only 1,500.

Though one city had 10,000 persons per square mile, another had only 1,500.

Note that the comma is correct if the editor removes the verb from the second clause:

One city had 10,000 persons per square mile, another city only 1,500.

Note also that a series of very short sentences can be connected with commas if it's clear to the reader that these sentences are a series. For example:

The sun beats, wildflowers rise, and rattlers coil in the shadows.

EXERCISE: Study two or three samples of published writing (one or two pages of each sample). Notice how all punctuation is used. Pay particular attention to complex sentences. How does punctuation separate parts of the sentence? How do punctuation and conjunctions show relationships between ideas? Note any ways in which the samples vary. ■

✍ **EXERCISE:** Study a draft of your own writing. Notice how you use punctuation to separate ideas, and punctuation and conjunctions to show relationships between ideas. Choosing particular sentences, rewrite them using various options for punctuation, syntax, and vocabulary. Observe how the rhythm of the sentence changes. Does the meaning change in any way? ■

HOW TO EDIT AND PROOFREAD: A FEW TIPS
Distance Yourself from the Text

If you edit your own work, you can't edit well if you are too close to the writing, that is, right after you write. (This goes for revision as well.) After completing your revised draft (whether it is the first revision or the fifteenth), don't begin editing the draft until you've given yourself enough of a break to achieve a fresh perspective on the writing. How long is enough? You'll have to learn by doing. In his *Ars Poetica,* the Roman poet Horace advised a friend to put his writing away for nine years before rereading it. Though Horace was joking, he was making a serious point about the writer's difficulty in getting far enough away from a work to be able to see it as another reader would (which is one reason why it's so important to have helping readers).

At the very least, give yourself a few hours when you pay no attention to the draft. Get involved in other work; play the piano; cook a meal; call a friend. Get far enough away from the writing so that you won't be able to remember the words, the commas, the sentences, the paragraphs. When you come back to the draft, you'll be better able to see where your text would confuse a reader, where you've used the wrong word or the wrong punctuation. If you are surprised by what you've written, you've gotten far enough away. If you don't feel the surprise, allow yourself more time away.

Don't Resist the Urge to Revise

Sure, it's your tenth draft; sure, the deadline is tomorrow. But if you're editing, and you find that you need more explanation or that one sentence should come before instead of after another one, don't hesitate to revise. Whenever we reread our texts, we're likely to find things we want to change. That urge is part of writing.

However, beware of fear of the reader. Sooner or later, we have to stop tinkering with our manuscripts and give them to our readers. Most writers I know like to work toward deadlines for two reasons. First, the deadline lets them plan their writing schedules: research, drafting, feedback, revision, editing. Second, the deadline forces them to let go. (Sometimes the publisher has to pry their hands loose; as they let go, they scream, "I know you won't like it. It still isn't right. I think I know how to change it.")

Look for Redundancy—and Cut

Probably the most common revision that editors make is to delete redundant writing. One pleasure of discovery drafting is that we can keep trying to state an idea until we're satisfied with the way we say it. But this means that our drafts overflow with repetitions. As you edit, keep asking yourself, "Does this sentence say the same thing as the previous sentence, just in different words?" Then, cut whatever is needed least.

Cut the needless repetitions in this example:

> Their charge accounts blew their budget away. VISA, MasterCard, American Express—they thought of them as money; not real money, but magic money that never grew less. Every month their pious plan to "spend just so much" was squashed by the magnetic force of those little rectangular decals in the store windows.

Look for redundancy within sentences as well. We often write pairs of words connected by *and* because the first word in the pair is the first one we think of, but isn't the one we want. Ask yourself, "Does each word really serve a purpose? What do I lose if I cut one of them?" Cut the redundancies in this example:

> The rules and regulations of the firm encourage and support the energy and ambition of the employees. We hope and pray that these guidelines and restrictions will not cause you any trials and tribulations.

Proofread as If You Were a Machine

Proofreading is the last part of editing, after all the revising and the editing for syntax and vocabulary. Proofreaders look for spelling, punctuation, and spacing errors. Period. Don't proofread earlier in the process, because you'll just have to do it again after all your other editing.

Proofreading a document, whether your own or someone else's, calls for a precise mind, no imagination, and a cold heart. Proofreading is devilishly hard work. If you don't find it tedious, you're doing it wrong. Why? Because to proofread well, you have to focus on one word at a time. You can't get interested in the writing because you'll read too fast. You have to understand the meaning of the text; otherwise you won't catch spelling or punctuation errors.

So, you have to proofread as if you were a machine. Unfortunately, no one has yet designed a machine that can proofread well because no machine can understand meaning. There are some computer programs that can be somewhat useful even though they do a poor job (more on these in the next section).

Always proofread a document more than once. Reading once through lets you find some punctuation errors, some spacing errors, and some spelling errors. Reading twice lets you catch almost all the rest of the errors. Reading three times is even better, and so on. Many writers, discovering a typo or omitted quotation marks in the printed copy two years later, will say that some errors can never be found.

To catch spelling errors, which seem to be the toughest to find, some proofreaders use the backwards method. After proofreading a document two or three times, they try reading it backwards: time a at word one. Because the backwards text means nothing, the proofreader focuses only on spelling without being tempted to read faster because of interest.

Mark Errors Clearly

If you are editing someone else's work or if you are marking your own text before recopying or retyping, be sure to indicate errors clearly: (1) use ink of a color different from the writer's and (2) place a check mark or other signal in the margin of lines containing marked errors. If you are editing in pencil (a good idea if you are only making suggestions to another writer), be sure to leave signals in the margins because pencil marks are easy to miss.

Respect the Writer

I noted earlier that you need to control your ego when you are editing someone else's work. Before marking an error, ask yourself whether it is really an error or just your preference. Some editors have been known to make changes just to show that they have the power to do so.

Remember that as an editor you are still a helping reader. What you mark and how you mark depend on what the writer has asked you to do. Above all, don't start editing if the writer is still in the revising stage. Many teachers and helping readers make this mistake, usually because it's easier to find spelling errors than to suggest ways to strengthen an argument or enrich a description.

If the writer really does want you to edit, remember that you are suggesting, not dictating. If you think a word or a punctuation mark is wrong, underline it, don't cross it out. Above it, or in the margin, suggest a substitution, perhaps with a question mark after it. For syntax errors, underline the problem, and write a substitution if there's room. Since correcting syntax errors might require rewriting whole sentences, you might want to use another sheet of paper. If you don't want to write out the substitution, you might just underline the error, write *syntax* or *dangling modifier* (whatever is appropriate) in the margin, and talk with the writer about the error.

SOME AIDS FOR THE EDITOR

Almost all writers have access to published works that can assist in editing. Many writers, particularly in colleges, have access to free or low-cost services that also can help. This section concerns both types of resources.

Writing Centers

Many colleges and universities have writing centers to which students in any program and at any level of proficiency can go for writing help. These centers have different names including *writing lab, writing clinic, writing tutorial center*. These centers are usually not editing services: you can't drop your revised writing into a box and pick it up later with the errors marked and corrected. Rather, the staff members of the center (either faculty, graduate students, skilled undergraduates, or members of the off-campus community) are trained helping readers. They are trained to find out what kind of help you need, to answer your questions, and to ask you questions about your reader, your purpose, and your format.

Staff members can help you edit by working with you to identify errors. Their goal, like the purpose of this chapter, is to help you understand why you've made mistakes, then to teach you how to correct the types of errors you make. Writing centers often use published guides to help you edit; more and more centers are equipped with computers and text analysis software to supplement the tutors' help.

If your college or university has a writing center, find out its location, hours, and policies. If your teachers don't seem to know about the center, mention it to them so that they can publicize it in class. If you don't know whether the college has a writing center, contact the English department, through which most centers are administered.

Remember that most writing centers are for all students, regardless of age, major, or proficiency. Sometimes writers fear that they'll be thought of as dumb for using the writing center, but competent writers, who understand the need for good feedback, are frequent clients of writing centers. The only dumb writer is the one who doesn't seek helping readers.

Teachers, Friends, and Other Fellow Writers

I've described ways to treat the person who asks you to edit. If the shoe is on the other foot, and you are asking for editing help, take the same care that you do in asking the helping reader for feedback toward revision. Indeed, your editor is a helping reader whose task is just somewhat different from that of the person who answers the earlier questions.

Above all, be clear about your needs. Don't just say to a person, "I want you to edit my writing." This means nothing in itself. Be specific. Do you have questions about particular words? About particular syntax? About particular uses of punctuation? Do you want only suggestions for changes, or does your editor have the freedom to make changes? How much freedom? It's not fair to your fellow writer to say, "Do whatever you think needs to be done," and then to say later, "What are you trying to do to me? I didn't want you to change that and that and that."

Remember that most editors will hesitate to change your writing very much, out of fear of hurting your feelings. That's why you have to ask questions. As mutual trust builds, the editor will take more initiative, and you will trust his or her judgment.

Beware of the opposite problem. An editor who is a highly competent writer but has little experience helping other writers to edit, might treat your piece as a challenge. This person might see your writing as raw material to be completely reshaped according to his or her style and opinions. Watch out. I've seen writers lose control of their work in the face of such overwhelming drive; the writers' own good ideas, tone, and vocabulary disappear, along with their confidence. If you state precisely what you want and don't want from an editor, you won't lose control.

Dictionaries, Grammar Guides (Including This One), and Thesauri

Dictionaries. Always keep at least one good dictionary handy to answer your questions about spelling and meaning. For most writing purposes, you don't need a ten-pound, hardback tome. However, dictionaries, such as *The American Heritage Dictionary* (Houghton Mifflin), can be useful introductions to names from history and terms from all disciplines. If you have had the pleasure of using such volumes, you know how good they can be for beginning research in almost any field. I recommend buying one, if at all possible, though you should also have a shorter, paperback version to carry with you.

A good paperback dictionary (with at least 50,000 entries) can answer your questions about all words except the very technical or the archaic (once-common words that are now rarely used).

As you get deeper into a discipline, you'll find that even the large all-purpose dictionaries won't include the specialized vocabulary of your field. Fortunately, every professional field publishes its own dictionaries and encyclopedias. If you don't know what these are, visit the reference room of your college or public library. The library will catalog these items by the name of the field (for example, medicine, sociology) under the topic *dictionaries*.

I've heard a few people complain that dictionaries are set up for people who already know how to spell; after all, the dictionary only includes correct spellings. Hence, a few dictionaries have been published for poor spellers. These list in alphabetical order common misspellings (for example, *definately*, *truely*, *relavent*, and *writting*) followed by the correct spellings.

However, most writers are able to manage with the regular dictionary because most spelling questions involve a simple either-or: "I can never remember whether 'traveler' has one 'l' or two"; "Is it 'independent' or 'independant'?" Usually no more than one page of the dictionary is needed.

Hint: Many spelling questions in English concern suffixes, letters added on to a root word as in *travel*er, *independ*ent, *writ*ing. Good dictionaries list words with their common suffixes, including the plural forms of nouns (*candy*, *candies*), the past tenses and participial forms of verbs (*write*, *wrote*, *writing*, *written*), and comparative forms of adjectives (*worthy*, *worthier*, *worthiest*). Words with their suffixes are usually not separate dictionary entries, but are part of the main word entry. Don't buy a dictionary that doesn't include this feature, since it won't help you with most of your spelling questions.

Grammar Guides (Including This One). Most companies in the United States that publish textbooks for writing courses publish handbooks or guides to SWE syntax, word usage, and punctuation. These can be especially useful to answer editors' questions about punctuation (for example, "Does the period go inside or outside the quotation marks?").

Be prepared to do some searching before you find the section of the book appropriate to your question. For example, you may have to read through many examples of usage of quotation marks before you find something relevant to your question. If you search under "uses of the period," you might not find anything relevant. These guides are organized in different ways; part of your search will involve learning the pattern of organization.

If you are comfortable with the rich vocabulary of traditional grammar (*nouns*, *predicates*, *intransitive verbs*, *relative pronouns*, and so on), you'll find it easier to use these handbooks. As with any other instruction manual, the grammar handbook will help you only if you have done enough outside reading to understand the technical terms.

Remember, though, that it may be just as efficient to read briefly through a few pages of any published book or article to see how that text handles a particular grammatical situation. My advice would be never to use the grammar guide, including the grammar sections of this chapter, instead of studying the syntax, vocabulary, and punctuation of actual essays, stories, reports, poems, and so on.

Thesauri. The Greek word *thesauros* means "treasure"; its Latin counterpart is *thesaurus,* the plural of which is *thesauri* (the sort of thing you can learn in a good dictionary). The language tool called a thesaurus is a book of synonyms and antonyms; it is not a dictionary. You don't look up meanings in a thesaurus; instead the thesaurus lists words that are similar in meaning to certain words, plus words that are close to the opposite in meaning of these words. The thesaurus helps to answer the question, "What's another word for ———?" It can also help you find the best word to indicate a certain idea: "I want a word that means ———, but I want something with more punch."

While I recommend that every editor have a dictionary, I'm more cautious about the thesaurus. Like the grammar guides, thesauri can be easily misused. There are a number of things to keep in mind to successfully use your thesaurus.

1. Understand that a synonym does not have exactly the same meaning as the word for which it is a synonym. No word can completely take the place of another. For example, *big* and *large* are synonyms, but you can't substitute *large* for *big* in the expression "Big deal!"; you can't substitute *big* for *large* in the sentence, "She ordered a large pizza to go." Be careful. Don't use a word from a thesaurus unless you already know that word well, where it fits and where it doesn't fit. I always can tell that an editor is misusing a thesaurus when I read such sentences as, "I disfavor to clean my room." If you want to use another word besides *hate*, be sure to use one that you know well.

2. Use the thesaurus to find the right word, not just a different word. I've heard writers say, for example, "I know that 'honesty' is the best word to express this idea, but I've already used it in three other sentences. I don't want to be boring." If your writing is boring, it's boring because your ideas aren't changing. You won't make your writing less boring by substituting one synonym for another. Follow the advice of Mark Twain, who told writers to keep using the same word as long as it was right.

3. When you find new words in the thesaurus, study them. Look them up in a good dictionary and be alert for them in your other reading. After a while, you'll be ready to try them out.

Word Processors, Spell-Checkers, and Text Analyzers

If you've spent any time working on a microcomputer with a word processing program, you've begun to learn how it changes your writing. Schools with computers that use word processing programs have found that writers revise more because the programs make it easy to insert, delete, substitute, and shift material without messing up the text! Editing becomes less tedious, even fun, when correcting a few typos means just striking a few keys, not retyping a whole document.

Computers have not only changed the physical act of revising and editing but they have also changed the way we analyze our texts for revision. Most companies that publish word processing programs also publish *spell-checker* programs that analyze texts for misspellings of common words (and any words that you add to their vocabularies). More and more companies are publishing programs that can analyze texts for grammatical errors and that can make suggestions about the readability of your style. Such programs still have (and perhaps always will have) serious flaws, but they can help your editing if you use them with caution.

Word Processors. For the editor, the advantage of word processors is the text editor feature. Good programs make it easy to

insert more text into a document,

delete unwanted text,

substitute one piece of text for another (to correct an error),
   and

move a piece of text from one place to another.

Most word processing programs allow you to do these things, so
don't consider using one that doesn't.

   If you are new to word processing, be prepared to spend a few
days getting to know each program you want to learn. Almost all
programs will appear bewilderingly complex at first; however, if
you have the patience to follow the manual step by step, you can
pick up the basics, including text editing, quite easily. Also, most
publishers include a tutorial disk that leads you, step by step,
through a series of exercises that teach you the basics. Finally, as
with every other aspect of your writing, don't hesitate to ask for
help.

   Many different programs are available; no program is exactly
like another. Some have more features than others; all differ in their
procedures for text editing. Though it will become easier to learn
each new program, because you'll know which questions to ask,
you'll still have to put in the time to learn the differences. Knowing
several programs allows you the flexibility to write on computers
that are not compatible with one another.

Spell-Checkers. Most commercial word processing programs either have a built-in system for proofreading for spelling or come
with a separate disk for this purpose. Spell-checking programs have
a vocabulary of commonly used words. Some vocabularies are
larger than others and many programs will let you add words (such
as technical terms in your field) to their vocabularies. When you
activate the spell-checker it scans your document and marks words
that aren't in its vocabulary. Some of the marked words will be
misspellings; most will likely be correctly spelled words, such as
proper names, that aren't in the program's vocabulary. The program doesn't correct the misspellings; it just marks them for your
attention. You have to make the corrections.

   Be careful. Besides marking as wrong a lot of words that are
correct, spell-checkers also miss some common misspellings. The
most common spelling errors at the college level involve homo-

phones (see the list earlier in this chapter in the section Some Commonly Broken Rules). If you mistakenly write *whose* instead of *who's*, the spell-checker won't pick up the error, because both words are in the vocabulary. Also, if you omit the *s* on *gives* or *houses*, the computer will just read *give* and *house*, both of which are correct in the vocabulary but wrong in your sentence. Lastly, because the spell-checker marks any technical terms or proper names that aren't in its vocabulary, you don't automatically know why a word has been marked. If you've written *Fyodor Dostoyevsky* or *staphylococcus aureus*, the program will mark it, but you won't know whether you've spelled those words correctly.

The spell-checker helps you edit, but it has essential limitations. You still need to proofread carefully and to keep the dictionary and your other technical sources handy.

Text Analyzers (Grammar and Style Checkers). Programs, called grammar checkers, are available that do the complex job of editing for punctuation and syntax. To such a program, an error is the presence of a certain word or punctuation mark in a place that the program expects to find it. For example, the program might be designed to mark a document when it finds a plural verb following a singular noun, as in "The boy go to the store." If this is a complete sentence, the program correctly marks it as an error according to the rules of SWE. However, the program might also mark it as an error in the sentence, "I saw the boy go to the store," in which the syntax is correct. Moreover, as with the spelling checkers, even the most sophisticated text analyzer will miss many errors. For example, the program may overlook the obvious error in "I saw the boy goes to the store" because it may have been set up to approve all singular verbs that follow singular nouns.

Because syntax is so much more complex than spelling, grammar checkers are necessarily less reliable than spell-checkers. Grammar checkers are useful for pointing out some constructions that might be wrong. You will still have to edit carefully and with wise judgment. No machine can take over your responsibility to learn correct syntax and to learn how to spot trouble.

On the other hand, another kind of text analyzer, popularly called a style program or readability program, can be used more reliably if you remain cautious. These programs don't look for errors in grammar or spelling. They look for elements that are easy to count and that determine how easy it is for someone to understand your writing.

For example, educational researchers tend to agree that it's relatively easy for people to understand short sentences with short words. Thus, says the theory, the shorter your words and the shorter your sentences, the better people will understand you. A computer can easily count the number of words between periods or the average number of letters in your words. If you run your draft through the style program, it can tell you, for example, that your average sentence length is 12.8 words and your average word is 4.3 letters long. According to some readability formulas, this means that your text would be understood by most people with at least a fourth-grade education.

These programs typically count other things as well, such as the number of being verbs (*is, could be, seemed*) versus the number of active verbs (*sit, run, count, understand*); or the number of passive voice constructions ("The prisoners *were released*") versus active voice constructions ("The warden *released* the prisoners"). If you believe that active verbs and active voice are easier for readers to follow than being verbs and passive voice, then this counting gives you useful information for editing.

Again, be careful. Don't change your text just because the program gives you a certain number. Read these two sentences:

> She said to the cop, "A red car hit her blue one."

> The victim's mother told the detective, "A maroon Cadillac side-swiped her light blue Volkswagen."

The first sentence is more readable according to formulas, but it's less meaningful than the second. The computer cannot read for meaning, so it can't tell you about clarity, accuracy, vividness, tone, appropriateness, and everything else that other humans can tell you about style and readability.

The bottom line is that these programs can give us statistical data about our writing that can be of use, as long as we realize the severe limitations of the programs.

✍ PROJECTS FOR WRITERS

Write Your Own. Within this book on writing there lies the theory that editing—concern for spelling, punctuation, and SWE correctness—is less fundamental than the skills explored in the earlier chapters. But you may have learned in earlier years that correctness in spelling, punctuation, and so on were the most important qualities of writing. For the subjects that you have been writing about in the Write Your Own assignments there may also be a controversy about which skills are fundamental. For example, in professional sports some managers place great emphasis on the appearance of the team, the style of the uniforms, the off-the-field behavior of the players, the spirit that the team shows in pre-game warmups; whereas other managers say these things matter little compared to how well the team performs when no one is looking, during the long hours of practice.

For this Write Your Own, identify the less fundamental aspects of your skill, craft, art, sport, or other activity: the matters of style and appearance that have some influence on your performance but are not basic. Is there something in your subject akin to Standard Written English, some standard of correct behavior that beginners should understand but should not overemphasize? Write about this standard, explaining its features and how important your reader should consider it.

Share this writing with your helping readers. Revise it according to their feedback.

Connecting with Fellow Writers. Brainstorm a list of people you know whom you consider good editors, good spellers, correct users of punctuation and SWE syntax. In every school and workplace, everyone seems to know who these people are. Interview at least two of these people. Do they think of themselves as good editors? How do they account for their ability? What do they do routinely to sharpen their skills with words and style? What advice can they give you to improve your editing skill? What do they see as the connection between writing and editing? Ask them about their writing: what do they wish they could do better?

Translate your interview notes into a report to share with others who have conducted similar interviews. What can the group conclude about the characteristics of good editors? How can you develop these in yourself?

Free Experiment. This chapter is full of examples of correct or incorrect usage. I try to offer several correct options to show that there are many correct ways to say anything. Experiment with sentences of your own or with sentences of published authors (note how I've used Woody Allen, Edith Hamilton, Arthur Schlesinger, and others in this chapter). Write version after version of the same sentence. Play with punctuation, dialect, vocabulary, syntax, using these features to change rhythm and tone. Read your sentences aloud to hear these changes. Show your versions to others and read their experiments.

As a next step, move from sentences to paragraphs, continuing to experiment with rhythm and tone by varying punctuation, dialect, vocabulary, and syntax.

Chapter Checklist ────────────────────────

Write and revise—then edit.

Learn the format before editing.

Learn format by
Studying pertinent samples
Asking questions

Note the rules of the format regarding
Spelling
Vocabulary
Punctuation
Graphic design
Syntax (including dialect)

Study the text for commonly-broken rules:
Spelling (homophones, phonetic spelling)
Vocabulary (watch out for pet peeves)
Punctuation (question marks, quotation marks, parentheses, conjunctions, commas)

Syntax (agreement, obscure reference, dangling modifiers, fragments, run-ons, comma splices)

To edit effectively:
Distance yourself from the text
Don't resist the urge to revise
Look for redundancy—and cut
Proofread as if you were a machine
Mark errors clearly
Respect the writer

Rely, carefully, on outside sources of help
Writing centers
Teachers, friends, other fellow writers
Dictionaries, grammar guides, thesauri
Word processors, spell-checkers, text analyzers

Words to Write By

Never edit too soon.

Respect the words of the person whose writing you edit: don't make
changes just because you have the power to do so.

9 Writing with Joy
(Some Success Stories)

*I wrote about old people long before I was anything like
as old as that, because I didn't know about them. I still
write out of an enormous sense of curiosity. As I get
older, I write more about children, because I've forgotten
what it's like to be a child.*

—*William Trevor Cox*

*In times of unrest and fear, it is perhaps the writer's
duty to celebrate, to single out some of the values we can
cherish, to talk about some of the few warm things we
know in a cold world.*

—*Phyllis McGinley*

THE JOY OF THE CHALLENGE

Maybe I overstate my case. Joy? If writing weren't difficult, if most
writers weren't staring at pages and knitting their brows most of the
time, there'd be no need for this or any of the hundreds of other
books about writing. But difficulty doesn't cancel joy. In fact, for
many of us the joy in anything is the joy of the challenge. Playwright Tennessee Williams wrote that human beings were made to

deal with tough problems; without problems to solve, he said, humans are like "swords cutting daisies."

As much as anything, this book has been about learning to know the difference between the problems necessary for the writer to solve and the needless problems we create for ourselves. The needless problems: fear of the reader, fear of error, isolation, and all the rest, rob us of joy. The problems that we must solve: turning our images into words, catching our feelings and thoughts before they disappear, reshaping our words for the eyes of others, keep pulling us joyfully back to the page. The confident writer says, with William Burroughs, "I don't make myself work. It's just the thing I want to do."

The following brief portraits highlight the joys of some confident writers. These writers are of different ages and backgrounds. They write in different settings, in school, on the job, in community affairs, in the privacy of the diary or journal. When I spoke with them, I focused on the fun. I asked questions such as:

> Why do you like to write? When? When writing is hard, how do you keep your confidence and joy? What made you a confident writer?

EXERCISE: Before reading the brief portraits, try the above questions on yourself and write your answers as an entry in your "History of a Writer." As you read the portraits, compare your views with those of the men and women interviewed. ■

SUCCESS STORIES

Mary Redenius

> If I get the response I intend, writing's a pleasure. If I get a different response, I revise.
> —Mary Redenius

Mary Redenius returned to college to complete her B.A. when her fourth child reached junior high. Even before returning to school, she was known to many friends and acquaintances as an avid, versatile writer of poems, letters, and short articles. Overcoming her initial anxiety as a returning student in a new school, Redenius went on to achieve her English department's outstanding student award. Currently she is pursuing a Master of Arts in English at the University of Colorado.

Where is the joy in writing for Mary Redenius? "I like to think of writing as a game—to try to say something really well, just as I want it to be. It can take me hours, say, to write a long letter to a friend, but if my friend calls to say she loved it, that's gratifying."

Redenius also finds joy in the voluminous writing she does for herself in her journals. "I keep several kinds of journals—travel, dreams, personal feelings. My journals are extremely intimate. I try to express how I really feel, especially my anger and worry. I used to suffer from insomnia, but keeping the journals cured it. When I'd awake at night with a problem on my mind, I'd realize that I'd already thought about the problem in my journal. Psychologically, I can write my worries in the book, close it, and leave them there."

She also brings confidence to the challenge of writing for teachers. She regards as one source of this optimism her fourth grade teacher in Galesburg, Illinois, who praised a poem she had written and had it published in the school newspaper. "Somehow I always felt thereafter that I'd succeed in any class where my grade depended on writing."

Consequently, she never enters into a class assignment afraid of the teacher's possible criticism. "What the teacher might want isn't really important to me. *I* know when I've done a good job. I've built my confidence through positive reinforcement in the past."

Her confidence doesn't always mean, however, that she wins nothing but praise from her teachers, though this is usually the case. "On my first paper as an undergraduate anthropology student, I thought I had done a wonderful job. But my professor didn't agree. He complained that the paper was too long and not scientific. I was a bit surprised, but I realized that I hadn't adjusted my accustomed style to his expectations as an anthropologist. With his advice and through revision, I pretty quickly learned the style he was looking for."

Her wealth of experience has given her high standards in her academic work. "I'm not satisfied just to receive an 'A' from a teacher. I want him or her to say, 'That's really a good idea!'" Her high standards also make her dissatisfied with the usual comments she receives from fellow writers. "Friends are always careful not to hurt your feelings. And, after all, every writer likes to get positive strokes: I know I do. The only way to get real help with your writing from a friend is to say, 'Here's a rough spot. I'm not happy with this. I need some help.' Then people will feel it's OK to make suggestions."

Basically, Mary Redenius is happy with her life as a writer. She loves the challenge of her academic work, finds real purpose and reward in her journals, and treasures her correspondence ("I've saved every letter I've ever received"). Still, she does have some unfulfilled goals. "I'd like someday to have an essay published in the *Hers* section of the *New York Times*. I've written some that are suitable but I've not sent them. Maybe I'm just not hungry enough—yet. Right now, it's satisfying just to have written." She also sees that publication is not the end of the writing process. "I like to read back over the poems I've published and papers I've written. Sometimes I pull out work I did years ago. I find that it's not where I am now. I change. I wouldn't want to be identified with ideas that I've grown beyond." The following are two poems by Mary Redenius.

NIECES

My brother's child, a small pink child,
has yellow curls and round blue eyes and tiny bones.
She is quick and chatty.
Three times a day she changes her clothes.
She sits at her table in the corner of the kitchen
and colors pictures in a neat book.
She walks down the road, leading her dog on the end of a string.
He is as big as a calf and he comes when she calls him.

My sister's child, a small pink child,
has silky saffron hair and eyes like lakes
that stare solemnly and blink slowly.
She shows me her red Mary Janes
by pointing a toe at the floor and looking away.
She asks for a cookie by standing in front of the cabinet
where they are kept and pushing her tongue into her cheek.
She walks through the grass around and around her house

on a serious search for something she cannot name.
She cries soundlessly, her shoulders shaking and her breath
  catching,
until she collapses in a pile of grief on the ground.
I recognize her. She is mine in a way my sons can never be.
My sister thinks she comes to my kitchen for cookies.

RELOCATION

Three days' droning drive,
hills and great plains away
from decades, decades of my life,
from waking at two in the dark,
drinking coffee after coffee
and doing the day;
Exchanging humming heat and swimming pools,
thick grass and my place
as a quilter at the bee,
for an herbal-spicy valley

cut from gray and purple silver layers
edged in gold,
clouds swept up in shapes of porpoises and spaceships,
canyons clear-creeked and sharp-shadowed,
meadows of elk and sparse grass,
skies of eagles,
and suddenly I miss a mockingbird.

Omar Altalib

> I like to write about social issues and personal ones—coping in
> school, peer pressure. I show my feelings when I write, then share
> them with others.
>
> —Omar Altalib

Now a Ph.D. candidate at the University of Chicago, Omar
Altalib double-majored in economics and sociology while in college.
Born in Iraq, Altalib moved with his parents to Ohio, to Saudi
Arabia for four years, and then to Virginia, where he completed
high school and attended George Mason University.

A person of high ideals, Altalib most enjoys writing "that

benefits people." He recalls, for example, an essay he wrote on the difficulties of parent-child relationships. "Some friends who read it said that it helped them resolve some differences with their parents. That made me happy." His interest in politics, he says, comes from his ideal of service. When I asked him to imagine himself in the future, he said he saw himself as a social commentator, one who studied and wrote about social issues to find answers.

Altalib sees a vital relationship between writing for himself and writing for others. He continues to keep the reflective journal he began four years ago in a college course, because the journal lets him express his "feelings, frustrations, and desires": "The writing I like to do for others comes out of my life and my reflections on it. If it's effective for others, it's because I put myself into the writing. The journal lets me articulate my thoughts in a physical way, more real to me than if I just talked about them. I also find that the more I write the better I get at expressing ideas. This gives me more confidence to write for others."

When is writing difficult for him? "Sometimes there is so much on my mind, so many things I want to write, that I don't know where to start. I manage to start somewhere, but it's frustrating to know that my writing can't capture it all."

Although he sometimes has difficulties with class assignments, he has ways to handle the problems. "If I receive written instructions from a professor, I try to make them concrete for myself by writing about the topic from several angles. Then I choose the one that sounds best. If I've written for this teacher before, the task is fairly easy. Otherwise, I try to write from as many angles as I can. If I'm still uncertain how to proceed, I'll go to the professor, show him or her the options I've tried, and get the professor's advice."

He says that he usually asks his teachers for clarification, since assignments are usually vague in some way. "I'll do some brainstorming before I talk with the professor. Then I'll ask, 'If I do it this way, is that OK?' Or I may offer the teacher several options and ask him or her to choose."

For his confidence as a writer, Altalib credits his regular writing and the influence of some teachers. While he doesn't recall a childhood event, he cites one of his high school English teachers. "She liked the students' writing and read it to the class." He also cites his teacheɪs iɪɪ the freshman and sophomore years of college. "Learning to keep a journal showed me that I could write as much as possible without having to critique it as I wrote. That really built up my confidence." The following is an entry from Omar Altalib's journal in his sophomore year:

FILM SHOWING: "THE PRECIOUS LEGACY"

This film was the story of a human atrocity and a shameful page in our history. It is about a people that were almost totally destroyed, and whose artifacts were collected to form a museum of "the lost race." The narration served to provide insight and meaning into what was shown on the screen. Although the photographic aspects were beautiful and captivating, the narration provided another dimension not offered by pictures: that of suggestion and introspection. The impressive array of intricate clocks with detailed designs, for example, reflected superb Jewish handiwork and aesthetic achievement. The narrator then gave us the historical and personal dimension, describing them as "clocks abandoned by time." If the visual aspects weren't able to get the film's message across to a particular viewer, then the narrator's words provided the missing link. The clocks were in a sense a personification of the film's meaning. The Jewish people were gathered in concentration camps to be exterminated. Mankind had turned its back on them, they were "forgotten by time," or at least that is how the Nazis wanted it. They were gathered from all over, tagged, identified, and catalogued. Meticulous records were kept on them in the true German tradition. The clocks were to be a record of a "lost people," the mass graves a record of our lost humanity. Music provided a background for the scenes and narration. Its purpose was to provide a flow for the film rather than distract from it, which is perhaps why classical music was chosen. Soft where it should be to let us contemplate the "precious legacy," and louder in other instances to make us realize the reality of what we were watching. The music, in a sense, drew you closer to the scenes while it softened the jarring impact of the holocaust being shown. Had there been no music, the impact of the film would have suffered because the viewer would have concentrated more on the pictures rather than the message. That is perhaps why there were also no personal interviews in the film, which I believe was intentional. The message was about people losing their heritage and their lives along with it, and had it been allowed to continue there would be no survivors to tell the story. It is a story told in the past tense, with implications for the future. Although it is making factual statements about a museum collection, it is intended to have an emotional impact. The filmmaker does not intend for you to get up and stop the holocaust, because it has already occurred. What he wants from you is to realize that man is capable of incredible destruction, and therefore we must learn a lesson from past holocausts to prevent future ones. "The Precious Legacy" is, as such, different than "E.T.A.," "Crossroads," and "The Turtle People," in that the latter are all stories of the present. Their intention in one way or another is to make you act, to mobilize you as part of an effort to prevent a serious situation from getting worse. "The Precious Legacy," at the same time, is a picture of a holocaust that has already occurred; the other three are holocausts in the making. Whether it be the destruction of a people, a culture, or a nation, the story is being repeated around the world. The Oromo of Ethiopia have suffered more from their fellow man than from the ravages of drought, in yet another instance where history repeats itself. The precious legacy of the Jewish people might have been preserved in a museum, but the legacy of mankind cannot survive in any form as a result of a nuclear holocaust. To put it cynically, our next holocaust might be our last.

Christine Sorge

> I have to be concise in my business letters. This has taught me to be concise in my college papers.
>
> —Christine Sorge

A recent graduate with a B.S. in economics, Christine Sorge now studies corporate and tax law. While she spent fall through spring working toward her bachelor's degree, she spent her summers in business, writing letters to her company's clients whose bills were overdue. During off hours from business or study, she enjoys writing other letters, personal ones to her friends.

"To my friends I'd rather write than talk. I can write as long as I want to—no phone bills! I use my letters to say what's on my mind, somewhat as other people might keep a diary. I'll start with an idea—about three or four sentences. By that time, more ideas are coming. Of course, I don't write the same kind of letter to every correspondent. I feel more comfortable going on at length with some friends than with others. It all depends on my audience."

Her work letters served a different purpose, so she used a different process. "In my personal letters I keep spinning out ideas; the business letters have to state all the necessary information, but concisely. Business people won't read a letter if it's longer than a page or two. So one skill I had to learn for writing collection letters was how to cut. I've found that the fastest way to write these letters is first to write a draft—get all the information on the page—then pare away. That's faster and easier than trying to write a short first draft."

Sorge enjoyed writing collection letters because of the creative challenge. "It may not sound creative, but it really is. Every situation is different. Often clients will argue that they don't owe us what we're claiming; it's our job to show that our claim is just. So I do research through the files to track down the right documentation, then use the documents to write the specific letter. Sometimes there's a good deal of back-and-forth correspondence. And, of course, sometimes the research shows that the client is right!"

Sorge says that when she began the job it took her about three months to learn the appropriate formats and tones for the letters. "My supervisor gave me good advice about what I could and couldn't say in a letter. The biggest problem for me was to learn the confidence to be aggressive, to assert the company's claim. It took a lot of reading letters and writing them to learn how to sound authoritative without sounding nasty."

How has her letter writing helped her academic writing? "I can think of two ways. First, I can express myself more easily when I have in mind a specific person as my reader, as I always do when I write letters. If the audience for my assigned paper isn't clear, I'll pretend that I'm writing to one person—a teacher, a friend, another student.

"Second, I learned how to revise for conciseness. I'll draft my papers, then cut. One can always cut."

Has academic writing helped her business writing? "Yes, in

doing research. Writing research papers in college taught me how to find sources, take notes, and then summarize the sources. That's essential in my business writing."

In looking back at her growth in confidence, she credits her high school history teachers. "I did a lot of writing in history and the teachers cared about our writing. We'd have tests on elements of style. We had to revise and edit. I thought it was pretty hard at the time, but I realize now how much I benefited."

Looking to the future, she expects that legal practice will call upon all the skills she has learned as a writer: "research, note-taking, summaries, reports, recommendations, notes for speeches, and lots of letters! I can see all my writing experience helping me in my work."

For the student entering college, Christine Sorge has this advice: "If an assignment is vague, use it to your advantage. Instead of asking the professor to be more specific, write out your idea for the paper, then propose it to the professor. If you take ownership of the project—if you show that you've done some thinking—the teacher will usually respond positively. Besides, you'll have much more fun doing the project in a way that challenges and excites you."

Christine Sorge wrote the following brief essay for an undergraduate economics course. "We were asked to evaluate a legal decision from an economist's perspective."

BROKAW V. FAIRCHILD

Brokaw in his argument in favor of demolishing the residence at number One East Seventy-Ninth Street tried to use the precedent set by the case of Melms v. Pabst Brewing Co. In the earlier case, it was ruled that the removal of the house was not simply "waste," but rather was "ameliorated waste," or a change in the physical structure of the occupied premises by an unauthorized act of the tenant which, though technically "waste," in fact increased the value of the land. Since circumstances beyond the control of Pabst permanently changed the condition of the area surrounding the house into a highly industrial (uninhabitable) area, the plot in question was more valuable after Pabst demolished the house and graded-down the land. Also affecting the ruling in favor of Pabst was the fact that the case was brought to trial after the deed was done.

Brokaw saw a similarity between the two cases. He claimed that since he has difficulty in renting the house, it was a similar situation to Pabst not being able to use the house received from Melms as a residence. However, this is not the case. Brokaw wasn't able to rent his house because there was no demand for it at the price he asked for it, not because it was uninhabitable. This is the major difference between the two cases.

The decision to enjoin Brokaw from tearing down the residence and constructing an apartment building does not meet Posner's efficiency criteria for maximizing value. The argument put forth by Brokaw is sound from an economic viewpoint. The costs incurred in maintaining the house were twofold. First there was the opportunity cost of renting out 172 rooms at $1,000 each per month, which calculates to $2,064,000 per year. The second cost was the cost of maintenance and taxes that had to be paid each year. These costs were incurred by the trust set up for the estate, and cost not only Brokaw, but also the succeeding life tenants of the residence. Clearly this judgment was not made in order to maximize value. In terms of optimality, the decision produced neither Pareto-superior nor Kalder-Hicks optimal results. If, however, the decision had been in favor of Brokaw, we might have witnessed Kalder-Hicks optimality, in that neither party would really be worse off, and a third party, the future inheritors, would receive compensation for the act.

The outcome of the Pabst case was prejudiced by the fact that Pabst had already torn down the residence and graded-down the land before the case came to trial. It would have been very inefficient to have Pabst pay double-damages for an act that had already benefitted the defendants. Had Melms brought the case to trial before Pabst changed the physical structure of the land, as is the case in Brokaw v. Fairchild, the judgment may have been ruled in favor of Melms. However, if that had occurred, as was the plight of Brokaw, an efficiency would also have occurred. It would have cost society much more if it ruled that Pabst must pay double-damages to Melms, since Pabst had already expended resources in improving the land. Brokaw, on the other hand, had not yet invested a great amount into his plan. If he had started the project, then the judge probably would have ruled in his favor since it would be inefficient and impractical to restore the house to its original condition.

Robert Clark

> Writing is artifice. In a world that seems formless and chaotic, writing shows us structure and meaning.
>
> —Robert Clark

The author of five books and editor of one, Robert Clark is Professor of Government and Public Affairs at George Mason University. He credits his mother, who was an elementary school teacher, and his father, a geologist, for his love of books and writing. "My mother gave me her fascination with language. My father, though not a well-educated man, loved literature and read voraciously. Books were holy in our home. Writing books has let me feel that I'm part of that community of authors. It has almost a magical quality for me."

Clark's writing has changed for him over the years. "Through much of my writing career I've thought mostly about audience and about the message I was carrying to others. All my books have had something of that inspiration. The book on the Basques [*The Basque Insurgents*, his most recently published book] I definitely felt to be a story I had to tell.

"But now I believe that that urge is secondary. I write for myself now. I pursue interests in my writing and feel free to write to new ideas as they develop. Hence, I've published a number of articles recently, though my book publication rate has declined. It takes single-mindedness, a kind of tunnel vision, to complete a book. I might find a topic to which I'll again devote that kind of discipline, but it's not something I currently need to do. Meanwhile, I love the freedom I feel in my writing."

The most enjoyable part of writing for Bob Clark is discovery: "I discover that I know something! I always find that I know more about something after writing about it. When I reread I find that what I know has form, structure, and meaning. People like to feel that they have the power to discover meaning."

Clark also appreciates the opportunity to revise. "I create lots of garbage. You can't discover anything unless you're willing to make a mess. That's one reason I like the word processor. With text editing, there's no limit to the amount of experimenting and re-shaping I can do."

But what happens to that freedom once a book is published? "I read something I wrote ten years ago that seemed good then and I now see it as pathetically written." Hence, he appreciates the infrequent opportunity to revise a published work. "When I revised for the fourth edition of my textbook [*Power and Policy in the Third World*], I not only corrected the factual errors and the clumsy phrases, but I also completely rewrote the third chapter because my understanding of the events had radically changed."

As a teacher, Clark tries to bring to his students some of the benefits that he has gotten from writing. Course assignments reflect his belief in two aspects of writing: discovery and collaboration. "I've seen some marvelous results from having students keep journals. When students write reflectively and personally about the cultures and political events we study, they reach insights they could not have discovered any other way." Clark also has some classes create research projects in small teams. "I feel that they must learn to plan and write in collaboration, since so much of the work of the world, including writing, occurs as conversation among people. Once they get into careers, they'll find that they do most of their writing in committees."

Clark's own writing is done within a network of people with shared interests. In his writing about the Basques, for example, he has sent copies of work-in-progress to people he has interviewed and to other scholars. "I not only want their ideas; I also feel that sharing my work with them somewhat pays them back for the time they have given me."

Is writing ever difficult for Clark? "No—because of how I do it. I like to immerse myself. As we say in the social sciences, I like to take off my shoes and wade around in the data. I begin my writing by making notes, drawing pictures, making graphs—I like to think visually. I keep doing this until I reach a sort of critical mass, ideas building inside me. When a pattern becomes clear, it's a kind of a 'Eureka!' experience. At that point, writing becomes irresistible. I can't keep from it."

He sees this process as being like that of the sculptor. "Sculptors say that the stone has a form inside it, and that it's the artist's job to help it come out. I feel the same way about data. They possess a meaning that it's my job to see and express. If I thought that I was imposing my *will* on the data, I'd say to hell with it. Anyone can do that. I discover meaning, I don't impose it."

Bob Clark describes the following sample: "Attached are some cards I doodled on while on an airplane trip last December. The third one is an attempt to visualize some linkage, and may lead to larger writing projects on the '*' topics."

Culture and Territory in
Advanced Indust. State

I. The Problem: The Clash between two
organizing principles — birth/culture
and territory
   A. Modes of Ethnic Politics

II. Territorial Devolution: The Mistaken Alternative
   A. The Roots of the Policy
   B. Examples
        North Ireland
        Spain
        Italy
        France

   Similarities to Federal System

   C. Reasons for failure
        Population is not homog.
        No auton.

III. Cultural Autonomy.
   A. Feasible Alternative?
        A. Essential Characteristics
        B. Obstacles to Realization
        C. Strategies

Nations, States, Europe: The Impact of
the EEC on Ethnic Peoples

1. The basic argument —
   Supra-national integration will not enforce
   the status of ethnic peoples, etc.
   Regional policies. Farming policies.

2. Case studies
   A. Basques fishing
   B. Basques dairy farmers
   C. Other — Scottish oil, Alsatian steel,
      Welsh coal, etc.

3. Conclusion

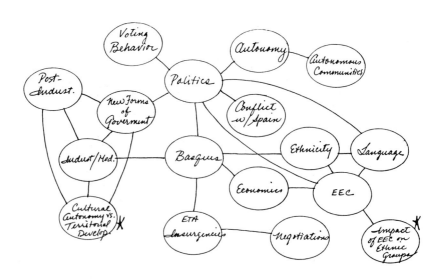

Ali Ghobadi

> When you write for others, you need feedback from people you respect. If you don't seek this, you'll just make more problems for yourself.
>
> —Ali Ghobadi

College freshman Ali Ghobadi, whose research essay on particle physics is included in Chapter 7, has recently embarked on a degree program in systems engineering. Bilingual in English and Farsi, he is a native of Iran, but has lived in the United States since age four.

I became acquainted with his writing through a journal I assigned in a freshman writing course. While frequently using the journal to record events and to explore his feelings and opinions, Ghobadi chose also to concentrate on what he sees as his main goal as a writer: "to express complicated ideas clearly to those less well informed in my field."

Ghobadi says, "I like to experiment. I try to find a style by which to communicate everything I know. Ideally, I'd like my reader to be able to read my mind—to know exactly what I'm thinking." He recognizes this goal as an extension of his goal in writing for himself. "I write for myself for two reasons. First, to clarify my own thoughts. As I write, I experiment. I'm never exactly sure of what I'm saying. But the writing is there so I can go back to it and see if it still sounds good to me. I revise to make it better, though I know it'll never be perfect."

Ghobadi's second purpose in writing for himself is to understand the thoughts of others, especially in reading. "After reading, I use writing to focus and summarize. At test times, I make long lists: two or three pages of important ideas, plots, formulas—whatever I'm studying. Rather than going back to the book and skimming pages, I find that this brainstorming helps me remember and keep the ideas clear. I think this method works best for me with math and chemical formulas, since writing the formulas lets me see what I know and where I'm still confused."

When is writing difficult for Ghobadi? "I don't like to be forced to write, as one often is in school, about a topic that doesn't interest me. But I've learned not to shut things out. It would be easy to say,

'That's not interesting,' and be turned off, but my method is to write about the topic until it connects with something that does interest me—this always happens. Once I feel some control over the project, then I no longer feel forced."

Like the other writers I've interviewed, Ghobadi recalls an early experience with writing that gave him confidence. "In elementary school, we did grammar exercises in which we were supposed to make up our own sentences. Besides trying to do these correctly—no run-ons and that sort of thing—I tried to make mine sound very adult. I remember getting praised for some of these. I guess that encouraged me to experiment."

Ali Ghobadi sees his future in systems engineering as totally involved with writing. "Systems are all about bringing together people who know different fields and speak different technical languages. I see myself constantly learning from others and getting their feedback. I also see myself continuing to search for ways to communicate clearly with those outside my field, as the systems engineer must."

Taejung Welsh

> To be sincere is the most important goal of writing. I revise until my reader can clearly see that I mean what I say.
>
> —Taejung Welsh

Taejung Kim Welsh was born and educated in Korea. Fascinated by her early exposure to English in Korean schools, she majored in this subject in college before going on to graduate school in art history. As one of three Korean students honored with the opportunity to intern at the United Nations headquarters in Geneva, Switzerland, in the early 1960s, she was daunted by the inadequacy of her English training and the linguistic difficulties faced by Korean diplomats in Western culture. Since coming in 1969 to the United States, where she has taught English as a second language and devoted her primary efforts to raising her family, she has maintained the goal of learning how best to aid others in becoming able speakers and writers in a foreign language. Taejung Welsh has just completed her doctoral dissertation in English as a Second Language at George Mason University. The eloquence of her writing testifies to her dedication and to her love of English.

Unlike others I have interviewed for this chapter, Welsh for many years lacked confidence as a writer. "I had done very well studying English in college, but my experience in Geneva disillusioned me about my proficiency. I knew grammar, but I had no fluency. I was afraid that I would never be able to communicate in this language." Nevertheless, she recalls one experience that gave her some confidence. "I took a creative writing course from a professor who was visiting from Yale. He greatly praised a descriptive piece of mine—about my brother's room in a boarding house—and read it to the class of over 100. Previously, I had had no idea that I could write acceptably in English."

She also credits a long-time friend, Oh Hye Ryung, now a well-known Korean playwright and essayist, with boosting her self-esteem as a writer. "We have corresponded for many years. She has sometimes cited our correspondence in her books. Last year, she actually published one of my letters. I felt truly honored."

Welsh asserts that her greatest breakthrough as a writer came while studying toward her doctorate. "I learned an entirely new theory of language. Studying Stephen Krashen, the linguist, and all the recent research on the writing process, I saw that I didn't have to worry about the errors in English I was making as I learned, but that I could concentrate on what I wanted to say. The theory taught me that if I wrote regularly—to express my thoughts, to record my experiences, to organize the images in my mind—then I would gradually, surely, become a better writer of English. And that has indeed happened."

In her dissertation, an except of which follows, Welsh describes her own struggle and breakthrough as one case study in her research. She goes on to show how her own success led her to create a method of teaching that used the theories she had learned. "It is amazing how a person's entire outlook can change. I recently tutored a Korean man who has struggled with English for years. I explained the theory of the writing process to him and encouraged him to begin by writing regularly without concern for error. The result has been miraculous. His writing teacher says that not only has his writing dramatically improved in every way, but he now actually enjoys writing."

Now that she has reached another milestone as a writer, she contemplates her future with a sense of serene wonder. "I do not want to plan what I will write. There are so many possibilities, some of which I can imagine but most of which remain to be uncovered. I have thought, for instance, that I might write about my culture and my people for Americans, who know so little about them. But I will remain open. All I know for sure is that now I am dedicated to rely on writing, so I will write, no matter the topic or the form."

The following is an excerpt from the doctoral dissertation of Taejung Welsh.

Suddenly I realized I had a false conception of freewriting. Its purpose is not floating about on the surface of the water—I had to go deep-sea diving for some archaeological treasures. Finally I had discovered the essence of good writing and I felt scared. I felt scared because throughout my whole school career I had learned "to psyche out the teacher" and not to make any mistakes, especially as a language specialist. Also, I had never had a teacher who explained the process of writing, let alone demanded to see evidence of it. To protect myself from such teachers, who looked only at finished products, I had been forced to hide early drafts. Gradually I came to rationalize my "fear" by analyzing its source.

Still in doubt, I started freewriting on a personal experience, determined to share my juicy ESL quirks, myself, and the "universals" in writing across languages, cultures, and systems of logic. I wrote for almost four hours continuously—the story of how my husband started running and of a quarter marathon (i.e., a six-mile run) day. I did not expect to make sense in the writing but determined to enter the pasture of my memory in neutral gear as I had seen others do with such excellent results. Suddenly the words began to flow. It was as if I had picked one end of yarn out of an old sweater and proceeded to unravel it. As I re-read now and then while writing, I found myself nodding at the way it was flowing. I trembled that I could taste for the first time what freewriting was. Once in that zone, my mind grew bold and free from the internal censor and form, the formulae and the worries about monitoring for correctness. It was the *story* that had become important.

The next day, as I handed in my illegible yellow pads with corrections, arrows, carets, and insertions, I saw Dr. Nelson's face bloom. "Read it to the group!" she said. When the class met in a few minutes, I read.

My foursome was sitting on the third row from the top of the bleachers in the main gym at Fort Leonard Wood. James had just finished his first marathon sponsored by the Ozark area which includes roughly St. Louis and Springfield, Missouri. We were simply proud of James because he was able to complete his run. We were drawn together like clouds, hugging and kissing him as if he had just returned home from his tour in Vietnam.

With the squeaking noise of the microphone, the award ceremony began. So many speakers, local and army representatives, tried to make the event meaningful. People looked distant and small from where we were sitting. We started applauding the winners as hard as we could. From a side glance I knew Moira was joining in applauding. Andrew was tired of doing it but by the peer pressure he clapped sporadically. I fully understood the symptoms, seeing Andy yawning at this overdue dinner time. I felt a bit exhausted, hungry and chilled, too. We hadn't eaten much since our pancake breakfast.

The next awards were for the division of men over 40. As Gen. Foreman was awarded the first place trophy, the crowd was suddenly animated with extra vigor and cheer. Over the microphone I thought I heard a familiar name, and then I saw James stood up and walking all the way down the bleachers. I couldn't see him any more because of my blurred vision along with a sensation of all my blood gushing into my throat and head, until James placed his trophy on my lap.

Looking up, I read expressions of approval on the group's faces. One by one they responded:

— "It doesn't sound like an ESL person's writing."
— "Look at that dramatic transition there."
— "It really started to flow from the second page."
— "I liked the expression 'we were drawn like clouds hugging.'"
— "You dealt with conflicting ideas and emotions, but it didn't sound melodramatic."
— "I feel I know who James is!"

As my fellow students spoke, I began to realize that I too was endowed with "deep structure" or innate competence," the so-called "universal" in human language, for I had paid no conscious attention to surface structure while writing that piece.

Thus I experienced freewriting for the first time and my story was christened by the group. It was truly exhilarating to get "OKAY" responses from that formidable writing group. Indeed, I felt elated with a sense of belonging to the group for the first time since I had joined the class. The quest for growth must be sticky stuff! After all those layers of pain, embarrassment, feeling out-of-place, inadequacy, and despair, I rejoiced at this moment of being newly hatched.

Douglas Ayers

> I learned to write well by reading essayists. The more good essays I read, the better I knew how to make a point with any reader.
> —Douglas Ayers

While still in high school, Douglas Ayers began working construction. He began college as an engineering major, but left after two years to work full-time as a field engineer with an interstate construction firm. A few years later, he returned to college—this time as an English major. Graduating in English literature and going on to do to master's work in this field, he continued to work in construction engineering, eventually becoming vice president of C. J. Coakley, Inc., a multi-million dollar subcontracting firm. As vice-president, Ayers supervises proposals, reviews and revises contracts, and carries on sensitive correspondence with clients and other construction firms.

"To be honest," he says, "most engineers don't communicate well in writing, even with other engineers." He sees his biggest advantage as his skill, sharpened over many years' experience, in writing clear, concise letters. "Much of the work we do requires careful spelling out of exact terms and specifications. Experience teaches one how to say things and how not to say them."

When Ayers considers his growth in confidence as a writer, he recalls an incident early in his career with the Coakley company. "We were not a large firm at that time and we were engaged in some sensitive dealings with a major contractor. I happened to see some of the correspondence and thought that our position could be improved through some revisions in our letters. I suggested these, Mr. Coakley thought they were good suggestions, and they worked out. After that, he began to rely on my advice in such matters."

In addition to his writing responsibilities on the job, Ayers, because of his enjoyment of writing, has served for three years as publications chair of the trade association to which his company belongs. "We put out a newsletter to members seven times a year. While we have a fine editor and staff, I review all the articles for their technical accuracy and make any revisions I think necessary. The editor and I work together to design the theme for each issue and choose the articles from those submitted, most of them having been written by the public relations people in the companies belonging to the association. My background in both engineering and writing definitely helps me do this job."

Douglas Ayers' writing also serves him in his family life. Similar to the personal essayists that he studied in college, he likes to write what he calls "impressions" of life at especially significant moments. "It's important to me to describe special events in the lives of my children—what they say, how I feel, what the events mean. I wish I had time to do this even more often."

How would he advise those now in college and planning careers in engineering? "I would tell them to take more writing. When I went to college, I was required to take one writing course, as a freshman. But I feel that I profited from all the writing and reading courses I took, so I'd urge other engineers to do more than what is required. Besides providing practical benefits for writing on the job, the courses also help to make one a more well-rounded person through contact with the ideas and arguments of others. I'd also highly recommend coursework in logic. I feel that the combination of formal logic, the essays I studied, and, of course, my own writing taught me how to understand the business documents I read and how to make sense to others."

The two samples of Douglas Ayers's writing which follow show his versatility as a business writer. Note how his format, his tone, and his language change from one writing situation to the other. Speculate how the formula Form = Time + Practice taught him how to write successfully in these diverse situations. Also, can you find a connection between the writing shown here and the essay reading that he found so beneficial to his writing in college?

The first sample he describes as "an everyday proposal." The second is his response to a questionnaire sent by the membership chair of a professional association to which his company belongs.

April 5, 1988

Centex-Rodgers Construction Company
P.O. Box 17911
Nashville, TN   37217

Attn: Mr. Carl L. Siddall, Jr.

   Project: Psychiatric Institute of Washington
   Location: 4228 Wisconsin Ave., N.W.
   Architect: Architecture Inc.
   Addenda: Addendum 2, Addendum 3

Gentlemen:

In accordance with the following information, we propose to furnish all labor and material for the sum of *Seven Hundred Seventy-Nine Thousand Nine Hundred ($779,900.00) Dollars.*

This proposal specifically includes the following:

1. Specifications 06100 — Rough Carpentry (Partial)
        Limited to plywood in coves (10/A5.5), plywood above seclusion room ceilings and metal blocking for accessories in patient toilets and kitchens.
    07200 — Insulation (Complete)
    08110 — Steel Doors and Frames (Partial)
        Limited to receiving and installing hollow metal door frames furnished by others.
    09200 — Lath and Plaster (Complete)
    09250 — Gypsum Drywall (Complete)
    09270 — Drywall Shaft System (Complete)
    09510 — Acoustical Ceilings (Complete)
    09951 — Acoustical Wall Panels (Complete)

2. Clean-up and removal of trash from site.

3. All work in accordance with Centex-Rodgers' *Drywall Pre-Bid Instructions.*

This proposal does not include temporary lighting, heating, ventilation, water, patching of finished work damaged by weather or other trades. 220 and 110 volt power for operation of equipment to be furnished to C. J. Coakley Co., Inc. at proper locations free of charge.

Please note that we have not reviewed the Subcontract Agreement with legal counsel. If we are the apparent low bidder, we would accept a standard agreement as previously negotiated between C. J. Coakley Co., Inc. and Centex or we accept annotation to the Centex-Rodgers' Agreement consistent with our company terms and conditions.

Respectfully submitted,

C. J. COAKLEY CO., INC.

Douglas P. Ayers
Vice President

DPA:em

July 15, 1987

Mr. Dennis Cohan
Pacific Ceiling Systems
6984 Sierra Court
Dublin, CA   94568

Dear Dennis:

In response to your letter of July 7, 1987, I'd like to take this opportunity to answer your questions:

"Why did you join?"

Up until 1981, C. J. Coakley Co., Inc. was strictly involved with drywall, plaster and sprayed-fireproofing. In 1981 we made a commitment toward a broader interior contractor and decided to add acoustical to our line of work. It was shortly after that time that we became members of CISCA. Just as AWCI had given us support in the drywall field, we were looking for an organization which would help us in our acoustical business.

"What benefits has CISCA given you and the members of your company?"

I think the biggest benefit CISCA has provided is that it remains through its operations and convention the one organization where new ideas, common concerns and industry problems are constantly being discussed and discovered.

"Why do you think other industry members should join CISCA?"

The main reason other industry members should join CISCA is that a CISCA membership demonstrates a company's commitment toward leadership and excellence within the industry. A commitment that will be rewarded with new people, new contacts and new experiences.

In closing, I'd like to say that you can definitely use any of the testimonial in CISCA's literature and if I can be of any further assistance, please let me know.

See you in October

Douglas P. Ayers

Doug Ayers
Eastern Regional Vice President

cc: Carl Wangman

REVIEWING "THE HISTORY OF A WRITER"

As you have progressed through the book, written some or all of the exercises chapter by chapter, and perhaps used the text toward completing tasks and projects, you will have grown, as we all grow through our work and our reflection on it. If you began this book with some of the fears described in Chapter 1, I hope that the book has helped you increase your confidence and enjoyment.

To chart this growth, try the following exercises, which review the concise history you have now written of yourself as a writer.

Back to the Beginning

The first exercise in the book asked you to explore your fears and problems as a writer. Reread your response. Now write a second response to the questions posed.

Observe the differences and similarities between the responses. Write your account of this comparison. Recall in writing specific events, people, and words of advice that can account for the changes. If a change has not occurred, or has not occurred to the degree you wish, speculate why.

Knowing Terms

This book uses many terms that may not have been familiar to you previously, at least not in the sense I use them. Focus on each of the following terms. What does it mean to you now? Think of a specific way in which your writing, or your approach to writing, has changed through your new understanding of this term. Write your responses.

> Experiment
> Knowledge
> Discovery
> Reader
> Revision
> Editing
> Research

After jotting down your responses, turn to a place in the text where I write about these terms. How does your understanding of the terms compare to mine? How would you revise my description in the light of your discoveries?

(If possible, compare your definitions of the terms with those of others. How do yours differ? On what do yours agree?)

Your Own Words to Write By

List one or more ideas from the book (or from another recent experience) that particularly strike you about writing. Are there one or more statements that help you when the writing becomes difficult? Or when you find yourself getting stuck or anxious? Formulate your own most helpful ideas into a statement to share with others.

Favorite Tricks and Techniques

Again, reflect on the stuck points in your writing, for example, the blank page, sticking with it, pleasing your teacher or another reader, and so on. Which tricks and techniques from the book (or that you've recently discovered elsewhere) do you now use to get out of the mud and keep going? Write about a particular stuck point in a recent writing and how you got through it.

The Big Wish

Apply the Big Wish (from Chapter 2) to your future as a writer. How do you see yourself using writing in your work and in your community and private lives? Assuming you have boundless confidence as a writer, what would you like to accomplish?

"THE HISTORY OF A WRITER": CHAPTERS TO COME

As I'm sure you've noticed already, keeping your history as a writer not only records your growth, but also helps growth occur, by showing you where you've been, where you'd like to go, and how you might get there. There's no reason to stop now. And you won't stop now, as long as you feel that the writing rewards your intellect and your emotions. Witness, for example, what student Kimberly Gray discovered through the journal she kept during a one-semester course:

> When I first started this journal, I thought it would be really boring, more of a pain than a pleasure. Slowly, however, as the weeks went by, I began to enjoy writing. It was nice sharing some of my stuff with others and getting opinions. . . . Perhaps that's also a way to get to know someone— through their writing.
>
> I began to realize that this journal was a real life saver during hard times, and happy times. It's hard to believe one can develop an attachment to an inanimate object. This journal has shared my joys and sorrows and has been a great sounding board I could use to release my anger and frustrations without hurting anyone's feelings. It also became a great way to think things through. Writing helped me to sort a lot out as I went along. It really surprised me.

Who knows? Someday, your history of a writer may become the inspiration for other writers, who will blazon your name in their books, so that still others may share the quiet joy that you knew as you wrote.

✍ PROJECTS FOR WRITERS

Write Your Own. The focus of the interviews for this Write Your Own will be on joy. Choose several people who are as enthusiastic about your favorite subject, skill, craft, art, sport, or other activity as you are. Interview them, using your adapted versions of the interview questions in the first section of this chapter (The Joy of the Challenge). Study the style of my interviews with writers as a possible model for your own reports. Feel free, of course, to use another style with which you are more comfortable. Try to include in each portrait some advice from your interviewee as well as a clear sense of the reasons for the interviewee's love of the subject.

Connecting with Fellow Writers. If this book has succeeded, it will have helped you produce a significant amount of writing, some of which you feel very good about and all of which you are confident can be made even better. You have already shared much of this writing with others. Here I'm suggesting that you connect with fellow writers by seeking a wider audience—through publication. Note that most of the writers interviewed for this book have had their work published and that this publication has taken many forms. For example, Ann Jeffries (Chapter 4) has published letters in local newspapers, as well as articles and poetry in national professional journals. The proposals of Ray Chapman (Chapter 3) are published by virtue of their broad dissemination at different levels of government. Douglas Ayers (Chapter 9) publishes in the newsletter of his professional association. Mary Redenius (Chapter 9) has published her poems in a variety of magazines devoted to the arts. Steve Gladis (Chapter 3), besides having published books about writing and speaking, achieves a form of publication of his team's speeches when they are presented by the director of the FBI. As these writers do, think of publication broadly, not in the narrow sense of books printed by major presses. Many writers are daunted hy the idea of publication, as if it means becoming one of a chosen few with talents not available to the rest of humanity. Publication means, literally, making the writing public, and this can be done in many undaunting ways.

You've already taken the largest step toward publication: you've become comfortable with the idea of getting feedback on your work. Once you overcome fear of the reader, publication becomes easy. You won't jump from sharing with your writing group to having your article accepted in *The New Yorker* or *The Reader's Digest,* but you can move easily from sharing with a helping reader to submitting pieces to the school newspaper or the office newsletter, and from there to publications that reach an even wider audience. If you've had some publishing experience, say in that school paper, literary magazine, or yearbook, you're already on your way.

The Project: Brainstorm publications that you read, local or national newspapers, newsletters, magazines, and so on. Focus on one or two that you know well. (If you've done the reading analysis exercises in Chapters 6 and 7, you should know several publications in your field of interest very well indeed.) Freewrite some ideas for pieces that would be suitable for these publications, or look through your journal and your other writings for work you've already written that could be revised for these publications. Share these pieces with your helping readers. Ask them for advice on revising your writing to meet the requirements of the publications you've chosen.

Procedure for Submitting Work: Before you draft or revise, be sure you know the form and format specifications of the publications for which you are writing. Many magazines include this information in the first few pages of each issue, on the same page as the staff and subscription rates; read the fine print carefully. If this information isn't available, or if you still have questions, don't hesitate to call the publication and ask to speak with someone who can answer questions about submitting manuscripts. All publications are on the lookout for good writers—publishers always need someone to publish—so you should be able to find someone who will answer your questions.

Always submit clean, typed manuscripts. Include a stamped envelope addressed to yourself (this is practical and courteous). You may wish to include a brief cover letter addressed to the editor (if the name of the editor is not listed in the publication, call and ask the name of the person to whom the manuscript should be sent). The cover letter should merely introduce you and your manuscript. At the very most the letter should state: (1) one fact about you that is relevant to this publication; for example, "I am president of the Sunrise Valley Homeowners Association," "I have been swimming competitively for eight years" (imagine the articles for which these statements would be relevant); and (2) a one-sentence summary of the piece; for example, "It argues for the banning of smoking in the halls of classroom buildings," "It describes how I modified my mountain bike for swampy terrain." Such a letter, no more than one paragraph of text, lets the editor know a bit about your qualifications to write the piece and lets the editor decide whether or not to read the entire piece. Don't use the cover letter to plead that the editor accept the piece; a good closing sentence might be, "Thank you for your consideration."

Expectations: If the piece is accepted, expect that you'll receive a request for revisions. As you've learned, that's how writing works. If the piece will be printed without revisions, appreciate your good luck.

If the piece is not accepted, expect anything, from a note explaining why it wasn't accepted to nothing (except the returned manuscript). If you get an explanatory note, read it carefully and learn from it. If your piece gets rejected, there's probably a good reason that has nothing to do with the quality of the piece: either the editor found it unsuitable to the style of the publication or the editor already had more good manuscripts than necessary. Don't ever use rejection as an excuse for not writing.

Keep Sending: Acceptance is a spur to submit further manuscripts. Rejection should also be a spur. Assume that the editor who rejected the piece just missed a good opportunity, and send the piece to the next publication on your list. The important thing is to believe in yourself. Theodore Geisel (known to everyone as Dr. Seuss) was rejected by twenty-eight publishers before one accepted his first book. Millions of children and parents are thankful that he persisted in sending out his work.

For Further Information: Writers turn to each other for tips and encouragement in getting published. Check your library shelves for the periodicals *The Writer* and *Writer's Digest* and for the latest edition of the annually-revised book, *The Writer's Market.* These publications are invaluable for information on places to publish and for good advice on writing in various forms and on various subjects.

Free Experiment. "Joy" is the theme, but not a haphazard, thoughtless joy. The writer's joy grows out of hard work, purposeful play; and most writers come through pain, doubt, and frustration to find the joy. What makes you happy? Has it always made you happy? If not, what occurred to make you change your mind? Write about this. When you've written enough to deepen and clarify your thinking about this theme, express your thoughts and feelings in some form that suits them: a story, a poem, an essay, an autobiographical sketch, a drawing, a collection of photographs, sculpture, music, dance, drama, and so on. Joyfully share your creation with others.

A Checklist of Checklists

The following lists summarize the checklists from Chapters 1 through 8. Refer to them when your writing day isn't going well or if you feel one of the common problems writers face coming on. If, when you read this list, any of the terms seems vague or puzzling, reread the appropriate section of the book as a refresher.

CHAPTER 1: GETTING STARTED AND STICKING WITH IT
Write regularly!
Try the tricks (freewriting, and so on) for getting started
Always remember to
    Relax, visualize, ignore the *have to's*
Stick with it
    Plan a schedule, set small goals for each day, meet mini-deadlines
Let incubation work for you

CHAPTER 2: THE BASICS OF WRITING: DISCOVERY, EXPERIMENT, KNOWLEDGE
Use writing to help you learn
Concentrate on what you are writing, not how
Write to the limit
Use writing to plan your reading, listening, viewing
Take questing notes—think, don't record
Write to summarize: Main idea? What doesn't make sense?
Reflect and speculate: "What if," Pros and Cons, Big Wish
Keeping the log: write for yourself first, others later

CHAPTER 3: HOW TO WRITE TO OTHERS
Write to yourself first, then revise for others
Follow the three-step method
To get good advice: learn to ask about format and form
To use models: dive in and swim around
To get good feedback: Make your reader your ally, not your enemy
    Write first, then ask the reader questions about the writing
    Take the initiative—don't wait for an invitation
    Form mentor relationships with trusted readers

CHAPTER 4: WRITING FOR THE TEACHER
Use the teacher as a resource
    Think of the teacher as a writer like you
    Ask for feedback: on your notes, on a draft
Ask the right questions: ask for exactly what you need to know
    Be specific to your writing
    Avoid vague, general questions
Train your helping readers: ask good questions, give specific praise
    Use the six starter questions if needed
    Avoid yes-no questions
    Be persistent in asking for the responses you need
Adapt to the special conditions of college writing

CHAPTER 5: FOUR COMMON TASKS FOR COLLEGE WRITERS
To observe and describe: use all the senses, use comparisons, use statistics, use change-location-purpose, rely on the reader's needs
To draw a conclusion: use writing to think, then revise for the reader
    Divide the process

In revising, include the three common elements
   as feedback on thesis, format, evidence
To make a plan of action: first plan, then revise for reporting
   To plan: use speculation, writing to the limit, graphic tricks
   To report: follow the three-step method, give your reader a sense
      of options, use presentation graphics
To write essay exams: use Chapter 2 tricks from day one, train
   yourself to read essay questions, plan time and organize, allow
   time for revision

CHAPTER 6: THE WRITING READER
To make you a better reader: use the reading response log and other
   Chapter 2 tricks
To analyze literature
   Use "key word," this reminds me of...," and other techniques
   Find something to look for with questions about point of
      view, tone, voice, format, sense of the reader
   Explore contexts
To report your analysis to a reader
   Use the three-step method (Chapter 3)
   Use the techniques for drawing a conclusion (Chapter 5)

CHAPTER 7: WRITING FOR RESEARCH
Choose a question, not a topic, to focus your search
Write to the limit
Brainstorm potential sources
Use reflective note-taking
Keep the research log: compare sources, evaluate sources, summa-
   rize
When using the library
   Remember the *LCSH*, get to know the reference room, and ask
      questions
Don't forget public records and special interest groups
When interviewing
   Plan questions, be flexible, be courteous, plan follow-up sessions
To write your research for others
   Dive in and swim around in sample research articles
   Follow the seven-step method

To use formal documentation
    Consult your reader, sample research papers, style guides
    Be consistent and use common sense

CHAPTER 8: GETTING HELP WITH EDITING
Write and revise—then edit
Study the format of your document; edit accordingly
Check your text for the most-commonly-broken rules
Get feedback
Proofread like a machine—it should be tedious
Use thesauri and spell-checkers with caution

Credits

Index